The New Poverty Strategies

Also by Anne Booth

AGRICULTURAL DEVELOPMENT IN INDONESIA

THE ECONOMIES OF ASIA, 1950–1998: Critical Perspectives on the World Economy, Volumes 1, 2, 3 (editor, with R.A. Ash)

ESSAYS IN INDONESIAN ECONOMIC HISTORY: Perspectives from the Late Colonial Era (edited with W.J. O'Malley and Anna Weldemann)

INDIRECT TAXATION IN ASEAN (with Mukul Asher)

INDONESIAN ECONOMIC DEVELOPMENT IN THE 19TH AND 20TH CENTURIES: A History of Missed Opportunities

THE INDONESIAN ECONOMY DURING THE SOEHARTO ERA (editor, with P. McCawley)

LABOUR ABSORPTION IN AGRICULTURE (with R.M. Sundrum)

THE OIL BOOM AND AFTER: Indonesian Economic Policy and Performance in the Soeharto Era (editor)

Also by Paul Mosley

AID AND POWER (with John Toye and Jane Harrigan)

DEVELOPMENT FINANCE AND POLICY REFORM (editor)

FINANCE AGAINST POVERTY (with David Hulme)

THE MAKING OF ECONOMIC POLICY

OVERSEAS AID: Its Defence and Reform

THE SETTLER ECONOMIES: Studies in the Economic History of Kenya and Zimbabwe, 1900–1963

The New Poverty Strategies

What Have They Achieved?
What Have We Learned?

Edited by

Anne Booth
Professor of Economics
School of Oriental and African Studies
University of London

and

Paul Mosley
Professor of Economics
University of Sheffield

palgrave
macmillan

First published 2003 by
PALGRAVE MACMILLAN
Houndmills, Basingstoke, Hampshire RG21 6XS and
175 Fifth Avenue, New York, N.Y. 10010
Companies and representatives throughout the world

PALGRAVE MACMILLAN is the global academic imprint of the Palgrave
Macmillan division of St. Martin's Press, LLC and of Palgrave Macmillan Ltd.
Macmillan® is a registered trademark in the United States, United Kingdom
and other countries. Palgrave is a registered trademark in the European Union
and other countries.

ISBN 0–333–91975–0

This book is printed on paper suitable for recycling and made from fully
managed and sustained forest sources.

A catalogue record for this book is available from the British Library.

Library of Congress Cataloging-in-Publication Data
The new poverty strategies: what have they achieved? what have
we learned? / edited by Anne Booth and Paul Mosley.
    p.   cm.
Includes bibliographical references and index.
ISBN 0–333–91975–0 (cloth)
1. Economic assistance—Developing countries. 2. Poverty—Developing
countries. I. Booth, Anne, 1946– II. Mosley, Paul.
HC60 .N4743 2002
362.5'526'091724—dc21   2002026759

10   9   8   7   6   5   4   3   2   1
12   11   10   09   08   07   06   05   04   03

Printed and bound in Great Britain by
Antony Rowe Ltd, Chippenham and Eastbourne

Contents

List of Tables

Preface

'Evidence-based policy' is much in fashion, but in relation to the most important policy target of all – the elimination of poverty worldwide – there has not been much evidence to go on in many parts of the developing world. Thus it seemed to the editors, asking themselves what we had learned about poverty reduction in the decade since the World Bank's path-breaking *World Development Report* (*WDR*) of 1990. In choosing a topic for the Development Studies Association's inaugural policy workshop – designed to bring members of the Association and their ideas closer to policy makers – we did not therefore have to hunt a long time for a theme.

In the process of planning the workshop we discovered that the World Bank was planning a second *World Development Report* for 2000–01 around the poverty theme. Accordingly we invited them to become involved in the planning of our own workshop. Several Bank staff presented papers at this event. We would like to thank, in particular, Christiaan Grootaert and Alison Evans of the World Bank for helping us to coordinate our work with theirs. For one reason and another the submission of the finished work to the publisher has been delayed beyond what was reasonable, at least to our long-suffering contributors. But this has at least made it possible to see both the pre-publication draft of the *2000/01 World Development Report* – and indeed the final published version. This second examination by the World Bank of the problems of global poverty, as explained in Chapter 1, looks at the issues through a rather different lens from its predecessor.

Our thanks go also to Judy Baggott, a superb conference secretary; to Blackwell Publishing for allowing us to reproduce Chapter 10, by Ann Whitehead and Matthew Lockwood; to the International Statistical Institute for permission to publish Chapter 5, by Graham Pyatt; and to Tim Farmiloe of Macmillan Press for responding with enthusiasm to the idea of the book. Since then Macmillan has become Palgrave Macmillan, with some inevitable upheavals along the way. We are grateful to Nicola Viinikka for her patience and support during the transition period. Our contributors also deserve thanks for their willingness to persevere with a project which has stretched over a much longer time horizon than was initially planned. We hope that the policy workshop idea will continue; indeed, a further workshop held at Easter 2001 on *Poverty and Social Exclusion in North and South*, has corrected some of the 'Southern bias' in the current book. The many abbreviations and acronyms used for books and aid programmes in the poverty strategies' debate are defined in the List of Abbreviations and Acronyms on page xv.

ANNE BOOTH
PAUL MOSLEY

Notes on the Contributors

Anne Booth is Professor of Economics at the School of African and Oriental Studies, University of London, and the author of a number of books and papers on the development of South-East Asia, particularly Indonesia.

Aidan Cox is a research officer at the Overseas Development Institute in London.

Stefan Dercon is a research officer at the Centre for the Study of African Economies at the University of Oxford.

Dag Ehrenpreis is on secondment to the OECD Development Assistance Committee, Paris, having previously been Chief Economic Adviser at the Swedish International Development Authority.

Lucia Hanmer is a research officer at the Overseas Development Institute in London.

John Healey is a research officer at the Overseas Development Institute in London. He was formerly Chief Economic Adviser at the Overseas Development Administration (now DFID), London.

Anuradha Joshi is Assistant Professor of Political Science, MIT, Cambridge, MA.

Pramila Krishnan is a research officer at the Centre for the Study of African Economies at the University of Oxford.

Matthew Lockwood is Social Development Adviser at the Department for International Development in London.

Andrew McKay is Senior Lecturer in Economics, University of Nottingham.

Mick Moore is a professorial fellow at the Institute of Development Studies, University of Sussex.

Paul Mosley is Professor of Economics at the University of Sheffield and formerly President of the Development Studies Association; he has published a number of books and papers on development and political economy issues.

Felix Naschold is a research officer at the Overseas Development Institute in London.

Graham Pyatt was formerly Professor of Economics at the Institute of Social Studies in The Hague.

Rolph van der Hoeven is Chief Economic Adviser at the International Labour Organisation, Geneva.

Ann Whitehead is Reader in Social Anthropology at the University of Sussex.

List of Abbreviations and Acronyms

AUSAID	Australian Aid Agency
CAS	Country Assistance Strategy
CBS	Central Board of Statistics (Indonesia)
CGE	Computable General Equilibrium
CGIAR	Consultative Group for International Agricultural Research
CPI	Consumer Price Index
CSO	Central Statistical Office (Ethiopia)
DAC	Development Assistance Committee (OECD/UNDP)
DFID	Department for International Development (UK)
DoEC	Department of Education and Culture (Indonesia)
DSA	Development Studies Association (UK)
EAS	Employment Assurance Scheme (India)
EC	European Community
EGS	Employment Guarantee Scheme (India)
ERHS	Ethiopian Rural Household Survey
ESRC	Economic and Social Research Council (UK)
EU	European Union
FDI	Foreign Direct Investment
FINNIDA	Finnish International Development Authority
FSU	Former Soviet Union
GAD	Gender and Development
GDP	Gross Domestic Product
HDI	Human Development Indicator
HIPC II	Highly Indebted Poor Countries (initiative of IMF/World Bank)
HRD	Human Resource Development
IDA	International Development Agency (World Bank)
IDB	Inter-American Development Bank
IDS	Institute of Development Studies (UK)
IDT	International Development Target
IFAD	International Fund for Agricultural Development
IFI	International Financial Institution
IFPRI	International Food Policy Research Institute
ILO	International Labour Organisation
IMF	International Monetary Fund
IMR	Infant Mortality Rate
INPRES	*Instruksi Presiden* (Presidential Instruction, Indonesia)
IRDP	Integrated Rural Development Project
ISS	Institute of Social Studies (The Netherlands)
ISWG	Inter-Secretariat Working Group (EU)

LFA	Logical Framework Approach (Sida)
LDC	Less Developed Country
LSMS	Living Standards Measurement Survey
NGO	Non-Governmental Organisation
OD	Operational Directive (World Bank)
ODA	Overseas Development Institute (UK)
ODC	Overseas Development Council (USA)
OECD	Organisation for Economic Cooperation and Development
OED	Operations Evaluation Department (World Bank)
OPK	*operasi pasar khusus* (Special Market Operations, Indonesia)
PA	Poverty Assessment (World Bank)
PPA	Participatory Poverty Assessment (World Bank)
PPP	Purchasing Power Parity
PR	Public Relations
PRA	Participatory Rural Appraisal (World Bank)
PRSP	Policy Reduction Strategy Paper (World Bank)
PTI	Poverty Targeted Intervention (World Bank)
ROSCA	Rotating Savings and Credit Association
SAL	Structural Adjustment Loan (World Bank)
SAM	Social Accounting Matrix (CBS, Indonesia)
SAP	Structural Adjustment Policy
SAREC	Swedish Technical Cooperation Agency
SIDA (Sida)	Swedish International Development Cooperation Agency
SIP	Sector Investment Programme
SMERU	Social Monitoring and Early Response Unit (Indonesia)
SUPAS	Inter-Censal Survey (Indonesia)
SUSENAS	National Statistical Office (Indonesia)
SWAp	Sectorwide Approach
TPF	Total Factor Productivity
UK	United Kingdom
UN	United Nations
UNDAF	UN Development Assistance Framework
UNDP	United Nations Development Programme
UNICEF	United Nations Children's Fund
UNRISD	UN Research Institute for Social Development
UNSFIR	United Nations Support Facility for Indonesian Recovery
UPE	Universal Primary Education (Uganda)
USA	United States of America
USAID	US Agency for International Development
WDR	*World Development Report*
WFP	World Food Programme (UN)
WHO	World Health Organisation
WID	Women in Development
WIDER	World Institute for Development Economics Research

Part I
Introduction

1

Introduction and Context

Paul Mosley and Anne Booth

Background

In 1990, following several years of pressure from humanitarian pressure groups and others disturbed by the human consequences of structural adjustment, the World Bank published a *World Development Report* (*WDR*) on poverty (World Bank 1990). Unlike the usual run of such Reports, this one did not serve purely to illustrate a theme in international development, but turned out to have a resonance which went far beyond its immediate context. The report became a basis for a range of policy changes which have altered the practice not only of the World Bank but of all development agencies. The Bank initiated, in poorer developing countries, a data-gathering effort (the *Social Dimensions of Adjustment* surveys) which, for the first time, made annual data on poverty in developing countries publicly available. World Bank office memoranda of 1991 and 1992, backed by a *Poverty Reduction Handbook* (World Bank 1993) placed poverty reduction at the head of the World Bank's priorities, and forbade the giving of adjustment loans to countries which did not already have an agreed poverty strategy in place. But also, far more than in the case of the previous Bank initiative in poverty reduction, by Robert MacNamara in the second half of the 1970s (Ayres 1980) this initiative has been emulated by many other development agencies. Several OECD countries, including Canada, Denmark, Norway, Sweden, the Netherlands, Switzerland and most recently Great Britain (United Kingdom 1997) have now also given priority to poverty reduction among their development objectives, and the International Development Targets announced by the OECD in 1996 began with a commitment to halve the number of individuals in extreme poverty by 2015. These announcements arguably imply a global policy shift even more dramatic than the movement towards liberalisation which began in the 1980s.

It is natural to ask what this policy shift has achieved so far, and what we can learn from the experience. That was the objective lying behind the policy workshop from which the chapters of this book are taken, which was held at the University of Reading, England, as the inaugural policy workshop of the Development Studies Association, between 8 and 10 April 1999. The original *World Development Report* (World Bank 1990) was based on a three-pronged approach, the three prongs being labour intensity, investment in the physical and human capital of the poor and the reinforcement of social safety nets; and all of these approaches continue to be pursued. The approach has a clear rationale: (1) to increase the command of the poor over resources it is necessary to begin by expanding demand for the resources which they currently possess, namely labour (in particular) and capital (very little, but essential to raise the productivity of the resources they do have); but (2) not all poor people, and in particular the old, the young and the disabled, can sell the product of their labour or skills directly, and thus a social safety net is needed to plug the gaps in a strategy mainly aimed to support the work and the enterprise of poor people.

One strand in this book, then, is to examine what those who have implemented such policies have learned from the experience. It is very clear that much work remains to be done. As shown in Table 1.1, numbers of poor people increased during the 1990s in all regions of the world except East Asia and the Middle East.

It is rational to begin with the World Bank itself which, through its Operations Evaluation Division, has been carrying out a comprehensive review of the coherence and effectiveness of the Bank's anti-poverty strategies. Alison Evans, of that Division, gave a verbal account at the 1999 Development

Table 1.1   Income poverty, by region, 1987–98, selected years

Region	Persons living on less than $1 a day (million; headcount index in brackets)			
	1987	*1990*	*1996*	*1998*
East Asia and the Pacific	417.5	452.4	265.1	278.3
	(26.6)	(27.6)	(14.9)	(15.3)
Europe and Central Asia	1.1	7.1	23.8	24.0
	(0.2)	(1.6)	(5.1)	(5.1)
Latin America and the	63.7	73.8	76.0	78.2
Caribbean	(15.3)	(16.8)	(15.6)	(15.6)
Middle East and North Africa	9.3	5.7	5.0	5.5
	(4.3)	(2.4)	(1.9)	(1.9)
South Asia	474.4	495.1	531.7	522.0
	(44.9)	(47.7)	(48.5)	(46.3)
Sub-Saharan Africa	217.2	242.3	289.0	290.9
	(46.6)	(47.7)	(48.5)	(46.3)
Total	1183.2	1276.4	1190.6	1198.9
	(28.3)	(29.0)	(24.5)	(24.0)

Source: World Bank (2001), Table 1.1.

Studies Association conference of the findings of this review. Among the main points highlighted were:

- That in spite of fairly rapid economic growth in most developing countries, even latterly in Africa, during the 1990–7 period, poverty trends were variable, with particularly serious deteriorations in a number of transitional and Latin American countries.
- That, reflecting this, the 'poverty elasticity' (the rate of change of headcount poverty divided by the proportional rate of growth of GNP) varies significantly between countries, and is significantly responsive to indices of inequality, of freedom from bureaucratic corruption and development of the 'social sectors' (education, health and social safety nets).
- That, within the World Bank's portfolio, the share of sectors with a 'direct poverty' focus (agriculture, human capital development, water and sanitation and social protection) had risen from 39 per cent to 45 per cent between 1980–4 and 1995–9.
- That Bank country assistance strategies had, however, been handicapped by too much focus on headcount poverty at the expense of both inequality and more fundamental measures of poverty.
- Finally, in a comparative review of a range of anti-poverty project options – special employment schemes, microfinance and social funds – the first scores highest on targeting on the poorest, the second on financial sustainability and the third on replicability, suggesting the need for a mix of strategies. This brief comparison draws attention to the crucial but underresearched issue of the relative effectiveness of different anti-poverty strategies, to which we shall return.

The *2000/01 World Development Report*

Ten years after the original *World Development Report*, the World Bank published another report on the poverty theme, very different in its recommendations, its process, and even its definition of poverty from its predecessor. (Poverty is now defined as 'pronounced deprivation of well-being', not just deprivation of income.) The conference on which this book reports was consciously planned as an input into this publication alongside the anti-poverty efforts of other donors, and several of the chapters here draw on background work for the *Report*.

Table 1.2 represents an idiosyncratic comparative summary of the main themes of the *1990* and *2000/01 World Development Reports*. Like the 1990 report, the later one is constructed on three 'pillars', which this time are *empowerment, security* and *opportunity*. Many of the policies associated with the security theme are developments of the *1990 Report's* emphasis on social safety nets, and the opportunity theme elaborates many of the possibilities for building up the human and physical capital of the poor contained in the

Table 1.2   1990 and 2000/01 World Development Reports: themes and associated policy recommendations

1990		2000/01	
'Pillars'	*Associated policies*	*'Pillars'*	*Associated policies*
Labour intensity	Small-scale industry; special employment measures; promotion of green revolution in small-farm agriculture		
Investment in the human capital of the poor	Promotion of primary health and education, especially among females; microfinance	Opportunity	Microfinance; land reform and other asset redistribution policies; fiscal, etc. measures to reduce inequality; 'pro-poor' public expenditure patterns
Social safety nets	Food subsidies; Social Funds	Security	'Tailor-made' social protection measures; measures to support asset diversification; insurance; 'international public good' defences against economic crisis – e.g. financial regulation; conflict prevention
		Empowerment	Democratisation, decentralisation; measures to build 'social capital'

earlier report, so two of the three pillars could be seen as organic growth from the lines of thinking initiated in 1990. By contrast, the empowerment theme of 2000/01 is new, and not at all foreshadowed in the earlier Report, and the labour-intensity approach so salient in 1990 is now relegated to the status of 'one possible approach' to poverty reduction (World Bank 2000: S6) rather than an approach sponsored by the Bank.

The Bank's exposition of the *opportunity* theme is notable for its emphasis on relative rather than absolute deprivation and for its espousal of the resulting inequalities as being themselves a cause of poverty. Among the measures recommended to reduce it is, for the first time in many years, land reform and other forms of asset redistribution, described here as having been 'central to poverty reduction in China, the Republic of Korea, Taiwan, Vietnam and the Indian states of West Bengal and Kerala' (World Bank

2000: 3.32). Strangely there was no mention of land reform in South Africa or any Latin American country. The long-standing Bank taboo against any form of asset transfer programme appeared, at least in the draft report, to have been laid to rest. There is an extended discussion of pro-poor patterns of growth, which not only reiterates the focus of the *1990 Report* on primary health care and education but also considers other budget headings such as physical infrastructure and agricultural research and extension: the CGIAR system is quoted as being 'the most effective use of overseas development assistance, bar none' (World Bank 2000: 9.18).

The *security* theme is treated at all levels from the insecurity of the poor individual and household to that of the nation-state. Central to the concept of security are the concepts of risk and vulnerability which in recent years have been used to extend the concept of poverty itself, and the complex of arrangements which, following the *1990 World Development Report*, we used to think of as social safety nets, are now re-presented as 'social risk management'. The phrase is carefully configured to avoid any presumption that poverty reduction and social protection are purely government responsibilities; nonetheless, it is a commonplace that security is not a thing which the free market provides (Mosley in Hubbard 2001) and one of the merits of the Report is its awareness that infinite gradations exist within the state of poverty and that many spontaneous group insurance arrangements, such as ROSCAs, are careful to exclude the poorest (World Bank 2000: 5.24). Grass-roots organisations, in other words, although an essential part of the structure of social risk management, are not to be idealised, and in particular fill only a small part of the very large gap left by the failure of insurance markets in developing countries. These insurance arrangements, and social safety nets generally, cannot be taken off the peg but must be tailored to the requirements of particular countries – and, indeed, target groups. There was an extended discussion, in Chapter 8 of the draft Report (World Bank 2000), of national economic security in the context of the recent East Asian–Russian–Latin American crisis, notable for its complete abandonment of the carefree approach to capital account liberalisation which characterised both the Bank and the Fund in the 1980s and 1990s. Reading the following passage, somewhat censored in the transition to the finally published draft of the Report, it might be possible to surmise that the commitment of the Bank, even if not yet the Fund, to a neo-liberal agenda in capital markets might now be defunct:

> Of all the reforms implemented, financial liberalisation stands out for having caused severe disruptions in economic performance. The combination of open capital accounts, weak regulation of the financial sector, and the volatility of short-term capital flows lie behind the major macroeconomic crises in the 1990s. The social costs of rescuing ailing financial institutions have been huge and regressive. During the height of the

'reform rush' the prevailing view was that reforms should be introduced as quickly as possible in order to take advantage of the 'window of opportunity' provided by reform-friendly governments. This view is now changing. The financial crashes of the late 1990s in particular revealed the importance of creating adequate institutions (rules and organisations) and codes of behaviour, or 'social capital' (voluntary compliance with established laws, trust, co-operative behaviour, and basic codes of conduct) before market-oriented reforms are adopted.

(World Bank 2000: 8.5)

The phrase 'social capital' is key to the new Report. It lies at the heart of the exposition of the Report's newest theme, that of *empowerment*. Here defined as 'the ability of individuals and households to secure benefits by membership of social networks', social capital now emerges as the key factor of production which enables the poor to empower themselves, just as the human capital of the poor was the key factor of production in the *1990 World Development Report*. Social capital is here presented as being of three kinds: 'bonding' (among the poor), 'bridging' (between the poor and other social and political organisations at the same level) and 'linking' (between the poor and organisations in higher political and social strata). Linking social capital is, for the poor, both the scarcest and the most vital of the three resources (Woolcock 2000), and it is strongly suggested by the Report that democracy and decentralisation may help to reinforce it, as well as overcoming other underdevelopment-inducing governmental pathologies such as corruption.

The anti-poverty efforts of donors

The 'new poverty strategies', as reviewed above, have by no means been the property of the World Bank, even if the Bank's two *World Development Reports* have played a key part in their making. Several chapters in Part II examine the anti-poverty experience of other donors. In Chapter 2 Aidan Cox and John Healey, summarising two large ODI studies, criticise donors in general for their continuing lack of coordination and their failure to evaluate poverty impact in a serious way, finding analysis of safety nets particularly thin. One of those donors, Dag Ehrenpreis, formerly of Sida and now of OECD, reviews the Swedish experience in Chapter 3 and, while demonstrating progress in terms of country allocations, also acknowledges limitations of rigour at the level of evaluation. In Chapter 4, Rolph van der Hoeven of ILO asks whether donors' continuing insistence on liberalisation (however nuanced it may now be) is undermining their anti-poverty efforts, and, in harmony with one of the main messages of the conference, answers 'yes, to the extent that they increase inequality'.

The link between inequality, growth and poverty works through various channels. The *economic* link runs through the pattern of demand: where inequality arises from a large proportion of the population being forced to live at subsistence level, no mass market for consumer manufactures can exist and possibilities for the development of domestic industries are reduced in proportion, as the experience of Brazil (pre-1980) and South Africa (pre-1990) bears witness. The *political* link runs through the feasibility and effectiveness of reform: where inequalities are high and, especially, the social and governmental capacity to manage the resulting conflicts is low, the payoff from otherwise promising reforms in the direction of greater openness may be much reduced. Arguably this happened in several fast-growing economies in South-East Asia (Thailand, Indonesia and Malaysia) over the 1990s, where governmental capacity to manage income inequalities resulting from rapid growth was weak. Finally, in the extreme case (Ethiopia and Mozambique in the 1980s, Rwanda and Burundi in the early 1990s and Angola, Congo and Sierra Leone at the present time), high inequality may at least contribute to a general breakdown of civil order which aborts the efforts of governments and even NGOs to reduce poverty. In other words, inequality, a word almost absent from the *1990 World Development Report*, is back on the agenda: neither labour intensity nor investment in the assets of the poor is sufficient.

The international aid effort has undergone a range of transformations in the process of implementing the new poverty strategies, including shrinkage over the 1990s. As discussed earlier, donors still have relatively scant evidence on the impact of the 'new poverty strategies' on which to base changes in policy, but this has not prevented a quite far-reaching reappraisal of the role of donors, which the *2000/01 World Development Report* attempts to summarise. It contains a chapter on aid (Chapter 11) heavily influenced by the paper by Collier and Dollar (1999) which produced the startling result that if aid were confined to poor countries with good policies, 30 million people per annum could cross the poverty line, compared with 10 million now being helped. (In the published version of the report this figure is reduced to 19 million compared with 10 million, see World Bank 2001: 196). The finding is of course heavily dependent on the 'new World Bank conventional wisdom' (World Bank 1998) which claims that aid is effective only in countries where policies are 'sound', a phrase which has had various meanings even within the World Bank literature, but which in the original 1998 report meant openness, low budget deficits and low inflation. Together with a set of findings purporting to show that conditionality is no longer effective (Collier and Gunning 1999) the vision now proposed is of donors forming long-term 'development partnerships' (World Bank 2001, see also DFID 1997) with those countries whose development policies they trust, and abstaining from *ex ante* policy leverage either in the interests of poverty reduction, or of any other cause. This of course contrasts dramatically with the role assumed by the Bank and other aid donors in the 1980s and 1990s. These findings have been quite influential, and are now colouring the debate about the future role not only of the Bank and aid donors, but also the IMF, which in the wake of the Asian crisis is hesitating between a continuation of its long-term, pro-poor role and a scaling back of that role to that of provider of short-term emergency loans only (Summers 1999; Mosley 2001).

It is therefore the more important to point out that these 'new views' of aid – both the correlation of aid effectiveness with policy quality in the Bank's sense, and the proposed abandonment of poverty conditionality – have been challenged on the basis of empirical evidence. Hansen and Tarp (2000) have demonstrated that aid effectiveness does not correlate robustly with the Bank's policy index, and correlates instead with the Adelman–Morris measure of human capital. The findings of 'ineffectiveness of conditionality', meanwhile appear to have been based on *Aid and Power* (Mosley *et al.* 1995), which in fact argues no such thing. Rather, it argues that conditional aid with downpayments can work perfectly well, if the policy recommendations are credible, and that donors' conditionality related in particular to the management of the budget has been increasingly successful in recent years – as demonstrated by Ehrenpreis' Chapter 3 in this volume. Even with highly effective conditionality, however, the World Bank estimates of 19 million a year taken across the poverty line (World Bank 2001: 196) depend on unrobust and wildly overoptimistic estimates of poverty elasticities. As can be seen from Table 1.1 which is extracted from the published version of the report, the fall in poverty during the worldwide boom of the 1990s was nowhere near this, even if one throws realism to the winds and ascribes all of it to the influence of overseas aid. The likelihood is that in the next ten years aid, however poverty focused, will run at lower levels than in the 1990s.

In practice, policy dialogue between aid donors and recipients is by no means devoid of conditionality. Rather, what is happening is that donors are looking for new conditionality in the form of *Poverty Reduction Strategy Papers* (PRSPs) to do for them, in the sphere of poverty, what old-fashioned conditionality used to do in the sphere of growth. PRSPs are medium-term poverty strategy documents agreed between the IMF, World Bank, donors and the recipient government, and aid in the form of debt cancellation is conditional on such strategies being agreed, just as old-fashioned aid for adjustment lending used to depend on the production of medium-term 'country strategy papers' agreed between the parties. On the ground, what is going on is very much an evolutionary rather than a revolutionary process. What has evolved is, first of all, the *process* – in each country, the production of a PRSP is supposed to involve exhaustive dialogue with different categories of poor people, such as landless workers, small farmers, the disabled, victims of discrimination and so on; secondly the *actors* – with NGOs now being routinely used as conduits for aid money and aid policies in the absence of pro-poor governments; and finally the *instruments of policy* – the heavily pro-agriculture investment strategies so frequently found in anti-poverty strategies of the 1970s now being conspicuous by their absence (Maxwell 2001).

The point remains that conditionality, in a less strident voice and in spite of the Bank's own claims of its uselessness, continues; indeed our simulations (Mosley and Hudson 2001) suggest that, provided that reasonable assumptions are made about response elasticities, this 'new conditionality' delivers more in terms of poverty reduction than the Collier–Dollar approach.

Agriculture, labour intensity and poverty reduction

The next group of chapters in the book (Part III) examines conceptualisations of poverty and the relevance of this one universal phrase to particular regions and, in some cases, countries. In Chapter 5, Graham Pyatt, in a critique of the World Bank's 1990 strategy and its poverty assessments, argues against a 'headcount' approach which groups all the poor together in one lump and argues for greater awareness of regional specifics, an approach with which the 2000/01 Report shows a great deal more sympathy than its predecessor. In Chapter 6 Anne Booth analyses the impact of the 1997–9 crisis in South-East Asia, which was at one stage seen as threatening the entire 'East Asian miracle' – the most successful pro-poor growth experience of the postwar period, if not of all time. Much as early reports of this threat may have been exaggerated, the downturn of the east Asian economies has had political consequences which are still working through, and Booth gives an indication of the policies which, under these new political circumstances, may be feasible as poverty reduction options for 2000 and beyond.

Prominent among these is intensification and labour absorption in agriculture, an issue heavily underemphasised by the 'new poverty strategies'. The Rural Poverty Report (2001) by IFAD is but one of several recent reports protesting at this tendency, and at the associated decline in aid volumes to agriculture. In Chapter 7, the first of two specifically agriculture-related African case studies, Mosley and McKay look at the so far rather weak spread of the green revolution to Africa. In so far as it has spread, they find none of the correlation between adoption and poverty intensification discovered by some authors in parts of South Asia. Where modern varieties have been adopted, they find, they have reduced poverty, partly through increases in farmer incomes and real wages, and partly through farm–non-farm linkages, but principally through one of the great driving forces stressed in the *1990 World Development Report* – the tendency of modern varieties to absorb more labour than traditional varieties, because of their higher yields, because of the correlation of labour-intensive husbandry and land preparation with adoption of modern varieties, and because modern varieties have less variance attached to their yields, which reduces the risk attached to the associated hiring of labour (Mosley forthcoming). The translation of this effect into poverty reduction, in Africa as in Asia, has been 'disappointing' to quote the word used by Lipton and Longhurst (1989) about the Asian green revolution, in relation to its potential, but in absolute terms it remains an important, and still under researched, engine of poverty reduction. The reasons why this absorptive capacity varies between regions and crops, why it is more responsive to assets than to income, and why it applies more to males than to females are examined by Mosley and McKay in Chapter 7. But rural poverty has fallen in some African countries without any green revolution at all – a classical case being Ethiopia, whose poverty reduction is decomposed by Dercon and Krishnan in Chapter 8, with human and physical capital and access to infrastructure emerging as the key determinants of poverty.

From all of the above, it will be clear that although none of the conceptual legs of the World Bank's original 'three-legged stool' have been kicked off, donors are very ignorant about what has been achieved with their support. Notwithstanding this they have in the 1990s, as we have seen, built on a number of additional conceptual legs, some of them emerging from the air rather than from the empirical work so far discussed. The second strand of the book is to enumerate, and as far as possible analyse, what the addition of these new ideas has achieved.

New approaches to poverty reduction

Particularly important among these new approaches, discussed in Part III of the book, are:

- The ability of governments and NGOs to reduce *inequality*. As we have seen this was emphasised by Alison Evans in her verbal presentation to the conference, and also by the *2000/01 World Development Report*. In an adaptation of one of the constituent studies for this Report, Hanmer and Naschold (Chapter 11) demonstrate that inequality levels are crucial to the achievement of the OECD's International Development Targets, the first of which is a halving in the numbers of those in extreme poverty by 2015. Their evidence suggests that a country with a Gini coefficient of 0.25 (indicating a relatively equal distribution of income) can expect a growth elasticity for the poverty headcount index of about – 3.3, whereas a country with a Gini index of 0.60 can expect an elasticity of – 1.8. One of the underlying factors behind the huge deterioriation in poverty in the Former Soviet Union (FSU) is that Russia went in the 1990s from having one of the most equal distributions of income in the world to a level of inequality greater than that of the United States (Mosley and Kalyuzhnova 2000).

- The ability of policies and institutions to reduce *vulnerability*, or the risk of loss, rather than simply increase current income. As we have seen, the *2000/01 World Development Report* works with concepts of poverty which go beyond deficiencies of current income to embrace households' vulnerability, social deprivation and exposure to risk, and the adoption of such a concept of poverty has implications for the design of social safety nets and protection arrangements, not only in the south but in the North also. The Report (Chapter 8) presents a typology of mechanisms for reducing risk (individual versus group versus public, risk-reducing versus risk-mitigating versus risk-coping) which enables them to make some progress towards the objective of tailoring social safety nets towards the requirements of their users. It concludes that whereas some risk-management instruments are multi-purpose and capable of addressing most types of risk (workfare, health insurance, social funds, microfinance) others, such as contractual saving and unemployment insurance, are relatively limited in scope.
- The emergence of the concept of *'social capital'*, as discussed earlier.
- Increasing emphasis on *governance*, the theme of the *1997 World Development Report* and already, as discussed in Chapters, 2 & 4, firmly established in donor approaches and conditionalities. In Chapter 9, Joshi and Moore link this theme with that of social capital by defining a range of range of governmental characteristics which will help build social capital – in particular, predictability, which however needs to be designed in different ways to sustain different types of collective action. The argument is sustained by reference to a number of Asian schemes, in particular the Maharashtra Employment Guarantee Scheme.
- Finally, an ever-increasing emphasis on *gender* and on broader dimensions of *intra-household* relations, including the welfare of children, the old and inter-generational contracts and relationships. These issues pervade all of the four 'new themes' discussed above, and once again are of relevance to both North and South: one sees poverty-related problems of the North, including an ageing population and an associated 'pensions crisis', invading the South, and poverty-related solutions made in the South, such as microfinance (Hulme and Mosley 1996; Rogaly 1998) increasingly used as key elements in welfare-into-work policies in the North. The gender issue is considered by Whitehead and Lockwood, in Chapter 10 who, like Pyatt, use a selection of the World Bank's poverty assessments as their basic raw material.

As we have shown, Part III of the book is able only to scratch the surface of these 'new approaches', many of which are so new, at any rate in their application to the policies of NGOs and aid donors, to defy proper evaluation at this stage. Worse, some important themes have been left out of the book completely. There is nothing here on Eastern Europe and the FSU which, for reasons intimately associated with the labour market, experienced a greater increase in poverty in the 1990s than any other region in the world. Education and health are not treated in depth, and although it may now be back in fashion, there is nothing at all on the main anti-poverty hope of the 1950s and 1960s – land reform, now broadened into more general asset redistribution. These gaps make it hard for us to claim to provide a credible answer to the question concerning the 'new poverty strategies' posed in the sub-title: What have they achieved? What have we learned? Nonetheless, we must try.

What have the 'new poverty strategies' achieved?

In their totality, we do not know. But we do know that:

(1) *Global poverty* did fall quite sharply between 1990 and 1996 (Table 1.1), and rose only marginally between 1996 and 1998, in spite of an economic crisis affecting much of Asia and some other countries.

(2) The *range of countries* in which poverty is falling has spread from East and South Asia and Chile to include also some African countries – notably Ethiopia, probably Ghana and Mozambique, and most dramatically of all Uganda, where headcount poverty fell from 56 per cent to 32 per cent between 1992 and 2000 (Uganda 2001), a faster rate of decline even than that achieved in China and Indonesia.

(3) *Aid effectiveness* has increased quite sharply (Mosley and Hudson 1999; Hansen and Tarp 2000), apparently due in part to shifts in the composition of aid away from physical capital and towards human and social capital, of which the shift towards poverty-focused aid is a part.

(4) An *oral tradition* has emerged, backed by the Operations Evaluation Department survey and by some quantitative evidence (see World Bank 2000) which asserts that within the set of anti-poverty instruments, relative effectiveness is more or less as shown in Table 1.3.

If these subjective impressions turn out to be correct, the implication is that donors and governments will continue to need to work with a range of policy instruments rather than specialising in one or two. The implication is furthermore that whereas instruments such as microfinance, social funds and welfare state measures such as unemployment benefit may be useful at dealing with *transient* poverty, they will be ineffective in dealing with *chronic* poverty. (The distinction is similar to that made in labour economics between frictional and long-term unemployment, and also to that made in Iliffe's historical study of Africa (1987) between 'structural' and 'conjunctural' poverty.) A research project at the University of Manchester (Hulme *et al.* 2001) now locates this kind of poverty particularly among the old and those with health problems; those who experience ethnic or gender

Table 1.3 Effectiveness of different anti-poverty instruments: subjective impressions

	Ability to exclude non-poor	*Ability to reach poorest*	*Financial sustainability*
Social funds	Moderate to poor; non-poor do slightly better in demand-driven systems	Little known, but employment effects generally moderate	Generally poor (dependent on aid flows); replication possible, scaling up more problematic
Special employment schemes/ public works/ food for work	Very good (mainly through low wage offered)	Good on a temporary basis	Generally poor
Food subsidies	Very good	Good	Poor
Microfinance	Generally poor; but type of loan, and whether supplied with complementary savings facilities, are an important determinant of reaching the poor	Generally very poor	Good; scaling-up often possible
Unemploy-ment benefit	Poor	Only in formal sector of urban areas (e.g. Eastern Europe/FSU)	Very poor

Source: Oral presentation by Alison Evans at the Reading Policy Workshop 'Reviewing lessons from poverty projects'; on microfinance, some impressions from Sebstad and Cohen (1999).

discrimination; and those living in remote rural areas. The existence of the chronically poor was acknowledged not only by Iliffe but also by the *1990 World Development Report*, which of course hoped to catch them in its famous 'social safety net'. From the more detailed analysis of the poor which has been made since 1990 it is clear that not one by but many different nets are needed; and for some categories of the chronically poor (e.g. nomads and pastoralists, those with mental health problems), the design of these nets has scarcely begun.

What have we learned?

Here we can be more specific. We have learned that we need broader definitions of poverty, a wider range of instruments of intervention and a perspective which takes note of the interconnectedness of North and South, rather than identifying 'the Southern government' as the locus of pressure and the focus of blame if things go wrong. *Definitions* of poverty which go beyond income into education, health, vulnerability, and political freedoms are still much more talked about than operationalised, even though for most poor people it is the lack of these things, rather their low income, which defines their poverty for them. A *broader range of instruments* implies not only the adoption of the ideas in the previous paragraph – many of which are not of themselves policy instruments – but also a range of instruments which alleviates those broader definitions of poverty – adult education, primary health care, rural savings schemes and even a revival of that much-maligned instrument for securing a better deal for the poor, the cooperative. Finally, a *broader perspective* requires us not only to repeat that many of the things which cause poverty in the South are made in the North – trade restrictions being only the most obvious example – but also to emphasise that many of the things which cause poverty in both North and South have common roots, in particular inequalities within *and between* countries. That these may need to be acted on for anti-poverty strategy to work properly is an insight which not only the 'new poverty strategies', but the revisions to them which have accumulated during the 1990s, have yet to assimilate.

Bibliography

Ayres, R. (1980), *Banking on the Poor*, Baltimore: Johns Hopkins University Press.

Collier, P. and D. Dollar (1999), *Aid Allocation and Poverty Reduction*, World Bank Policy Research Working Paper 2041.

Collier, Paul and J.W. Gunning (1999), *Economic Journal 109* (December).

DFID (1997), *Eliminating World Poverty*. White Paper on Overseas Development. London: The Stationery Office.

Fine, B. (2000), *Social Capital versus Social Theory*, London: Routledge.

Hansen, H. and F. Tarp (2000), 'Aid effectiveness disputed', Chapter 4 in F. Tarp (ed.) *Foreign Aid and Development: Lessons Learnt and Directions for the Future*, London: Routledge, printed with amendments as H. Hansen and F. Tarp, 'Aid and growth regressions', *Journal of Development Economics*, 2001.

Hubbard, M. (ed.) (2001), Complete Issue of *Journal of International Development*, essays by Hubbard, Shepherd, Chambers, Mosley, Moore, Maxwell, White, Amis, Moser, Barnett and Whiteside, Vol. 13(3).

Hulme, D. and P. Mosley (1996), *Finance against Poverty*, 2 Vols, London: Routledge.

Hulme, D. *et al.* (2001), Prospectus for Chronic Poverty Research Centre, University of Manchester (www. chronicpoverty.org).

IFAD (2001), *Rural Poverty Report 2001*, Rome: International Fund for Agricultural Development.

Iliffe, J. (1987), *The African Poor*, Cambridge: Cambridge University Press.

Kanbur, R. (1999), *World Development Report 2000/01: A Very First Cut*, Ithaca: Cornell University and World Bank.

Lipton, and R. Longhurst (1989), *New Seeds and Poor People*. London: Allen & Unwin.

Maxwell, S. (2001), 'Heaven or hubris: reflections on the new poverty agenda', Oral presentation at Development Studies Association Conference, 10 September.

Mosley, P. (2001), 'The IMF after the Asian crisis: merits and limitations of the "long-term development lender" role', *The World Economy*.

Mosley, P. (forthcoming), *A Painful Ascent: The Green Revolution and Poverty in Africa*, London: Routledge.

Mosley, P. and J. Hudson (1999), 'Has aid effectiveness increased?', Universities of Sheffield and Bath, unpublished paper.

Mosley, P. and J. Hudson (2001), 'Aid, poverty reduction and the new conditionality', Universities of Sheffield and Bath, unpublished paper.

Mosley, P. and Y. Kalyuzhnova (2000), 'Can poverty and social goals be met in the transition region?', *Development Policy Review*, March.

Mosley, Paul, Jane Harrigan and John Toye (1995), *Aid and Power*, 2 Vols. London: Routledge.

Narayan, D. with R. Patel, K. Schafft, A. Rademacher and S. Koch-Schulte (2001), *Voices of the Poor: Can anyone Hear Us?*, New York: Oxford University Press for World Bank.

Rodrik, D. (1999), *The New Global Economy and Developing Countries: Making Openness Work*, Washington, DC: Overseas Development Council.

Rogaly, B. (ed.) (1998), Special Issue of *Journal of International Development* on microfinance in industrialised countries, Vol. 9: 6, December.

Sebstad, J. and M. Cohen (1999), 'Microfinance, risk management and poverty', Background Paper for *WDR 2000/01*, Washington, DC: USAID and World Bank.

Singh, I. (1990), *The Great Ascent*, Baltimore: Johns Hopkins University Press.

Summers, L. (1999), 'The IMF: possible future roles', Transcript of speech at London Business School, 14 December.

Uganda (2001), *Fighting Poverty in Uganda: The Poverty Action Fund*, Kampala: Ministry of Finance, Planning and Economic Development.

United Kingdom (1997), *Eliminating World Poverty* (White Paper on International Development), London: The Stationery Office.

Wade, R.H. (2001), 'Making the World Development Report 2000: attacking poverty', *World Development*, Vol. 29: 8.

Woolcock, M. (2000), *Using Social Capital: Getting the Social Relations Right in the Theory and Practice of Economic Development*, Princeton: Princeton University Press.

World Bank (1990), *World Development Report 1990: Poverty*, Washington, DC: World Bank.

World Bank (1993), *Poverty Reduction Handbook*, Washington, DC: World Bank Poverty Network.

World Bank (1998), *Assessing Aid: What Works, What Doesn't and Why*, Washington, DC: World Bank in association with Oxford University Press.

World Bank (2000), *World Development Report 2000/01: Attacking Poverty*, Consultation Draft, 17 January.

World Bank (2001), *World Development Report 2000/01: Attacking Poverty*, New York: Oxford University Press.

Part II
Donor Perspectives

2

The Poverty Reduction Strategies of the Development Cooperation Agencies in the 1990s: Their Record and What They Need to Do

Aidan Cox and John Healey

Introduction

The purpose of this chapter is to make a judgement on the *record* of the OECD development cooperation agencies in relation to poverty reduction objectives during the 1990s, based on the following six broad criteria:

- Their *commitment* to poverty reduction goals
- The way they have *conceptualised* poverty
- The *strategies* they have adopted
- The *effectiveness* of their country strategies
- The *nature* of their partner relations and programming
- The degree of *impact* of their interventions on poor people.

Then, based on this record and the weaknesses revealed, *suggestions* are made for improving the agencies' performance.

The views presented in this chapter are based on two major studies led and coordinated by the Overseas Development Institute (ODI, London). One study which involved collaboration with a group of European Research Institutes, examined 10 European Union (EU) member agencies as well as the European Commission in 1997 (Cox and Healey 2000). This involved some fieldwork on the operations of the European agencies in seven poor countries. The second study in 1998 led by the ODI and Associates for International Resources and Development (AIRD, Boston), looked at the policies, approaches and practices of all the OECD development cooperation agencies, mainly through studies made in the headquarters of the agencies (OECD/ DAC 1999).

Poverty reduction goals, concepts and strategies

Agency goals and commitment to poverty reduction

The majority of development agencies now have a *formal commitment* to poverty reduction as an overarching goal or as one of their two or three priority goals (Table 2.1). There was evidence of increased attention to poverty goals by agencies throughout the 1990s. In some sense, all agencies can be seen as having an implicit commitment to poverty reduction, since all have subscribed to the International Development Targets. However, there remains some variation in degree of donors' formal commitment. Although there is little doubt that agencies with no formal commitment at all can still contribute to poverty reduction, a single overarching poverty reduction goal is more likely to be reflected in a greater degree of attempted 'mainstreaming of such a goal' within the organisation (i.e. the extent to which all activities and all levels of the organisation are committed to work to this end).

Among the agencies which identify poverty reduction as an overarching goal, however, only a minority of agencies go on to articulate the *potential linkages* between their operational objectives and benefits for poor people. A few of these (e.g. BMZ, Germany; SIDA, Sweden; DFID, UK; and the World Bank) envisage three broad types of actions to help poverty reduction:

- Those which focus directly and predominantly on *identified groups of poor people*
- Those wider actions which are intended to include benefits to poor people among others: sometimes termed *indirect or inclusive types* of action and
- Those which help create a *policy and political environment* which allow the poor to participate more.

A pervasive difficulty here – which will emerge later – is that clear links between these types of actions and their potential impact on the poor are rarely clearly specified in advance nor is their impact on the poor established or measured afterwards.

Table 2.1   Formal commitment to poverty reduction

PR[a] is sole overarching goal	PR is one of two (or three/four) overarching goals	PR is not an overarching goal
Australia, Canada, Denmark, Ireland, Luxembourg, Netherlands, Norway, Spain, Sweden, UK, UNDP, World Bank	Austria, Belgium, EC, Finland, Germany, Italy, Japan, New Zealand, Switzerland	France, IMF, Portugal, USA

[a] PR = Poverty reduction.

Conceptual framework for poverty

The way in which agencies conceptualise poverty can assist them in developing poverty-reduction strategies and ensure their successful operationalisation in developing countries. This conceptual framework involves defining the nature of poverty, its causes and how the poor can best be identified and targeted for assistance. All agencies now embrace a multi-dimensional definition of poverty, though the weight they attach to different dimensions varies across agencies. In contrast to the early 1990s, the majority of donors consider the right to individual dignity, autonomy and social inclusion to be important dimensions of poverty. Similarly, far more agencies than in the past demonstrate an awareness of the *dynamics of poverty* – that poverty is often not a permanent state and that people move in and out of poverty, often as a result of seasonal or random shocks.

However, there is some confusion within agencies concerning the *causes and effects* of poverty. In part, this is due to the complexity of the phenomenon but it also results from a lack of conceptual clarity. This might be redressed by a greater focus on the processes of poverty, whereby cause and effect are examined simultaneously. Very few agencies explicitly address the different levels at which causes of poverty may be found and the connections between those levels. Making such links may be important in order to clarify the agencies' underlying understanding of social processes and also to help anchor activities in concrete contexts. Finally, while many donor agencies can give a long list of very different and, on the face of it, equally important causes of poverty, there is little discussion among donors of their relative importance and the linkages between them.

The *identification and targeting of the poor* by donors is often broad-brush with a tendency to treat target populations as homogeneous socio-economic groupings. Thus, for example, a number of agencies associate the poor with the agricultural sector and, as a result, assume that working with agricultural smallholders is poverty-focused, without recognising that smallholders are often a highly heterogeneous group. A similar tendency to see the poor as homogeneous often applies to gender and poverty issues. Some agencies equate the two, failing to recognise that not all the poor are women and neither are all women poor. The relation between gender equality and poverty reduction needs clarification – a task for independent analysts as much as the agencies.

While a number of agencies identify vulnerability as a dimension of poverty, very few seem to explore this issue in any depth in relation to targeting for poverty reduction. However, agencies need to focus on both entries and exits from poverty if they are to decrease the overall numbers of the poor. This requires a much broader understanding of *poverty processes* and an ability to identify not just the currently poor but those groups that may be vulnerable to becoming poor. Overall, to convey a real sense of the multi-dimensional and interlocking constraints which the poor experience and which poverty- reducing efforts have to confront, a more comprehensive social analysis is required which allows agencies to develop a greater understanding of poverty and gender dynamics and to better identify the poor and vulnerable.

Although agencies have clearly improved and broadened their understanding of poverty in recent years, many agencies are still grappling with translating this into effective actions on the ground. Agencies recognise the potential value of a *multi-dimensional definition of poverty* which directs attention to the wider issues of social exclusion and away from narrower income–consumption definitions. However, in practice multi-dimensional definitions sometimes generate little more than a taxonomy of characteristics of poverty, and their very breadth leads to difficulty in separating the poor from the non-poor at the operational level. Some agencies seek to resolve this by retaining a multi-dimensional understanding of the causes of poverty, but adopting a narrower definition for operational purposes. An example is in Germany:

> People are poor if they do not have the minimum monetary or non-monetary income necessary to meet their food requirements and satisfy other basic needs... [But] The social, economic, cultural, political and ecological causes of poverty are inextricably interlinked.
>
> ((submission) to DAC Annual Report, quoted in Cox and Healey (2000))

Although not all agencies have an entirely rigorous multi-dimensional conceptualisation of poverty, the priority concern is how existing multi-dimensional approaches can be more effectively operationalised. A few agencies such as Sweden, which is currently developing 'operationally-relevant guidelines' are already grappling with this.

Agency strategies for poverty reduction

The broadening conceptualisation of poverty is reflected in the range of agency strategies for its solution. No agency has a single strategy, but instead they tend to adopt a 'mix and match' approach, aiming to prioritise different strategies according to the country context. There are several distinguishable strategies in the current repertoire.

All agencies see *economic growth* as important for poverty reduction, but most attach the condition that growth should be 'pro-poor' or broad-based. Only a very few still subscribe (implicitly) to the view that trickle-down from growth patterns inherited from the past is enough. Yet, there is much uncertainty as to what 'pro-poor' growth actually is and what its implications are for policy change and actual donor interventions. The World Bank three-pronged strategy for poverty reduction dating from 1990–1 was of course important and the extent to which it has been pursued by the World Bank is currently being evaluated by the Operations Evaluation Department. The UNDP has also been developing perspectives in recent years. However, among most bilateral and multilateral agencies there is a distinct lack of precision regarding the content of favoured pro-poor policy. This has limited their effectiveness as advocates for pro-poor policy change (see below).[1]

Gender relations influence the growth process through their impact on macro aggregates, meso institutions and the actions of economic agents at the individual and household levels. Addressing gender can thus have a strategic and indirect effect on poverty but it is *not* necessarily identical to addressing poverty. Some agencies have made considerable progress in developing a gender-focused analysis for micro-level interventions, but at the meso and macro levels greater efforts need to be made to draw out gender-policy linkages and to address their implications for poverty reduction interventions.

Investment in human capital features in all agencies' strategies. Some agencies tend to view expenditure on education and health as equivalent to a pro-poor strategy in assisting improved productivity and economic growth. However, it is more likely to favour poor people if there is some redistribution of public social services towards the basic levels, and in some cases the secondary levels. While a number of agencies have indeed focused on supporting primary-level education and health services, this appears to have had little impact on shifting the overall balance of public expenditure (see below). Most envisage a gender component to their social sector work as a key to the success of poverty reduction strategies. However, attention to redistribution needs to go beyond efforts to address gender inequalities, to include a broader analysis of socio-economic inequalities. Social sector investment strategies sometimes fall into the trap of assuming that the same approach will suit all in countries where 'everyone' is poor. However, even in 'mass poverty' countries important socio-economic differences exist which may limit the extent to which the poorest benefit from a 'one size fits all' approach. A further gap relates to the distribution of *natural assets*. Few agencies have articulated a clear position on the importance of the redistribution of ownership or usage of natural assets (especially land and water) or what role the external agencies might play here.

There is also a growing interest among the agencies in issues of *governance and human rights* because they have become increasingly aware that the domestic attack on poverty requires a strengthening of the 'voice of the poor' and a governance system that is more responsive to them, if pro-poor policies are to become a reality. This is entirely consistent with the agencies' dominant perspective that this evolution cannot be achieved by donor conditionality, at least in the way it has been practised so far. However, there is a tendency to believe (without much historic evidence) that the introduction of more 'democratic' or 'accountable' political systems by themselves will ensure more participation by the poor. Few agencies have yet clarified what kinds of participation or types of domestic institutional arrangements and procedures are most likely to empower the poor or articulate their demands effectively at all levels – national, meso and local – and what role an external agency can play in this process.

Paralleling the easy equation drawn between governance, democracy and power to the poor majority is the assumption that government decentralisation/devolution strategies (which many donors have supported) will bring decision making closer to the poor and have greater impact on them. However, some observers currently express some scepticism about this. Such linkages deserve far closer scrutiny if political strategies are to bring concrete benefits to the poor. Similarly, growing rhetoric on a *rights-based approach* to poverty reduction requires closer examination if it is to provide an effective framework for operations. These issues are undoubtedly a new challenge not just for the agencies themselves but also for those independent political and sociological analysts and researchers who might hope to indicate some leads to follow.

Safety net strategies to reduce poverty have been less prominent in approaches to poverty reduction, especially by the bilateral agencies. For some, safety nets are seen as a short-term measure particularly associated with mitigating the immediate adverse effects of structural adjustment, whereas others see them as part of the underlying fabric of society. Although traditional or indigenous social safety net systems are often the most important for the poorest people, donors appear to have attempted little analysis of what they can do to strengthen or preserve existing structures and practices. Indeed, some donor practices may be worsening the poverty situation by undermining such systems. A few agencies, however, are developing ideas in this area looking particularly at supporting and developing local institutions and social processes in order to reduce vulnerability. There appears to be a strong case for reassessing the role of safety net approaches as part of a poverty reduction strategy, and identifying more clearly the role which external agencies can usefully play.[2]

The DAC's *Shaping the 21st Century* document reflects renewed concern for the importance of ensuring the *coherence* of industrialised country policies with the goal of poverty reduction. This is born out of a growing understanding of how agricultural, trade, investment and other policies of OECD countries can limit the scope for developing countries to capitalise on the opportunities afforded by globalisation and increase the risks associated with increasing international economic integration. Yet despite some positive steps taken at the OECD level, only a small minority of agencies and their governments have taken concrete steps to ensure that their domestic policies and their positions on international policies are consistent with poverty reduction. This largely stems from the domestic political weakness of development cooperation agencies, which limits their scope to lobbying other domestic ministries. Similar efforts to achieve policy coherence are also required at the developing country level, where inconsistencies threaten to undermine pro-poor developmental processes. These latter issues are being explored by the DAC Informal Poverty Reduction Network in the preparation of DAC Guidelines on Poverty Reduction.

Poverty reduction at the country level

Are donor country assistance strategies effective vehicles for poverty reduction?

For the vast majority of agencies, Country Assistance Strategies (CASs) are the main vehicle for translating poverty reduction goals into effective actions on the ground. However, the content of CASs and the process by which they are prepared reveals serious shortcomings in many cases.

First, out of 26 agencies only nine unambiguously require country pro-gramme managers to focus on poverty reduction strategies in their CAS (Table 2.2). Very often inclusion of poverty strategies and objectives is left to the discretion of individual managers. This is reflected in weaknesses or the absence of senior management systems for screening the poverty *content* of CASs. Ten agencies do have some kind of screening mechanism, but often senior sector expertise is not involved sufficiently or early enough to ensure a multi-disciplinary and cross-sectoral approach is taken. More widespread rigorous scrutiny of the genuine poverty content, whereby weak CASs are rejected, would help to create incentives for staff to prioritise poverty reduction.

Second, part of the value of CASs lies in the *process* by which they are developed as well as the content. Dialogue with developing country govern-ment and civil society can contribute to bolstering pro-poor policy reform and a more open discussion of public expenditure priorities. The donor case studies reveal examples of participation by partner governments (e.g. DG VIII, Germany, IMF, Japan, Norway, Sweden, Switzerland, UK, UNDP, USA, World Bank), and commitment to increase this. Nonetheless, efforts to involve partner governments substantially in the process of developing donor strategies remains patchy, and attempts to go wider and involve other stakeholders (e.g. trade unions, NGOs, the private sector) have been very rare. Only Sweden, the World Bank and (since 1998) the UK have made reasonably systematic efforts (Table 2.3). It is essential, however, that

Table 2.2   Is poverty reduction required in Country Assistance Strategies?

Yes	*Some*	*No*
Australia, EC (DG VIII), Germany, Ireland, Luxembourg, Netherlands, Sweden, UK, UNDP, World Bank	Canada, Denmark, Finland, Japan, Switzerland	Austria, Belgium, EC (DG IB), France, IMF, Italy, New Zealand, Norway, Portugal, Spain, USA

Table 2.3   Participation in the Country Assistance Strategies process

Yes	Some	No
Participation by government:		
Australia, EC (DG VIII), IMF, Japan, Norway, Sweden, Switzerland, UK, UNDP, USA, World Bank	Austria, Canada, Finland, Ireland, Italy, Luxembourg, New Zealand, Portugal	Belgium, Denmark, Netherlands, Spain, Germany
Participation by civil society partners:		
Sweden, UK, UNDP, World Bank	Austria, Canada, Finland, IMF, Ireland, Japan, New Zealand, Norway, Switzerland, USA	Denmark, Germany, Italy, Netherlands, Portugal, Spain

attempts by donors to increase government and civil society participation are managed on a collective basis to avoid overburdening partners. Where possible this should be centred on national poverty reduction strategies developed by partner governments in conjunction with civil society representatives. Some agencies have begun to support this, but more could be done.

Third, the effectiveness of poverty reduction strategies contained in donor CASs depends in part on the quality of the *poverty data and analysis*. Far more CASs include references to poverty data than in the past, and only a minority of agencies make no systematic use of poverty assessment data. However, often the use made of poverty data is superficial, in part because poverty assessments have in the past been overly descriptive, with insufficient attention to possible policy prescriptions.[3] This partly reflects insufficient effort to articulate the linkages between the nature and extent of poverty and the strategies and interventions set out by the donor. Poverty data do not appear to be fundamentally shaping the approach of many CASs, and the extent to which the data is feeding into inter-sectoral and intra-sectoral priority setting is unclear. Too often strategies continue to provide *ex post* rationalisations of existing practice, rather than fundamentally reappraising priorities in the light of a systematic assessment of the needs of the poor and the causes of their poverty. Sometimes country programmes are informed by gender analysis, but this tends not to consider poverty–gender inequality linkages. However, a number of agencies are increasingly trying to build partner capacity to undertake high-quality poverty assessments and monitoring rather than seeking to improve the quality of their own data and analysis.

Preparing a carefully crafted CAS, developed in a participatory fashion and based on good poverty analysis, is an important first step for agencies seeking to maximise their impact on poverty. However, it will amount to no more than window-dressing unless the CAS results in a programme of dialogue and interventions that result in practical benefits being delivered to poor people. This aspect is examined further below.

Finally, from a management perspective, CASs could become more effective instruments for mainstreaming poverty reduction at the country level if more attention were given to monitoring how far the poverty reduction objectives set out in the CAS are in fact achieved. No agency appears to have a comprehensive system for holding country programme managers accountable for performance against CAS poverty objectives. Although many agencies use logical frameworks as part of the CAS documents, performance indicators are often vague, there is no indication who is responsible for collecting these indicators, nor is there a senior management committee to scrutinise them.

Overall, CASs are becoming more effective instruments for translating poverty goals into real benefits for the poor especially in the case of the World Bank (see oral presentation by Alison Evans at the Reading policy workshop). CASs tend to be more informed by dialogue with developing country partners than ever before and make more use of poverty data and analysis. However, there need to be stronger incentives to programme managers in many bilateral and multilateral agencies to ensure a poverty orientation to their programming and more accountability for what they actually implement.

Partnership to promote poverty reduction?

The development community increasingly emphasises that solutions to poverty must be found through effective *partnerships* with developing country actors characterised by a higher quality and more equal relationship and enhanced coordination. However, there is no consensus on what 'partnership solutions' imply. For some, partnership is centred on the development of a closer and more reciprocal relationship with selected governments – those which share a common commitment to poverty reduction (e.g. Denmark, Finland, the Netherlands, Norway, Sweden, Switzerland, the UK). This approach leads to an interest in more flexible, less 'hands-on' forms of financing such as budgetary support and sectorwide approaches, and to ensuring that the national government is 'placed in the driver's seat' with respect to aid coordination. A DAC review of development cooperation in Mali appears consistent with this interpretation of partnership, recommending the 'progressive adoption of a programme approach where activities are managed by Malian institutions' (OECD/UNDP 1998).

An alternative approach to partnership, which is somewhat less recent but still strongly defended, seeks to avoid too narrow a focus on government by giving significant weight to building partnerships in civil society, and with private or voluntary organisations and community-level structures. This is favoured by many smaller donors, for which a modest scale of operations is suitable. It is also supported by several large agencies – especially in Germany and to some extent the USA – which have never embarked on using programme aid as a lever for influence through concerted dialogue. Partnership approaches which privilege relations with civil society have obvious appeal as a means of coping with the corruption and lack of accountability of some partner governments. The World Bank's Report *Assessing Aid* found that if the policy environment is not right and government does not work then nothing works (World Bank 1998). This provides a strong case for giving at least some attention to relations with government and not adopting 'civil society' partnerships on an exclusive basis. A pragmatic approach to government-centred partnerships also recognises that governments are not monolithic, and it may be possible to seek out those parts of government where potential exists for pursuing pro-poor policy and practice.

Some agencies are now reluctant to use the language of *conditionality*. This is the result of prolonged criticism that it has been heavy-handed and ineffective. Recent research suggests that neither criticism is fully justified, but does indicate that conditionality is not effective in promoting longer-term policy or institutional transformation. Faced with this mixed picture, some agencies attempt to use some form of political conditionality. Germany and Finland, for instance, favour criteria such as respect for human rights and popular participation in political decisions. There is no consensus, however, that new partnerships should include specifically pro-poor conditionality and few appear to have adopted it in practice. However, the HIPC II initiative links the provision of debt relief to eligible countries to their progress in alleviating poverty, in other words some form of performance criteria on poverty reduction which will be judged. Interestingly an opinion survey undertaken in five partner countries conducted as part of the research for OECD (1999) elicited quite favourable views on conditionality in relation to good governance and democracy, gender and the environment, and accountability for aid.

A third source of thinking on partnership relates to the tendency for agencies to be dominantly involved in ad hoc projects rather than wider sector-based and budgetary modes of delivering development cooperation. The multiplication of projects, even when formally managed by government staff, has been found by some to be institutionally corrosive, diverting officials' effort from more central tasks and creating enclaves seen as 'islands of excellence'. Some conclude that as long as agencies channel funding outside of the partner government's budget process they will remain 'part of the problem rather than part of the solution' (Foster and Merotto 1997). Partnerships are seen as providing solutions by favouring large disbursements in support of poverty reduction through official budgets (see below).

Some issues in partnership approaches to poverty reduction

Although there is no consensus on what partnerships entail, agencies are increasingly adopting the view that the purpose of building partnerships is poverty reduction. Given this shift, there is an urgent need to clarify the mechanisms for achieving pro-poor partnership. Four important issues here concern selectivity, ownership, mechanisms for dialogue/coordination and finally the appropriateness and deployment of agency skills.

The principle of *selectivity*, given a boost in the World Bank's Report *Assessing Aid* involves agencies abandoning traditional conditionality and instead selecting governments with whom they share a commonality of purpose and which have an effective policy framework or a commitment to develop one. Selectivity is seen as affording some leverage over policies through the 'gentler and more effective' means of ongoing dialogue (Mosley and Hudson 2002) about implementing shared principles. Nevertheless, the appropriate criteria for determining selection needs clarification, since countries may share a commitment to poverty reduction but not meet other criteria (e.g. they may declare war on their neighbours). How do agencies recognise a pro-poor government when they see one? Given that governments are not homogeneous, even where the overall environment is not promising for poverty reduction, should not agencies select to work with individual ministries where prospects are reasonable?

Ownership. By definition, partnership involves donors agreeing to fund government-led expenditure plans, reflecting government vision and subject to national accountability. A key constraint is the shortage of governments or even sectoral ministries with both the commitment and the capacity to move into 'the driver's seat'. There are, however, obvious dangers that technical cooperation to build capacity will result in donor dominance by another route, undermining the ownership that it is designed to foster. Currently, where governments are unable or uninterested in projecting their own vision, the bilaterals and the Bank show an unhealthy tendency to push ahead regardless, particularly in the area of sector programmes, partly as a result of disbursement pressures (Oxford Policy Management 1997).

Stronger mechanisms for *dialogue and coordination* are needed for effective approaches to poverty reduction at the country level. Evidence on this is not systematically available for all agencies. However, the main European agencies' record in bilateral or collective dialogue on poverty issues with their partners, has been rather patchy and generally weak. Much of the coordination effort centres on narrow technical issues, limiting duplication and the exchange of experience with little specific focus on poverty reduction. Also, much coordination remains donor-driven and can leave developing country governments disempowered. The partner country perspectives' study (OECD/DAC 1999) draws attention to insufficient efforts to include civil society representatives in dialogue and coordination, as well as a lack of knowledge on poverty of government negotiators and the need for more donor support to build government capacity. Some efforts have been made to raise the profile of poverty reduction in coordination fora, through Round Table meetings, for instance, and a recent evaluation in Zambia concluded that Consultative Group meetings gave substantially more attention to poverty in 1997 than they had in 1990 (Atkinson *et al.* 1999). UNDP and the World Bank have played a leading role in coordination. Although the extent of World Bank dialogue on pro-poor policies and approaches in sub-Saharan Africa has been modest (World Bank 1996), there now seems to be greatly increased momentum for pro-poor coordination and dialogue. UNDP began piloting the UN Development Assistance Framework (UNDAF) in an attempt to ensure strategic coordination within the UN system and with government. Important innovations have also been made by some bilaterals (e.g. Germany in India) in initiating a broad dialogue within national society on poverty reduction issues, and this is something that could be developed more in the future.

Finally, developing strong and effective pro-poor partnerships calls for a reappraisal of agency skills and their deployment. On balance, decentralisation of donor skills and decision making to field offices is likely to be more effective in pursuing poverty strategies in terms of closer local understanding of the constraints and opportunities and more continuous and improved quality of dialogue (as well as helping to reduce administrative delays and complexities). Table 2.4 indicates that although a few agencies

Table 2.4 Estimated degree of decentralisation of staff and decision making

Highly decentralised	Moderately decentralised	Mainly centralised
Germany: process of decentralising underway but partial	**Canada**: authority remains at HQ, but field staff have large leeway	**Australia**
Ireland	**Denmark**: some decentralisation of staff, but authorisation at HQ	**Belgium**
Netherlands	**EC DG VIII**: substantial system of country Delegations, with some but limited formal authority.	**EC DG IB**: delegation system but understaffed and limited authority
Norway	**Switzerland**: informal system giving considerable autonomy for field staff	**Finland**: staff allocation and decision making highly centralised at HQ
Sweden	**USA**: fair amount of decentralisation for regional bureaux	**Italy**: has local units, but very understaffed
UK (all large country programmes)	**World Bank**: some country directors now in-country, but only a minority in Asia, Africa and Latin America	**Japan**: value of decentralisation recognised but actual reform is slow **Portugal** **Spain**

are highly decentralised, most are only moderately so and there are quite a number that remain centralised. Partnership approaches place a premium on sophisticated stakeholder analysis skills and organisational development expertise, but a range of economic, social and technical skills is also vital. General deficiencies vary from agency to agency but there is often a lack of economists with a micro analysis background in relation to households, firms and farms who can interact with social development experts. Attention to widening the range of skills and decentralising their location and decision making are important priorities if agencies are to be properly equipped to meet the challenges of partnership for poverty reduction.

Prioritising poverty reduction in agency-country portfolios

Studies of the OECD agencies indicate that there are no common criteria to assess even the broad poverty orientation of donor country programmes. A few agencies do have marker systems for their commitments which provide an entry point for assessing poverty focus, while for others the extent to which interventions are shown to have linkages with poverty reduction provides an alternative criterion.

CASs, however, reveal little explicit prioritisation of poverty reduction relative to other development and non-development (e.g. commercial) objectives. The portfolio of interventions is generally justified; usually implicitly on the basis of past experience, perceived comparative advantage and dialogue (generally without a poverty focus) with partner governments. Few attempts are made to assess the poverty reducing 'bang per buck', or impact per dollar spent, of different sectors. There are nonetheless, individual examples of agencies providing clear, poverty-based justifications for their choice of interventions.

Development agencies have widely varying views on the value of seeking to target poor people specifically. The World Bank's policy is to directly target the poor in countries where poverty is concentrated and sufficient government administrative capacity exists, though the policy is not systematically applied in practice. Some donors, notably the Nordics, reject targeting in principle, as undermining the political acceptability and sustainability of interventions, or because they consider it to be unnecessary in very low-income countries where 'all population groups are poor'. Others have no clear policy but implement targeting on an ad hoc basis. Generally the impression is that agencies make relatively limited, though varying, use of poverty targeting mechanisms. Often interventions do not select the poorest regions, districts or villages, or the poorest groups, such as the landless.

When considering the merits of universal versus targeted approaches it is useful to distinguish between basic service provision and interventions in the productive sectors (e.g. agriculture, fisheries, manufacturing). Targeting mechanisms appear to be particularly important in the productive sector, where untargeted support can empower the better-off at the expense of the poor and actually exacerbate the concentration of assets in the hands of the non-poor (Cox *et al.* 2000). In contrast, in the social sectors the long-term benefit of the poorest may be best served by providing good-quality services on a populationwide basis. However, it is often essential to consider the need for complementary measures to ensure that constraints specific to the poor do not prevent them from sharing in the benefits from populationwide approaches. A good example is Germany's support for drinking water provision in Burkina Faso which coupled the objective of universal provision with a careful analysis of the particular constraints facing poor groups, particularly poor women, in accessing water.

The project mode remains the preferred instrument for pursuing poverty reduction objectives for small donors and most larger donors. Recognised weaknesses of the project approach lie in the donor's temptation to retain a 'hands-on' management style, the difficulty of relating satisfactorily to the wider institutional context and policy environment, and resulting problems of sustainability. Recently, some donors have begun seeking a shift to sector investment programmes (SIPs) or sectorwide approaches (SWAps), which are intrinsically different. SIPs retain the identification of individual donors with the particular components of the programme which remain, in this sense, projects, with the Bank often playing a strong brokering and coord-inating role. The SWAp approach is intended to ensure that government plays a more active role in coordinating donors, formulating policy and setting priorities. Funding is not 'earmarked' against components but placed in a 'common basket'. While these wider approaches to poverty reduction are currently favoured by some agencies, to date, there have been few examples of SWAp approaches. Experience and guidance on how to make them work is in its infancy. Because they take (and should take) a long time to develop effectively, lessons of best practice may take some time to emerge. Problems that need to be highlighted and given more reflection, are:

- The strain on national governments' capacities for developing the neces-sary vision and systems
- The need for a patient, disciplined and self-effacing approach on the donor side
- The need to meet the challenge of combining upstream policy and system oriented interventions with action downstream which directly involves communities in the improvement of their own health and education status or wellbeing.

When selecting between different modes of intervention for poverty reduc-tion there has been a renewal of interest among some agencies, such as in Germany, the UK and World Bank, and continued interest by some others in area-based interventions. This return to more 'integrated' or multi-sectoral designs may be explained by the fundamental changes that have taken place in political and economic contexts in developing countries and worldwide since a line was drawn under the experience of Integrated Rural Development Projects (IRDPs) more than a decade ago. It is likely to be strengthened by the influence of thinking about the multi-dimensionality of poverty and 'livelihoods' approaches. It is part of a response by agencies to the fact that 'the poor do not live in a sector'. Despite the change in context, the relationship with local government needs attention if the new area projects are to avoid the 'enclave development' that was one of the negative features associated with the old IRDPs.

Agency policies indicate increased support for decentralisation measures within developing countries, designed to bring decision making and resource allocation processes closer to poor people. Practice is less widespread, but there are examples of successes in institutionalising more responsive, participatory planning in a local government framework. In many countries, giving these efforts national scope calls for legal and administrative reforms to decentralise resources and authority. However, experience with such reforms has been very mixed. A balance sheet urgently needs to be drawn up on the precise conditions under which decentralisation may be expected to assist poverty reduction.

The effectiveness and impact of agency interventions on poor people

The poverty orientation of agency portfolios

There is no systematic information on the poverty orientation of agency portfolios because most agencies do not have marker systems for their activities and commitments. However some indications are available for the World Bank and a few bilateral agencies.

There were some shifts in the World Bank's portfolio during 1992–5, partly in a pro-poor direction. The proportion of (annual) aid commitments for Poverty Targeted Interventions (PTIs) rose from 18 per cent to 24 per cent in the Bank as a whole but remained static at 28 per cent for IDA during this period. Interventions with specific mechanisms for targeting the poor, which are usually participatory and community based, remained limited (in 1995 only one out of 24 of the PTIs in sub-Saharan Africa and three out of eight in South Asia). During 1993–5 there was an increase in the proportion of spending commitments for primary education, while the proportion of social sector interventions aimed at women and girls also rose. The percentage of funds targeted on poor farmers for improvement of agricultural productivity also increased. However, over the same period, programme composition in sub-Saharan Africa did not always shift in a pro-poor direction. There was still limited agricultural assistance and little of it was targeted, and there was a further decline in rural spending on water and roads.

Most bilateral donors do not publish information even for directly poverty-focused intervention. No agencies publish the pattern of their operations for individual recipient countries. Nonetheless, available information suggests that, notwithstanding their stated objectives, the poverty orientation of European agencies' interventions are modest, measured by the share of specific poverty-focused interventions in total bilateral aid portfolios. The share for the Netherlands in 1994–5 was 19 per cent, while for the UK those projects with a direct (targeted) poverty focus accounted for 11 per cent of classified expenditure during 1995–6 to 1996–7. Germany provides technical cooperation for self-help projects which have a mainly PR focus and the share of expenditure on this mode rose from 8 per cent in 1991 to 19 per cent in 1995. It is independently estimated that poverty-focused expenditures by Italy were a mere 7 per cent of total grant aid in 1995. It is unlikely that the proportions were significant for the EC, France or Spain. Information is not available for USAID, Canada and Japan, among the larger donors.

Commitments for basic education and health can be used as a proxy for anti-poverty orientation. Incomplete information indicates that as a proportion of their total bilateral commitments (unweighted average), OECD bilateral donors' contributions to basic education were negligible in 1990 and even by 1996 constituted less than 3 per cent of total aid. For basic health care, nutrition, infectious disease control and health education, the picture was similar (under 3 per cent usually), although some agencies achieved considerably higher levels. Among the multilateral agencies, only the World Bank's IDA window appears to have achieved a high commitment (over 10 per cent) in recent years. Overall, the effort appears very modest.

How much difference have the donors made to the welfare of the poor?

The evidence here is particularly weak because most donors' monitoring and evaluation systems have not given much attention to the distributional impact of interventions. The chapter therefore draws on some limited evidence pertaining only to the World Bank and major European donors, in order to make some judgement. However, it should be added that agencies are now well aware of the lack of impact assessment and this issue is being addressed methodologically and operationally by a range of donors, of which some of the most prominent are the World Bank, DFID and USAID.

The impact of directly and indirectly focused poverty reducing interventions

For the World Bank, there has been an independent evaluation of the performance ratings of 67 IDA PR projects approved in 1988–90. As a group, these had better ratings than other projects, in terms of achievement of objectives and overcoming problems of implementation (Carvalho and White 1996). There were some cases of model poverty reducing projects, such as IDA's National Leprosy Elimination Programme in India, which, although in its early stages, already manifested a clear impact in reducing infection among poor people. A World Bank Evaluation (World Bank 1997) for programmes in 1995 concludes that progress has been made in reducing poverty but the gains are modest when set against the challenge.

European agencies provide little evidence on the effects of their interventions on poor people. Impressionistic evidence comes from the ODI-led European comparative research programme which looked at seven poor countries. A sample of 73 specific interventions were mainly chosen by the agencies themselves to represent their most poverty-focused efforts. It is not a random sample and may not necessarily be representative for the agencies or countries concerned (Table 2.5).

These results suggest that nearly three-quarters of all the selected PR interventions had brought, or were likely to bring, some benefits to the poor. A quarter were judged likely to have a large impact. If these judgements were correct, donor PR interventions were far from having been a failure. However, the figures also underlined the considerable scope for improvement, given that a quarter of the projects were thought to have had a negligible impact on the welfare of the poor, even though the projects studied were those selected by donors as having a poverty orientation.

It was possible to judge four different elements in the overall judgement of impact: the extent to which the poor benefited from improvements in their livelihoods, from improved access to resources, from enhanced knowledge and skills, and improved rights and empowerment.

The greatest impact was through increased access of the poor to resources: over 90 per cent of all sample interventions contributed in some degree. The interventions were also judged to have made a significant impact on levels of knowledge. Nearly a third of all projects were regarded as having substantially raised levels of knowledge and skills, and only a fifth as having made no contribution at all. However, under a quarter of projects were viewed as making a large contribution to increasing livelihoods, with two-fifths making

Table 2.5 Impact on poverty of EU agencies' interventions (per cent of observations in each class)

	Size of impact			Sample (no. of projects)
	Large	*Moderate*	*Negligible*	
Overall impact	25	48	27	73
Dimensions of impact				
Livelihoods	24	36	40	72
Resources	34	57	9	77
Knowledge	31	49	20	71
Rights	15	51	33	72

Source: Cox and Healey (2000).

no impact. Unsurprisingly given the difficulties external agencies are bound to experience in such sensitive areas, the record was the weakest in relation to enhancement of the rights of the poor, with only about one project in seven thought to have empowered the poor substantially, although half of projects were judged to have made some contribution.

What explained these variations in the degree of impact? Although there was considerable variation between countries, the sample was not large enough to test whether country context was a dominant influence. However, impact emerged as positively associated with the degree of targeting though this outcome must be qualified by the greater difficulty of tracing benefits to the poor in the more indirect or widely targeted interventions. There was a strong correlation between those interventions which had participation of some kind by the poor and the degree of estimated impact on them. This helps to confirm that the participatory approach now favoured by donors is justified. There is a trend towards greater participation in these agency projects, though there is scope to do a lot more still. Other possible influences not systematically confirmed were the degree of past experience of the donor in the country and the shortness of the gestation period of projects on the hypothesis that the poor are 'impatient'.

Enabling policy actions

To trace the impact of policy changes on the poor from interventions by external agencies is particularly difficult at any time. Since there has been limited dialogue of the bilateral agencies (at least) on issues relating to an enabling environment for the poor it seems an unfruitful path to pursue. In most of the poorest countries a regressive pattern of public subsidies in the education and health sectors persisted through the 1990s despite much rhetoric from donors on the need to shift the incidence of public subsidy towards primary and preventive health and basic education where the poor are thought to gain greatest access. The apparent inertia here may owe something to lack of outside pressure or financial support so far. Nevertheless there are signs of change here with greater financial commitment to public social spending of this kind not only from the World Bank but also from some bilateral donors including DFID. While fungibility may place some limits on external impact, this should not be exaggerated and there is much scope for dialogue and contribution to improvement in administration and quality of services from the agencies.

What ought the agencies do to improve their performance in poverty reduction activities?[4]

Effective anti-poverty action is difficult to achieve

The problem is complex and location-specific. Its roots go deep into the social fabric and into the distribution of economic and political power. The resource and other practical constraints on effective intervention are considerable, and there is an ever-present danger that provisions intended to raise the welfare of the poor will become captured by the less-poor. Moreover, external aid donor agencies do not have a strong comparative advantage in the PR area. There is a danger that agencies may lack an in-depth knowledge of the specific local context of poverty and its causes. This may be due to their remoteness from local socio-political realities, the centralisation of personnel and decision-making authority in donor capitals, or their top-down structure.

Some ingredients of change to improve performance are set out below – some of which have already been indicated earlier:

- In any specific country, the external agencies need to have *a clearer conceptualisation* of the nature of the poverty which they wish to redress and *better identification* of the poverty groups they are seeking to assist than they have so far displayed. Further work by them is needed on the multi-dimensional nature of the problem and the heterogeneity of 'the poor'. In countries where poverty is endemic, a donor will have to make choices among poverty groups. The choice and prioritisation of measures adopted should be consistent with the chosen view of the nature of the poverty problem.
- Actions which leave the *causes* of poverty largely untouched are unlikely to be effective in the long run. More work needs to be done on the causes and dynamics of poverty to give more insight into where interventions might be more effective.
- Agencies have recognised that growth alone is not enough and a more *pro-poor pattern of growth* than in the past needs to be stimulated. However, agencies need to work with their partners on a more precise idea what a pro-poor set of policies is for each country and to pursue the implementation of these through more dialogue than they have done in the past.

Effective poverty reduction is essentially a matter of domestic political attitudes and governance

This has three major implications which some agencies have recognised:

- *Ownership* of a pro-poor strategy or set of policies by the partner government is essential and conditionality, as practised in the past, is not a convincing way forward. Yet at the same time a lot of governments do not give poverty objectives high priority. Some governments have proved indifferent, occasionally hostile, as the World Bank (1996: 16) found especially in Africa.
- For the external agencies *selectivity in the choice of partner governments* to assist then becomes central to greater effectiveness. This has been recognised especially by DFID, Sida and the World Bank but also by other agencies.

This approach however, will have to be taken with caution because of the risk of throwing the baby out with the bath water.

- The pursuit of relationships of *'partnership'* based on mutual commitment and ownership should be pursued, preferably between all the agencies and not just bilaterally. The ultimate objective must be consensus among them on a *single strategy* for the country. Institutional mechanisms need to be developed through which such exchanges of views can be focused nationally (high-level political and societal involvement) and sectorally on poverty orientation of actions. While local ownership of PR policies and programmes is the key, the use of conditionality nevertheless may be effective if commitment to poverty reduction is limited to specific parts of government, and where donor leverage can tip the balance among domestic policy makers in favour of reformers.

- The agencies need to enter into more constructive dialogue with their partners on the causes of poverty and pro-poor policies and measures, preferably at both national and meso/sectoral levels. They have shown limited signs of this so far. Greater *coordination* among the agencies is even more important in the pursuit of partnerships and the search for a commonly agreed set of policies to allow the poor to participate more. To achieve this requires greater decentralisation to the field of skills and decision making by the agencies. Since many donors have low staffing levels in-country and lack the full range of specialist skills, there is a challenge for a number of them here.

Agencies' CASs and portfolios could become far more effective, through changes to both process and content

Possible improvements include the following:

- Agency personnel need to better understand the local *cultural and historical context* of poverty. Agencies should improve their own analytical capacity and cooperate more in supporting local research on poverty and pro-poor policy.

- Agencies should provide more assistance to recipient governments for the formulation and, even more importantly, the *implementation and monitoring* of pro-poor strategies.

- Agencies need to formulate more precisely their own country strategies for achieving PR, draw them up with wide local consultation processes and use them more effectively as a *management instrument* for poverty reduction.

- Agencies' own country strategies should give clear *operational guidance* to programme managers for drawing up their portfolios and monitoring performance.

- There should be greater incentives for programme managers to increase the poverty orientation of their strategies and disciplines that ensure they account for their *implementation*.
- Ad hoc project interventions which have been the dominant mode so far in poverty reduction, are unlikely alone to contribute to the ambitious international targets to which the agencies now subscribe. Some donors are shifting towards *sectorwide approaches*. to have wider potential impact than projects. However, this approach demands considerable changes in the behaviour of donors and recipient governments to be effective. First, donors need to work according to a *locally owned strategy* and follow a less 'hands-on' management style than they have often pursued for projects. Second, the sectoral approach requires provision of budget support, including perhaps recurrent budget funds in coordination with other donors. Third, donors need to follow flexible long-term approaches with partner governments who share the same poverty objectives. The major challenge is to ensure that attention to upstream administration reform does not undermine sensitivity to, and focus on, the needs of the poor.
- The emergence of a 'Governance and Poverty' agenda from some donors is new, logical but demanding. The aim is to strengthen the 'voice of the poor' and the responsiveness of governments to their needs. But the agencies will need to be more clear than they are at present on what are the types of *participation* and types of *institutional strengthening* that might serve this purpose as well as the ways in which they can assist from outside. This is a major challenge not only to the agencies but also the research community to come up with leads.

The issue of 'mainstreaming' the poverty reduction objective throughout agencies from top to bottom

- While senior management commitment was observed to be positive on this objective in about half of the OECD agencies there was still a predominantly 'permissive' management culture. The mechanisms for *transmitting poverty reduction objectives* to the field need strengthening. As the World Bank (1996: 14) has recorded, it is all too easy to start with good intentions but to have lost the poverty reduction focus by the time an intervention is executed. Even for donors that publicly embrace a poverty reduction goal, most provide weak operational guidance and inadequate staff orientation training and it often remains a vague objective for many programme managers. Only the World Bank, Germany and more recently the UK and Sweden seem partial exceptions to this generalisation.
- *Incentives* for programme managers and their staff, or at least minimum disincentives, are vital to encourage them with the difficult problems of understanding poverty and designing effective poverty-focused interventions. Benchmarks for judging the poverty reduction performance of

their managers would seem necessary so that those who make a more serious attempt to increase the poverty impact of their interventions are more likely to be recognised or rewarded. Since poverty reduction activities often involve an extended phase of awareness creation and institutional development prior to investment of significant funds, they are time-consuming and run counter to another incentive characteristic of donor agencies – the need to disburse country aid budgets often within an allotted time. This is a major challenge for some agencies to overcome.

Notes

1. There has also been surprisingly limited independent research work in the field though current research work for the *2000/01 World Development Report* (World Bank 2001) may help to remedy this.
2. Substantial work on safety nets is going on currently under the 2000/01 *World Development Report* research agenda (World Bank 2001).
3. More recent poverty assessments have improved in this respect.
4. This section draws on Healey, J. and T Killick (1999).

Bibliography

Atkinson, S. and K. Bird, D. Booth, J. Milimo, V. Seshami, and H. White (1999), *Evaluation of ODA/DFID Support to Poverty Reduction: Zambia Country Study*, Report for the Evaluation Department, Department for International Development, London.

Carlsson, Jerker, and O. Sassa (forthcoming), *Poverty Reduction in Zambia: Context, Policies, Strategies and Experiences with Aid from Members of the European Union*, ODI/NAI Working Paper, London: ODI.

Carvalho, S. and H. White (1996), *Implementing Projects for the Poor: What Has Been Learned?*, Washington, DC: World Bank.

Cox, A. and J. Healey (2000), *Promises to the Poor: The Record of European Development Cooperation*, London: Macmillan.

Cox, A., S. Folke, L. Schulpen and N. Webster (forthcoming), *Do the Poor Matter? A Comparative Study of European Aid for Poverty Reduction in India*, ODI/CDR Working Paper, London: ODI.

de Boisdeffre, L. (1998), *L'aide française á la réduction de la pauvrété au Burkina Faso: étude comparative des approaches européennes de l'aide à la réduction de la pauvrété au Burkina Faso*, Paris: DIAL, mimeo.

Foster, M. and D. Merotto (1997), *Partnership for Development in Africa: A Framework for Flexible Funding*, London: DFID, Africa Economics Department, mimeo.

Freres, C. and José Luis Rhi Sausi with S. Donoso (forthcoming), *European Donors and Poverty Reduction in Bolivia*, ODI\AETI\CeSPI Working Paper, London: ODI.

Gsaenger, H. and T. Voipio (1999), *European Aid for Poverty Reduction in Nepal*, ODI\GDI (Berlin)\IDS(Helsinki) Working Paper, London: ODI.

Healey, J. and T. Killick (1999), *Using Aid to Reduce Poverty*, London: ODI, Report to Danish International Development Authority (DANIDA).

Hoebink, P. and T. Voipio (1999), *European Aid for Poverty Reduction in Tanzania*, ODI Working Paper 116, London: ODI.

Killick, T., J. Carlsson and A. Kierkegaard (1998), *European Aid and the Reduction of Poverty in Zimbabwe*, ODI Working Paper 109, London: ODI.

Loquai, C. and K. Van Hove (1997), *Preliminary Findings on EU Donor Approaches Towards Poverty Reduction in Burkina Faso*, Maastricht: ECDPM, mimeo.

Mosley, Paul and John Hudson (2002) *Aid, poverty reduction and the 'new conditionality'*, Sheffield: OFID Programme on Pro-Poor Growth.

OECD/DAC (1999), *Donor Poverty Reduction Policies and Practices*, DAC Informal Network on Poverty Reduction, A Synthesis Report prepared by the Overseas Development Institute (ODI) and Associates for International Resources and Development (AIRD).

OECD/UNDP (1998), *Review of the International Aid System in Mali: Synthesis and Analysis*, Paris: OECD, Development Cooperation Directorate.

Oxford Policy Management (1997), *Sector Investment Programmes in Africa: Issues and Experience*, 2 Vols, Oxford: Oxford Policy Management.

World Bank (1996), *Taking Action for Poverty Reduction in Sub-Saharan Africa: Report of an Africa Region Task Force*, Washington, DC: World Bank.

World Bank (1997), *1995 Evaluation Results*, Washington: Operations Evaluation Department, Washington, DC: World Bank.

World Bank (1998), *Assessing Aid: What Works, What Doesn't, and Why*, Oxford: Oxford University Press for World Bank.

World Bank (2000), *World Development Report 2000/01: Attacking Poverty*, New York: Oxford University Press.

3
Poverty Reduction in Swedish Development Cooperation: Policies and Practice

Dag Ehrenpreis *

Introduction

During the almost forty years of Swedish official development assistance, solidarity with the poor and destitute has been the *leitmotif* of Sweden's aid policies. However, there have been both gradual and abrupt changes in emphasis between different sectors and ideas in Swedish development cooperation policies, reflecting oscillations between the interests of different stakeholders and the influence of different schools of thought. The balance has usually been struck at a point closer to humanitarian than commercial interests. This may indeed have been the case more in Sweden than in most other donor countries, at least in terms of policy statements if not consistently in budget allocations.

An aid programme needs wide political support, and thus must represent both the idealistic solidarity motive and the demands of more or less enlightened self-interest. In good times in Sweden, the former motive has held the upper hand, but when the economy turns sour and problems of trade or budget deficits and unemployment dominate the political stage, export and employment considerations dominate. Policy makers always have to balance between these interests and motives. Broad-based popular movements representing the NGO community have consistently provided political support for increasing the aid budget to, and maintaining it at, 1 per cent of GDP. This political support base has strongly supported an aid programme oriented to poverty alleviation, while the corporate sector, more

---
* Senior Adviser on Poverty Reduction, OECD/DCD, on secondment from Sida, Sweden. This chapter draws mainly on Ehrenpreis (1996) and Carlsson (1999). The usual disclaimer applies.

discreetly but with often overwhelming economic power, has been lobbying for increased industry and infrastructure investments financed through the aid budget.

In measuring Swedish aid allocations and disbursements at the sector and country levels, the bias towards poverty alleviation seems to be confirmed. But if we look more closely at the degree of mainstreaming of poverty reduction and gender equality in institutional management incentives, or in learning, monitoring and evaluation systems, the case for declaring Sweden an ideal donor is considerably weakened. It is rather one of several donors making serious efforts to achieve poverty reduction and other humanitarian objectives, but much has yet to be done to assure that the good intentions are realised and confirmed in practice. This chapter will argue that, until recently, insufficient attention has been given to developing the organisational, methodological and quality control aspects of an aid policy oriented to poverty reduction. It is important to analyse the conditions for effective poverty reduction in different countries, to encourage the active participation of poor people in designing and monitoring projects and programmes, and to enhance Sida's institutional culture and learning systems. Mainstreaming the poverty reduction objective requires clear leadership commitment, as well as new systems and procedures, including monitoring and evaluation of results.

Objectives of Sweden's development cooperation

The overarching objective of Sweden's development cooperation policies was stated in the first official policy statement on development assistance, a Government Bill in 1962. It was formulated as follows:

> The aim of giving aid is to raise the level of living of the poor peoples. In concrete terms, this means abolishing starvation and mass poverty, eliminating epidemic diseases, reducing child mortality and on the whole creating possibilities for decent living conditions.

This objective is still valid. It has been complemented with four official goals concerning resource growth, economic and political independence, social and economic equity, and democratic development. Since then, further goals have been added by the Swedish Parliament relating to environmental sustainability and gender equality. A Parliamentary Commission on Swedish Policy for Global Development with broad representation was appointed in 1999 to undertake an overall review of development cooperation objectives and policies, and to present its report by the end of 2001. In the forty years since a mixed government and civil society commission published the first Swedish policy statement on foreign aid, this small and non-aligned country has adopted a high international profile in promoting development cooperation for poverty reduction. Sweden launched a rapidly growing bilateral aid programme, while initially mainly channelling aid through multilateral channels. Strengthening and supporting the UN system has always been a priority area in Sweden's foreign policy.

This chapter will review Sweden's implementation of development cooperation since the 1960s. The focus is on the extent to which Swedish aid has systematically emphasised the poverty objective in policy formulation, organisation and management, programming, implementation and monitoring/evaluation. The case of Sweden is chosen as an example to complement the overall DAC Scoping Study review (see Cox and Healey's Chapter 2) since it is one of the countries with a reputation for stressing the altruistic 'solidarity' motive for development cooperation. The hypothesis to be tested in the chapter is whether Sweden is an appropriate role model for other DAC members in formulating and implementing poverty oriented aid policies.

The evolution of Swedish aid: an overview

In the first, semi-official policy report from 1959 entitled 'Sweden Helps', the motives presented for Swedish aid were solidarity, social fervour, humanitarianism and egalitarianism. There was an increasing awareness of the needs of the rapidly growing populations in underdeveloped areas and of the increasing international importance of these areas at the threshold of decolonisation. The export opportunities of aid and development in an expanding world market were also recognised. In the 1962 Bill, the humanitarian motive for helping the poor was also emphasised. Based on the ideas of human dignity and social equity, the growing feeling of international solidarity and responsibility were seen as an expression of a more profound insight that peace, freedom and wellbeing are not exclusively national matters, but increasingly universal and indivisible. This indirectly introduced self-interest as a motive for development assistance. Poor people and nations may become a threat to international stability and peace, and therefore to our own security and life-style. The 1962 Bill stated: 'The idealistic motives for giving aid are thus at the same time highly realistic.'

During the 1960s, the Swedish aid budget grew quite rapidly. In 1968, a new Bill set out a plan to reach the 1 per cent of GDP target in seven years by annual increases in the aid budget of 25 per cent. The goals of the 1962 Bill were reconfirmed, with increased emphasis on social and economic equality. But in the 1970s, major changes were made in Swedish development assistance policy. In the Budget Bill of 1970, the new Department for International Development Co-operation in the Ministry for Foreign Affairs replaced the project approach by a new partner country selectivity criterion, favouring those countries that carried out egalitarian structural reforms. This new principle was reinforced by the international tendency to introduce country programming as the main planning model for development assistance, raising the policy focus to the country or state level. However, SIDA (as it was then known) and the Swedish Parliament resisted any radical policy change. Parliament approved the Bill only with the amendment that 'the aims of Swedish aid policies are possible to attain in countries with different political and economic systems'. It further stated that the equity goal could be achieved by designing projects in agriculture, water supply, health, school construction and vocational training so as to reach ordinary people.

From the beginning of Swedish development cooperation, the situation of women was given attention, primarily as a result of the efforts of Swedish women's organisations. The initial focus was on women's subordinate and impoverished situation. There were special projects for women, mainly in the area of education. As part of the overall increased emphasis on social equity, a study of the position of women was carried out in the early 1970s, which recognised women as being among the poorest of the poor. It established that special projects for women were necessary but insufficient. A complementary strategy of integrating a review of the position of women in all aid analyses, and in policy and programme development, was also needed.

SIDA stated in its 1973 budget petition to the government that the lowest income groups required increased attention in coming years. An important task was to improve the planning and implementation of projects which improved the level of living of the lowest income groups and the poorest areas. Thus the problems of the neglected groups attracted increasing attention in SIDA's country analyses and country programmes over the 1970s. SIDA followed the research in this field and intended to contribute, in cooperation with recipient countries and voluntary organisations, to the design of concrete development programmes and projects, so that the foreign assistance really would reach the poorest groups. A SIDA Task Force was established in 1973 to study how aid funds could best contribute to improvements in the living standards of the least developed groups and areas, in the light of international and Swedish experience. The Task Force reviewed recent SIDA-funded programmes and projects in order to find out to what extent they had been explicitly targeted toward low-income groups, and the results evaluated. In fact, the Task Force did not find much information about the impact of Swedish aid on the target groups. Some evaluation reports, however, provided evidence of success in reaching the poor through projects such as rural water supply schemes, health centres and primary schools. In the flagship CADU agricultural development project in Ethiopia, small farmers had doubled their yields of cereals and many useful innovations had been developed and implemented.

One conclusion of this review was that more efforts should be made to integrate monitoring and evaluation systems into aid programmes and projects, in order to trace their impact on the target groups. Emphasis was also placed on the need to integrate all projects into regional and national development programmes, on local participation and control in project planning and implementation and, furthermore, on broadening the perspective from the project level to an analysis of the structural causes of poverty and underdevelopment. Simply alleviating the symptoms was seen as insufficient, and perhaps even counterproductive.

A Parliamentary Commission on Development Co-operation Policies in its 1977 report strongly emphasised social and economic justice as the principal aim of development cooperation, which should dominate both the form of assistance and the choice of partner countries. Swedish assistance should attack poverty and its causes directly, and it must reach the poorest and most disadvantaged groups. In the subsequent Aid Bill, the non-socialist coalition government confirmed the proposed objectives, which together 'would promote social justice for poor people'. In a typical political balancing act, the government appointed an Industrial Development Assistance Commission, which in 1977 reported that the industrial sector had grown very rapidly during the 1970s and proposed the establishment of a new agency to support joint ventures for industrial development in low-income countries. The Aid Bill approved the proposal, and SIDA's Industry division was also expanded.

In 1980, SIDA adopted an integrated Rural Development Strategy. Through a package of interacting efforts covering a wide range of activities, such as agriculture, social forestry, road construction, education and health, it was envisaged that the standard of living of the vast majority of the population could be improved in such a way as to generate a self-sustaining development process. In practice, the main effect of this policy shift towards basic needs and equality was a stronger rural emphasis than before in several country programmes and within sectors such as health and education. The programme in India, for example, was transformed from one stressing mainly import support into a series of sector programmes in social forestry, health and rural drinking water plus energy projects. This matched India's plans as well as the interests of Swedish suppliers.

Swedish development assistance continued also in other important areas, especially in industrial development, infrastructure, public administration and import support. In terms of disbursements, infrastructure was the major sector in Swedish aid until 1976–7. For the following six years, industry and construction took first place. The implementation of the Rural Development Strategy meant that from 1982–3 until the mid-1990s, agriculture, forestry and fishery became the major sectors, except in one year when the health sector took first place. However, general import support was much larger than any single sectoral programme until 1992–3. This was a result of the rapidly growing aid budget, while the staff and other administrative overhead costs were kept at a much lower growth rate. To a considerable extent, it complemented direct industry sector support and assisted Swedish exports, although import support was not generally tied to Swedish products.

The 1980s were a period of economic crisis and adjustment in most partner countries, which deeply affected Sida programmes. Rehabilitation of industry and infrastructure, safeguarding social progress and relieving the worsening balance of payments and foreign debt problems of aid recipients were major areas of attention. SIDA was particularly concerned by the negative development of the priority agricultural sector during this period. Since the major problems seemed to stem from inadequate policies, Sweden found it necessary to enter into policy dialogue with aid recipients, covering both agricultural and broader economic policies, including issues such as producer prices, private sector incentives, exchange rate policy and budget deficits. This was a major policy shift, since Sweden had not wanted to interfere in the policy making of sovereign partner countries (except in the special case of Ethiopia). Supporting the independence of developing countries was after all one of the main objectives of Swedish aid.

Over the 1980s, Swedish aid in many countries was redirected in order to ameliorate the negative effects of structural adjustment policies (SAPs) and ensure that important social development programmes could be maintained. Sweden's substantial involvement in the social sectors of several countries was a dilemma. In countries such as Tanzania and Zambia the economic crisis had undermined the financial solvency of the social services built up since independence, with Swedish assistance. Schools were in poor condition, lacking textbooks, materials and teachers with the minimum qualifications. Many health centres had become empty shells lacking even the most rudimentary equipment and medical supplies. Water pumps no longer functioned owing to lack of spare parts, fuel and an effective maintenance system. Industries were operating at a fraction of installed capacity. SIDA then shifted the emphasis away from new investments towards operation and maintenance, which involved provision of basic supplies, transport, essential training programmes and other recurrent expenditures, except wages and salaries. Import support was provided to help fill the widening balance-of-payments gaps.

The economic crisis of the 1980s meant increasing Swedish cooperation in internationally coordinated SAP financing. The poverty impact of these programmes was, and to some extent remains, a controversial issue in the Swedish aid community. Debt relief measures were introduced bilaterally even in the 1970s, and became an increasing part of Swedish aid after 1980. Emergency relief and NGO support also sharply increased their shares of Swedish aid after the 1980s. In the public debate, it had been argued that such funding should increase faster than normal development assistance because of the large needs and the more direct benefits for impoverished and distressed people, such as disaster victims and refugees.

In the 1990s, the poverty focus re-emerged in Swedish (and international) aid. The Swedish government welcomed the UNDP *Human Development Report* in 1990, and the World Bank's *1990 World Development Report* as indications of a renewed focus on poverty reduction in the international community. SIDA adopted an aid strategy for the crisis-ridden African countries in the 1990s, which concentrated on increasing the focus on direct poverty reducing measures, including support to health care, education and local infrastructure. Furthermore, aid should support democracy by encouraging local and popular participation in the development process, public sector reform, real debt reduction for the poorest countries and improved competence of national and local institutions. Aid should also promote increased local influence on SAPs and better coordination of their conditionality requirements.

In 1995, SIDA was merged with other Swedish ODA agencies such as SAREC, BITS and SWEDCORP to form the new unified Swedish International Development Cooperation Agency, Sida. In 1996, Sida's Programme of Action for Poverty Reduction was adopted. It stressed that every strategy document and project proposal must clearly explain how the activities proposed were designed to reduce poverty. Inputs could be made at different levels and be oriented to target groups to a greater or lesser extent. The impact on poverty was the main criterion in the project assessment. The programme distinguished four levels of impact: direct (targeted), inclusive, policies and institutions, and other indirect impacts. The selection of types of interventions should be determined by the assessment made in the country strategy. This should make clear the extent to which a country's development efforts were likely to enhance poverty reduction and in what ways a contribution by Sida could help in this respect.

The rather extensive Programme of Action included an analytical approach, stressing principles and priorities, methods of work and division of responsibilities within Sida. It also had a summary of experience as well as action plans and reference projects for the different Sida departments. In order to make it more operational and user-friendly, simple Implementation Guidelines for Sida's Programme of Action for Poverty Reduction were issued in 1998. The Swedish government presented a policy report to Parliament in 1997 on combating poverty in Sweden's Development Cooperation, entitled *The Rights of the Poor – Our Common Responsibility* (Government of Sweden 1997). This Report stated that the primary objective of Sweden's international development cooperation was to combat poverty, both by responding to acute emergencies and by creating opportunities for the poor to help themselves escape from poverty in the long term. The objective was to further strengthen the fight against poverty, thereby achieving a world living in peace and concord, where poverty had been eliminated and international assistance would no longer be necessary. Thus, the original motives for Swedish development cooperation were reconfirmed.

Measuring the poverty focus of Swedish aid

SIDA's social sector disbursements increased from under 21 per cent in 1990/91 to around 34 per cent in 1994–5. Included in the definition of social sector aid were projects embracing education, health, population, water and sanitation, as well as social housing and human rights. This spending was mainly aimed at the provision of primary-level social services to poor people. Emergency assistance, which by definition is directed towards especially affected hardship groups, increased to become SIDA's largest expenditure line, representing nearly 21 per cent of total SIDA expenditures in the mid-1990s. Thus, a total of nearly 55 per cent of SIDA's disbursements in 1994–5[1], went to the poverty-focused social and emergency relief sectors.

Another way of measuring the poverty focus of foreign aid is to calculate the degree to which it goes to the poorest countries. An analysis of DAC statistics indicates that Sweden, along with Denmark, Finland and Switzerland, disburse the highest proportions of their aid to the poorest countries. Over the ten-year period 1985–94, about 75 per cent of Swedish bilateral aid disbursements were made to countries whose populations were among the poorest half of the population in all developing countries, on a country *per capita* income basis. Over these ten years 50 per cent of the Swedish aid which went to the poorest countries was concentrated on the bottom 12 per cent of the total population in all developing countries, measured on a country *per capita* income basis. Thus, Sweden has disbursed extremely high shares of its assistance to the poorest countries, whereas countries such as Australia, France, Germany, New Zealand and, especially, the USA provided their aid mainly to developing countries with much higher *per capita* incomes. The difference would be even larger if Sweden's large contributions to those international organisations that mainly support the low-income countries are taken into account (e.g. IDA and the similar 'soft loan' funds of regional development banks as well as UN agencies such as UNDP, UNICEF, WFP and IFAD).

But does the strong poverty focus of Swedish development assistance at the country level necessarily imply similar achievements in poverty reduction? Do the high figures for social sector expenditures, emergency assistance, NGO support and rural development imply that Sweden's aid reached the poorest of the poor? In fact doubts have been expressed about the extent to which Sweden's aid does focus on social spending. More generally, the measures used by the DAC of the OECD and the UNDP to measure the poverty impact of aid can be disputed. Figures published in UNDP's *Human Development Report* have indicated that Sweden had the lowest allocation for 'total social investment' of all the member countries of OECD/DAC. This result was disputed by the Swedish authorities, which claimed that it was the result of a gross misinterpretation of Swedish aid statistics. Both the UNDP and the DAC definitions are unclear and misleading about the extent to which different kinds of aid has a sustainable impact on improving the level of living of the poor. For instance, providing technical assistance to a ministry for developing more effective poverty reducing policies is not included in the definition, only strictly targeted service deliveries.

The remainder of this chapter will look more closely at what has actually been done to achieve the poverty reduction objectives of the Swedish aid programme.

Institutional mainstreaming, change and learning

The planning system

The current procedures for planning and implementation of Swedish development aid were introduced in 1995. They place the country strategy process at the centre of the Swedish system of bilateral development cooperation. The process was reviewed and revised after a few years of experience, with new guidelines adopted in 2000. The revised guidelines do not strongly emphasise poverty reduction as an overarching goal, but highlight poverty, democracy and human rights, gender equality and sustainable development as areas which the country strategy process should deal with.

The purpose of the country strategy is to facilitate efficient management of Sweden's development cooperation, in conjunction with the recipient partner country. It is to present the viewpoint and intentions of the Swedish government and to determine the orientation, organisation, and expected results from cooperation. The strategy should be designed in such a way as to facilitate a policy dialogue not only with the recipient partners, but also in multilateral forums and in donor coordination meetings. A country strategy is to be prepared for all programme countries, and other major recipients of Swedish aid (for example, the countries of Central and Eastern Europe).

A country strategy implies a long-term commitment, and its point of departure should be the six objectives of Swedish aid. It should also take into consideration Swedish interests in a wide sense, as well as the needs of the recipient partner country. This holistic approach requires an intensive dialogue between the Ministry of Foreign Affairs, Sida and the recipient partner country. The country strategy should express Swedish priorities and objectives. The participation of the recipient country is required in order to achieve a real sense of ownership. The purpose of the country strategy process is to achieve a consensus among its major stakeholders – the Ministry of Foreign Affairs, the relevant embassy, Sida and the recipient partner country. The country strategy provides concrete guidance on how Sida's programmes of development cooperation with a country should best be organised to contribute to poverty reduction. This is done by:

(1) Stating how the areas for Swedish development cooperation that have been identified are likely to *contribute to poverty reduction.*
(2) Supporting reforms and capacity building at the *policy and institutional levels*, stating the anticipated effects of the planned interventions for poverty reduction.
(3) Providing guidance at *sector policy level* in respect of programmes of cooperation that have not yet been identified.

The *country analysis* is the most important instrument and basic document for producing the country strategy. Its core is an analysis of the causes of, and remedies for, poverty. It should ideally incorporate the following:

(1) A brief *history of the country* during recent decades.
(2) *Government policies*, including economic and social development policies; poverty reduction, gender equality and environmental policies; democratic developments, peace and conflict policies.
(3) *Poverty.* An analysis of social and economic issues, e.g. income inequality, regional differences, ethnic and socio-cultural conditions. More specifically, Sida instructs its programme officers to include the following information (*Guidelines for the Application of Sida's Poverty Programme* Sida 1998: 3)

   (a) Statistics on *who is poor* (broken down by gender, age group and other attributes)
   (b) The *views of the poor* on their poverty
   (c) Where the poor *live*
   (d) Poverty reduction *actors* and their *capacity* (the government, NGOs, local associations, etc.)
   (e) An analysis of the *causes of poverty*.

(4) *Economic development.* Analysis of macroeconomic conditions and policies, structural adjustment, environmental economic issues relating to development, the microeconomy and aid dependence.
(5) *Democracy and human rights.* Human rights, including the rights of women and children. Freedom of the press and of assembly, democratic elections.
(6) *Gender equality.* An analysis of political, economic, social and cultural conditions and potential from a gender perspective.
(7) *Environment and sustainable development.* An analysis of political, economic, social and cultural conditions and prospects for environmentally sustainable development. This would include a discussion of natural

resources, production and consumption patterns, ownership situation, legislation, environmental plans, etc.
(8) *Public administration.* The partner country's administrative systems and administrative capacity. Also an analysis of the situation regarding corruption.
(9) *Development cooperation.* Other donors, general objectives, government policy, donor coordination, significance and impact of international support.

Incentives and skills

Sida's staff incentive and promotion system is flexible and partly the result of periodic negotiations between management and unions in connection with recurrent salary negotiations. General skills and abilities – including, in recent times, gender considerations – have been more important criteria than proven dedication to poverty reduction. It would appear that quality of performance is assessed in terms of *managerial and social competence* rather than in terms of proven analytical, preparatory or monitoring skills for longer-term sustainable poverty reduction. On the other hand, emphasising poverty reduction has not been discouraged. The Sida Director-General has actively encouraged risk taking as a general management rule.

Historically, Sida never had many highly trained economists, social anthropologists or other specialists among its staff, and has never had very attractive salary levels, which has made it difficult to recruit qualified professionals. This has recently changed and the agency has made efforts to recruit young people with a strong technical competence, but not necessarily with a long experience in development cooperation. Financial market analysts and environmental specialists are examples of such targeted recruitment. There is a small cadre of specialists on cross-cutting issues in the agency, known as 'advisers'. They work as focal points for internal and external networks in disseminating information and maintaining the collective identification with the particular cross-cutting issue – e.g. poverty reduction, popular participation and democracy, gender equality and environmental sustainability. A Senior Poverty Adviser, working with a social anthropologist, leads the focal point unit for poverty reduction in the Policy Secretariat. A new post has now been added to facilitate the coordination of Sida's poverty work.

In the case of gender equality, there are two or three people organised as a small unit, also housed in the Policy Secretariat. Sida has reduced its locally employed expertise on gender in the embassies in partner countries; experience showed that they tended to become marginalised by programme officers who were regular Sida staff members. Instead, gender mainstreaming of the work of regular programme officers and managers has become the main strategy. Sida is has also experimented with posted advisers on socio-cultural issues, conflict, democracy and human rights, but their tasks are often transformed into operational work.

Training courses play a central role in Sida's gender and poverty strategies. Gender courses have been ongoing for many years. However, the two training courses on poverty organised by the Overseas Development Institute (ODA, London) and the Institute of Development Studies (IDS, University of Sussex) were the first examples of consistent agencywide training in poverty analysis. The idea is that this course package will form the starting point for a recurrent training programme in Sweden, and possibly for coordinated poverty training with other aid agencies,

Thus the average Sida staff member gets some training in cross-cutting issues such as poverty and gender issues. Expertise in these areas is available in the agency, but not necessarily within the operational departments. The current pattern has been that of employing such expertise at the policy level. At the same time, expertise on the environment, conflicts, human rights and democracy is centred in the operational departments with corresponding areas of responsibility, although these issues are also, to varying degrees, cross-cutting.

With the establishment and subsequent strengthening of the focal point for poverty reduction in the Policy Secretariat, Sida's poverty work has made substantial strides. An agencywide poverty network has been established and one-week intensive top-class training for this group has taken place. A series of Management Committee poverty seminars have also been held. These activities are part of an overall formal poverty reduction project, commissioned by top management and involving both HQ and field office managers, which are aimed at enhancing Sida's poverty reduction work and instilling a poverty reduction focus in Sida's organisational culture. The project was concluded in 2002; it has produced a large number of studies on Sida's experience of working with poverty issues since 1996 – on economic growth and poverty reduction, on institutional dimensions, livelihoods and employment, participatory approaches, democracy, and on health, gender and methodological aspects of poverty reduction.

Monitoring poverty reduction performance

For several years, Sida has used the Logical Framework Approach (LFA) as an instrument for planning, as well as monitoring interventions. Today, partly as a result of an intensive training programme, the method is generally accepted as useful, not only as a tool for improving quality, but also for easing the workload of the staff. In practice, efforts have been made to integrate the LFA method in the various departments' work procedures, revisions of appraisal systems, issuing of new guidelines, etc. However, the application of the LFA method during the full project cycle is not consistently implemented. Currently, it is mainly a tool for appraising project proposals.

It has also been found that the quality of project documents leaves a lot to be desired. (Carlsson and Eriksson-Baaz 1998). This is important, since it is the project document which provides the basis for effective monitoring and evaluation. The study by Carlsson and Eriksson-Baaz concluded that the quality of appraisal analysis was weak: the documents were characterised by description rather than analysis. Monitoring has traditionally meant project monitoring. At present, it is unclear how the poverty objectives of country strategies will be monitored: there is no system in place, although the need is recognised. The LFA method is a useful instrument since it helps in formulating measurable indicators, but at present few departments make any consistent use of this potential. Monitoring, as distinct from evaluation, means following up activities in work plans and budget outcomes. Partly this reflects organisational priorities; partly it reflects the impact of weak concepts that are difficult to operationalise into measurable indicators of performance.

Sida, like other donors, has a system for evaluating the performance of its various programmes. The value of such a system depends on quality criteria against which performance can be measured. However, Sida does not have any explicitly accepted and agreed quality requirements that can be used for judging its various projects. Criteria such as local ownership, relevance, feasibility and sustainability are only implied in Sida's concept of quality. In 1998, Sida initiated a quality improvement project with a chief controller in the Director-General's office, and a network of controllers in Sida's departments. A new management performance assessment system has also been introduced, and stronger emphasis placed on organisational and management development. However, it remains to be seen whether poverty reduction will be central to the quality criteria selected.

An overall assessment

A 1990 Sida Poverty Project study on the agency's experience of working with poverty reduction tackled five issues (Booth, Conway and Silfverstolpe 2001):

(1) Whether, in spite of not being poverty-focused in the strict sense (having poverty reduction as a main goal, in logframe terms) the selected programmes may be considered broadly relevant to poverty reduction.
(2) What learning there has been, and what gaps remain, in thinking about how to reach poor people, directly or indirectly, in a more effective way.
(3) What the project and programme experience suggests about the institutional conditions for effective poverty reduction, and what issues remain to be clarified.
(4) To what extent poor people have been treated as actors in Swedish-supported programmes, and with what costs and benefits.
(5) Why Sida's poverty reduction work has suffered from the gaps and limitations identified, and what mix of changes in policy and practice – including in the area of country strategies – is needed at this point.

The first study's major finding is that many, if not most, of the programmes considered are at least potentially relevant to poverty reduction in some way, when poverty is conceptualised as a multi-dimensional problem. This is curious in view of the observation, demonstrated more systematically by Peck and Widmark (2000), that Sida programme documentation does not generally make poverty reduction an explicit overarching objective. The study confirms the belief that Sida has plenty of relevant experience to work with if and when the agency turns more decisively towards poverty reduction – viewed multi-dimensionally – as the overall objective of everything it does.

On the study's second major topic, the study suggests that at least one of the central ideas of SIDA's 1996 Action Programme on poverty is well established. That is that there are valid ways of approaching poverty reduction directly (through more or less closely targeted operations) and indirectly, by acting on poverty's underlying causes. Although poverty reduction is often not formally and specifically named as the goal of the activity, the study finds examples of critical thinking and analytical effort on both targeting and the rationale for indirect forms of action.

The study's third set of findings centres on national ownership and new forms of partnership, which are coming to be recognised as the key issues in the institutional framework for poverty reduction. The study confirms that Sida's policy focus on country ownership is right. On the other hand, even when this takes the form of a fully fledged sectorwide approach, big questions are raised about viability and poverty orientation. Like other agencies and partners, Sida needs to be open to rapid learning from international experience in this field.

The study's fourth question relates to participation by poor people, and the study finds actual practice to be fairly limited among the sample programmes, in both form and range of application. To some extent this is legitimate, if compensated by imaginative promotion of broader stakeholder participation, with probable spin-offs for the poor. However, some missed opportunities have been identified. A stronger requirement to carry out a stakeholder analysis, and justify which actors are involved in programme design and management, is recommended in the preparation of major programmes.

Fifth, the study argues that there is a substantial 'guidance deficit' on poverty reduction in Sida. There is wide agreement that this guidance deficit has arisen from the failure of the various Action Programmes and directives issued since 1996 to agree on the current meaning of the 1962 Act's statement of the goal of Swedish development cooperation. The inconsistency between the different documents has led to a widespread perception that for Sida management and the Swedish government, poverty reduction is just one objective among many. This is indeed the most crucial matter raised by the study as a whole. There are a number of areas where the guidance material and training available to Sida staff could be improved, and various points of entry into operational processes can be identified. However, as stated in the DAC *Guidelines on Poverty Reduction*, (1999) a clear general signal from the highest level is generally a precondition for other changes to be effective.

A previous study came to similar conclusions (Tobisson and de Vylder 1998: 23):

> It is far easier to talk about poverty reduction and gender equality in a politically correct way than to do something about it. While Country Analyses and Country Strategies pay lip service to poverty and gender issues, the actual design of projects and programmes indicates that while poverty reduction and gender may get 'priority' the funds tend to go somewhere else.

Conclusion

Swedish development cooperation policies and programmes have to a considerable extent emphasised the poverty reduction motive and objective. In measuring aid allocations and disbursements at the sector and country levels, this inclination seems to be confirmed. However, looking more closely at the institutional management incentives and the learning, monitoring and evaluation systems, Sweden does not stand out as a model but rather as one donor among others, with a lot remaining to be done to ensure that the good intentions are realised and confirmed in practice. This concerns in particular the need to develop Sida's capacity for poverty analysis and for the necessary institutional change and learning.

The underlying thinking has been that allocating aid to very poor countries and to sectors of particular and direct importance to poor people would ensure the achievement of poverty reduction objectives, if the resources provided were of high quality. However, until recently insufficient attention has been given to developing the methodological requirements and quality control aspects of aid. Important factors include analysing the conditions for effective poverty reduction in different countries, encouraging the active participation of poor people in designing and monitoring projects and programmes and improving institutional learning and mainstreaming of the poverty reduction objective and achievements.

Note

1. The last year before SIDA merged with other Swedish ODA agencies to form the new Sida.

Bibliography

Booth, D., T. Conway and A. Silfverstolpe (2001), *Working with Poverty Reduction in Sida*, Stockholm: Sida Poverty Project.

Carlsson, J. and M. Eriksson-Baaz (1998), *Two Years After – A Review of the Introduction of the LFA Method in Sida*, Stockholm: Sida.

Carlsson, J. (1999), *Swedish Aid for Poverty Reduction*, Unpublished working paper for DAC Informal Network on Poverty Reduction Scoping Study.

Ehrenpreis, D. (1996), 'Poverty reduction in Swedish assistance: policy and practice', Working Paper 6, Sida Task Force on Poverty Reduction, Stockholm: Sida.

Government of Sweden (1997), *The Rights of the Poor – Our Common Responsibility. Combating Poverty in Sweden's Development Cooperation*, Stockholm: Government of Sweden.

Peck, L. and C. Widmark (2000), 'Sida documents in a poverty perspective. A review of how poverty is addressed in Sida's country strategy papers, assessment memoranda and evaluations', Sida Studies in Evaluation 00/2, Stockholm: Sida.

SIDA (1998), *Guidelines for the Application of Sida's Poverty Programme*, Stockholm: Swedish International Development Authority.

Tobisson, E. and S. de Vylder (1998), *Poverty Reduction and Gender Equality: An Assessment of Sida's Country Reports and Evaluations in 1995–96*, Stockholm: Sida.

UNDP (1990), *Human Development Report*, New York.

World Bank (1990), *World Development Report 1990: Poverty*, Washington, DC: World Bank.

4
Poverty and Structural Adjustment: Some Remarks on Tradeoffs between Equity and Growth

Rolph van der Hoeven *

Introduction

The adjustment experiences of the 1980s and the adjustment and liberalisation experiences in the 1990s have led to renewed attention being paid to poverty and inequality in debates about economic development. Inequality was a topical issue in the 1970s when major attention was given to it by scholars and international organisations such as ECLA and ILO. The emphasis on adjustment policies in the 1980s relegated inequality discussions to the sidelines, notwithstanding a greater concern for poverty at the end of the 1980s and in the 1990s. One stream of thought continues to argue that the best way to tackle poverty is to grow out of it. According to this view, income inequality is often the consequence of deep-rooted societal structures, which will take time to change. Others have regarded measures to reduce inequality as detrimental to growth and therefore not warranted during periods of adjustment when all emphasis must be placed on the speedy return to sustainable growth. Such views have not, of course, been uncontested (van der Hoeven 1995; ILO 1996; Ravallion 1997) but only recently has a concern for inequality entered into mainstream discussion of structural adjustment and liberalisation (Rodrik 1998; Stiglitz 1998; Tanzi and Chu 1998). This renewed attention can be partly explained by very specific socio-political reasons. Not only may large inequalities be harmful to growth (following the analysis of the so-called 'new growth theory') but also large

* This chapter is a revision of an invited paper for the policy workshop of the Development Studies Association on 'New Poverty Strategies', Whiteknights Hall, University of Reading, 8–10 April 1999. The views in this chapter are those of the author and do not necessarily reflect those of the International Labour Office. I benefited from comments by participants at the DSA workshop and by John Weeks, Fahrad Mehran and Claire Harasty.

inequalities may promote coalitions of different groups in various countries to oppose measures designed to liberalise both trade and capital flows.

In the light of these debates, three themes are explored in this chapter. First, I present a review of literature on the effects of stabilisation and adjustment policies on poverty and inequality. Second, I discuss the impact of adjustment and liberalisation on labour markets, looking especially at issues such as informalisation of employment, wage inequality, human capital formation and workers' organisations. It will be argued that stabilisation, adjustment and liberalisation policies have not infrequently contributed to greater inequality (see, e.g., Cornia 1998). This in turn casts doubt on the argument that inequality should not be a policy concern as long as countries have a good growth performance which permits a decline in numbers of persons in poverty ('a rising tide will lift all boats').

The last part of the chapter explores in more detail the effects of growth and equality on poverty. It is argued that a reduction of inequality can greatly reduce the number of households in poverty and that efforts to reduce poverty simply by stimulating growth are not sufficient and need to be complemented by efforts to reduce inequality. Policy-makers should therefore shift to policies which increase equality if the goal of poverty eradication set at the 1990 World Summit for Social Development is to be achieved.

Stabilisation, adjustment and poverty: a literature review

The question whether stabilisation and adjustment policies are aggravating poverty cannot be answered in a straightforward manner. It is difficult to define poverty, but for our purposes, it suffices to define it using the headcount measure – i.e. as the percentage of households with an average income below a certain poverty threshold (Fields 1994: 3). Although there are some objections to such a simple definition of poverty (Foster, Greer and Thorbecke 1984; Kanbur 1987), this definition is much more clear cut than any definition of stabilisation and adjustment. What do such policies comprise? One easy answer is a very practical one, namely that stabilisation and adjustment policies are defined as the set of policies adopted by those countries which have accepted one or more structural adjustment loans (SALs) from the World Bank since this term was introduced. Such a definition will be used here.

Based upon various evaluation reports (e.g. World Bank 1992), we can define structural adjustment policies (SAPs) as a set of policies which combine short-run stabilisation measures and longer-run adjustment measures, which are either applied sequentially or simultaneously or overlap each other. The set of stabilisation policies consists of the following four elements:

(a) Fiscal policies designed to reduce the budget deficit
(b) Monetary policies designed to reduce the money supply

(c)   Wage and price policy designed to control inflation
(d)   Exchange rate policies to reduce balance of payment deficits.

The complete set of adjustment policies contains policies to make product and factor markets operate more smoothly by removing 'obstacles' such as price controls and subsidies. A further important element is often the reform of trade policies in order to achieve freer trade. A restructuring of the public sector and privatising publicly owned enterprises to reduce the fiscal deficit and to make such enterprises more profitable is often also a part of a SAP.

The above description makes it clear that it is much more difficult to delineate a set of adjustment policies than it is to delineate the components of stabilisation policies. For example, one could question to what extent a change of trade regime is part of 'normal' stabilisation policy and to what extent it is part of an adjustment effort. It is here that the concept begins to lose analytical precision. We therefore discuss in this section the relation between stabilisation policies and poverty and postpone until the next section a discussion of adjustment, poverty and developments in labour markets.

Stabilisation policies and poverty

The stabilisation policies most commonly applied are fiscal policies and monetary policies, coupled with wage policies and devaluation. Fiscal and monetary policies implemented as part of a stabilisation programme reduce domestic absorption in the economy, which often lowers growth rates or even results in an absolute decline in national income. The simulation models used by Khan (1990) point to reduced growth of usually one or two years' duration in the wake of stabilisation measures. How do such deflationary policies affect poverty? If one assumes that income distribution does not change, then policies which reduce income in an absolute sense must by definition increase poverty, and policies which reduce the rate of growth of income must over time reduce the rate of decline of poverty incidence. How much poverty increases, or poverty decline slows down, depends not only on the reduction in the real rate of growth, but also on the parameters which determine the slope of the income inequality function around the cut-off point for poverty. It is difficult to maintain the assumption that income distribution remains unchanged during a process of stabilisation, since the very policy instruments applied in the stabilisation process frequently alter income before tax (wages, profit, rents), income after tax and net incomes which include the imputed benefits of public services. In other words stabilisation policies usually affect the primary, secondary and tertiary income distribution (Ndulu 1992).

How stabilisation policies affect income distribution depends not only on the nature of the policies but also on the forces which drive income inequality, or what Taylor (1988) calls the social matrix and Khan (1993) calls the interface between the institutional organisation and the policy regime of the country applying stabilisation policies. Based upon an overview of stabilisation experiences in the mid-1980s of 17 countries, carried out by UN/WIDER, Lance Taylor concludes:

> The moral is that getting into and out of economic stabilisations are not processes independent of major groups in the country, their political role, and insertion in the economic system. On the whole, professional economists deal uneasily with these issues, and often carry through their analyses of economic classes and their political roles ineptly. But such factors have been vital to the successes and failures of many stabilisations 'with a human face'. This can only be realized on the basis of a serious analysis of the social matrix.
>
> (Taylor 1988)

Early analysis of the effects of stabilisation policies pointed to an adverse effect on the poor which was at least equal to the initial disinflationary measures, and often larger (PREALC 1985; Cornia, Jolly and Stewart 1987; van der Hoeven 1987). The contraction in the economy has also frequently led to a decline in the wage share in national income, as Pastor (1987) has demonstrated. Some authors (e.g. Sahn 1992) argue that poor people do not take part in the formal economy and especially do not make much use of government services, and hence are less (either negatively or positively) affected by stabilisation policies than non-poor groups which used to profit much more from public services. Thus stabilisation policies, and especially fiscal contraction, results in a more equal tertiary income distribution. These views are however questioned by many observers. In general it is accepted that the deflationary component of stabilisation policies results in increased poverty, although the intensity depends both on the relative weight and intensity of the policies adopted as well as on the initial conditions, as Khan has demonstrated. Khan (1993: 15) classifies countries into four groups which are characterised by the degree of efficiency (that is, having basically the right policies and institutions to adapt to world market conditions and changes, and hence a positive growth of labour and/or total factor productivity, TPF) and by the degree of egalitarian structure (that is, a fair distribution of income and assets).

In an *efficient, egalitarian* country a balance-of-payments deficit which requires adjustment is typically caused by an external shock or by overheating of the domestic economy. In such a situation the correct policy response is often stabilisation policy, rapidly implemented, of a deflationary nature which will result in a temporary increase in unemployment and a temporary drop in real wages. The efficiency of the economy will permit rapid adjustment, leading to recapturing of world market share and the egalitarian welfare system will act as a brake on poverty increase. However, few countries fall in this category. A much larger number fall in the *efficient inegalitarian* group. In this group, stabilisation and deflationary policy will increase poverty and unemployment and some segments of the population will be worse off after the policy is implemented. Institutional and policy changes are needed to reverse this situation. The deflationary elements of the stabilisation programmes should be scrutinised for their poverty-enhancing impact. Corrective measures should be taken by retargeting public expenditure, by the provision of compensatory programmes for the most adversely affected groups, and by an alteration of production patterns and ownership structures so that poorer groups such as peasant farmers and small-scale manufacturers can improve their output and productivity.

A third group of countries falls into the category of *inefficient egalitarian* economies. In this type of economy, adjustment programmes ought to concentrate on long-term structural changes and changing incentive structures and institutions, so that the various economic actors can better respond to world market signals. Stabilisation programmes will in this situation not bring about a resumption of growth, but they will put the egalitarian system under strong pressure. Indeed they often cause its breakdown, so that these countries often end up in the fourth category. This category consists of countries which are both *inefficient and inegalitarian*. The main challenge for countries in this group which implement stabilisation policies is to achieve both resumption of growth and a reduction in inequality, which will permit the whole population to benefit from growth. In these economies, adjustment programmes often break down and emphasis on stabilisation and deflationary policies will frequently not lead to the desired results. Countries need simultaneously to remove those structural impediments which lead to inefficiency and also to remove structural impediments which prevent reasonably egalitarian growth. Adjustment policies should therefore be part of a comprehensive, continuous development process which combines adaptation to foreign competition, industrial and agricultural policies for small- and large-scale producers with programmes of land redistribution, and investment in human capital.

Macroeconomic efficiency and growth

It is, especially in the context of discussing stabilisation policies, important to distinguish between short-term and long-term effects on growth. As argued above, adjustment policies dominated by stabilisation have not infrequently been characterised by a contraction in the economy, which leads to a fall in GDP *per capita*. Such a contraction is accompanied by lower rates of capacity utilisation. Several economists have therefore argued that the first task of macroeconomic stabilisation policy is to increase capacity utilisation, as this will contribute to non-inflationary growth. Taylor (1988, 1993) has criticised the financial accounting in most stabilisation packages for failing to take account of the importance of increases in capacity utilisation. Monetary policies and income policies can play an important part in a process of increasing capacity utilisation and of reviving non-inflationary growth.

More attention has been given in the literature to the relation between macroeconomic policies and long-term growth. Fischer's overview article (Fischer 1991) is a good example of this. Fischer starts from the premise that current thinking among economists differs from thinking in the 1970s, when it was generally accepted that short-term cyclical movements should be dealt with through Keynesian-type effective demand policies, while structural policies should be used to accelerate rates of growth. In the 1980s, these ideas were upset by the experience of adjustment policies as well as by the emergence of 'new growth theory' which, although emphasising the role of structural phenomena in explaining growth and the acceleration of growth, also takes into account variables relating to macroeconomic policy climate (Romer 1986; Lucas 1988).

Cross-country regression analysis, using variables which concur with neoclassical growth theory and the 'new growth theory' as well as macro-economic variables (usually a mixture of outcome variables such as the inflation rate, or the current account deficit, and policy variables such as the government budget surplus or deficit) suggests some relationship between macroeconomic policies and growth. To quote Fischer, 'the evidence supports the view that the quality of macroeconomic management reflected in these regressions in the inflation rate, the external debt ratio and the budget surplus, matters for growth' (Fischer 1991: 342). However, Fischer also points out that, although it would be logical to try to tie down precisely which macroeconomic indicators are most robustly associated with growth, this would not lead to instructive results (see also Levine and Revelt 1991 for the same argument). The main reason why it is difficult to draw lessons about individual policy instruments is that the macroeconomic variables, especially variables such as the debt ratio, the budget surplus or deficit, and the current account surplus or deficit are not truly exogenous with respect to growth. Faltering growth can affect the level of each of these variables, lead-ing, for example, to larger current account deficits, larger budget deficits and higher debt ratios. In short, there is a large degree of simultaneity in the relationship between growth and macroeconomic variables.

The result of most cross-section analysis is that, broadly speaking, good macroeconomic policies contribute to growth. But determining what exactly constitutes good macroeconomic policy is frequently very difficult, as it depends very much on the specific situation in each country. In order to solve the problem of causality, Fischer (1991) resorts to emphasising the relation between some macroeconomic variables and investment, which is an important determinant of growth, in order to establish, in an indirect way, the relationship between macroeconomic policies and growth. He adduces evidence which shows that inflation is negatively correlated with investment. He also shows that budget surpluses are negatively correlated with investment, a result which Fischer interprets as counter-intuitive, since a negative relationship between a budget surplus and investment would imply a positive relationship between deficits and investment, which does not tally well with the crowding-out hypothesis of budget deficits. But Taylor (especially Taylor 1988) would accept such results as plausible, since in many instances public investment crowds-in private investment, especially where political stability prevails, and ownership rights are respected.

A further attempt to establish a more robust relationship between macroeconomic policy and growth has been made by combining country studies and time series analyses, in which again investment is treated as the most crucial variable. The major conclusion of the more qualitative analysis is that uncertainty or instability in macroeconomic variables reduces investment, and hence growth. Work by Serven and Solimano (1992) confirms these conclusions. Dornbusch (1990) analyses the policies needed to move from stabilisation to growth, and puts forward the same line of argument. He concludes that responsible macroeconomic policies contribute to growth, but he also finds it difficult to define exactly what 'responsible macroeconomic policies' are. Is a 20 per cent annual inflation rate responsible or not? This is difficult to answer. What seems to be important in the work of Dornbusch is the degree of uncertainty.

Most of the analyses discussed in the previous paragraphs relate macroeconomic policies to growth in terms of aggregate variables such as the fiscal deficit, the inflation rate, money supply, etc. and usually only weak relationships were established. However, what is important in assessing these relationships is not only the absolute levels of these macroeconomic aggregates, but also the content of macroeconomic policy, and especially fiscal policies. Buffie (1994) and Stewart (1992), for example, indicate that fiscal contraction can have a negative effect on economic growth when essential investments in infrastructure and in human capital are curtailed. Buffie (1994), using a general equilibrium model, shows furthermore that short-term contractionary policies may force the economy into a low-level equilibrium trap.

Macroeconomic efficiency and income distribution

Macroeconomic policies must, by definition, have an effect on income distribution. This becomes immediately apparent when one considers the distinction between primary income distribution, which relates to total income earned, secondary income distribution, which relates to income after tax and transfers and tertiary income distribution, which includes the imputed income of government services. Tight monetary policy, insofar as it relates to interest policy, will be beneficial to holders of interest-bearing assets who are usually found in the higher-income groups. Furthermore, to the extent that higher interest rates depress (at least initially) economic activity, strict monetary policies result in more unemployment and lower wages. Thus for at least two reasons, a more unequal primary income distribution can be expected to result from strict monetary policies. The effects on income distribution of a more relaxed monetary policy which results in higher inflation are more difficult to gauge. It depends on whether wage incomes and pensions are properly indexed in order to keep them constant in real terms (Marinakis 1993). Experience shows that high rates of inflation are often regressive (and therefore not much liked by electorates). However, the redistributive effect of lower levels of inflation is more difficult to determine and research outcomes are ambiguous (Dornbusch 1990).

Fiscal policies have, by definition, an effect on income distribution since taxes determine the net disposable incomes of families. Indeed, one of the aims of tax policy is precisely to bring about a redistribution of income or of assets in the economy, although the extent to which this is possible has often been questioned (see, for example, the discussion in Newbery and Stern 1987). The effect of different tax measures on secondary income distribution depends on the tax mix. In many developing countries, tax systems rely heavily upon indirect taxes, and this reliance makes the tax system regressive rather than progressive. For example, in Latin America direct taxes are equal to some 3 per cent of GDP, compared with 10 per cent of GDP in Europe. A switching of the tax base to favour direct taxes could make secondary income distribution much more equal.

Public expenditure policy which is aimed at providing services to poorer groups can change the tertiary income distribution considerably. A sizeable literature existed at the end of the 1970s and in the early 1980s on the distributive aspects of government expenditure (Paukert *et al.* 1984; see also Jiminez 1986). In this literature, the effects of government expenditure on household welfare was often dealt with in a static way. In the light of the 'new growth theory', the issue of the distributional impact of government services becomes more important, since access to government services (such as education) is not considered as a means of increasing consumption, or as an imputed income element but contributes directly to growth. Whether such growth will be more or less egalitarian (or whether a given tertiary income distribution will affect the primary income distribution in the future) cannot be determined *a priori*. This will depend on whether poorer groups can profit from increased growth rates – through, for example, increased access to income-earning assets or to greater factor rewards.

Adjustment and poverty

The major effect on poverty of a stabilisation package is often felt not only through the deflationary policies, but also through the switching policies which include devaluation of the national currency, in order to change the price ratio between tradeable and non-tradeable goods. Exchange rate devaluations are adopted not only to stabilise the economy, but also to change production patterns. They thus can be classified as both a stabilisation and an adjustment policy. In considering their impact on poverty, the key question is to what extent the poor are producers of tradeable or non-tradeable goods and services, and to what extent they are consumers of both types of goods and services. The theory is rather agnostic. The application of the Salter–Swan type of analysis is now widespread (see, e.g., Demery and Addison 1993; Sachs and Larrain 1993), but the difficulty with this analysis lies with its practical application. First, the definition of tradeables is not as clear as the theory might suggest. Second, the production patterns and consumption patterns of the poor cannot easily be mapped using the categories of tradeables and non-tradeables. This complication is well explained in Jamal and Weeks (1993) and in Stewart (1995: 26–35). Stewart argues that initial conditions determine whether or not switching policies lead to more employment and poverty reduction. In the absence of growth, employment and income distribution (and thus poverty) are likely to worsen following a devaluation in economies with the following characteristics:

(1)   Specialising in mineral exports or agricultural products whose production is unequally distributed.
(2)   Where urban poverty is high in relation to rural poverty.
(3)   Where there is a large, oligopolistic modern sector, specialised in import substituting production.

Employment, income distribution and the poverty situation are most likely to improve in economies where:

(4)   Tradeables are labour-intensive relative to non-tradeables (i.e. in economies specialising, especially at the margin, in labour-intensive manufacturing or in labour-intensive agriculture).
(5)   Rural poverty is high in relation to urban poverty, and rural incomes (and tradeable production) are fairly evenly distributed.

The effects of other adjustment policies on poverty are more difficult to judge. For example, the effect of privatisation on poverty or of a decrease in public sector employment depend very much on whether, for example, dismissed civil servants belong to poor groups or not, whether they can find other jobs and whether the privatisation process will result in a decline in the tax burden on the poor. Also, the effect of deregulation cannot be predicted in advance. If deregulation reduces rent-seeking by wealthy and influential groups and this results in lower prices of products consumed by the poor, then adjustment policies can over time contribute to a decline in poverty. However, if deregulation results in the creation of natural monopolies, then the effect of deregulation on the poor can be negative. The effects of adjustment policies on poverty depend therefore much more on the initial social and economic setting in the country undergoing adjustment and on the types of adjustment policies applied. The next section will therefore review the impact of adjustment policies on poverty, especially in relation to some labour market issues.

Poverty and labour market developments: some trends

In order to get a better appreciation of the effects of adjustment policies on poverty, we must look particularly at the effect on the quality and quantity of employment, on wages and on income distribution in general and on human resource development. One can of course question to what extent observed trends in the operation of labour markets are the consequences of adjustment policies. Some argue that with so many adjustment policies adopted in so many developing countries, many carried out for a decade or more, a causal link must exist between these policies and labour market trends. Others argue, however, that adjustment policies prevented a fall in production and income and that without them the situation would have been much worse and, as a consequence, poverty also. This debate on the so-called 'counterfactual' is very difficult to settle. Carefully undertaken country studies which involve the use of general equilibrium models to generate hypothetical outcomes with and without adjustment have been used to clarify the issues. Such methods have their drawbacks. Robinson (1990), in discussing a set of general equilibrium models, argues that while they are useful in improving our understanding of how economies react to particular policy packages, they should not be used for policy evaluation and advice. This is because of the assumptions involved in the choice of parameter values and reaction coefficients. In what follows, I provide a broad overview of some of the issues involved.[1]

Changes in employment patterns

In Africa the percentage of the labour force working in formal sector jobs has declined since the introduction of adjustment programmes (Table 4.1). This decline is mainly due to the falling number of workers in state enterprises and the inability of the economic and social system to generate sufficient jobs in other sectors to accommodate the retrenched workers. Industrial and formal service employment has, in total, hardly increased (van der Hoeven and van der Geest 1999). The aim of the liberalisation and reform programmes has been to create conditions for stronger formal sector growth and some impressive policy changes have been made in many parts of Africa. Exchange rates have been adjusted, currencies have become almost fully convertible and budget deficits have decreased. In many countries *per capita* growth has become positive. However despite all these policy changes the recovery in Africa has not yet resulted in massive creation of new jobs. Of course adjustment takes time, and many programmes have been extended from an initial period of two–three years to five years and

Table 4.1   Sub-Saharan Africa: evolution of employment in the formal sector during the adjustment phase, 1990 and 1995 (as per cent of the active population)

Country	1990	1995
Kenya	18.0	16.9[1]
Uganda	17.2	13.3
Tanzania, Rep. of	9.2	8.1
Zambia	20.7	18.0[1]
Zimbabwe	28.9	25.3

Note: [1] 1994.
Source: Van der Geest and van der Hoeven (1999).

longer, in order to implement the necessary structural reforms. But nevertheless results are very slow in emerging, which often puts the stabilisation measures under pressure. International markets have sensed this ambivalence in African adjustment programmes. Despite the richness of many economies in terms of primary commodities, climatic conditions and low labour costs (especially following successive devaluations in English-speaking Africa), foreign domestic investment, which is needed to provide the financial backing for the necessary structural changes, has not been forthcoming. This makes it even more difficult to manage the transitional costs of adjustment programmes.

Employment experiences in Asia have differed substantially between East and South-East Asian countries on the one hand and Southern Asian countries on the other. In the former countries there has been sustained formal sector employment growth in most countries, resulting in increases in manufacturing employment. In South Asia, on the contrary, there are strong indications that employment in the informal sector has expanded (see ILO 1996 for more details). Also in Latin America, transitional costs of liberalisation policies have been high. As Lee (1996: 489) points out:

> The experience of Chile in the early 1980s illustrates the severe effects of overshooting in terms of stabilisation policy. Output contracted by 23 per cent in 1982–83 and unemployment remained above 23 per cent for 5 years. Similarly the Mexican crisis of 1994–95 illustrated the devastating effect of the wrong monetary and exchange rate policies.

Strong recovery took place in Latin America in the 1990s, with almost all countries experiencing a positive GDP growth rate, but the ILO has pointed out that unless the GDP growth rate is robust and sustainable at levels well above the growth of the labour force, growth in formal sector jobs will

Table 4.2 Informal employment as per cent of labour force (non-agricultural), 1990–7, selected countries in Latin America

Country	1990	1991	1992	1993	1994	1995	1996	1997
Latin America	51.6	52.4	53.0	53.9	54.9	56.1	57.4	57.7
Argentina	47.5	48.6	49.6	50.8	52.5	53.3	53.6	53.8
Brazil	52.0	53.2	54.3	55.5	56.5	57.6	59.3	60.4
Chile	49.9	49.9	49.7	49.9	51.6	51.2	50.9	51.3
Colombia	55.2	55.7	55.8	55.4	54.8	54.8	54.6	54.7
Mexico	55.5	55.8	56.0	57.0	57.0	59.4	60.2	59.4
Paraguay	61.4	62.0	62.2	62.5	68.9	65.5	67.9	59.4
Uruguay (Montevideo only)	36.3	36.7	36.6	37.0	37.9	37.7	37.9	37.1
Venezuela	38.8	38.3	37.4	38.4	44.8	46.9	47.7	48.1

Source: ILO (1998).

remain limited (ILO 1995; see also Fanelli and Frenkel 1995, Amadeo 1996). In most countries in Latin America one detects an increase in the number of workers in the informal sector (Table 4.2). This trend makes many workers understandably fearful of further liberalisation measures. Investigations by the Latin American Regional Office of the ILO confirm that growth in formal sector jobs is correlated with high economic growth, irrespective of the type of labour market regulations implemented (ILO 1995).

Changes in wage and income inequality

Another phenomenon which has been observed in many countries is an increase in wage and income inequality. In those economies where reliable data are available in the 1980s, income inequality increased in Asia in six out of twelve countries monitored (Bangladesh, Indonesia, Thailand, China, Singapore and Sri Lanka). In Africa, inequality increased in four out of six countries (Nigeria, Tanzania, Kenya and Ethiopia), and in Latin America in nine out of fourteen countries (Bolivia, Mexico, Argentina, Brazil, Panama, Venezuela, Guatemala, Honduras, Peru) (World Bank 1996). Changes in income inequality are in themselves often a cause for concern, although these changes must be seen in a wider perspective. First, some countries start from a low base. Income inequality is low in many Asian countries and slight increases in inequality, especially when accompanied by strong growth, will not usually result in worker unrest. Even in countries with high income inequality, strong growth may diffuse unrest among poorer workers. Second, income inequality figures give only a limited indication of wider social inequalities. A rich person paying for expensive medical treatment abroad, which is paid for in other countries by the state, may not in fact be better off than a sick person in one of those other countries, who does not have to worry about high medical bills. However, in general, changes in income inequality reflect broader changes in social inequality, which can have important effects on the social climate and on the willingness of the population to accept change.

Theoretical discussion of the link between income inequality and adjustment and trade liberalisation often argues that declining inequality should result, as adjustment and trade liberalisation will favour the production of goods which use intensively the factor in which a country has comparative advantage. For most developing countries this is unskilled labour (Berry *et al.* 1997). However, the evidence does not always support these arguments. Research reported by the ILO (1996) indicates, for example, that in most countries in the 1980s which underwent SAPs, wage dispersion increased with falling real wages (Table 4.3). Also the World Bank (1997) argues that 'information on wage inequality in developing countries is sparse and mixed... evidence from East Asia supports the view that greater openness in countries with an abundance of unskilled labour benefits this type of labour' but 'even for these countries however, the picture of relative wages is more complex, reflecting the interplay of the increase in relative demand for unskilled labour and the supply of skilled labour'. For Africa 'greater openness and policy changes in the 1980s are associated with recovery in growth and some reduction in poverty, but with an increase in equality in some cases'. This Report concludes that:

> the generally favourable verdict on East Asia in the 1960s and 1970s has been brought into question by analysis of experience in Latin America in the 1980s. In some countries increased openness has been associated with widening wage differentials.
>
> (World Bank 1997: 61)

The evidence regarding increasing inequality may lead to different policy conclusions. One conclusion is that the liberalisation measures have not been sufficiently comprehensive, and that domestic labour market constraints have often inhibited the impact of liberalisation measures on employment creation. This is the view adopted by the World Bank (1997). But one might also conclude that the liberalisation process is influenced by other factors which are not explained by the traditional Heckscher–Ohlin theory which lies at the heart of theories of comparative advantage. Alternative explanations for increased inequality introduce more than two categories of labour (no education, basic education and higher education) and argue that for successful export production at least basic education is necessary (Berry *et al.* 1997: 14; see also Owens and Wood 1997). Other explanations are that manufacturing tends to be dominated by large companies in the formal sector where wages are higher, and which have weak

Table 4.3 Wage dispersion and real wage changes in manufacturing, 1975–9 to 1987–91 (US$)

Country	Wage dispersion	Change in real wage
Asia		
Singapore	– 12.5	58.5
Taiwan China	– 9.8	151.5
India	– 9.3	– 2.5
Korea, Rep. of	– 8.2	116.9
Indonesia	4.7	– 22.0
Philippines	7.4	12.5
Sri Lanka	8.2	– 10.2
Pakistan	14.7	17.9
Malaysia	19.8	2.8
Thailand	49.2	29.5
Africa		
Mauritius	– 25.1	– 37.3
Zimbabwe	– 8.8	– 32.2
South Africa	6.8	– 7.4
Kenya	17.2	– 40.4
Tanzania	38.0	– 83.1
Latin America		
Colombia	– 5.3	– 31.5
Uruguay	1.8	– 3.9
Mexico	15.1	– 44.5
Guatemala	25.3	– 41.2
Peru	26.5	32.7
Argentina	26.5	– 29.1
Panama	27.2	– 17.1
Brazil	34.2	– 15.5
Chile	55.4	– 16.6

Source: ILO (1996).

linkages to the small scale sector ('globalization accentuates the disadvantage of small scale producers'). In addition, liberalisation makes it easier to import capital goods (especially if exchange rates are overvalued) which increases labour productivity and raises the demand for skilled labour (UNDP, 1997). Furthermore Amsden and van der Hoeven (1996) observe that the distribution of income between labour and capital in industry has shifted in the direction of capital in the 1980s which has led to changes in consumption patterns and life-styles adding to inequity (see also ILO 1996). Liberalisation has also resulted in the decline of trade union membership which has weakened the bargaining power of workers (this point is taken up again below).

Changes in human capital formation

Liberalisation and adjustment programmes in developing countries have tended to place social expenditures under strong pressure. However in some countries downward pressure on government expenditures on education, health and social welfare had already begun during the economic crisis before adjustment programmes were applied. Adjustment programmes are therefore not necessarily the principal cause of decline in social expenditure, although they failed in most cases to reverse the decline. An evaluation of adjustment programmes published by the World Bank (Jayarajah, Branson and Sen 1996) pointed out that especially in Latin America and Africa, adjustment programmes were accompanied by a decline in social expenditure as a percentage of total government expenditures (Table 4.4) Given the fact that total government expenditure often declined in absolute terms, this resulted in declining *per capita* expenditure figures. Declining government expenditure will not necessarily be detrimental to poorer classes. Alesina (1998) points out that often middle classes and more vocal political groups profit most from government expenditure and that therefore a decline in government expenditure might hurt them more than the poor. But when we examine educational and health indicators, including those which measure primary and secondary school enrolment and infant mortality, we notice a deterioration in education standards and a slowdown in the decline in infant mortality rates during adjustment and less than full recovery after

Table 4.4   Composition of social sector expenditures, 1996 (per cent of GDP)

	Asia			Latin America[a]			Sub-Saharan Africa[a]		
	Before	*During*	*After*	*Before*	*During*	*After*	*Before*	*During*	*After*
Expenditure									
Total social spending	2.7	3.3	3.4	7.1	7.3	7.8	5.9	5.6	5.3
Education	1.8	2.2	2.2	3.0	2.7	2.6	3.4	3.3	3.1
Health	0.5	0.6	0.6	1.7	2.1	2.4	1.3	1.2	1.1
Percentage of total expenditures									
Total social spending	17.9	19.6	19.6	23.7	23.4	19.3	26.1	22.4	19.9
Education/total expenditures	11.8	12.9	12.6	19.6	16.9	14.3	16.3	14.2	13.5
Health/total expenditures	3.6	3.4	3.7	9.2	10.9	11.0	6.0	5.4	5.2

Note: [a] Only countries with data for the post-adjustment period.
Source: Jayarajah, Branson and Sen (1996), Table 4.3.

Table 4.5 Trends in selected social indicators, 1996

Indicator	Asia			Latin America[a]			Africa[a]		
	Before	During	After	Before	During	After	Before	During	After
% change in gross enrolment ratio	1.3	0.5	0.3	1.4	−0.4	1.0	4.7	−0.5	−0.4
% change in infant mortality rate	−2.5	−3.1	−3.6	−5.6	−2.5	−2.4	−1.8	−1.7	−1.4

Note: [a] Only countries with data for the post-adjustment period.
Source: Jayarajah, Branson and Sen (1996), Table 4.8.

adjustment (Table 4.5). This trend is most obvious in Africa, where in a number of countries primary school enrolment rates actually declined. This affected large parts of the population especially in poorer areas (van der Hoeven and van der Geest 1999). In Latin America, the middle class suffered large setbacks in providing their children with accessible quality education.

Limited or non-existent progress in education has not only had serious implications for efforts to improve productivity, but also for income inequality. Londono (1996: 16) argues, for example, that the increasingly uneven distribution of human capital in Latin America has increased income inequality. His estimates suggest that the dispersion in human capital increased the Gini concentration coefficient by 5 points. Furthermore he finds a strong correlation between the growing number of households in poverty and the growing number of households headed by illiterate household heads. UNCTAD (1997) reports on educational attainment and the skill intensity of exports in a number of countries. Their analysis:

> lends support to the hypothesis that educational attainment is a necessary but not a sufficient condition for skill-intensive production...all countries with a high share of skill-intensive exports also have a relatively high educational attainment while evidence from countries such as Argentina, Chile, Peru and Uruguay suggests that relatively high educational attainment does not automatically translate into skill-intensive exports... almost all countries where high educational attainment has translated into skill-intensive exports are those that have sustained a rapid pace of capital accumulation, technological upgrading and productivity growth over many decades. (UNCTAD 1997: 158)

The relation between adjustment, education, skills and productivity increases are thus complex, but the data are sufficiently robust to support an argument that a slowdown or reversal in primary, lower secondary and vocational education contributes to greater inequalities in societies and that this hampers the ability of many countries to take full advantage of increased production for exports.

Poverty inequality and growth: a guide for policy-makers

A tradeoff between growth and equity?

I have reviewed briefly the relationship between stabilisation policy and adjustment policy on growth and equality. This section discusses in more detail the linkages between growth, inequality and poverty. The existence of a tradeoff between growth and income equality is often based upon the concept of accumulation – i.e. lower income inequality would lower national savings rates and hence, hamper future growth. Evidence from research in the 1970s has shown rather convincingly that the savings argument for a tradeoff between income equality and growth is often not valid. Also, were it to be valid, it would still be only a weak explanatory variable. Country studies have provided examples of economies which have combined high income equality with high growth rates.

The discussion on inequality and growth has received an impetus in recent years from authors who have combined the 'new growth theory' – which endogenises technical progress – with political economy models – which endogenise political decisions. These authors argue that inequality is harmful to growth. Alesina and Perotti (1994) discuss several causal links which underlie this argument. Some of these links are based on traditional economic arguments, such as the effect of income inequality on the composition of demand and the effect of inequality on the supply of human capital. A more equal income distribution leads to increased demand for industrial goods which stimulates innovation and growth. Growth is further enhanced by increased investment in education by low-income groups; here the argument is that increased equality in both income and asset distribution allows the poor to build up stocks of human capital more rapidly. Among the political explanations, two seem to figure prominently. The first postulates that inequality leads to voting behaviour which sanctions higher taxes and larger budget deficits with a consequent negative impact on growth rates. This in turn forces the government to adopt redistributive policies which are growth-destructive (Persson and Tabellini 1994). The second explanation is that inequality causes political instability, which hampers effective macro-economic management. This point is also made by Stern (1990) in discussing the relevance of growth policies. However, Alesina and Perotti (1994) show rather convincingly that the argument that inequality causes higher taxes which harm growth does not find much empirical support. They explain this mainly on the basis of a weak link between inequality and taxation levels. The policy uncertainty argument has found some support; it is most recently confirmed by the unwillingness of private investors to continue to finance capital flows to countries with looming conflicts on land redistribution and poverty programmes.

The experiences of the 1980s and the findings of the 'new growth theory' cast new light on the growth and equity debate. On the one hand higher taxes and deficit financing can affect negatively decisions on savings, and thus distort growth. On the other hand a higher level of government expenditure (which results from higher taxes or deficit financing) can increase investment in human resources, support the development of markets and better infra-structure which in turn, following the 'new growth theory', can contribute to higher levels of growth. The 'new growth theory' thus injects a more dynamic element than traditionally was the case into the relationship between income equality and economic growth, especially through the link between tertiary income distribution and the generation of future primary incomes.

As argued earlier, macroeconomic policies can have a positive redistributive impact, especially when emphasis is simultaneously placed on tax policies and on expenditure policies, with monetary policies playing a more minor stabilisation role (Pyatt 1993). Macroeconomic policies can especially be more poverty-focused if 'sound' macroeconomic policies are carried out in tandem with a set of incomes policies, including minimum wage policies and other mesopolicies which reinforce the redistributive impact of the macroeconomic policies. Incomes policy, when based upon consultation with employers and workers, can contribute to a better social climate and can therefore reduce inflationary pressure. Countries which reduced income inequality and have had a reasonable growth record have often relied on a set of incomes policies which have included an active minimum wage policy.

Mesopolicies include targeted public expenditure, microeconomic policies (involving the integration of labour and product markets), and the redistribution of ownership of assets (Stewart 1995: 50–81). However, despite the potentially redistributive role of fiscal policies, their implemen-tation often frustrates this impact. Tax policies are often less redistributive than originally intended, and budget deficits are often dealt with through reducing expenditure rather than through increasing taxes. In addition, the redistributive impact of government expenditure is often less than it is claimed, since many public service programmes benefit the rich more than the poor and the application of priority ratios, in order to increase those expenditure items which benefit the poor, is often not well developed. Yet some countries have combined high priority ratios with high growth rates (UNDP 1991).

It can be argued that pro-poor macroeconomic policies depend not on the policies themselves but on the social situation in the country and especially on whether a society is willing to give priority to distributional issues in times of economic crisis (Khan 1993). Politically it is often more difficult to develop, or maintain, a distributional strategy in times of economic difficulty than in times of rapid growth. The paradox is therefore that macroeconomic policies can include elements which favour the poor, especially in those countries which are already relatively egalitarian, but that applying more poverty oriented macropolicies in a less egalitarian society is probably doomed to fail. Changes in the distribution of assets and human capital should become a necessary complement of macroeconomic policies to reduce inequality and stimulate growth. This issue is discussed in Stiglitz (1998) and will not be further pursued here. This conclusion thus weakens the case often made that income distribution policies are less important in a poverty alleviation strategy than stimulating overall growth, because steady-state growth will gradually lift all people above the poverty threshold. In the next section we will argue that redistributive measures can have an important impact on poverty reduction.

A policy maker's guide to the tradeoff between growth and equity

One elegant way to consider the relation between equity and growth, and its impact on poverty levels, is to construct a poverty measure which takes into account simultaneously growth and distribution. Ravallion (1997) has investigated this by running combined time series country data analysis and estimating for certain groups of countries the elasticity of poverty reduction with respect to growth. This confirms that countries with lower inequality have a higher elasticity of poverty reduction. McKay (1997) has also argued that a dynamic poverty count, which expresses a poverty index over time, should be split up between a growth component and a equity component, although he does not present an integrated measure.

In this section we show that, by using a perhaps somewhat restrictive assumption regarding the shape of the distribution function of inequality, a composite index can be developed which can deal with tradeoffs and complementarities between distribution and growth. The restrictive assumption is that the distribution of inequality follows a log normal distribution. Various authors (e.g. Aitchison and Brown 1973) have argued that this assumption can be made for inequality in developed countries. The proposition has not been tested for developing countries but, pending further research, it is assumed here to be valid. Based on this assumption that incomes are lognormally distributed, we can calculate the head count index of poverty, expressed as a fraction of the population below the poverty line, as follows:

$$P\left(X \le \frac{1}{\sigma}\log f + \frac{1}{2}\sigma\right) \qquad X \text{ is } N(0, 1) \tag{4.1}$$

This is the probability of a standard normally distributed variate X where f is the poverty line expressed as a fraction of *per capita* income and σ is the variance of the lognormal distribution, and a measure of inequality. There is a one to one relation between σ and the Gini ratio, one of the most frequently used measures of inequality.

Table 4.6 indicates, for various values of the poverty line (f) and various values of inequality (s and G), the percentage of the population below the poverty line. What is striking is that inequality does matter. For example, in countries with high income inequality (a Gini ratio of around 0.6, such as Brazil), a poverty line set at 15 per cent of *per capita* income will result in 16.3 per cent of the population in poverty, but if that country were to reduce its inequality to that which is typical of a low-inequality country (a Gini ratio of 0.30), less than 1 per cent of its population would fall under the poverty line. Another example from Table 4.6 of the tremendous effect which inequality reduction can have on poverty is that with a poverty line equal to 50 per cent of *per capita* income, a high-inequality country (with a Gini ratio of above 0.6) has over 50 per cent of its population in poverty while a country with a low inequality (a Gini ratio of 0.3) has only 16 per cent of its population in poverty.

It is obvious that in (4.1) f (the poverty line as a fraction of average *per capita* income) will decrease as the average *per capita* income (y) increases. Thus we have:

$$f = a/y \tag{4.2}$$

where $a =$ the absolute poverty line expressed in money terms and $y =$ average *per capita* income in money terms:

$$y = y_0 \, e^{gt} \tag{4.3}$$

where y is growing per year at a growth rate g and y_0 is the *per capita* income in the base year.

By substituting (4.2) and (4.3) in (4.1) it can be easily deduced that the fraction of the population below the poverty line is:

$$P\left(X \leq \frac{1}{\sigma}\left(\log \frac{a}{y_0} - gt\right) + \frac{1}{2}\sigma\right) \tag{4.4}$$

Equation (4.4) thus represents a poverty measure which depends on the absolute poverty line (a) and *per capita* income (y_0) in the base year, the degree of inequality (σ) and the growth of *per capita* income (g) as well as the time period (t) over which the growth is considered. That inequality matters in the growth process is confirmed by a glance at Table 4.7 where we have indicated for an initial poverty line of 75 per cent of *per capita* income (a quite normal assumption, see Ravallion and Chen 1997), and a range of

Table 4.6 Per cent of population below the poverty line as a function of inequality (G, σ) and the poverty line (f) (expressed as a fraction of per capita income)

| G | 0.28 | 0.30 | 0.33 | 0.35 | 0.38 | 0.40 | 0.43 | 0.45 | 0.48 | 0.50 | 0.52 | 0.54 | 0.56 | 0.58 | 0.60 | 0.62 | 0.64 | 0.66 | 0.68 |
f / σ	0.5	0.55	0.60	0.65	0.70	0.75	0.80	0.85	0.90	0.95	1.00	1.05	1.10	1.15	1.20	1.25	1.30	1.35	1.40
0.05	0.0	0.0	0.0	0.0	0.0	0.0	0.0	0.1	0.2	0.4	0.6	1.0	1.5	2.1	2.9	3.8	4.9	6.1	7.5
0.10	0.0	0.0	0.0	0.1	0.2	0.4	0.7	1.1	1.7	2.6	3.6	4.8	6.1	7.7	9.4	11.2	13.1	15.1	17.2
0.15	0.0	0.1	0.2	0.5	0.9	1.6	2.4	3.5	4.9	6.4	8.1	10.0	12.0	14.1	16.3	18.6	20.9	23.3	25.6
0.20	0.1	0.4	0.9	1.6	2.6	3.8	5.4	7.1	9.0	11.1	13.4	15.7	18.1	20.5	22.9	25.4	27.8	30.3	32.6
0.25	0.6	1.2	2.2	3.5	5.2	7.0	9.1	11.4	13.8	16.2	18.8	21.3	23.9	26.4	28.9	31.4	33.9	36.2	38.6
0.30	1.5	2.8	4.4	6.3	8.5	10.9	13.5	16.1	18.7	21.4	24.1	26.7	29.3	31.8	34.3	36.8	39.1	41.4	43.6
0.35	3.2	5.1	7.4	9.9	12.5	15.3	18.1	20.9	23.7	26.4	29.1	31.7	34.3	36.8	39.2	41.5	43.7	45.9	48.0
0.40	5.7	8.2	11.0	13.9	16.9	19.9	22.8	25.7	28.5	31.2	33.9	36.4	38.9	41.2	43.5	45.7	47.8	49.9	51.8
0.45	8.9	12.0	15.1	18.3	21.5	24.5	27.5	30.3	33.1	35.7	38.3	40.7	43.0	45.2	47.4	49.4	51.4	53.3	55.2
0.50	12.8	16.2	19.6	22.9	26.1	29.1	32.0	34.8	37.4	40.0	42.3	44.6	46.8	48.9	50.9	52.8	54.6	56.4	58.1
0.55	17.2	20.8	24.3	27.6	30.7	33.6	36.4	39.0	41.5	43.9	46.1	48.2	50.3	52.2	54.1	55.8	57.5	59.2	60.8
0.60	22.0	25.7	29.1	32.2	35.2	38.0	40.6	43.0	45.3	47.5	49.6	51.5	53.4	55.2	56.9	58.6	60.1	61.7	63.1
0.65	27.0	30.6	33.8	36.8	39.5	42.1	44.5	46.7	48.9	50.9	52.8	54.6	56.3	57.9	59.5	61.0	62.5	63.9	65.3
0.70	32.2	35.9	38.4	41.1	43.7	46.0	48.2	50.2	52.1	54.0	55.7	57.4	58.9	60.4	61.9	63.3	64.6	65.9	67.2
0.75	37.2	40.2	42.9	45.3	47.6	49.7	51.6	53.4	55.2	56.8	58.4	59.9	61.4	62.7	64.1	65.4	66.6	67.8	69.0

Table 4.7 Per cent of population below the poverty line as a function of inequality (G, σ) and a five-year annual growth of per capita income (g) from an initial poverty line of 75 per cent of per capita income (f=0.75) at year t=0

G	0.28	0.30	0.33	0.35	0.38	0.40	0.43	0.45	0.48	0.50	0.52	0.54	0.56	0.58	0.60	0.62	0.64	0.66	0.68
σ	0.5	0.55	0.60	0.65	0.70	0.75	0.80	0.85	0.90	0.95	1.00	1.05	1.10	1.15	1.20	1.25	1.30	1.35	1.40
Year 0	37.2	40.2	42.9	45.3	47.6	49.7	51.6	53.4	55.2	56.8	58.4	59.9	61.4	62.7	64.1	65.4	66.6	67.8	69.0
Year 5 0.25	36.2	39.3	42.1	44.6	46.9	49.0	51.0	52.9	54.6	56.3	57.9	59.4	60.9	62.3	63.7	65.0	66.2	67.5	68.6
0.5	35.4	38.5	41.2	43.8	46.1	48.3	50.4	52.3	54.1	55.8	57.4	59.0	60.5	61.9	63.3	64.6	65.9	67.1	68.3
1.0	33.5	36.7	39.6	42.3	44.7	47.0	49.1	51.1	53.0	54.8	56.4	58.1	59.6	61.1	62.5	63.9	65.2	66.5	67.7
1.5	31.7	35.0	38.0	40.8	43.3	45.7	47.9	49.9	51.9	53.7	55.5	57.1	58.7	60.2	61.7	63.1	64.5	65.8	67.0
2.0	30.0	33.4	36.5	39.3	41.9	44.4	46.6	48.8	50.8	52.7	54.5	56.2	57.8	59.4	60.9	62.4	63.7	65.1	66.4
2.5	28.3	31.7	34.9	37.8	40.5	43.0	45.4	47.6	49.7	51.6	53.5	55.2	56.9	58.6	60.1	61.6	63.0	64.4	65.7
3.0	26.6	30.1	33.4	36.4	39.2	41.7	44.2	46.4	48.6	50.6	52.5	54.3	56.0	57.7	59.3	60.8	62.3	63.7	65.1
3.5	25.0	28.6	31.9	34.9	37.8	40.4	42.9	45.3	47.4	49.5	51.5	53.4	55.1	56.9	58.5	60.1	61.6	63.0	64.4
4.0	23.4	27.0	30.4	33.5	36.4	39.2	41.7	44.1	46.3	48.5	50.5	52.4	54.2	56.0	57.7	59.3	60.8	62.3	63.7

different inequality figures, the percentage of population below the poverty line in the initial year and after five years following various hypothetical *per capita* growth rates (*g*) ranging from 0.25 per cent to 4 per cent per annum. With a *per capita* growth rate of 2 per cent per annum, a quite acceptable figure in the 1990s, a country with high inequality (Gini of 0.60) reduces the percentage of its population living below poverty from 64 per cent to 61 per cent. However a country with low inequality (a Gini ratio of 0.3) reduces the percentage of the population under the poverty line from 40 to 33 per cent. Thus when inequality is low (and the income distribution curve flatter), a given growth rate will reduce poverty faster than when inequality is high.

There would seem to be a powerful case for emphasising inequality reduction in poverty reduction programmes, even if this will reduce growth somewhat. For example, it can be seen from Table 4.7 that in the case of an initial poverty line of 75 per cent of *per capita* income, reducing inequality from a Gini ratio of 0.60 to 0.40 with a 1 per cent *per capita* growth rate over five years reduces poverty more compared with a situation where the *per capita* growth rate is 4 per cent and inequality remains unchanged. It is often argued that social and cultural factors prevent such rapid reductions in income inequality, except at very high costs. But Table 4.8 indicates that changes in income distribution do take place over time (some countries improving, others deteriorating), which refutes the argument that income distribution is a more or less fixed parameter.

Table 4.8 Gini ratios and *per capita* growth for selected countries, 1970s–90s

	Gini ratios			Per capita growth		
	1970s	1980s	1990s	1970–80	1980–90	1990–5
Taiwan	20.9	21.1	–		–	–
India	30.9	31.4	31.1 –		3.7	2.8
China	–	31.5	36.2		8.7	11.7
Indonesia	36.6	33.4	33.1		4.3	5.9
Pakistan	35.5	33.4	–		3.2	1.7
Korea	36.1	35.6	–		8.2	6.2
Bangladesh	34.8	37.3	–		1.9	2.5
Jamaica*	–	43.2	39.8		0.8	1.9
Côte d'Ivoire	–	39.1	41.4		– 3.7	– 2.2
Singapore	–	33.0	41.0		0.7	3.5
Uganda*	41.5	42.9	44.4		– 1.6	0.2
Venezuela*	40.8	36.1	40.7		– 5.2	3.4
Jordan*	38.8	43.7	–		2.8	3.6
Sri Lanka	–	44.0	48.6		0.3	0.2
Tanzania*	44.0	43.0	41.0		0.8	2.1
Tunisia	41.9	45.0	45.0		– 1.6	0.0

Philippines*	41.9	41.4	45.0	–	–
Hong Kong	48.2	44.4	43.0	–	–
Bahamas	46.1	45.1	–	0.2	3.0
Costa Rica					
Trinidad and Tobago	48.5	41.7	–	– 3.8	0.2
Thailand	41.9	47.4	50.1	5.9	7.2
Senegal*	49.0	45.1	54.1	0.2	3.0
Chile	48.0	51.0	50.3	2.5	5.7
El Salvador*	46.1	48.4	50.0	– 0.8	3.9
Guatemala	–	58.6	59.5	– 2.0	2.8
Malaysia	51.5	48.0	–	2.6	6.4
Colombia	52.1	51.2	–	1.8	2.8
Honduras	–	54.0	52.7	– 0.6	0.5
Mexico*	55.0	52.7	57.0	– 1.3	– 0.7
South Africa	51.0	49.0	62.3	– 0.9	– 1.1
Brazil	57.0	58.7	60.6	0.5	1.0

Source: *Gini ratios*: Bruno and Ravallion and Squire (1998); WIDER data base (*).
GDP per capita: World Bank, *World Development Indicators 1997; 1988/89 World Development Report 1998/99*.
Thanks are due to Mr Kiiski for providing the data from UNU/WIDER.

The second objection to active policies aimed at reducing income inequalities is that there are costs to reducing inequality. On the other hand, as argued earlier, there are strong indications that greater income equality will contribute to faster growth and hence that at least some of the costs incurred in achieving higher equality will be gained back over time, although more research is needed to substantiate this. It is nevertheless clear that increased attention to inequality and policies to reduce inequality should be a primary objective of development policy.

Note

1. For more specific country analyses of adjustment and labour market issues, the reader is referred to, for example, Garcia (1993), Islam (1994), Khan (1993), Toye (1995) and van der Geest and van der Hoeven (1999).

Bibliography

Aitchison, J. and J. Brown (1973), *The Lognormal Distribution, with Special Reference to its Use in Economics*, Cambridge: Cambridge University Press.

Alesina, A. (1998), 'The political economy of macroeconomic stabilisations and income inequality: myths and realities', in V. Tanzi and K.Y. Chu (eds), *Income Distribution and High Quality Growth*, Cambridge, MA: MIT Press.

Alesina, A. and Perotti, R. (1994), 'The political economy of growth: a critical survey of the recent literature', *The World Bank Economic Review*, Vol. 8(3).

Amadeo, E. (1996), 'The knife-edge of exchange rate based stabilisation impacts on growth, employment and wages', UNCTAD Review, No. 1, Geneva: UNCTAD.

Amadeo, E. *et al.* (1997), *Costos Laborales y Competividad Industrial en America Latina*, Lima: International Labour Organisation.

Amsden, A. and R. van der Hoeven (1996), 'Manufacturing output, employment and real wages in the 1980s: labour's loss until century's end', *Journal of Development Studies*, Vol. 32(4), pp. 506–30.

Arrow, K.J. (1962), 'The economic implications of learning by doing', *Review of Economic Studies*, Vol. 29, pp. 155–73.

Berry, A. *et al.* (1997), 'Globalization, adjustment, inequality and poverty', Background Paper for UNDP Human Development Report, University of Toronto, Department of Economics.

Bruno, M., M. Ravallion and L. Squire (1998), 'Equity and growth in developing countries: old and new perspectives on the policy issue', in V. Tanzi and K.Y. Chu (eds), *Income Distribution and High Quality Growth*, Cambridge, MA: MIT Press.

Buffie, E. (1994), 'The long run consequences of short-run stabilisation policy', in S. Horton, R. Kanbur and D. Mazumdar, *Labour Markets in an Era of Adjustment*, EDI Development Studies, Washington, DC: World Bank.

Burgess, R. and N. Stern (1993), 'Taxation and development', *Journal of Economic Literature*, Vol. 31, June.

Cornia, A. (1998), 'Liberalization, globalization and income distribution', Helsinki: UNU/WIDER, mimeo.

Cornia, G.A., R. Jolly and F. Stewart (1987), *Adjustment with a Human Face*, Oxford: Oxford University Press.

Demery, L. and Tony Addison (1993), 'The impact of macroeconomic adjustment on poverty in the presence of wage rigidities', *Journal of Development Economics*, Vol. 40(2), pp. 331–48.

Dornbusch, R. (1990), 'Policies to move from stabilisation to growth', in *Proceedings of the Annual Conference of Development Economics*, Washington, DC: World Bank.

Fanelli, J.M. and R. Frenkel (1995), 'Micro–macro interaction in economic development', *UNCTAD Review*, No. 1, Geneva: UNCTAD.

Fields, G. (1994), 'Poverty changes in developing countries', in R. van der Hoeven and R. Anker (eds), *Poverty Monitoring: An International Concern*, London: Macmillan.

Figueroa, A. (1997), 'Equidad y competitividad international en America Latina: una primera aproximacion', Working Paper 41, Lima: ILO Regional Office for the Americas.

Fischer, S. (1991), 'Growth, macroeconomics and development', in *National Bureau of Economic Research Macroeconomic Annual*, Cambridge, MA: MIT Press.

Fitzgerald, E. (1997), 'The theory of import substitution', Centro Studi Luca d'Agliano, Working Paper 108, Oxford: Queen Elizabeth House.

Foster, J., J. Greer and E. Thorbecke (1984), 'A class of decomposable poverty measures', *Econometrica*, Vol. 52, pp. 761–5.

Garcia, N. (1993), *Lessons from Structural Adjustment Processes of Costa Rica, Chile and Mexico*, Santiago: ILO PREALC.

van der Geest, W. and R. van der Hoeven (1999), *Adjustment, Employment and Missing Labour Market Institutions in Africa*. London and Geneva: James Currey and International Labour Organisation.

Grossman, Gene M. and Elhanan Helpman (1991), *Innovation and Growth: The Global Economy*, Cambridge, MA: MIT Press.

van der Hoeven, R. (1987), 'External shocks and stabilisation policies: spreading the load', *International Labour Review*, Vol. 126 (2).

van der Hoeven R. (1995), 'Structural adjustment, poverty and macroeconomic policy' in G. Rodgers and R. van der Hoeven (eds), *The Poverty Agenda: Trends and Policy Options*, Geneva: International Institute for Labour Studies.

van der Hoeven, R. (1996), 'Implications of macro economic policies for equity and poverty', in UNCTAD, *Globalization and Liberalization Effects of International Economic Relations on Poverty*, Geneva: UNCTAD.

van der Hoeven, R. and W. van der Geest (1999): 'The missing institutions of Africa's adjusted labour markets', in W. van der Geest and R. van der Hoeven (eds), *Adjustment, Employment and Missing Labour Market Institutions in Africa*, London and Geneva: James Curry and International Labour Organisation.

ILO (1995), *The Employment Challenge in Latin America and the Caribbean*, Lima: International Labour Organisation.

ILO (1996), *World Employment Report 1996/97*, Geneva: International Labour Organisation.

ILO (1997a), *1996 Labour Overview Latin America and the Caribbean*, Lima: International Labour Organisation.

ILO (1997b), *World Labour Report, 1997/98*, Geneva: International Labour Organisation.

ILO (1998), *1998 Labour Overview Latin America and the Caribbean*, Lima: International Labour Organisation.

IMF (1997), *World Economic Outlook*, Washington: International Monetary Fund, May

Infante, R. and V. Tokman (1997), 'Crecimiento con empleo: la experiencia de los paises Latino Americanos y del Sud-Este Asiatico', Working Paper 43, Lima: ILO Regional Office for the Americas.

Islam, R. (ed.) (1994), *Social Dimensions of Economic Reform in Asia*, New Delhi: ILO/SAAT.

Jamal, V. and J. Weeks (1993), *Africa Misunderstood or Whatever Happened to the Urban–Rural Gap?*, London: Macmillan.

Jayarajah, C., W. Branson and B. Sen (1996), *Social Dimensions of Adjustment: World Bank Experience 1980–93: A World Bank Operations Evaluation Study*, Washington, DC: World Bank.

Jiminez, E. (1986), 'The public subsidization of education and health in developing countries: a review of equity and efficiency', *World Bank Research Observer*, Vol. 1(1).

Kaldor, N. (1957), 'A model of economic growth', *Economic Journal*, Vol. 67, pp. 591–624.

Kanbur, R. (1987), 'Measurement and alleviation in poverty', *IMF Staff Papers*, Vol. 34(1), pp. 60–85.

Khan, A. (1993), *Structural Adjustment and Income Distribution: Issues and Experiences*, Geneva: International Labour Organisation.

Khan, Mohsin H. (1990), 'The macroeconomic effects of Fund-supported adjustment programmes', *IMF Staff Papers*, Vol. 37(2), pp. 195–231.

Lee, E. (1996), 'Globalization and employment – is anxiety justified?', *International Labour Review*, Vol. 135(5).

Levine, R. and D. Renelt (1991), 'Cross-country studies of growth and policy: methodological, conceptual and statistical problems', World Bank Policy Research Working Paper, No. 608.

Londono, J.L.L. (1996), 'Poverty, inequality and human capital development in Latin America 1950–2025', *World Bank Latin American and Caribbean Studies*, Washington, DC: World Bank.

Lucas, R. (1988), 'On the mechanics of economic development', *Journal of Monetary Economics*, Vol. 22.

Marinakis, A. (1993), 'Wage indexation, flexibility and inflation: some Latin American experiences in the 1980s', Occasional Paper, No. 6, Geneva: ILO, Interdepartmental Project on Structural Adjustment.

McKay, A. (1997), 'Poverty reduction through economic growth: some issues', *Journal of International Development*, Vol. 9(4), pp. 665–673.

Ndulu, B. (1992), 'Enhancing income distribution and rationalizing consumption patterns', in G.A. Cornia, R. van der Hoeven and T. Mkandawire (eds), *Africa's Recovery in the 1990s*, London: Macmillan.

Newbery, D. and Stern (1987), *The Theory of Taxation for Developing Countries*, New York: Oxford University Press.

Owens, T. and A. Wood (1997), 'Export-oriented industrialization through primary processing', *World Development*, Vol. 25(9), pp. 1453–70.

Pastor, M. (1987), 'The effects of IMF programmes in the Third World: debate and evidence from Latin America', *World Development*, Vol. 15(2), pp. 249–62.

Paukert, F. *et al.* (1984), *Income Distribution and Economic Development*, Geneva: International Labour Organisation.

Persson, T. and G. Tabellini (1994), 'Is inequality harmful to growth?', *American Economic Review*, Vol. 84(3), pp. 600–21.

Pieper, U. (1998), 'Openness and structural dynamics of productivity and employment in developing countries: a case of deindustrialization', *Employment and Training Papers*, No. 8, Geneva: International Labour Organisation.

Pio, A. (1994), 'New growth theory and old development problems', *Development Policy Review*, Vol. 12, pp. 277–300.

PREALC (1985), *Beyond the Crisis*, Santiago: International Labour Organisation/PREALC.

Pyatt, G. (1993), 'Fiscal policies, adjustment and balanced development', Occasional Paper No. 8, Geneva: ILO, Interdepartmental Project on Structural Adjustment.

Ravallion, M. (1997), 'Can high-inequality developing countries escape absolute poverty?', World Bank Policy Research Paper, 1775, Washington, DC: World Bank.

Ravallion, M. and S. Chen (1997), 'What can new survey data tell us about recent changes in distribution and poverty?', *World Bank Economic Review*, Vol. 11(2), pp. 357–82.

Robinson, S. (1991), 'Macroeconomic, financial variables and computable general equilibrium models', *World Development*, Vol. 19(11), pp. 1509–26.

Rodgers, G. and R. van der Hoeven (1995), *The Poverty Agenda: Trends and Policy Options*, Geneva: International Institute for Labour Studies.

Rodrik, D. (1998), 'Globalization, social conflict and economic growth', *The World Economy*, Vol. 21(2), pp. 143–58.

Romer, P. (1986), 'Increasing returns and long-term growth', *Journal of Political Economy*, Vol. 94.

Romer, P. (1992), 'Two strategies for economic development: using ideas and producing ideas', in World Bank, *Proceedings of the Annual Conference of Development Economics*, Washington, DC: World Bank.

Sachs, J. and F. Larrain (1993), *Macroeconomics in the Global Economy*, New York: Harvester.

Sahn, D. (1992), 'Public expenditures in sub-Saharan Africa during a period of economic reforms', *World Development*, Vol. 20(5), pp. 673–93.

Serven, A. and A. Solimano (1992), 'Economic adjustment and investment performance in developing countries: the experience of the 1980s', in V. Corbo *et al.*, *Adjustment Lending Revisited: Policies to Restore Growth*, Washington, DC: World Bank.

Shaw, G.K. (1992), 'Policy implications of endogenous growth theory', *Economic Journal*, Vol. 102.

Somavia, J. (1995), 'Some political and social issues and international aspects', in D. Turnham *et al.* (eds), *Social Tensions, Job Creation and Economic Policy in Latin America*, Paris: OECD.

Stern, N. (1990), 'The determinants of growth', *Economic Journal*, Vol. 29.

Stewart, F. (1992), 'Short term policies for long term development', in G.A. Cornea, Rolph van der Hoeven and T. Mkandawire (eds), *Africa's Recovery in the 1990s*, New York: St Martin's Press for UNICEF.

Stewart, F. (1995), *Adjustment and Poverty: Options and Choices*, London, Routledge.

Stiglitz, J. (1998), 'Distribution, efficiency and voice: designing the second generation of reform', Paper presented at the Conference on Asset Distribution, Poverty and Economic Growth, Brasilia, 14 July.

Tanzi, V. and K.Y. Chu (eds) (1998), *Income Distribution and High Quality Growth*, Cambridge, MA: MIT Press.

Taylor, L. (1988), *Varieties of Stabilisation Experience*, Oxford: Clarendon Press.

Taylor, L. (ed.) (1993), *The Rocky Road to Reform*, Cambridge, MA: MIT Press.

Touraine, A. (1995), 'The political conditions for development in Latin America', in D. Turnham *et al.* (eds), *Social Tensions, Job Creation and Economic Policy in Latin America*, Paris: OECD.

Toye, J. (1995), *Structural Adjustment and Employment Policies: Issues and Experiences*, Geneva: International Labour Office.

Turnham, D. *et al.* (eds) (1995), *Social Tensions, Job Creation and Economic Policy in Latin America*, Paris: OECD.

UNCTAD (1996), *Globalization and Liberalization Effects of International Economic Relations on Poverty*, Geneva: UNCTAD.

UNCTAD (1997), *Trade and Development Report*, New York: United Nations.

UNDP (1991), *Human Development Report*. New York: Oxford University Press.

UNDP (1997), *Human Development Report*, New York: Oxford University Press for UNDP.

World Bank (1992), *Report on Adjustment Lending III*. Washington, DC: World Bank.

World Bank (1995), *World Development Report*, Washington, DC: World Bank.

World Bank (1997), *Global Economic Perspectives and the Developing Countries*, Washington, DC: World Bank.

Part III

Poverty, Crises and Agricultural Development

5

Poverty versus the Poor

*Graham Pyatt**

Introduction

Reference is increasingly being made among economists, and more widely, to a 'Washington Consensus' on poverty in developing countries. It refers not only to a perceived need to do something about the poverty that can be observed throughout the world, especially in Latin America and sub-Saharan Africa, but also to the policies that respond most appropriately to that widespread perception. Thus, for example, in their substantial contribution on 'Poverty and Policy' to the *Handbook of Development Economics*, Lipton and Ravallion have noted that:

> Central to the consensus is the World Bank's [1990] two pronged strategy of labour-demanding growth combined with investment in poor people's human capital. The growth is to be based on private production, realised in part by the removal of state-imposed market distortions that discriminate against agriculture and exports, and fostered by state-facilitated physical infrastructure. The human capital is to be expanded through primary education and basic health care, largely provided (though not necessarily

---

* This chapter is based on an address delivered on the occasion of the 44th *Dies Natalis* of the Institute of Social Studies. While some glimmer of the thoughts expressed here had been in my mind for some years, the argument as presented has been brought to the surface and otherwise stimulated by Lucia Hanmer and Howard White with whom I have recently been collaborating in an evaluation of Poverty Assessments for more than 20 countries in sub-Saharan Africa that have been undertaken since 1990 by the World Bank on behalf of a donor consortium known as the Special Programme of Assistance for Africa. The opportunity to evaluate these Assessments was presented by the Ministry of Overseas Cooperation in The Hague. I have drawn freely here on the findings of that evaluation and would like to express, accordingly, my thanks and appreciation to all concerned and, most especially, to my co-authors. Equally, I must absolve them all from any responsibility for my text or for the point of view that I have sought to articulate here.

produced) publicly. Additionally, there is a perceived need for well-targeted social safety nets provided by the state, to guard the poor and vulnerable against food and other insecurities.[1]

These same authors go on to note that, the 'Consensus' notwithstanding, there remain 'some unsettled issues [which] still disturb the waters of consensus'.[2] On a number of these issues I share their concerns and several will be touched on in this chapter. However, my main purpose is not to develop a critique of the Consensus since I am more concerned with methodology on account of the policies it suggests, rather than with the policies themselves. To be more precise, I want to explore here the methodology of poverty analysis which underpins the Consensus because I want to show how this methodology admits – I put it no stronger – the promotion of policies that are not always persuasive, and circumnavigates others that might be thought to be relevant. In developing this position, I also want to point to an alternative methodology which might be more robust.[3]

In embarking on this agenda, my point of departure is a set of more than 20 *Poverty Assessments* for countries in sub-Saharan Africa that I have reviewed in collaboration with colleagues at the ISS.[4] Our review was focused on the question of what could be learned from these Assessments, all of which have been undertaken with donor sponsorship by the World Bank since 1990. One of the overall conclusions that we reached was that, in an important sense, there was surprisingly little to be learned; and this has inevitably prompted some reflection on how that could be the case. There is no doubt that the Assessments (which cover some 23 countries in sub-Saharan Africa) contain many useful insights. Yet these individual insights do not seem to take us very far in seeking to develop a corpus of knowledge. At the risk of oversimplifying the matter, we have evidently gathered a lot of facts but learned relatively little. The hypothesis I have formed to explain why this might be so is that the conceptualisation that underpins these Assessments is excessively stylised and academic: the bones on which we were trying to put some flesh did not constitute a sufficiently well-articulated skeleton. Accordingly, I maintain that there is a need to reconsider the conceptual framework which underpins the policy dialogue between the World Bank and its member countries, and the staff work which supports it, before we can anticipate that more persuasive development policies will be forthcoming. This, then, is a challenge for the research community in the first instance, and not for the World Bank itself.

The thesis is developed in four sections, following this Introduction. In the next section, three preliminary topics are covered: (1) what is meant by poverty; (2) the dependence of causation on the level of aggregation; and (3) alternative ways of approaching a discussion of poverty from the initial perspective of GDP *per capita* (the level of the gross domestic product of a country in proportion to its population).

Then, the money metric approach to poverty analysis which underpins the Consensus position is elaborated in stages that cover the definition of the metric; problems of measurement; the determination of one or more poverty lines; the development of a national poverty profile; and the method of benefit-incidence analysis which has been developed to elucidate who benefits most, and by how much, from public expenditures, and especially from expenditures on health services and education.

Following this, policy and the Washington Consensus are discussed, starting with an overview of the Consensus prescriptions and their preconditions. Then, each of the main elements of the Consensus policy package is reviewed in the broader context of economic growth, structure and performance, transfers and targeting.

The final section of the chapter attempts no more than to indicate an alternative way forward, starting with a reformulation of supply-side economics and moving on from this to an alternative perspective on poverty analysis.

Some preliminaries

What is poverty?

The fact that there is an extensive and often challenging literature which seeks to define poverty is ample testimony to the difficulties of doing so and may even be a warning that one should not attempt to be too precise about the matter. It may suffice here, therefore, to make some general observations which are hopefully not controversial. Refinements can then be introduced subsequently as necessary to the argument.

There are two initial points, of which the first to mention is that being poor is essentially a personal matter, as are its manifestations such as malnutrition, ignorance and morbidity. Of course, whole families can be impoverished and extreme variations within a household are unusual. But some intra-household variation is apparently commonplace in many cultures, often along gender lines. If we are to avoid glossing over these differences then our starting point must be with the individual, not the household.

Secondly, I have recently learned that most, if not all languages recognise a distinction between poverty and destitution. Both are of concern here, but so is the distinction, which seems to turn on whether an individual has the capacity and sufficient resources to function in a sustainable way, albeit at a low level. Those who depend on others within the family, the community or the state in order to remain viable are therefore at risk of becoming destitute, with the degree of risk depending on the reliability of their support systems.

There is, of course, an enormous difference between remaining viable and having the opportunity to realise one's full human potential. It follows that there can be many levels of poverty or relative deprivation within this range and that it is perfectly possible for whole societies to be poor relative to the standards of others. In this sense, all development is about the eradication of poverty and there is no need to talk separately about poverty as such within the context of development policy.

So, if the notion of poverty is to have a narrower meaning which is distinct from that of destitution, then the use of the word 'poverty' should perhaps be restricted in one or other of two senses. One possibility is to use the word in a relative sense so that poverty and inequality become more or less synonymous in suggesting that not everyone in a given society is equally well-off. The alternative usage would then be to define poverty as an absolute lack of particular opportunities and/or necessities which are thought to be critical within a particular social context. This is the approach of the basic needs literature, which must ultimately rest on some value judgements about which needs are more important than others.

A variant of this last approach which I find attractive is to define basic needs relative to the capacity of a society to do something about them.[5] The poor are then those who lack certain specifics which the society is committed to making good, one way or another. What these specifics might be should be decided politically and relative to the resources available. The first claimants, presumably, are those who are destitute or at some risk of becoming so because life is uncertain and the support networks on which they depend may be unreliable. And here we can note that such an approach is consistent with the general conclusion of Rawls that the primary concern of society should be to raise living standards for the poorest group.[6]

The opposite of poverty is wellbeing. Wellbeing is founded in rights, which include property rights and entitlements, which implies a somewhat broader foundation than the real asset base – land, housing, tools, etc. – on which economists tend to focus. This asset base is a stock and the main role of the economic system is to use this stock to generate a flow of goods and services via production activities and also include reproduction, i.e. the raising of the next generation. How well this process works must depend on the context within which production and reproduction take place, i.e. on the efficiency of markets, on the institutional framework (including the family), on the quality of governance, etc.

At the next level up we arrive at individual capabilities and opportunities, which have been promoted by Sen as the essential objectives of development. His approach is endorsed by the UNDP, not least through its annual series of *Human Development Reports*.[7]

There has been some discussion of the extent to which this approach ultimately leads to different policy priorities to those of the World Bank as set out in the *1990 World Development Report*.[8] In relation to this, two general points may be helpful. First, it is clear that Sen's notion of 'capabilities' is a broader one than that of the conventional consumption opportunity set, since it includes opportunities and entitlements which cannot be delivered by conventional markets and derive instead from family ties and community. It then follows that the expansion of the opportunity set is a part of what Sen means by 'development', but not the whole story. In this sense, economic growth is characteristic of development but not synonymous with it.

A second and different point is that the way in which economic growth is conventionally measured is exceptionable. This is in part a reflection of current conventions as to what to include and what to leave out of measures of individual incomes or, at the national level, of GDP. One can go some way towards meeting these concerns by suggesting that much more attention should be paid by economists to non-market activities and that comparisons between individuals and countries should be based on purchasing power parities (PPPs).[9]

However, it is unlikely that such advances would be seen by the authors of the *Human Development Report* as being sufficient to meet their objections, which relate not only to what is included and what is left out when GDP is calculated, but also to the aggregation of individual capabilities using as weights market prices as determined through the interaction of demand, market structure and opportunity costs. To date, no alternative system of weighting has been proposed. Yet, without some system of weighting or valuation, there is no way of adding together the various ingredients of wellbeing into a single measure or metric. Accordingly, the alternative to an explicit system of values is to analyse options in terms of vectors of capabilities and to accept the implication that policy options can, at best, be weakly ordered. Faced with this prospect, most economists – among whom I would include myself, together with those who subscribe to the Washington Consensus – would prefer to accept the opportunity cost of scarce resources as being a useful value system and hence a way of arriving at aggregates, such as total consumption; to accept that total consumption so determined is a useful index of wellbeing; and that it is far from being the only measure that is interesting. For example, Sen must be correct in suggesting that life expectation might be a useful alternative measure and that these alternatives are not perfectly correlated. It therefore makes a difference which one is chosen.

Causes of poverty and levels of aggregation

One considerable advantage that follows from a willingness to entertain a single, metric measure of living standards, based on consumption, say, is that it simplifies the quest for causes of wellbeing or the lack thereof, which is poverty. However, this does not mean that causes are easy to identify. On the contrary, this is a difficult area and the more so because the causes of poverty have to be understood relative to a level of aggregation if the fallacy of composition is to be avoided.

To clarify these concerns, Table 5.1 indicates four levels of aggregation, each of which is relevant to poverty analysis and all of which can usefully

Table 5.1   Multiple levels of aggregation at which causation can be identified

Level of aggregation	Sub-strata/policy areas
International	Trade policy International debt
Macro	Monetary policy Fiscal policy Governance, *including* the respective roles of government, NGOs and private enterprise
Meso	Socio-economic groups Communities Production sectors Product and factor markets
Micro	Households Individuals

be disaggregated to give more detail. Thus, at the most basic, micro-level disaggregation can lead to an explicit recognition of individuals as distinct from the households in which they live, and this distinction is important, as we have seen, if analysis is to address the inequality that maintains within households, often along gender lines. An example of the fallacy of composition at this level would be to suggest that because those women who have relatively more children may be better-off (because their land entitlement under traditional systems may be greater and or because their older children can help with productive and reproductive responsibilities) then all women might be better-off if they had more children. Similarly, while it is true that those who are better educated tend to have higher living standards, it does not follow that increasing human capital will cause an economy to develop: it may instead lead to the pervasive unemployment of educated youth, depending on the balance between education, on the one hand, and the creation of job opportunities on the other.

At the next level up from the micro, i.e. at the meso level of analysis in Table 5.1, we find all the structural features of an economy, which include the communities in which people live, the productive sectors into which economic activity can be divided and the markets through which goods and services change hands.

The distinction between the micro and meso levels of analysis is important because it reflects the distinction between prices and quantities. At the micro level commodity prices and wage rates are typically exogenous, so it may be reasonable to claim that low wages and high prices are causes of poverty at this level.[10] However, at the meso level and above, wages and prices are endogenous: they depend on the interplay of demand and supply. Thus, from a meso perspective, the level of wages, and hence poverty, is determined by whatever it is that determines demand and supply in the labour market. It would then be a major fallacy of composition to suggest that, if all wage rates were higher, there would be less poverty. On the contrary, it can be suggested that higher wage rates would most likely increase unemployment and, therefore, increase poverty. Similarly, at the micro level, smallholders who achieve high yields tend to be better off. But if all smallholders were to achieve higher yields then they would all be better off only if the price elasticity of demand for their produce was greater than one. This condition will often be satisfied, but it is not out of the question for higher output to lower prices drastically by glutting the market.

Many of the mechanisms which operate at the meso level are a translation to the sectoral and local level of policies and attitudes which are set at the macro level. These include political attitudes towards the role of the private sector (NGOs and business), to law and order, and to good governance, all of which affect poverty via, for example, their influence on investment, and, hence, on growth. More importantly, they can also affect poverty and wellbeing directly – through human rights, for example. Otherwise, it is at the macroeconomic level that monetary and fiscal policies are determined. These are the foundations on which the system of economic incentives which operates throughout a society are built. The best efforts of private entrepreneurs and of the self-employed in the informal sector can all be frustrated by bad macroeconomic policies which prejudice their chances of thriving. In sub-Saharan Africa in particular it is argued by many who subscribe to the Washington Consensus that bad economic policies through the 1970s and 1980s, if not before that, are the main cause of poverty today. They may have a point and certainly it is the case that most of the countries in that region have yet to regain the highest level of income per head that they have previously enjoyed at some time within living memory.

But these same pundits who put the blame on bad macroeconomic policies may also be wrong in the sense that some blame might also be apportioned at a level of aggregation above that of the nation state, viz. the international economy. In that largest of arenas, the countries of sub-Saharan Africa are small players and can hardly be responsible for the changes in the international environment which took place around 1980–2. At most they could be blamed for not having foreseen these changes, for not having made appropriate contingency plans or for reacting too slowly. But this is a blame that must evidently be shared in some measure with their advisors. And, whatever the verdict of history might be on this matter, the legacy of international debts and the need to service them remains as a major problem. This is not the only cause of poverty today, but the ability of governments to alleviate poverty, both now and for the foreseeable future, is undoubtedly constrained by it. Sound macroeconomic policies have that much less to offer in mobilising resources for a poverty alleviation strategy if such a strategy is crowded-out by obligations to service debt.

What, then, are the causes of poverty, and where are they to be found ? The answer must be that they are to be found at every level from the individual to the global. It then follows that the design of strategy needs to address each and every level in turn. But the ordering is potentially crucial because, for any given level, what happens at a higher level of aggregation is (more or less) exogenous and, therefore, has to be taken as given. It follows that the quest for appropriate policies must begin at the highest level and work down. Solutions to the problem of poverty must therefore start at the global level with trade issues, debt and the international migration of labour and capital, and only then work down to the lower levels as the potential for making progress at each higher level starts to be realised: good micro policies will not take a country very far if macro policy is distorted. And, as we follow such a procedure, working down through the various levels of aggregation, we will eventually be left with those individuals who, for one reason or another, have not been able to catch the drift of the mainstream of development as it emerges by some combination of chance and the policies that have been selected at levels beyond their influence. These are the individuals who, probably through no fault of their own, have been marginalised by the tide of affairs. These are the poor who are potentially destitute and therefore in greatest need of help.

The three-pronged approach to policy that has been endorsed by the Washington Consensus and described at the beginning of this paper can be reviewed against this background. An obvious comment is that it starts at the macro level and works down to the micro, in line with the previous argument. However, this also means that the international level tends to be overlooked. A second observation is that it has little or nothing to say about structure. And a third, less obvious comment which derives from reading the Poverty Assessments and other relevant documentation is that the Consensus policy rarely penetrates all the strata so that the destitute and those who are marginalised by the mainstream of development are not necessarily recognised as having some claim to priority. In this sense, the Washington Consensus is a development strategy but not a poverty alleviation strategy.

From GDP to poverty analysis: alternative routeings

Setting aside for the present the international level of affairs, our point of entry for discussion of causes and policies is at the macroeconomic level with the determination of GDP.

This is generated by capital services (assets) and labour services, which are valued in terms of their time use. This allows for the possibility of taking a broader view of human capital services than is usual without necessarily imposing such a generalisation on the analysis.[11] However, as we will eventually elaborate, this possibility is important if one wants to capture the time-use dimension of gender discrimination in African households. Arguably this is one, if not the key distortion in the use of resources south of the Sahara. Building on this, we may suggest two different ways of approaching poverty analysis: on the one hand a structuralist approach and on the other the Washington Consensus. This latter terminology seems to be appropriate for two reasons. One is the heavy dependence of the associated methodology on (tailor-made) data sets and, especially, on household survey data. The other is the dependence of the methodology on a money metric measure of living standards and its distribution across all households.

Details of how the money metric is derived and the methodology of poverty analysis that can be based on it are to be developed in the next section of this chapter. But before turning to that it is appropriate to say something about the alternative, structuralist approach. And the first thing to be said is that it depends crucially on a characterisation of society as being made up of a set of mutually exclusive and exhaustive socio-economic groups which are defined in relation to the assets they own and the work that they do. Hence, we see, time use and assets are shown as influencing the determination of socio-economic groups, which define the critical disaggregation for policy analysis at the meso-economic level. It was suggested in Pyatt and Thorbecke (1976) that socio-economic groups might be defined primarily in relation to location, ethnicity or language and assets. The subsequent literature on social accounting matrices and earlier work on Sri Lanka offers some interesting examples of how those general principles might be applied and this theme has now been taken up within the context of the latest international guidelines on national income accounting.[12]

However, the all-time favourite example must be that shown in Table 5.2 which, it can be noted, was compiled without the advantage of a large-scale household survey. Instead, the author relied largely on common sense, participatory appraisal methods and, no doubt, a good deal of intelligent guesswork to produce his seminal contribution to 'politikal arithmetik'.

Table 5.2 Abstract from a scheme of the income and expenses of several families in England, calculated for the year 1688

Number of families	Ranks, degrees, titles and qualifications	Heads per family	Yearly income per head (£)	Expenses per head (£)	Increase per head (£)
160	Temporal lords	40	70	60	10
26	Spiritual lords	20	65	55	10
800	Baronets	16	55	51	4
600	Knights	13	50	46	4
3,000	Esquires	10	45	42	3
12,000	Gentlemen	8	35	32/10/-	2/10/-
5,000	Persons in offices	8	30	27	3
5,000	Persons in offices	6	20	18	2

Table 5.2 (Continued)

Number of families	Ranks, degrees, titles and qualifications	Heads per family	Yearly income per head (£)	Expenses per head (£)	Increase per head (£)
2,000	Merchants and traders by sea	8	50	40	10
8,000	Merchants and traders by sea	6	33	28	5
10,000	Persons in the law	7	20	17	3
2,000	Clergymen	6	10	9	1
8,000	Clergymen	5	9	8	1
40,000	Freeholders	7	12	11	1
140,000	Freeholders	5	10	9/10/-	10 shillings
150,000	Farmers	5	8/15/-	8/10/-	5 shillings
16,000	Persons in science and liberal arts	5	12	11/10/-	10 shillings
40,000	Shopkeepers and tradesmen	4½	10	9/10/-	10 shillings
60,000	Artisans and handicrafts	4	10	9/10/-	10 shillings
5,000	Naval officers	4	20	18	2
4,000	Military officers	4	15	14	1
511,586	**Sub-totals**	5¼	12/18/-	12	18 shillings
					Decrease
50,000	Common seamen	3	7	7/10/-	*10 shillings*
364,000	Labouring people and outservants	3½	4/10/-	4/12/-	*2 shillings*
400,000	Cottagers and paupers	3¼	2	2/5/-	*5 shillings*
35,000	Common soldiers	2	7	7/10/-	*10 shillings*
849,000	**Sub-totals**	3¼	3/5/-	3/9/-	*4 shillings*
..	Vagrants	..	2	3	*1*
849,000	**Sub-totals**	3¼	3/3/-	3/7/6	*4/6 pence*
	So the general account is				
511,586	Increasing the wealth of the Kingdom	5¼	12/18/-	12	18 shillings
849,000	Decreasing the wealth of the Kingdom	3¼	3/3/-	3/7/6	4/6 pence
1,360,586	**Net totals**	4¼	7/18/-	7/11/3	6/9 pence

Source: King (1696).

There are several features of Table 5.2 that are worthy of comment and some will be mentioned later. Here, just one point will be noted, which is that government as such does not appear in the table, nor is there any corporate sector. The first omission is potentially an error.[13] The second is explained by the fact that the concept of limited liability had yet to be recognised when this table was compiled. Today governments and companies are much in evidence and they need to be added to the set of socio-economic groups which are recognised in the structuralist approach if this is to capture a complete disaggregation of GDP into the disposable incomes of different institutions (plus net international transfers). This is important because the distribution of income between households, companies and governments is an important aspect of structure and therefore of the context in which individual poverty arises.[14] There is no difficulty in doing this in the environment of a social accounting matrix and, again, the literature provides many examples. But in relation to the statistical approach it is a somewhat different matter.

More generally, there is evidently no recognition of the institutional and production structure of society in the statistical approach. This is in contrast to the structural approach which can, through social accounting, be rich in such details.

The money-metric approach to poverty analysis

Defining the metric

The money metric is a sophisticated notion which builds on the proposition that the living standard of a household depends on its membership and on the commodities they consume. The latter in turn depend on the level of total consumption expenditure, c, and the vector of prices that the household faces, to be denoted here by $\mathbf{p}$. Hence, for each household there is a representation of welfare given by the indirect utility function $V(c, \mathbf{p}; \theta)$ where θ is a vector of household characteristics which includes details of its composition. If we now define γ_i by:

$$V(\gamma_i, \mathbf{p}_i; \theta_i) = V(c_j, \mathbf{p}_j; \theta_j) \tag{5.1}$$

then γ_i can be interpreted as what it would cost household i, which has characteristics θ_i and faces prices $\mathbf{p}_i$ to achieve the same welfare as that which is enjoyed by household j. Evidently γ_i will depend on $\mathbf{p}_i$ and θ_i as well as on the choice of j, the reference household, i.e.

$$\gamma_i = \gamma(\mathbf{p}_i, \theta_i | c_j, \mathbf{p}_j; \theta_j) \tag{5.2}$$

The money-metric measure of the living standard of household i can now be defined as:

$$m_i = c_i / \gamma_i \tag{5.3}$$

i.e. by the actual consumption expenditure of household i divided by what it would cost this household to sustain the same living standard as the reference household, given that household j has a different composition and has to face different prices.

A number of virtues can be claimed for this measure of living standards, starting with its firm grounding in theory. This is reinforced by more elaborate formulations in which households are expected to maximise their welfare over time. For those who can raise loans and for those who do not need them, this theory suggests that the current living standard is a reflection of permanent income, in which event consumption levels are to be preferred to current income in seeking to understand wellbeing.

Empirical implementation

This last result is helpful because it is also the case that consumption is easier to measure than income from sample survey results. However, other aspects of measurement are more problematic, starting with the need to define a household. The *de jure* definition which is favoured by statisticians excludes domestic servants and lodgers but generally includes students and spouses who are temporarily absent. A *de facto* approach reverses these positions so that whether or not a household is female-headed when the husband is working away from home and living in a hostel is a moot point. Similarly, it is not clear whether polygamous arrangements should be treated as multiple households and, if so, whether all or none of these should be characterised as having a household head.

Similarly, while it is not difficult to approximate the cost function γ_i, it is extremely difficult to get it right. The usual approximation is to allow for household composition by assuming that γ_i is proportional to household size, and to further assume there are no price differences except, perhaps, some differences as between rural and urban areas. These are gross simplifications. With respect to household size, some analysts measure size in terms of equivalent adults on the grounds that women and children have fewer needs than adult males. But it is unusual for any allowance to be made for economies of scale; and this despite the fact that any suggestion that poorer families are larger may be crucially dependent on the omission.

Equally serious, if not more so, is the problem of allowing for variation in the prices that families face. As noted above, some allowance may be made in practice for regional price variations. But this does not address the problem of variations which are correlated with income. Thus the price of potable water can easily vary by a factor of 10 as between the piped water supplied by a public utility to an affluent suburb and the street vendor with a handcart in a shanty town. Even more challenging is the likelihood that some goods and services are not available at all to the very poor.

For these reasons the metric is especially hard to establish for the richest and poorest households, who may well be under-represented in any actual survey, if only because the rich are less likely to be willing to be interviewed while those who have no fixed abode are less likely than others to be selected by most sampling procedures. Hence it is the two tails of the distribution that are most likely to be inaccurately measured.

There are other difficulties also, one of which is to decide whether or not, in estimating c_i, to include an estimate of the (imputed) value of individual benefits arising out of public consumption expenditure and, if so, how such estimates should be constructed. Similar problems arise in relation to do-it-yourself activities such as fetching water and the consumption of own production. Opportunity costs in these cases include the value of non-market time and can vary from household to household. This has several significant implications, of which the increased sensitivity of the metric to the choice of reference household is only one.

Enough has been said, to establish the estimation of a distribution of living standards which is not an exact science. Moreover, this distribution maintains at the level of the household and therefore by-passes the individual. Accordingly, the metric approach tends to gloss over the equity and efficiency issues that arise within the household.

Drawing poverty lines

The next step in the metric approach is crucial. It is to identify one or more critical values of m_i as poverty lines. These values are usually denoted by z or by z_u (for upper) and z_l (for lower) if there are two of them. Those for whom the metric is less than z (or z_u) are identified as being 'the poor', and those for whom the metric is less than z_l (in those cases in which a lower poverty line is defined), are the 'ultra-poor' or 'core-poor'. The location of the poverty line(s) will determine how many households are poor and, more generally, the extent of poverty. It is of some interest, therefore, that the World Bank does not recognise any set rules for drawing poverty lines for individual countries, neither in relation to their motivation nor their level. The consequent variation as to where these lines are drawn in practice for countries in sub-Saharan Africa is discussed in detail in Hanmer, Pyatt and White (1996). It emerges that in roughly half of all cases the World Bank invokes a relative measure of poverty by choosing the second quintile to define the poverty line, with the obvious result that 40 per cent of the population is deemed to be poor. Or the line may be drawn at a point which is, say, two-thirds of the average value of the metric, which has more or less the same effect. In the other half of the cases investigated, poverty lines are drawn on the basis of some absolute criterion, usually related to food expenditures. As an illustration of this genre, one can envisage calculating the calories available to each household by inference from their pattern of food consumption. Norms can then be set for individual household members which allow a poverty line to be defined as that level of total expenditure which will typically allow the norms to be achieved. If the same norms were set for different countries, this latter approach would give meaning and motivation to comparisons across countries of the incidence of poverty. But in practice the norms vary, tending to be set at higher levels in richer countries. Consequently, a considerable degree of relativity enters into the setting of poverty lines with this approach also.

The empirical consequence of all this is that when only one poverty line is set, between 30 and 50 per cent of the population emerge as being poor in most countries, irrespective and largely independent of considerable variation between countries in GDP *per capita*. Similarly, when a lower line is drawn, 10–20 per cent are typically found to be ultra-poor. These are all essentially meaningless numbers when taken at face value. The fact that 40 per cent of the population in country X is poor should be read as saying that the poverty line has been drawn for country X in such a way that 40 per cent of the population is poor. And, since the rationale for this is not apparent, the concept of poverty as articulated in the Poverty Assessments is devoid of any apparent motivation which goes beyond a general concern to suggest that the distribution of living standards is important, as well as their average value. The ultra-poor are not necessarily those who are destitute and those who are poor are not necessarily those households that have insufficient food to eat or lack secure employment. They are not that part of the population which is 'decreasing the wealth of the Kingdom' in the language of Table 5.2, i.e. those who are not managing to accumulate. They are simply the bottom slice of the statistical distribution; they are not members of any identified socio-economic group.

Poverty profiles

It is implicit in the foregoing discussion that the poor as identified by the statistical approach may not be the poorest as judged by some other standards or procedures. It is therefore of interest to know who the poor are, how many there are of them, and some of their salient characteristics. A poverty profile is developed within each of the Assessments to answer these questions.

The obvious starting point for the development of a poverty profile is to ask how much poverty there is and then to investigate how this poverty is distributed across households of different types. However, the amount of poverty and the proportion of poor people are not necessarily the same thing: they will be so only if the latter, which is known as the headcount ratio, is used to measure the former. But there are other measures of poverty, such as the Sen index and the family of indices, of which the headcount ratio is one, introduced in Foster, Greer and Thorbecke (1984).[15] Each of these different measures, other than the headcount ratio, makes some allowance for inequality in the distribution of the metric among the poor.

All assume that some meaningful poverty line can be taken as given although, as we have seen, the money metric theory does not suggest any particular way of doing this. It is therefore of some interest to note that theorists have arrived at the conclusion that, in comparing two different populations, or the same population at different points in time, it does not matter (within limits) where the poverty line is drawn or which measure of the extent of poverty is used: so long as one situation shows what is called generalised Lorenz dominance relative to the other, then there will always be less poverty in the dominant case, irrespective of where the line is drawn. This potentially powerful result may explain why the Assessments take an apparently casual attitude towards the location of the poverty line. But it does not explain why generalised Lorenz dominance is not used to develop poverty profiles. For this the Assessments are mainly dependent on a single poverty line and the headcount ratio as the measure of incidence.

The approach that is in fact adopted within the Assessments can be elucidated with reference to Table 5.3, which suggests that the total population is to be divided into different types (or socio-economic groups) and the number of poor people of each type is to be computed. The table also includes the average level of consumption per head, for reasons that will be explained below.

A typology of households which is often investigated within the Assessments is one based on location: urban versus rural is the simplest version but other, more detailed, disaggregations are obviously possible. Relative to each of these the data included in Table 5.2 allow some simple calculations from which one can deduce, for example, whether rural or urban households are more likely to be poor or which district is the poorest. Similarly, with an alternative typology defined by characteristics of the household head, one can calculate whether female-headed households are more likely than others to be poor according to the definition chosen.

Table 5.3   Schematic representation of a poverty profile

Types of individuals or households	Consumption per capita	Headcount ratios		Total number of individuals
		Very poor	*Poor*	
Type A Type B Type C etc.	Consumption *per capita* for each type of household	Proportion of the households of each type that is very poor	Proportion of households of each type that is poor	Numbers of individuals by type or socio-economic group
Totals/ National averages	Consumption *per capita*	Proportion of the population that is very poor	Proportion of the population that is poor	Total population

There are at least four difficulties with this approach, which is typical of the Assessments. The first is that the metric is sufficiently ambiguous at the conceptual level and difficult to implement empirically that inferences such as those used by way of illustration – the poorest district, or the relative circumstances of female-headed households – cannot necessarily be derived with confidence.

Secondly, the proliferation of alternative typologies is not very interesting or helpful. An example to emerge in the course of research some years ago using Malaysian data can illustrate this point. These data confirmed the common understanding in Malaysia at the time that poverty was associated with ethnicity and a two-pronged strategy was in place to reduce poverty and to redistribute wealth towards Malaysians and away from foreign ownership. However, the data also suggested a rural–urban dimension to living standards and a strong association with educational attainment within the household. Moreover, when all three typologies were analysed simultaneously, the ethnic dimension ceased to be significant, suggesting that ethnic differences could be explained by differences in access to educational opportunities according to where people lived.[16] The policy significance of this finding was, of course, considerable.

A third limitation of the approach which is commonly adopted by the Assessments is that it discards useful information. The characterisation of a household as scoring 1 if it is poor and 0 otherwise wastes much of the information that is contained in the ratio m_i/z. Accordingly, the approach makes it unnecessarily difficult to identify correlates and the potential causes of living standards at the micro level. We observe that probit analysis is coming to be used in the development of poverty profiles and this is an improvement to be welcomed. However, it must also be the case that much more could be extracted from the data if standard analysis of variance or covariance techniques were to be invoked, with the metric m_i/z (or its logarithm) as dependent variable.

Fourthly, it seems somewhat arbitrary to focus exclusively on the poorest third of the population, say, in a country where most people are poor, and to treat all those who are poor as equal. To do so implies that the dominant characterisation of who the poor are becomes a function of where the poverty line is drawn.

These *various* arguments suggest that the poverty lines constructed within the framework of the Poverty Assessments have a limited role to play in the development of a poverty profile and can even be misleading. A better way to proceed is to seek to identify a socio-economic classification of households such that differences in living standards (and potential causes) are captured between the groupings. This can be developed using analysis of covariance techniques as noted above with either (the logarithm of) the money metric or consumption expenditure as the dependent variable. It seems that nothing would be lost by proceeding in this way and something might be gained, since there would be less chance of losing sight of the poorest groups in society. Moreover, it is likely that such an approach will lead to a socio-economic classification of households that are differentiated *inter alia* by their assets in relation to household composition and savings behaviour. Table 5.2 can be revisited in this context to recall that the major division in the table is between those who are accumulating and those who are not. And among the former it can be observed that those who are saving at the fastest rate are the 'Merchants and traders by sea'. It would seem, therefore, that the structuralist approach may have more potential than the statistical alternative as a way of moving forward from the poverty profile to an investigation of the causes of poverty and the design of policy to stimulate development.

At this stage in the argument it should be noted that the poverty profiles developed in the Assessments do not always depend entirely on household surveys: increasingly they include the findings of participatory studies in which individuals are asked to characterise who the poor are and what it means to be poor. Typically these studies are consistent with the survey results. They identify the destitute and those who are most vulnerable – widows and orphans, for example. Otherwise they tend to associate poverty with lack of assets – a shortage of land, for example, or a house with a mud floor and no toilet – and not being able to accumulate, even in the form of sending the children to school. There would therefore seem to be no difficulty in reconciling the participatory and structuralist approaches. Indeed, it is quite likely that they can be deployed in ways that reinforce each other.

Benefit-incidence analysis

With suitable adjustments and re-calibration, both the structuralist and statistical approaches can provide a complete accounting for the aggregate level of private consumption as recorded in the national income accounts.[17] But, as we have noted previously, this leaves out of account the national savings and public consumption components of GDP. Benefit-incidence analysis is a technique for allocating public consumption expenditures, and, in particular, expenditures on health and education, to particular households, i.e. for computing their imputed income arising out of public transfers.[18] The method is quite straightforward. It involves computing the cost per beneficiary of a particular service, such as primary education, and then attributing an amount equal to that cost as a benefit to each household in proportion to the number of their children who are attending primary school. Hence the distribution of benefits across the various quintiles of the distribution of living standards can be estimated. When plotted on a Lorenz diagram, these details describe what are known as a *concentration curve*. This will approximate a straight line if primary school enrolment is evenly distributed across households *or* if it is uncorrelated with the size of their metric, as it must be when enrolment is high.

Unfortunately, such results do not mean very much because they make no allowance for the quality of service delivery. If expenditure per pupil on rural schools is only half that on urban schools, then this would show up if benefit-incidence analysis was conducted in relation to socio-economic groups that are defined to distinguish between rural and urban households. But the metric concentration curve approach will show a difference only to the extent that urban households, say, are significantly richer than their rural neighbours. Thus disaggregation of service supplies, in this case on urban–rural lines, is a necessary but not a sufficient condition for revealing what may, in practice, be substantial differences in the quality of services, as distinct from some sort of access. Accordingly, the finding within the Assessments that concentration curves tend to approximate straight lines does not necessarily tell us much and one is likely to learn more about the distribution of income below the line from casual empiricism, participatory analysis and the common knowledge that, in many countries, there is considerable urban bias in the provision of services and the allocation of such provision is often subject to political influence. Such features are much more likely to emerge if a structuralist approach is adopted.

Policy and the Washington Consensus

Prongs and preconditions

As we have noted in the Introduction, the *1990 World Development Report* provided the initial articulation of what is now referred to as a three-pronged approach to development policy. The first prong is economic growth which has been variously qualified as needing to be 'pro-poor', 'labour-intensive' or 'broad-based'. The second is to develop human capital, not least through primary education and basic health care. And the third prong, which has only achieved 'full-prong' status since 1990, is to provide safety nets, especially to protect those who are temporarily disadvantaged by change, and not least by the changes involved in establishing the preconditions for growth.

The preconditions for economic growth are essentially a set of macro-economic policies which are designed to establish and sustain internal and external balance and otherwise to create an attractive climate for private investment through deregulation and clear understanding as to the respective roles of government and the private sector, not only in those sectors which produce goods but also in supplying services, including health and education, perhaps through NGOs. Another important area for understanding is the commitment of governments to the strategy overall. This cannot be taken for granted.

The non-economic preconditions for growth include all those other things which influence risk from the point of view of the private entrepreneur –

political stability, the rule of law, honest government and personal safety are all important factors in this context which lose none of their significance in also being important determinants of wellbeing in their own right. Accordingly, their role as part of an effective development strategy is potentially critical despite the fact that the Washington Consensus has relatively little to say about them.

Similarly, the Consensus does not include a position on the external support which countries can expect to enjoy or, indeed, could expect to rely on if they were to embrace the policy advice that is now on offer. Yet it is clear that some countries in sub-Saharan Africa have no chance of achieving external balance while continuing to service foreign debt. Export-led growth is essential, but there is no realistic prospect of sufficient growth being generated without substantial private investment which, more than likely, will need to be attracted (or crowded-in) by public investments in infrastructure of various sorts and other, more direct fiscal incentives. To the extent that the Consensus position does not explain how the considerable difficulties of achieving all this are to be resolved, the policies proposed are incomplete and perhaps unsustainable.

The importance of growth

The emphasis that is placed within the Consensus strategy on economic growth is largely a result of the observed success of a number of countries, notably South Korea and others in East Asia. However, an *ex post* rationalisation of the importance of growth in reducing poverty can be articulated. If growth is neutral, so that the living standard of everyone increases by the same percentage amount, then the distribution of living standards will be stretched to the right. Consequently, if the poverty line is fixed, the incidence of poverty will decrease as a result of growth.

This simple result can be formalised and extended in various ways. If growth is neutral then inequality as measured by, say, the Gini coefficient will not be affected by the growth process. And if, on the contrary, growth is not neutral and inequality goes down as growth proceeds, then growth is said to be pro-poor. Alternatively, if inequality increases, then the growth process is anti-poor, which does not mean that poverty will necessarily increase, but only that poverty, if it does decrease, will decrease by less than it would have done had growth been neutral.

These qualifications on the impact of growth are important because the rates of growth which are otherwise required to reduce the absolute number of poor people are very high, given that population growth rates in sub-Saharan Africa are approaching 3 per cent per annum. Thus in Hanmer, Pyatt and White (1996) it is estimated that neutral growth rates of the order of 6 per cent per annum are needed to avoid increases in the number of those who are poor relative to some fixed poverty line.

Such simple calculations define a formidable task. It is therefore of some interest that the size of this task is modified by three considerations:

(1) The trend in inequality
(2) The need to adjust for savings
(3) The location of the poverty line.

With reference to the first of these, the point has already been made that if growth is pro-poor so that inequality is declining, then less growth is required to achieve a given reduction in poverty than would be needed if growth was neutral. However, in practice, pro-poor growth is hard to achieve, if only because those who are marginalised are less likely to benefit from the economic growth because, by definition, their links to the mainstream are tenuous at best.

Next, we can note that if an economy is going to achieve faster growth rates, then it is likely that the domestic savings rate is going to have to increase. In the case of sub-Saharan Africa, this increase is going to have to be substantial. Hence the GDP growth rate is going to have to be significantly higher than the growth rate of aggregate consumption. One of the more disturbing findings reported in Hanmer, Pyatt and White (1996) is that in Ghana and Uganda, two countries which might now have the best chance of evolving from adjustment to sustained growth, domestic savings have been negative in recent years. In any country, to raise the domestic savings rate, it may be necessary to encourage a redistribution of factor income towards land and other capital assets and away from labour. Doing so is likely to inject an anti-poor bias into the economic growth path.

The third consideration noted above is the purely technical one that the relative importance of achieving growth in the average living standard versus the reduction of inequality as ways of reducing poverty also depends on where the poverty line is drawn. To be specific, the higher (within limits) the poverty line is set relative to the average level of living standards, the less important is the trend in inequality relative to the importance of the rate of economic growth. Hence the adoption of a relative poverty line, such as two-thirds of the mean living standard, while it has no motivation in terms of identifying the extent of poverty in relation, say, to malnutrition, nonetheless has very clear implications for the relative importance of the tradeoff between economic growth and the reduction of inequality if reducing poverty is the ultimate goal. By setting the poverty line at a level which is equal to two-thirds of the mean the trade-off recognises that reductions in inequality can reduce poverty, but such reductions are at less of a premium relative to economic growth than they would be if the poverty line had been set at a lower level, equal, say, to one-third of the mean. Thus setting a relatively high poverty line reinforces the importance of economic growth irrespective of the scope for inequality to be reduced. This may be unfortunate in so far as the causes of high inequality may well militate against the achievement of development.

These mechanics of the Consensus approach are important in the real world. In *The World Bank Research Observer*, Demery and Squire (1996) analysed trends in poverty over time for five countries in sub-Saharan Africa, chosen on the basis of data availability. Their results, which are reported at greater length in Hanmer, Pyatt and White (1996), are sum-marised in Table 5.4, which shows that in three of their five cases (Kenya, Nigeria and Tanzania) poverty was seen to go down when the poverty line was set at high levels and to go up when poverty was more tightly defined. Two inferences might be drawn from their findings. The first is that results based on high levels of poverty – the initial levels of poverty in the high case for these three countries were 51.5 per cent, 43.0 per cent and 64.4 per cent, respectively – should not be accepted without further examina-tion. This may take the form of looking at what happens when a more stringent definition of poverty is adopted, which is a special case of the conclusion previously noted as having been reached by theorists, namely that analysis should be based on movements of the generalised Lorenz curve when there is no particular reason for focusing on a particular pov-erty line. This same conclusion is reinforced by the results of Demery and Squire (1996) for the two additional countries in their set of five. In both these cases the high poverty line suggests significantly less poverty initially in comparison with the three other cases: poverty is initially 36.9 per cent in Ghana and 30 per cent in the Côte d'Ivoire. Hence the upper and lower poverty lines are closer together for these two countries. For that reason it is not surprising that in these instances poverty moves in the same direc-tion whichever line is used; it goes down in Ghana and increases in the Côte d'Ivoire.

The second conclusion to be drawn is that if results in practice are so sensitive to where the line is drawn and there is no particular motivation for

Table 5.4 Trends in headcount ratio measures of poverty in five countries

Country	Percentage change in the headcount ratio measure of poverty relative to an absolute poverty line that is initially:	
	Low	High
Côte d'Ivoire	*Increase* from 10.0 to 14.1	*Increase* from 30.0 to 45.9
Ghana	Decrease from 10.2 to 6.0	Decrease from 36.9 to 31.4
Nigeria	*Increase* from 10.0 to 12.5	Decrease from 43.0 to 34.1
Kenya	*Increase* from 10.1 to 14.1	Decrease from 51.5 to 48.7
Tanzania	*Increase* from 10.3 to 20.9	Decrease from 64.4 to 50.5

Source: Demery and Squire (1996).

choosing a particular location, then it might be best not to draw a line at all. Analysis could then still proceed within the statistical approach using generalised Lorenz curves. The only differences would now be that any claim to a focus on poverty would be lost. It seems, yet again, that the poverty line, as articulated by the World Bank in the context of Poverty Assessments serves a limited purpose at best and can be misleading.

What sort of growth?

A case has been made for the importance of growth and the desirability that whatever growth is stimulated should be pro-poor. However, the notion of 'pro-poor growth' is somewhat academic, perhaps, and alternative characterisations such as 'labour-intensive' and 'broad-based' are potentially more tangible. However, that does not imply that either 'labour-intensive' or 'broad-based' growth is necessarily feasible. And, if they are feasible, then they may not be sustainable.

The question of whether the growth of any particular economy is sustainable is central to the question of whether the Consensus policy package actually works. In sub-Saharan Africa it may be too soon to say. Half the countries covered in Hanmer, Pyatt and White (1996) are in decline and in most of the remainder the growth rate is insufficient to offset the impact of population growth on the number of poor people. In these cases, therefore, the policies have failed, or they have not been adequately implemented, or it is too soon to judge.

For the remaining fraction of cases it can be noted that actual growth is in part the result of efficiency gains which are a direct consequence of macro- and meso-level policies. They represent movements towards the production opportunity frontier, therefore, not a movement of the frontier itself. Such growth is not, therefore, sustainable. It can be supplemented by balance-of-payments support or by remittances from abroad. The latter may be sustainable but the former will not be to the extent that debt has to be serviced and cannot, therefore, be allowed to increase indefinitely.

Sustainable growth requires continuing investment which is financed out of domestic savings or by sustainable inflows from abroad. Such inflows should preferably take the form of direct foreign investment (FDI) in local ventures or grant aid. Otherwise, the servicing of these inflows must be covered by the sustainable growth of export revenue. Hence, the conclusion can be drawn that sustainable growth requires both a high domestic savings rate and the sustained growth of export earnings at a substantial rate.

How 'labour-intensive' or 'broad-based' growth might fit into this picture is not entirely clear. The second prong of the Consensus strategy is to develop human capital, which implies an increasingly efficient labour force. Therefore, if wages are restrained in the sense that wage costs per unit of output remain low, a comparative advantage in the production of labour-intensive goods can be developed provided that the real exchange rate remains competitive. Hence a labour-intensive growth scenario might be initiated. But this is not inevitable and will depend crucially on investment in the traded goods sectors and the cultivation of overseas markets.

Broad-based growth is somewhat different. It suggests that there should be widespread participation in the growth process and its benefits. And if this is the focus, then two things will be important. One is the need for strong intra-sectoral linkages to avoid duality. The other is a widespread distribution of stakes in the asset base. Neither is easy to achieve in the early stages if only because some individuals must be the first to benefit from new opportunities in education and the labour market. Several countries in East Asia, notably Taiwan, (for which the data are probably the best), have experienced increasing inequality in the early stages of their economic development which persisted until such time as the slack in the labour market was absorbed.

While slack in the labour market may be unavoidable, it can also be significant, not only as a waste of resources but also because it may have political consequences, especially when the unemployed have gone beyond the primary stage and completed their secondary education. Some criteria are needed, therefore, to decide how much investment in human capital should be undertaken and how such investment should be kept in balance relative to other types of investment opportunities. It is at this point that the ideas of balanced development that have been worked out by UNDP become relevant.[19] Building on basic concepts of cost-benefit analysis, they provide a simple criterion as to how far to go in correcting for urban biases and the complementary bias towards tertiary levels of service provision at the expense of the basic or primary levels. They also address the imbalances between recurrent and capital account funding, emphasising that it is often better to maintain the flow of services offered by existing facilities than it is to create new infrastructure. The problem of low quality and deteriorating services comes up frequently in the Poverty Assessments for sub-Saharan Africa, but the obvious solution of reallocating resources from the development budget to bolster the funding of recurrent expenditures is never mentioned.

Proposals for redistributing the asset base incrementally through education and the creation of human capital go at least as far back as the work of Chenery *et al.* (1974) on *Redistribution with Growth*. However, this is not the only way in which foundations can be built for broad-based growth. Other methods, notably the granting of title to land on an individual or collective basis were important in Taiwan and also in countries as different as South Korea and Malaysia. The Washington Consensus does not offer any specific points of entry into a discussion of these alternatives, being more concerned with the balance between human and physical capital and land in aggregate than with their distribution among potential stakeholders.

Transfers and targeting

If individuals or families cannot sustain an acceptable standard of living on the basis of their existing assets and skills then the only way to raise their living standards to a higher level is through transfers. Capital transfers such as land redistribution or the public provision of educational opportunities have already been noted as possibilities. Current transfers are the only remaining option.

The exercise of this option is one measure of the extent to which the Washington Consensus departs from a pure growth strategy. Arguably it is the only measure since the reinforcement of macroeconomic policies by public investment in human capital is clearly a part of what is needed to implement an optimal growth strategy. This applies especially to investment in the education of girls to the extent that there is a private bias against doing so (perhaps because the advantages to parents that result from educating daughters are thought to be that much less).

Current transfers are a charge against the budget and, as such, they involve a potential tradeoff between current and future welfare. And, no matter how this tradeoff may be struck, it is important that any funds that are allocated to current transfers are used efficiently, which translates, first, into the question of how transitory the need for targeting may be and, secondly, into the cost-effectiveness of the transfers made.

There is less risk that transfers which are temporary will become a regular charge on the budget, but this consideration does not apply to seasonal relief which can easily be both temporary and regular. It does apply, perhaps, to those who are adversely affected by structural adjustment. Indeed, temporary or one-off payments to such individuals and, especially, to retrenched civil servants, have become a regular feature of SAPs. Potentially they are highly cost-effective if one is reasonably confident that the adjustment policy package will work if only it is given a chance to do so, and that the chances of adjustment being politically acceptable would be enhanced by making these transfers (at which point the transfers become part of an optimal growth strategy and there is no tradeoff involved).

Other forms of transfers which are likely to be temporary are various kinds of emergency relief and support for those who can be identified by particular morbidities, pregnancy, etc. In all these cases it is relatively easy to target those whom it is intended to benefit so that resources are not wasted on individuals who are outside the target group (except, in so far as all such schemes attract corruption and administrative overheads). But, when the identification of the target is less obvious, as is the case when the target is 'the poor' as determined by a somewhat arbitrary poverty line, the identification of the potential beneficiaries and how to pin-point them becomes much more problematic. It depends, in the first instance, on the poverty profile, the purpose of which is to identify who the poor are. It follows that the limitations of the poverty profile that have previously been noted carry over to third-prong policies which are directed at what to do about the problem of poverty as identified at the micro level.

The relatively permanent costs of caring for orphans, the destitute, handicapped and displaced members of society may be one reason why the Washington Consensus is apparently unable to afford them the priority that their need would otherwise seem to justify. This is ultimately a political judgement, of course, and therefore lies beyond the economic calculus. However, it can be noted that if the multilateral agencies were able to provide reliable assistance to governments in seeking to coordinate and control the NGO sector then some additional funding might well be achieved, to the benefit of those in greatest need.

If the poor are defined more broadly, then there are two ways in which a particular policy might be deemed to be inefficient. On the one hand, the policy might give benefits to those who are not poor through 'leakages' (which include any unavoidable administrative costs) and, on the other hand, some of those who are poor may fail to be included in the set of beneficiaries. Whether or not these are serious concerns can be checked in any particular case. For example, giving milk to children at school will not benefit those who do not go to school, it may discourage parents from feeding their children as well as they might otherwise do and there will undoubtedly be administrative costs to offset the benefits to farmers, the children who receive the milk and their parents. To evaluate all this potentially requires a full cost-benefit analysis, and there is no reason why such analysis should not be distributionally sensitive. However, the distributional weights implicit in poverty targeting – score 1 for the poor and zero for the non-poor – do seem to be extreme. They imply, for example, that the benefits of a universal public health service to those who are not poor should be ignored, even in very poor countries. It is one thing to say that such a country could not afford a public health service. It is another thing entirely to assume that, say, half the population would get no benefit at all if the service were provided. Yet again, it seems, there are implications of drawing a poverty line which are quite unhelpful in a situation in which a poverty line is unnecessary.

An alternative perspective

It has been suggested in this chapter that the statistical approach to development policy and the analysis of poverty has a number of limitations. In this final section I want to argue that these limitations are not unavoidable. An alternative, more robust methodology can be developed in the spirit of the structuralist approach. In conclusion, therefore, I want to attempt no more than to outline this alternative.

The starting point for the structuralist approach is to define a set of mutually exclusive and exhaustive socio-economic groups in the spirit of Gregory King's pioneering effort which is reproduced in Table 5.2. The groupings in Table 5.2 refer mainly to households with the exception being the reference to those of no fixed abode – i.e. the vagrants. These groupings are characterised by the socio-economic status of the head of the household and classified, *inter alia*, according to whether, on average, the group achieves some savings out of current income or is running into debt. This, then, is not very different from a classification which seeks to distinguish those who are destitute from households that can sustain a subsistence level of existence but are otherwise unable to accumulate assets, and a complementary category of households who do indeed manage to save some fraction of their income. Evidently a classification based on the ownership of assets is likely to go a long way towards identifying these categories in any particular society, as illustrated 300 years ago by Gregory King. Then, as now, participatory techniques can be of some value in deciding on the details, which need to recognise the existence of government, NGOs and the corporate sector in modern societies.

Given a suitable socio-economic classification it is conceptually straightforward to develop benefit-incidence analysis to see which groups benefit most or least from particular types of public expenditures and otherwise to explore which groups are poorest as judged by various indicators such as nutritional status, morbidities and the overall consumption level. The findings of such analysis can help to identify not only which socio-economic groups should be targeted by meso-level policies but also which households and individuals within any individual group might constitute a particular cause for concern. Thus meso-policies can address differences between groups while micro-policies are directed at variations which arise within particular groups and may cut across them.

The next stage of analysis is to attempt to link socio-economic groups to the production structure in relation to both sources of income and patterns of expenditure. This can be achieved most straightforwardly via a social accounting matrix framework, which can support both macroeconomic and mesoeconomic analysis of alternative policies. Thus, at the meso level, the interdependence of production structure and the distribution of income across socio-economic groups can be explored for linkages that might usefully be strengthened and leakages that it would be wise to control. Moreover, such analysis, with or without the support of a general equilibrium model, can be developed in relation to the external constraints which the economy has to accommodate – and, in particular, the obligation to repay debt.

Two developments of the methodology beyond this point are potentially useful. One is to introduce separate details for individuals as factors of productions. Again, a typology is needed and it is most likely that this should recognise age and sex. Beyond that, education is probably the single most important dimension to capture.

The classification of individuals by type can be incorporated within a social accounting format. It has the effect of introducing details of household composition by age, sex and educational level if these are the variables that are used to classify individuals. And it has the further effect of introducing details of the demand for labour services of different types that is generated by production activities. Thus the multiplier process could be elaborated in relation to the standard circular flow of demand from institutions to activities, then on to factors and, hence, back to institutions. The demand for labour of particular types is generated within this process which, consequently, captures the sense in which labour-intensive growth may be effective in raising the living standards of the poorest socio-economic groups.

The final elaboration to consider here is the extension of the production boundary beyond that which is usually assumed by the national income accounts to include all forms of time use. Pyatt (1990) shows how this can be done at the conceptual level, with the main difficulties in practice being the need to estimate the return to domestic durable goods and the shadow price of time.

Conventional national income accounts make some attempt to impute a value to some production activities which provide goods and services that are domestically consumed rather than being sold on the market for cash. However, for the most part, the national accounts and the associated measure of GDP are restricted to cash transactions. And, as a result, that part of economic activity which involves time use within a domestic setting goes unrecorded and largely ignored. This is a serious omission for several reasons which include the social and political implications of this omission, not least for women. It seems entirely possible that the preoccupation of structural adjustment policies with efficiency in that part of the economy that is monetised and a natural reluctance to focus on policies for improving the efficiency of time-use within the household is one reason why the supply response of GDP to structural adjustment is low in sub-Saharan Africa.

Something else I learned from reviewing the Poverty Assessments is that leisure is a concept to which many women in Africa have difficulty relating. There is much to be said, accordingly, for the proposition that development is the amelioration of the lot of women.

Notes

1. Lipton and Ravallion (1995. 2571). The reference to the 'World Bank [1990]' within this quotation is a reference to the *1990 World Development Report*.
2. Lipton and Ravallion (1995), p. 2571.
3. Some earlier thoughts which move in the same direction are to be found in Pyatt and Thorbecke (1976).
4. See the note on the opening page of the chapter above for an acknowledgement of the contribution of my colleagues to this effort. The report of the study which is referred to in the text is cited here as Hanmer, Pyatt and White (1996).
5. See Pyatt and Thorbecke (1976) for a discussion of this approach.

6. See Rawls (1971).
7. See UNDP (1990 and later years).
8. In Pyatt (1991) I have compared the *Human* and *World Development Reports* for 1990 while Vol. 48 of the *American Economic Review* contains a set of three papers by Srinivasan, Streeten and Aturupane, and Glewwe and Isenman, all of which were included in a symposium organised by Amartya Sen which sought to clarify the differences. See Aturupane, Glewwe and Isenman (1994), Srinivasan (1994) and Streeten (1994).
9. See Pyatt (1990) on the first of these points.
10. Such a claim was in fact the proximate cause for calculating the first cost of living index in the UK in 1904. See Pyatt (1968) for a general discussion of the development of data as a response to policy issues.
11. See Pyatt (1992) or UNDP (1992) for an elaboration of this possibility.
12. See ISWG (1993).
13. Born, perhaps, of a sense that it might be indiscreet to estimate and publish the required details for the royal family.
14. See Pyatt (1977) for discussion of this point.
15. See Sen (1976)
16. See Pyatt and Round (1984). The simultaneous analysis of alternative typologies can be developed using multi-way χ^2 contingency tables.
17. This is potentially much easier to realise within a Social Accounting Matrix (SAM) structuralist framework since the institutionalised population – those in hospital, hostels, barracks, camps and prisons, etc. – can be treated as one or more separate socio-economic groups that are distinct from the household sector as usually defined.
18. In the 1950s literature, such transfers were categorised as 'income below the line'.
19. See Pyatt (1992) and UNDP (1992).

Bibliography

Aturupane, H., P. Glewwe and P. Isenman (1994), 'Poverty, human development and growth; an emerging consensus', *American Economic Review*, Vol. 48(2), pp. 244–49.

Chenery, H., M. Ahluwalia, C. Bell, J. Duloy and R. Jolly (1974), *Redistribution with Growth*, Oxford: Oxford University Press.

Demery, L. and L. Squire (1996), 'Macroeconomic adjustment and poverty in Africa: an emerging picture', *World Bank Research Observer*, Vol. 11(1), pp. 39–59.

Foster, J., J. Greer and E. Thorbecke (1984), 'A class of decomposable poverty measures', *Econometrica*, Vol. 52, pp. 761–65.

Hanmer, L., G. Pyatt and H. White (1996), 'Poverty in sub-Saharan Africa: what can we learn from the World Bank's Poverty Assessments?', The Hague: Institute of Social Studies Advisory Services mimeograph.

Inter-Secretariat Working Group (ISWG) (1993), *System of National Accounts 1993*, Commission of the European Communities – Eurostat; Brussels/Luxembourg: International Monetary Fund; Washington: Organisation for Economic Cooperation and Development; Paris: United Nations; New York: and World Bank; Washington, DC.

King, G. (1696) 'Natural and political observations and conclusions upon the state and condition of England', originally printed as an appendix to Sir George Chalmers, *An Estimate of the Comparative Strength of Great Britain* and reprinted in *Two Tracts by Gregory King*, Baltimore: Johns Hopkins University Press, 1936.

Lipton, M. and M. Ravallion (1995), 'Poverty and policy', Chapter 41 in J. Behrman and T.N. Srinivasan (eds), *Handbook of Development Economics, III*, New York: Elsevier Science, pp. 2553–657.

Pyatt, G. (1968) 'On official economic statistics', *Journal of the Royal Statistical Society, Series A (General)*, Vol. 131, Part 1, pp. 35–44.

Pyatt, G. (1977) 'On international comparisons of inequality', *American Economic Review*, Vol. 67(1), pp. 71–5.

Pyatt, G. (1990) 'Accounting for time use', *Review of Income and Wealth*, Series 36, No. 1.

Pyatt, G. (1991) 'Poverty: a wasted decade', *European Economic Review*, Vol. 35, pp. 358–65.

Pyatt, G. (1992) 'Towards balanced development in Pakistan', *Pakistan Development Review*, Vol. 31(4), Part 1, pp. 407–29.

Pyatt, G. and J.I. Round (1984), 'Improving the macroeconomic data base: a SAM for Malaysia, 1970', World Bank Staff Working Papers, No. 646, Washington, DC: World Bank.

Pyatt, G. and E. Thorbecke (1976), *Planning Techniques for a Better Future*, Geneva: International Labour Office.

Rawls, J. (1971), *A Theory of Justice*, Cambridge, MA: Harvard University Press.

Sen, A.K. (1976), 'Poverty: an ordinal approach to measurement', *Econometrica*, Vol. 46, pp. 436–46.

Srinivasan, T.N. (1994), 'Human development; a new paradigm or reinvention of the wheel?', *American Economic Review*, Vol. 84(2), pp. 238–43.

Streeten, P. (1994), 'Human development: means and ends', *American Economic Review*, Vol. 84(2), pp. 232–37.

United Nations Development Programme (UNDP) (annual from 1990), *The Human Development Report*, New York: Oxford University Press.

United Nations Development Programme (1992), *Balanced Development: An Approach to Social Action in Pakistan*, Islamabad: United Nations Development Programme.

World Bank (1990), *The World Development Report 1990, Poverty*, Oxford: Oxford University Press.

6

The Impact of a Severe Economic Crisis on Poverty and Income Distribution: An Indonesian Case Study, 1997–9

*Anne Booth**

Introduction

To many people, both in South-East Asia and elsewhere, the crisis which struck a group of South-East Asian economies (Thailand, Indonesia, Malaysia and the Philippines), as well as South Korea, in mid-1997 appeared to arrive like a meteor from outer space, crashing onto what had been some of the most dynamic economies in the world. More than three years later, it was very clear that the legacy of the crisis would be lasting and serious, especially in Indonesia. Not only did the crisis result in a devastated banking system and a heavily indebted non-banking corporate sector but also in a severe contraction in real GDP. In 1998, GDP contracted by over 13 per cent, and in 1999 there was an increase of under 1 per cent (Bank Indonesia 2000. Table 1). For an economy which grow at 6 per cent in terms of *per capita* GNP in the decade from 1985 to 1995, a contraction of this magnitude posed enormous problems of adjustment. These problems were exacerbated by the after-effects of a very serious drought, which ravaged parts of the country in 1997–8.

Not surprisingly, given the extent of the real GDP decline in 1998, the debate about the impact of the crisis on popular welfare was, and continues to be, very intense in Indonesia. By mid-1998 when the effects of both the financial crisis and the severe drought were already becoming very obvious, the government of President Habibie was under great pressure to take action to alleviate what was viewed as, potentially, a major famine. It was argued that many workers who had lost their jobs in the cities would go back to the villages where they would become an extra mouth to feed for families

* This is a revised and expanded version of Booth (1999a). Assistance from many colleagues in Indonesia and Australia is gratefully acknowledged.

whose incomes were falling because of the contraction in rural non-farm employment opportunities, combined with the impact of the drought. Many millions would thus not be able to afford to buy whatever food was available. As prices of rice and other basic needs soared in the third quarter of 1998 these predictions took on added force. Unfortunately there was a lack of reliable data with which to monitor trends; the SUSENAS household expenditure module was not carried out until February 1999, and there were few other data sources available which could be used to monitor household consumption trends in both urban and rural areas.

The debate about the welfare effects of the crisis thus took place, at least in the latter part of 1998, largely in a factual vacuum. Much of the argument tended to be based on *a priori* reasoning about what the impact of the crisis was likely to be on particular regions and social groups. The following issues emerged as crucial:

(a) How would the contraction of GDP (and the severe drought) in 1998 affect different sectors of the economy, and the workers employed in those sectors?
(b) How would the contraction in GDP affect different categories of expenditure; in particular would the contraction in total GDP be reflected in a similar, smaller or larger contraction in household consumption expenditures, which in the short run at least determine levels of welfare?
(c) What would be the effect on welfare of the rapid increase in inflation which occurred in the middle months of 1998?
(d) What effect would the substantial devaluation of the rupiah have on the incomes of different categories of producer and consumer in different parts of the country?
(e) What effect would the crisis have on school attendance and on utilisation of health facilities?
(f) What forms of government intervention would be most effective in mitigating the impact of the crisis?

Obviously the answer to (f) would depend on the answers to questions (a)–(e). But given the fraught political climate in 1998, the government of President Habibie, not to mention a large number of domestic and international NGOs, as well as both bilateral and multilateral development agencies, felt compelled to implement remedial programmes, even if there was no compelling evidence that the target beneficiaries were those most severely affected by the crisis. By early 1999, debates became more vociferous not just about how many, and who, were severely affected by the crisis but also about the effect of the various intervention policies, which were known under the general rubric of 'social safety net' (*jaring pengaman sosial*) programmes. With the assistance of the World Bank (using ASEF funds) and AUSAID, a Social Monitoring and Early Response Unit (SMERU) was established in late 1998 to coordinate work on the effects of the crisis, and to examine the effectiveness of government intervention programmes. By the latter part of 2000, several studies were available from this unit which together with reports from the Central Board of Statistics (CBS), and other domestic and international sources, had clarified the debate and produced answers to at least some of the questions listed above.

The purpose of this chapter is threefold. The first section sets out what, by 2001, we had learned about the impact of the crisis on living standards and access to public services in Indonesia. This is followed by a discussion of the effectiveness of the various social safety net programmes. Finally, the chapter gives at least a tentative answer to the six questions posed above, and examines the longer-term policy implications of the debate over social safety nets and provision of social welfare in Indonesia. It also draws some wider lessons about how developing countries should respond to the impact of severe economic crises on living standards and popular welfare.

The World Bank, CBS and ILO/UNDP estimates: July–August 1998

In spite of the lack of data, in July and August 1998, three separate sets of estimates of poverty in Indonesia for 1998 were published. The first was included in a World Bank report published in July (World Bank 1998); the second was prepared by the Indonesian Central Board of Statistics, and the third was published by the International Labour Organisation and the United Nations Development Programme (ILO/UNDP 1998). These three estimates used different methodologies, which I have discussed in detail elsewhere, to evaluate the effect of the crisis on poverty (Booth 1999a). They came up with rather different answers to the fundamental question: what will be the impact of the crisis on the poor and vulnerable groups in Indonesian society?

The World Bank Report argued that in mid-1997, before the crisis hit, around 10.1 per cent of the population was below the official poverty line[1]. This can be compared with the official estimate of 11.3 per cent below the poverty line in early 1996 (Booth 1999b: Table 6). According to the World Bank, a contraction of GDP of around 12 per cent in 1998 could push the incidence of poverty up to 14.1 per cent of the population in 1999. This would imply 29 million people in poverty (World Bank 1998: 32–3). The World Bank argued that the most visible effects of the crisis would be in urban areas, and numbers in poverty would increase more rapidly in percentage terms in urban than in rural areas. But the increase in absolute numbers of poor would be higher in rural areas, and especially in those areas most affected by the *El Nino* drought. These areas included provinces such as East Nusatenggara, Irian Jaya and East Timor where the incidence of poverty was already much higher than the national average, and where large numbers of households were very vulnerable to declines in output and incomes.[2]

A much more pessimistic set of estimates were prepared by the CBS and incorporated in the Appendix to the State Speech of President Habibie, published in August 1998. These data indicated that by mid-1998 the proportion of the population below the official poverty line would jump to 39.9 per cent, compared with 11.3 per cent in 1996. This percentage translated into 79.4 million people, compared with 22.5 million in 1996 (Department of Information 1998: Table IV-1). This dramatic increase was based on the key assumption that the poorer groups in both urban and rural areas would experience a sharper decline in income than the fall in *per capita* GDP. These were followed by an even more alarming set of estimates prepared by the ILO/UNDP, which indicated that the proportion of the population under the official poverty line could rise to 48 per cent by the end of 1998, and 66 per cent by the end of 1999. Both the CBS and the ILO/UNDP figures indicated that absolute numbers below the poverty line would be higher in 1998 than at any time since the mid-1970s (Booth 1999b: Table 6).[3]

The ILO/UNDP and CBS estimates received considerable publicity in Indonesia in the latter part of 1998, and were not at the time subjected to much critical scrutiny, although they were clearly based on rather extreme assumptions. Certainly it was not immediately obvious why a reduction in GDP of around 13 per cent in 1998 would lead to such a huge increase in the proportion of the population under the poverty line. National accounts data published in 2000 showed that real *per capita* GDP in 1998 was around 14 per cent lower than that in 1997, while real *per capita* consumption expenditures was around 7 per cent lower (Table 6.1). In other words, the severe GDP contraction had

Table 6.1   Trends in *per capita* GDP and *per capita* private consumption expenditures, 1993–2000[a] (Rp. 000 *per capita*: constant 1993 prices)

Year	Per capita GDP	Per capita GNP	Per capita household consumption expenditures
1993	1,749.8	1,683.2	1,023.9
1994	1,851.0	1,800.3	1,086.0
1995	1,970.6	1,909.4	1,202.8
1996	2,100.1	2,036.7	1,304.4
1997	2,173.3	2,095.7	1,390.1
1998	1,866.1	1,727.4	1,289.2
1999[b]	1,860.0	1,751.5	1,333.3
2000[b]	1,926.2	1,807.0	1,365.7

Notes: [a] Population estimates for 1993 and 1994 interpolated from 1990 Population Census data and 1995 Inter-Censal Survey data as reported in Central Board of Statistics (2001a), Table 3.1.1. Population for 2000 assumed to be 206,456,005, as reported in Hull (2001: 107). Data for 1996–9 interpolated from this figure and the Inter-Censal Survey figure.
[b] Figures are provisional.
Sources: Central Board of Statistics (1998a), Table 4; Bank Indonesia (2000), Table 1.

a much more adverse effect on the investment component of national expenditure than on household consumption expenditure.[4] In the short run at least, poverty estimates are driven by changes in real consumption expenditures rather than changes in real GDP. Preliminary data for 2000 indicated that real *per capita* consumption expenditures were in fact slightly higher than in 1996, and much higher than in 1993 when the CBS estimate of the proportion of the population below the official poverty line was 13.7 per cent (Table 6.1). Thus the CBS estimate of almost 40 per cent of the population falling below the poverty line in 1998 (and presumably little change by 2000) was almost certainly an exaggeration, unless the crisis had brought about a very sharp increase in expenditure inequalities.

Further studies in 1999 using data sources from 1998

The World Bank estimates: January 1999

By early 1999, a 'revisionist' view of the impact of the Indonesian crisis on poverty was gaining ground. According to press stories, a World Bank Report circulated in January 1999 endorsed the predictions of its previous Report for Indonesia (World Bank 1998) and criticised some of the more pessimistic estimates which were circulated in Jakarta in the latter part of 1998. World Bank officials were quoted as stating that the middle classes in urban areas had taken the brunt of the crisis, and that young relatively well-educated workers had suffered far greater income declines than the least educated and poorest workers in rural areas.[5] The Report acknowledged that many people who had lost relatively well-paid jobs in the formal sector had been pushed into less secure and less well remunerated work in the informal sector, and many young high school and college leavers were finding it difficult to get any kind of employment at all. But the net effect of all these developments on the incidence of poverty was, according to the World Bank, unlikely to be very dramatic, at least in the short run. The proportion of the population under the official poverty line would certainly be higher in 1999 than in 1996, but by only a few percentage points.

The Rand study

Another set of poverty estimates circulated in early 1999 were derived from the Indonesian Family Life Survey, the second stage of which was carried out in Indonesia in 1997–8. Because of the severity of the crisis, it was decided to implement a further survey in late 1998, which followed up 25 per cent of the 7,730 households visited in the second stage survey (Frankenberg, Thomas and Beegle 1999: 5). This survey found that the headcount measure of poverty had risen from around 11 per cent in 1997 to between 14 and 20 per cent in 1998. The range of results was due to the use of two different deflators, and the study cautioned that the results were very sensitive to the inflation rate used. The crux of the problem lay in the fact that the incidence of inflation was not uniform across expenditure groups. As would be expected given the magnitude of the devaluation over 1998, the price of traded goods in the Consumer Price Index (CPI), especially food, had risen more rapidly than the prices of non-traded items such as housing. Thus any adjustment to the poverty line between 1996 and late 1998 or early 1999 had to take into account not just the overall rate of inflation but also the sharp change in relative prices of traded and non-traded goods. Because the poverty line basket of goods and services is more heavily weighted towards traded items such as food, compared with the CPI basket, it was to be expected that the poverty line would increase at a faster rate than the CPI.[6]

By early 1999, there was plenty of evidence that the very high inflation in Indonesia in 1998 had had a more severe effect on the poor and those close to the poverty line because food prices rose faster than other prices. The composite 44-city CPI showed that by January 1999, food prices had risen 133 per cent compared with December 1997, but housing prices had risen by only 49 per cent.[7] As food accounts for a higher share of the consumption basket of the poorest groups, the effect of the higher inflation of food prices would have been much more serious for them than for better-off groups.

The obvious solution would be to take the poverty line basket of goods and services and value it at prices prevailing in late 1998. This was in effect what the Rand study did, which produced a much higher poverty line, and thus a much higher headcount estimate of poverty than if the 1996 poverty line had simply been increased by the rate of inflation indicated by the CPI. But as the authors of the Rand study pointed out, the rate of price increase of a fixed bundle of goods would not necessarily reflect the 'true changes' in the cost of living of poor households because, as a result of the rapid inflation, it is probable that many households substituted less expensive food items for more expensive ones, and cut back on non-food expeditures in order to maintain essential food purchases. But to anyone who regards poverty line concepts as essentially prescriptive in nature, this point should be disregarded; what headcount (or other) indicators of poverty are intended to measure is the proportion of the population who cannot afford to buy a basket of goods and services deemed to be essential basic needs. On this view the Rand estimates, which showed an increase in the incidence of urban poverty from 9.2 to 15.8 per cent, and in rural areas from 12.4 to 23 per cent between 1997 and late 1998, would appear to be valid (Frankenberg, Thomas and Beegle 1999: Table 2.2).

Analysis of the 100-village surveys

The 100-village surveys were sponsored by UNICEF, and carried out by the CBS in May 1997, August 1998 and December 1998. Although the sample was quite large (12,000 households), it was not designed to be statistically representative of the whole country; rather it was meant to focus on rural, and relatively poor areas. Major urban areas both in Java and elsewhere were excluded, and the selection of villages was not random (Skoufias, Suryahadi and Sumarto 2000: 98). Nonetheless because of their bias, the surveys proved useful in monitoring the effects of the crisis on vulnerable rural populations across the country. The analyses carried out by SMERU selected as the poverty line for 1997 the consumption expenditures of the 11th percentile of the expenditure distribution. This obviously yielded a head-count measure of poverty of 11 per cent in 1997. Inflating the poverty line by an appropriately weighted price index, and applying it to the August 1998 expenditure distribution, yielded a headcount measure of poverty 7 percentage points higher, although by December, the headcount measure had dropped back by 2.8 percentage points (Suryahadi, Sumarto and Pritchett 1999: Table 4). A second, and higher, poverty line was also used but the basic conclusion, that the headcount measure rose sharply between May 1997 and August 1998, then fell slightly between August and December 1998, was still valid.[8]

Estimates based on the SUSENAS surveys

A discussion paper circulated by the United Nations Support Facility for Indonesian Recovery (UNSFIR) in April 1999 argued (as did the Rand study) that the assumption of constant nominal incomes contained in the UNDP/ILO/UNDP Report circulated in August 1998 was clearly incorrect, and that the very high poverty estimates based on this assumption were thus unreli-able. Acknowledging that 'the debate on the social effects of the Indonesian crisis is not easy to resolve', the UNSFIR Report cautioned against drawing conclusions from small-scale surveys restricted to particular locations.[9] This was no doubt intended as a criticism of the Rand study and indeed the World Bank estimates circulated in January 1999. The UNSFIR Report argued that the World Bank's 'it is not so bad after all' scenario could not be uncritically accepted (UNSFIR 1999: 55–6).

On 10 July 1999 the Director of UNSFIR and the Head of the CBS announced that an analysis of a special 'SUSENAS-type' survey carried out by the CBS in December 1998 indicated that 49.5 million people (24.2 per cent of the population) were below the poverty line. Of these, 17.6 million were in urban areas and 31.9 million were in rural areas. These results immediately gave rise to demands that the CBS clarify the methodology used to estimate the poverty line.[10] The key problem here was that the poverty line in both urban and rural areas used by the CBS is divided into a food and non-food component. While the food poverty line had risen rapidly in step with inflation, several commentators argued that the non-food component had been increased by far more than the rate of change in non-food prices.

A subsequent clarification issued by the CBS pointed out that the non-food poverty line estimates used in the calculations were not strictly comparable with the 1996 data as more items had been introduced 'to allow for the changing environment' (Sutanto 1999: 2). For example a larger amount was needed for the education component of the basic needs bundle to allow for the fact that compulsory education now lasted for nine years rather than six. Whether it is sensible to use a 'dynamic poverty standard' is in itself a contentious issue. But it can fairly be pointed out that in the context of the debate about the impact of the crisis on living standards, introducing changes into the composition of the basket of basic needs led to even more confusion in what had already become a rather heated discussion. To clarify matters, the CBS published some revised estimates of poverty in both 1996 and 1998; the revised 1996 estimates used the same non-food bundle as the 1998 estimates announced in July; the revised 1998 estimates used the same poverty line bundle as the original 1996 estimates. The two revisions produced the same conclusion; that between 1996 and 1998 the number of poor in Indonesia increased by around 11.5–12 million people.

The CBS/UNDP data showed that the overall headcount measure of poverty in 1998 was about the same as in 1987, although the absolute number of poor was larger because of population increase (Booth 1999b: Table 6). This appeared to be a conclusion with which most participants in the debate were reasonably happy; broadly it confirmed the results of both the Rand study and the analysis of the 100 village survey, as far as the impact of the crisis was concerned. But the debate was far from concluded; by early 2000 the results of the SUSENAS Household Consumption Module, conducted by the CBS in early 1999, were available for analysis. A paper by Suryahadi, Sumarto, Suharso and Pritchett (2000) found that the headcount measure of poverty was higher in early 1999, compared with early 1996 when the last SUSENAS Household Expenditure Module had been conducted. But the increase depended crucially on assumptions about changes in prices; not surprisingly these authors found a much lower increase in the headcount measure of poverty when the CPI was used to measure food and non-food inflation rates. Putting together estimates from a range of sources from February 1996 to August 1999, these authors found that an 'index of poverty' based on headcount estimates fell from 148 in early 1996 to 100 in August 1997, and then rose again to a peak of 264 in November 1998. By August 1999 the index had fallen back to 151, which was slightly higher than in February 1996 (Suryahadi, Sumarto, Suharso and Pritchett 2000: Figure 2).

During 2000, the CBS also released poverty estimates for 1996 and 1999 based on the full SUSENAS Module results from February 1999, and using the new poverty lines, incorporating a wider range of non-food goods and services (Central Board of Statistics 2001a: Tables 12.5–12.7). These showed

Table 6.2 Comparison of CBS and SMERU poverty estimates from the SUSENAS Household Survey Modules, 1996 and 1999

	1996		1999	
	CBS	*SMERU*	*CBS*	*SMERU*
Percentage of the population below the poverty line				
Urban	13.6	7.2	19.4	16.3
Rural	19.9	20.5	26.0	34.1
Total	17.6	15.7	23.4	27.1
Numbers in poverty (million)				
Urban	9.6	5.1	15.6	13.2
Rural	24.6	25.3	32.3	42.4
Total	34.2	30.5	48.0	55.6

Source: Pradhan *et al.* (2000), Tables 2, 4; Central Board of Statistics (2001a), Tables 12.5, 12.6, 12.7.

an increase in the headcount measure of poverty from 17.7 per cent in 1996 to 23.4 per cent in 1999, and an increase in the absolute numbers below the poverty line of some 13.8 million people (Table 6.2). The headcount measure of poverty reported by the CBS for 1999 was rather lower than that estimated in a further SMERU Report published in 2000 (Pradhan, Suryahadi, Sumarto and Pritchett 2000). There were very considerable differences between the CBS and the SMERU estimates of the headcount measures of poverty for urban and rural areas. Furthermore the SMERU Report calculated that numbers below the poverty line had increased by some 25 million between 1996 and 1999 which was almost twice the CBS estimate (Table 6.2).

How could such different results be derived from the same data set? The answer lay in the different methodologies used to estimate the urban and rural poverty lines in the two studies. In particular the two studies used different approaches to estimating the non-food component of the poverty line. Thus the urban poverty line used by the CBS was higher relative to the rural one than was the case in the SMERU study. As a result, although the total number of poor people estimated by SMERU from the 1999 SUSENAS data was only about 3.7 million higher than the CBS, in rural areas the SMERU estimate exceeded that of the CBS by around 8 million. It is not my purpose to argue that either estimate is the 'right' one; rather the results of the two studies are a salutary reminder that different approaches to the estimation of the poverty line can give very different results. The two sets of estimates also differed at the provincial level; I return to this point below.

Table 6.3   Trends in employment and unemployment, 1997–2000[a]

	Male	Female	Total
Economically active population (million)			
1997	55.027	34.191	89.218
1998	56.516	35.822	92.338
1999	58.433	36.414	94.847
2000	58.780	36.871	95.651
Unemployment rates			
1997	4.1	5.6	4.7
1998	5.0	6.1	5.5
1999	6.0	6.9	6.4
2000	5.7	6.7	6.1
Employed in agriculture (million)			
1997	21.089	13.437	34.526
1998	23.708	15.437	39.145
1999	23.764	14.614	38.378
2000	24.600	16.076	40.676
Growth in agricultural employment as percentage of total employment growth			
1997–2000	131.7	123.4	128.0

Note: [a] Estimates refer to August in each year. To ensure comparability, data on East Timor have been removed from the 1997 and 1998 estimates and data on workers aged between 10 and 15 have been removed from the 1997 estimates. Since 1998 the labour force data refer to the population over the age of 15 years.

Sources: Central Bureau of Statistics (1998b, 1999c, 2000, 2001b).

The impact of the crisis on employment and real wages

In addition to the rather extreme predictions about increasing poverty which were current in the latter part of 1998, there were also widespread predictions that there would be a rapid increase in unemployment. Prior to the crisis, the 1996 Labour Force Survey showed that slightly fewer than 5 per cent of the labour force was unemployed and looking for work; many of these were young, relatively well-educated, first-time job seekers. As the crisis deepened in late 1997 and early 1998, there were fears that many workers in sectors such as construction, manufacturing, wholesale and retail trade and financial services would become unemployed. In fact the Labour Force Survey for August 1998 indicated that, compared with the same survey from the previous year, the overall rate of unemployment increased only slightly, from 4.7 to 5.5 per cent (Table 6.3). Urban unemployment increased from 8.0 to 9.3 per cent, and rural from 2.8 to 3.3 per cent (Manning 2000: Table 3). There was little change in the labour force participation rate (in fact it increased slightly for women), so it seemed unlikely that those who have lost jobs as wage or salary workers had withdrawn in large numbers from the labour force.

The most striking trend revealed by the comparison of labour force data prior to and post-crisis has been towards greater 'informal sector' employment, where the informal sector is defined as workers in agriculture, all family workers and the non-professional self-employed. The data from the four Labour Force Surveys carried out between 1997 and 2000 show that over these three years, the male agricultural labour force increased by around 3.5 million and the female agricultural labour force by 2.6 million (Table 6.3). In both cases, the absolute increases in the agricultural labour force were higher than the increases in the total employed labour force; in other words, it would appear that the non-agricultural sectors of the economy were shedding labour, which was falling back on agricultural employment.

It is likely that the rapid growth in agricultural employment since 1997 has been exaggerated. Labour force surveys such as the SAKERNAS can easily mis-classify workers displaced from a non-agricultural occupation as employed in agricultural activities when in fact most of their time is engaged elsewhere. Given the pre-crisis evidence that a majority of rural households in parts of Java did not own agricultural land, it is likely that many migrants who lost jobs in sectors such as manufacturing and construction did not have much land to return to.[11] On the other hand, to the extent that there was an operated holding, however small, to occupy at least part of their time, such workers are more likely to have been categorised as working in agriculture than in another occupation.

Inevitably given the numbers of workers surging back into the agricultural sector, real wages in that sector fell sharply in 1997–8. Papanek and Budiono (1999: Graph 8) plotted trends in real wages for unskilled farm workers in the three large provinces of Java from 1996 to 1999; the downturn began in mid-1997, and continued until September 1998. The early months of 1999, when inflation slowed, saw some recovery but in all three provinces real wages in early 1999 were little more than half their 1997 peak. Real wages also fell sharply for construction workers employed by the PWD, and for production workers. The decline in real wages over 1997–8 was not owing to cuts in nominal wages but rather to the very high inflation over calendar 1998. The implication of these falls is clear: those wage workers who kept their jobs or found new wage employment in agriculture had to accept real wages which were substantially lower than before the crisis.

Manning (2000: 130–2) has argued that the labour market adjustments which occurred in Indonesia over the crisis period demonstrated that Indonesian labour markets were still very flexible, and workers displaced from urban formal sector employment found jobs in other sectors (especially in agriculture), albeit at lower wages. The fact that urban unemployment did not increase as rapidly as in Thailand or indeed in Latin American economies during severe economic downturns certainly helps to explain why poverty outcomes were not as dire as originally predicted. But at the same time the crisis threw into reverse the trend towards labour market formalisation which had been obvious in the early 1990s. It is doubtful that many who have taken temporary employment in the agricultural sector will wish to stay there, and many workers will move back into manufacturing and service sector occupations as soon as they can. How soon this will be must depend on a return to the kind of growth in the non-agricultural sectors which occurred in the decade up to 1996.

The impact of the crisis on the distribution of income

When the full impact of the crisis on the Indonesian economy became apparent during 1998, it was argued by some observers that while the impact on poverty and living standards would be adverse, the impact on distribution could well be positive. These predictions were in fact borne out by the SMERU analysis of the 1996 and 1999 SUSENAS Modules (Suryahadi, Sumarto, Suharso and Pritchett 2000: Table 8). But once allowance was made for the differential impact of inflation on different expenditure groups, the reduction in inequality was quite small.[12] Certainly the contraction in GDP was most severe in urban areas, especially in sectors such as financial services, and thus the incidence of the contraction would be most severe on the incomes of the relatively prosperous middle classes. By contrast, rural producers of export crops would benefit from the effects of the massive devaluation of the rupiah.

But at the same time there was considerable evidence that some groups already vulnerable before the crisis suffered greatly after it struck. As was pointed out above, many of those who lost their jobs as unskilled workers in construction or trade surged back into agriculture, with the inevitable result that real agricultural wages fell. The decline in wages was of course aggravated by the high inflation in mid-1998; as has already been emphasised, prices of basic food staples rose more quickly than those of goods and services consumed more intensively by the better off. Some evidence supporting the argument that the crisis did aggravate income disparities between social classes in Indonesia can be found in the Social Accounting Matrix (SAM), published by the CBS (1999b). The gap between the incomes of the poorest category of workers in Indonesia (farm labourers) and other categories (especially medium and large farmers and the non-poor non-agricultural workers in rural areas) widened fairly consistently over the 1990s (Table 6.4). Certainly there was no evidence of the gap narrowing between 1995 and 1998. In urban areas, the gap between the urban poor and non-poor workers also widened. By 1998 the most affluent group in Indonesian society (urban upper income) on average had a *per capita* disposable income over nine times that of the poorest (farm labourers), compared with less than five

Table 6.4 Trends in relativities: real *per capita* disposable incomes, by social class, 1990-8

Category of household	1990	1993	1995	1998
Rural				
Farm labourers	1.00	1.00	1.00	1.00
Poor farmers	1.32	1.62	1.58	1.65
Medium farmers	1.60	1.93	2.02	2.12
Large farmers	2.49	3.14	2.97	3.15
Poor non-farmers	1.18	1.35	2.98	2.98
Non-poor non-farmers	2.52	3.96	5.79	7.90
Rural non-working	2.24	2.83	2.82	2.67
Urban				
Urban low-income groups	1.94	2.18	3.85	3.59
Urban upper-income groups	4.53	6.63	8.82	9.53
Urban non-working	2.14	2.64	3.45	3.33

Source: Central Board of Statistics (1999b), Table 3.14.

times in 1990. In interpreting the data in Table 6.4 we also have to bear in mind that all the comparisons are in nominal terms. If we allow for the higher incidence of inflation on the lower income groups, the disparities between the categories of people shown in Table 6.4 could well have been greater in 1998.

The impact of the crisis on school attendance

By mid-1998, at the time when both the CBS and the UNDP/ILO/UNDP were circulating their estimates suggesting that the effect of the crisis on income poverty was of catastrophic dimensions, there were also grave concerns about the impact of the crisis on education. In 1994–5, at the beginning of the sixth Five Year Plan of the Soeharto era, the Indonesian government had committed itself to a target of universal education for all children up to lower secondary school by 2004. This implied a compulsory nine-year cycle encompassing six years of primary education and three years of lower secondary education. This was a bold target, especially in view of the fact that lower secondary enrolments had declined over the previous five years. But between 1993–4 and 1997–8 numbers of children in the lower secondary system (Department of Education schools only) increased from 5.7 to 7.6 million; numbers in the *madrasah tsanawiyah* increased from 1.2 million to 1.8 million over the same period. Crude enrolment ratios increased over this period from 52.7 per cent to over 70 per cent of the age cohort (Booth 1999b: Table 9). There was also a steady improvement between the mid-1980s and 1992–3 in the percentage of children enrolling in primary school who completed the six-year cycle (Jones and Hagul 2001:

Table 1). These were impressive achievements, but there were fears that as a result of the crisis, numbers at both the primary and lower secondary level would drop sharply.

A survey carried out by the Department of Education and Culture (DoEC) and the World Bank in October 1998, two months after the school year began, found that while the worst scenario of large-scale drop-outs did not appear to have materialised, there were some worrying trends. For the country as a whole, primary school enrolments changed very little, although there were substantial declines in the poorer urban areas (over 8 per cent in parts of Jakarta). At the lower secondary level, total enrolments fell by only 1.6 per cent but in the poorer areas of Jakarta, there were much larger declines in first-year enrolments (Filmer *et al.* 1999: 2). The Rand study cited above also found evidence of declining enrolments in the sample of households which were reinterviewed in 1998. In urban areas the percentage of young people aged 13 to 19 who were out of school had risen from 33 to 38 per cent between 1997 and 1998, 'a change that is statistically significant' (Frankenberg, Thomas and Beegle 1999: 50). They also pointed out that 'children from poorer households are more likely to be out of school than children from better off households – a phenomenon that intensified between 1997 and 1998'.

Already in July 1998, the government had responded to fears of large-scale drop-outs from the school system by issuing a decree abolishing entrance fees for public schools; this was followed by a widely publicised programme of scholarships which I will discuss further below. Oey-Gardiner (1999: Tables 13 and 14) used two rounds of the 100-village survey (August and December 1998) to examine trends in gross and net enrolment ratios by level of education and by income group; she found that while there was a fall in both gross and net enrolment rates for 13–15-year-old between 1997 and 1998 (August), there was some improvement between August and December 1998. More striking, net enrolment rates at the lower secondary level improved between August and December 1998 for all income groups. This provided at least some support for the argument that government persuasion, fee abolition and the availability of scholarships together enabled the poor to keep their children in the system, although as will be argued below, there are doubts about the accuracy of the targeting process.

By August 1999, official (although preliminary) data on enrolments for the 1998–9 school year seemed to confirm the findings of the above studies. At the primary level, enrolments in both the DoEC schools and the *madrasah ibtidaiyah* increased marginally in 1998/99 compared with the previous year; as numbers of children in the 7–12 age cohort were now stable, this meant that both crude and refined participation rates at the primary level increased slightly (Department of Information 1999: Table V.1.17). At the lower secondary level, numbers enrolled in the schools under the control of the DoEC fell slightly but numbers in the *madrasah* rose, so the overall decline in enrolments was quite modest. Crude enrolment rates fell only slightly, but the refined enrolment rate in DoEC schools fell rather more sharply, as did the continuation rate from the primary into the lower secondary system. These trends were also obvious at the upper secondary level, although at this level there was little change in total enrolments. The refined participation rate in DoEC upper secondary schools fell slightly (Booth 1999b: Table 9). Taken together, these data indicate that the crisis probably did discourage some students from continuing to the next level of education. In some cases families who felt they could not afford the costs associated with attendance at a government lower or upper secondary school appear to have decided to sent their children to the *madrasah*. This choice was almost certainly influenced by financial considerations rather than by the superior quality of tuition available in the *madrasah*.

Other studies have confirmed that the net impact of the crisis on school enrolments was quite muted, at least until 1999. Jones and Hagul (2001: Table 2) use the SUSENAS Module on education to examine trends in age-specific and sex-specific enrolment rates by expenditure quintiles for the school years 1996–7, 1997–8 and 1998–9. They found little sign of declines even for the poorest quintile. Cameron (2001: Table 1) used the 100-village survey data to look at trends in school enrolment rates between May 1997 and May 1999. Her results confirmed those of other studies in that there appeared to be little change over the two years, either for the country as a whole or by region and by gender. But although there is little evidence of sharp declines in attendance, there was also little evidence of the kinds of increases which would be necessary if the compulsory nine-year target was to be met by 2004 (Jones and Hagul 2001: 218). Delaying the attainment of this target may indeed be the main consequence of the crisis for school enrolments in the medium term.

The regional impact of the crisis

By mid-1998, it was frequently being asserted that 'Krismon' (the financial crisis) was primarily a crisis afflicting urban Java, and that the outer islands were either relatively untouched, or actually benefiting from the effects of the massive rupiah devaluation.[13] As would be expected, the most optimistic reports of rising incomes came from regions where a substantial part of the population was involved in cash crop production for export. It would appear that rupiah prices of most export crops (rubber, coffee, pepper, cocoa, tea, spices, palm oil, copra) increased rapidly in the wake of the rupiah devaluation, and indeed the rate of increase was considerably faster than the increase in rice prices, at least in the year from May 1997 to May 1998 (Booth 1999a: Table 2). While it is true that not everyone even in those regions where export production predominates would have benefited from these higher prices, many millions would have done so, and more would have been able to benefit indirectly from the expenditure effects of the increase in producer incomes.[14]

On the other hand, it would be incorrect to assume that all rural producers continued to enjoy increases in real, as distinct from nominal incomes, after mid-1998, even in regions where export production is important if not dominant. The cost of living increased rapidly in rural areas in the latter part of 1998, as did prices of key agricultural inputs. The data on the farmers' terms of trade (output prices deflated by input prices and the cost of living) for 14 provinces suggest that in the three large provinces of Java, their terms of trade stagnated or declined after the rupiah began to slide (Booth 1999b: Table 10). Outside Java, the picture was far more mixed; in some provinces (South Sumatra, Bali, West Nusatenggara, North and South Sulawesi) farmers did experience some improvement in their prices, relative to costs, in the year from June 1997 to June 1998, while in Bali, West Nusatenggara and South Kalimantan, the terms of trade improved in the 11 months from June 1998 to May 1999. But elsewhere, the terms of trade over these 11 months either did not change appreciably or actually fell. It is likely that for many farmers, the initial price boost which occurred as a result of the devaluation was reversed in the latter part of 1998 and early 1999 as prices of inputs and basic necessities rose and the rupiah began to appreciate again from the low point reached in the early months of 1998.[15]

Both the CBS and the SMERU poverty estimates derived from the 1996 and 1999 SUSENAS Household Expenditure Modules showed that a large part of the increase in numbers of poor people between 1996 and 1999 took place in Java and Bali (Table 6.5). This supports the view that the impact of

Table 6.5 Percentage breakdown of the increase in numbers of poor people, and total population, 1996–9

	CBS poverty	SMERU poverty	Total population
Sumatra	16.3	18.9	23.3
Java and Bali	69.5	65.2	55.9
Jakarta/West Java	30.4	27.1	33.2
Central Java	18.7	16.7	11.6
East Java/Bali	20.4	21.4	11.0
Nusatenggara	3.6	3.1	4.3
Kalimantan	4.7	5.3	6.6
Sulawesi	3.1	5.3	7.6
Maluku/Irian Jaya	2.9	2.1	2.3
Indonesia	100.0	100.0	100.0

Sources: Pradhan *et al.* (2000), Tables 2, 4; Central Board of Statistics (2001a), Tables 12.5, 12.6, 12.7.

the crisis was most severe in these provinces. In both Kalimantan and Sulawesi, the share of the increase in numbers of poor between 1996 and 1999 was less than the share of the increase in total population. Both the SMERU and CBS estimates agreed that by 1999 the highest headcount measures of poverty were to be found in the provinces of East Nusatenggara, Maluku and Irian Jaya (now called Papua), while the lowest were in Jakarta, West Sumatra and Riau (Pradhan, Suryahadi, Sumarto and Pritchett 2000: Table 2; Central Board of Statistics 2001a: Table 12.5).[16]

The social safety net programme

As concern about the effects of the crisis on living standards mounted in the second part of 1998, the Indonesian government, with support from several multilateral and bilateral donors, launched an ambitious set of programmes intended to provide 'social safety nets' *(jaring pengaman sosial)*. This term was new to the vocabulary of the Indonesian development discourse, as indeed were most of the programmes. Rather than build on existing programmes, the government decided to launch new initiatives. Given that fears of famine were widespread in the first part of 1998, food security programmes were an important part of the new social safety net programmes, especially the OPK *(operasi pasar khusus)* or special market operations which injected low-quality, mainly imported rice into key markets across the country at a subsidised price (Rp 1,000 per kilo, or about 10 US cents at the exchange rate prevailing in the latter part of 1998). Each eligible household was permitted to purchase 20 kg at this price per month; since the programme began the criteria for eligibility were widened, and by mid-1999 250,000 tons of rice were still being sold at the subsidised price, even though most authorities agreed that the danger of widespread famine had passed.[17]

Monitoring the impact of such a policy is obviously difficult, but an analysis of the 100-village survey carried out by SMERU indicated that, in at least some *kabupaten* (the level of government below the province), there was clear evidence that poor households had benefited from the programme, although plenty of non-poor households were also obtaining subsidised food (Suryahadi, Suharso and Sumarto 1999: 7–9). In August 1999, the Minister of Food and Horticulture, A.M. Saefudin, was quoted in the press as saying that 17.5 million families still could not afford to eat twice a day.[18] He also stated that 350,000 tons of rice was in stock but only 250,000 tons could actually be distributed each month at the subsidised price. This implied that if each family took the full 20kg, then only about 12.5 million families were benefiting from the cheap rice, or only about 70 per cent of those households who were able to eat only once a day.[19]

The school scholarship and block grant programmes appeared by late 1999 to have been reasonably successful in reaching poor families, although the SMERU study found that the effectiveness of the targeting varied considerably by region (Suryahadi, Suharso and Sumarto 1999: Tables 5a and 5b). Although every *kabupaten* in the country received an allocation of both block grants and scholarships, the amount varied according to the '*kabupaten* poverty index'. Allocation to *kecamatan* (sub-district) and individual schools was carried out by both the education authorities and NGOs, while within the school, scholarship recipients were selected by school committees of parents and teachers.[20] In the 1998–9 school year, almost 4 million scholarships were granted, and 131,975 block grants allocated.[21] Although comprehensive guidelines were produced on scholarship allocation, it was far from clear in 1998–9 to what extent they were being followed, and if so, what criteria local officials and parent-teacher groups were using to identify the most needy housholds. Certainly further analysis of the programme will be needed before any firm conclusions about its efficacy can be drawn.

Of the other social safety net programmes, the most ambitious and also the most highly criticised have been the employment creation schemes. It appears that, rather than expand existing INPRES (regional development) programmes, a decision was made to direct funds towards new programmes designed to create new jobs for workers in urban areas (where it was assumed millions would become unemployed) and rural areas which were especially affected by drought and harvest failure.[22] The urban programmes were much criticised and seem to have largely failed in their objectives; fewer workers became unemployed than was originally envisaged and many of those that did appear to have made their own arrangements for finding alternative employment. In addition it appears that several of the urban-based programmes paid above-market wages; had lower wages been paid more jobs could have been created, and they would have been better targeted to the very poor (Cameron 1999: 28). In rural areas, the *kecamatan* Development Programme and the Village Infrastructure Programme were slow to get under way, at least partly because of donor demands regarding their implementation, although in some districts poorer households did benefit from some employment creation schemes.[23]

Lessons and reflections

It is now time to return to the questions raised at the beginning of the chapter concerning the impact of the crisis, and the effectiveness of government measures implemented to protect the incomes and living standards of the most vulnerable groups. It is clear that the contraction in GDP which occurred in 1998 was most severe in the non-agricultural sectors of the economy, especially in construction, the financial sector, wholesale and retail trade, non-oil manufacturing and transport. All these sectors registered contractions of more than 5 per cent; it was also in these sectors, especially construction and financial services where employment fell (Manning 2000: Table 5). In the agricultural sector, by contrast, real output grew slightly in 1998 while employment grew by close to 5 million workers.

Clearly agriculture played a crucial role as the employment sector of last resort over the crisis period. It is also clear from the national income data that the contraction in investment expenditure was far greater than the contraction in personal consumption expenditure; this indeed was the main reason why the initial impact of the crisis on poverty and living standards was less than predicted in mid-1998. But there can be little doubt that the surge in inflation in the middle months of 1998 had an especially serious effect on the poor, because food prices rose more rapidly than non-food prices. This indeed was what had happened in previous inflationary episodes in Indonesia. Thus while the crisis itself might not have affected the incomes of the poor more seriously than those of the better off, the ensuing inflation certainly did.[24]

Similarly, the lessons of previous devaluations in Indonesia were useful in predicting the likely effect of the very substantial rupiah devaluation of 1997–8 on incomes of various categories of producer. There can be no doubt that the devaluation led to a rapid increase in the rupiah prices of a range of agricultural products in the last part of 1997 and early 1998, and that the supply response was positive. The GDP data indicate that output of tree-crops grew by more than 2 per cent between 1997 and 1999, in spite of the lingering effects of the drought. But the rapid inflation of 1998 led to a surge in the cost of living for farmers, and thus an erosion of the effects of the devaluation. Because of the magnitude of the inflation, the erosion almost certainly took place more quickly than in past devaluations. In addition of course the rupiah began to appreciate in late 1998 and early 1999. Thus by mid-1999 much of the positive effect of the devaluation on the real incomes of rural producers had been dissipated.

As far as most wage and salary workers were concerned the effects of the rupiah devaluation and the ensuing inflation were almost wholly negative. Real wages in all sectors of the economy fell steeply in late 1997 and 1998, and made only a partial recovery in 1999. Thus it may well be correct to argue that, relative to rural producers of export products, some urban dwellers did suffer a greater decline in income especially in the initial phase of the crisis. But given the large increase in the agricultural labour force that has occured between 1997 and 2000, it is unlikely that there will be a strong upward pressure on agricultural wages for some time to come.

It is hardly surprising, given the suddeness and severity of the downturn in Indonesia, that the question of enhanced social security should be getting far more attention from independent analysts and policy makers than at any time over the past three decades. As in many other parts of the Asian region, Indonesian policy makers have in the past voiced their hostility to 'Western-style' social security provision which is supposed to destroy entrepreneurial initiative and lead to a culture of welfare dependency. But in reality, given the combination of rapid economic growth, rapid growth of employment opportunities and a favourable dependency ratio owing to the speed of the fertility decline in most parts of the country, policy makers have not been under pressure from any powerful constituency to concern themselves with comprehensive social security provision. Now with the possibility of slower economic growth, together with the demographic inevitability of a higher proportion of the population moving into the older age groups, issues such as social security, and the provision of 'social safety nets' are suddenly at the forefront of the policy debates in Indonesia.

They are likely to stay there in coming decades. The implementation of the social safety net programmes since 1998, however inadequate the targeting has been, has built up a set of expectations that the government should provide basic goods and services such as food, health and education at prices which all sections of the population can afford. Future Indonesian governments will have to deal with these, and other, expectations. Experience from other countries indicates that it is politically very difficult to remove welfare entitlements once they have been conceded, even if the initial granting of the entitlements was made under conditions of severe economic distress. However reluctantly, future Indonesian governments will have to transform emergency social safety net programmes into more comprehensive social programmes aimed at giving all citizens access to basic needs and services. Thus it is likely that debates over implementation and targeting, far from ending once the economy begins to recover, will intensify.

Does the Indonesian experience of 1997–9 offer any lessons to other countries coping with the aftermath of a severe financial crisis, leading to a substantial decline in real output? Perhaps the most obvious lesson is that such crises can burst out of what might appear to be a clear blue sky with little warning.[25] While preventing a crisis from happening in the first place is obviously the best method of preventing crisis-related social ills, the experience of countries such as Indonesia, Thailand, Malaysia and South Korea in 1997–9 does confirm the views of at least some economic historians that financial crises are the inevitable 'childhood diseases' of capitalism (Goldsmith 1982: 42). Governments in other parts of the developing world would do well to realise that being hailed as a 'miracle economy' by leading international development experts does not immunise a country from such diseases. In fact, to the extent that the overhyping of the economic performance of Indonesia, Thailand, Malaysia and South Korea in a number of publications in the early 1990s bred an attitude among policy makers in these countries that they were somehow exempt from the risks and dangers that beset other developing economies, the international development establishment, led by the World Bank, has to take some of the blame for the

Asian crisis.[26] Policy makers in other parts of the developing world would do well to ponder these lessons, and make prudent allowance for the fact that such crises will almost certainly affect them at some stage in their evolution into mature capitalist economies.

A second important lesson is that the effects of a severe economic downturn in an economy as large and heterogeneous as Indonesia are very difficult to measure. Most of the initial judgements which were made by a number of agencies and individuals in 1998 have had to be modified as more data have come to hand from different parts of the country. Even three years after the crisis hit, the effects were still working through to millions of households across the country. In addition, as was pointed out in the discussion of the SUSENAS surveys, different analysts have drawn quite different conclusions from the same body of data about trends in poverty, depending on how the poverty line is estimated. In addition it can reasonably be argued that none of the data sets pressed into service between 1998 and 2001 to estimate the impact of the crisis on poverty, income distribution and unemployment was suitable for the purpose. Household surveys such as the SUSENAS by their very nature ignore that part of the population who do not live in registered households. To the extent that numbers of unregistered street dwellers have increased in urban and peri-urban areas since 1997, and to the extent that many of them have expenditures below the official poverty line, they are excluded from the poverty estimates. Other data sets such as the 100-village survey, while useful as far as they go, were deliberately skewed to poorer rural areas and ignore not just urban areas but also the more developed rural hinterland.

Thus debates about the impact of the crisis on poverty and living standards are likely to continue in Indonesia for some time to come. It will probably be at least a decade before we can draw final conclusions about the effects of the crisis on poverty and welfare, let alone evaluate the efficacy of the various policy measures which have been implemented to alleviate these effects. One can only hope that by then, living standards will have improved for the poorest and most vulnerable groups in Indonesia and the grim years at the end of the twentieth century will be a distant memory.

Notes

1. Another report prepared under World Bank auspices found that in 1995 11.4 per cent of the population in Indonesia was under a poverty line of 1 dollar per day in 1985 international dollars (Ahuja, Bidani, Ferreira and Walton 1997: Table 2.1). Using a comparable poverty line, 22.2 per cent of the population of China was poor in 1995, and 18.2 per cent in East Asia excluding China.

2. See Department of Information (1998: Table IV-4) for estimates of poverty by province for the years 1990, 1993 and 1996. The highest incidence of poverty in 1996 was recorded in East Timor where the headcount measure was 31.2 per cent compared with a national average of 11.3 per cent of the population below the

official poverty line. It should be noted that the CBS revised its poverty estimates by province for 1996; see Central Board of Statistics (2001a: Tables 12.5–12.7).

3. The ILO estimates assumed that average wage rates and household incomes would not change *in nominal terms* over 1998–9, in spite of the accelerating inflation. As in the CBS estimates, the ILO assumed that the distribution of expenditures would not change compared with 1996, but that cumulative inflation over 1998 would lead to an 80 per cent increase in prices of basic staples. In 1999 prices of basic needs were projected to increase by a further 25 per cent. Adjusting the official poverty line to allow for these price increases, the ILO Report found that by the end of 1998, the proportion under the poverty line would rise to 48 per cent (39 per cent of the population in urban areas and 53 per cent in rural areas). By the end of 1999 (assuming further inflation of 25 per cent and stagnating nominal incomes) 66 per cent of the population could fall under the poverty line (57 per cent in urban areas and 72 per cent in rural areas). This indeed would imply that the incidence of poverty would be much higher than at any time since 1976, when the CBS began to publish poverty estimates. In that year the CBS estimated that 40 per cent of the total population fell below the official poverty line.

4. Imports of goods and services into Indonesia fell in 1997 and 1998 far more rapidly than exports; this reflects the sharp decline in investment expenditures which are import-intensive. In 1995, imports of goods and services, as reported in the national income accounts, were around 9 per cent higher than exports; by 1998 exports were slightly above imports. For further information, see Central Board of Statistics (1999a).

5. For a summary of the World Bank Report issued in January 1999, and also some discussion of criticisms on the part of Bank officials of previous estimates, see Keith B. Richburg, 'World Bank: Jakarta crash less severe than feared', *Washington Post*, January 25, 1999; Evelyn Iritani 'Indonesian fiscal crisis now seen as less severe', *Los Angeles Times*, 23 January 1999; and Jeremy Wagstaff, 'Good news? bad news? Who can tell?', *Asian Wall Street Journal*, 25 January 1999.

6. This differential impact of inflation is in fact quite well known in the Indonesian context. Asra (1989: Table 3) demonstrated that during the early part of the 1970s when food prices rose rapidly, the cost of living index of the poorest 40 per cent increased faster than for other groups in both urban and rural areas.

7. *Buletin Ringkas*, January 1999 (Jakarta: Central Board of Statistics), Table 1.

8. Skoufias, Suryahadi and Sumarto (2000) extend the analysis by estimating other poverty indicators, as well as the headcount measure.

9. The Rand study was based on two rounds of the Indonesian Family Life Survey which has been carried out by the Rand Corporation in conjunction with the University of California at Los Angeles and the Demographic Institute of the University of Indonesia. Although the sample was small (under 2,000 households), the same households were interviewed in both late 1997 and late 1998, giving a longitudinal picture of how their incomes and expenditures were changing as a result of the crisis. See Frankenberg, Thomas and Beegle (1999) for details.

10. See *Kompas*, 10 July 1999.

11. The 1995 Inter-Censal Survey (SUPAS) reported that in West Java 53 per cent of all rural households did not own agricultural land. The percentage was rather lower in other parts of Java, and lower again for most provinces outside Java. The national percentage was 37 per cent. See Central Bureau of Statistics (1996), Table 60.2.

12. Skoufias, Suryahadi and Sumarto (2000), using the 100-village survey, found an increase in most indicators of inequality between 1997 and 1998.
13. Wetterberg, Sumarto and Pritchett (1999) used the results of a survey of sub-districts *(kecamatan)* carried out in the latter part of 1998 to examine the regional impact of the crisis and reached the conclusion that urban areas and Java were the hardest hit.
14. The 1993 Agricultural Census (Central Bureau of Statistics 1995: Table 3) indicates that in 10 provinces outside Java average farm household income from smallholder treecrop cultivation exceeds income from foodcrop cultivation. In a further four provinces, income from treecrop cultivation is only slightly lower than from foodcrop cultivation. In such households a rapid pass-through of the effects of the devaluation should have led to an increase in real incomes, although subsequent inflation would then have eroded these gains.
15. For a careful analysis of the impact of the crisis on smallholders in Sumatra and Sulawesi, see Potter (2000). Sunderlin *et al.* (2001) argue that for a sample of small farmers in five provinces in forest areas outside Java there was little sign of any improvement in real incomes. Rapid inflation eroded whatever nominal increases in income had occurred as a result of the rupiah devaluation.
16. Pradhan, Suryahadi, Sumarto and Pritchett (2000: 14–15) point out that the Spearman rank correlation coefficient between their estimates of the headcount measure of poverty by province in 1999 and those based on the CBS method was over 0.9. But it was lower for urban and rural areas taken separately.
17. A critical assessment of the use of food aid in late 1998 and early 1999 is given in Li Kheng Poh *et al.* (1999). This Report argues that the cheap rice programme was targeted at cities and particular provinces as a means of 'pacification' and to consolidate political support in the run-up to the 1999 parliamentary elections.
18. *Jakarta Post*, 21 August 1999.
19. Further analysis of the targeting of the cheap rice programme is given in Sumarto, Suryahadi and Pritchett (2000). They found that the sales were targeted at the 'permanently poor' rather than to those households which had fallen into poverty after 1997.
20. A *kabupaten* is the level of government below the province; the *kecamatan* is the level of government between the *kabupaten* and the village.
21. Figures from officials in the Department of Education and Culture, September 1999.
22. INPRES is an acronym for *Instruksi Presiden* (Presidential Instruction). The term is used to embrace a number of labour intensive public works programmes which were initiated between 1969 and 1975.
23. Sumarto, Suryahadi and Pritchett (2000: 26) found that participants in the employment programmes were more likely to be from households which had experienced changes in income, rather than from permanently poor households. They also argued that the employment programmes were much less cost-effective than the cheap rice programmes, in terms of costs per dollar of benefit to the recipients.
24. The inflation was much higher in Indonesia than in the other crisis-affected Asian economies. Although the magnitude of the rupiah devaluation was in part to blame, the main reason for the inflationary surge in mid-1998 was the huge increase in money supply in late 1997 and early 1998 which was due to the attempt by the central bank to shore up via liquidity credits those banks who

were experiencing massive deposit runs. The IMF has conceded that its insistence on the closure of 16 banks in late 1997 may have triggered these runs.

25. Kenward (1999) discusses in detail the extent to which warning signals of the crisis were visible in Indonesia, and should have been heeded in the months before the rupiah began to slide in the latter part of 1997.

26. Apart from the *East Asian Miracle* Report (World Bank 1993), a number of other publications took the view that the rapid growth in East and South-East Asia would continue unabated; see for example World Bank (1996: 126). It now appears that the predictions about the pace of recovery made in World Bank (2000) were probably too optimistic, both for Indonesia and for other affected countries.

Bibliography

Ahuja, V., B. Bidani, F. Ferreira and M. Walton (1997), *Everybody's Miracle? Revisiting Poverty and Inequality in East Asia*, Washington, DC: World Bank.

Asra, A. (1989), 'Inequality trends in Indonesia 1969–81: a re-examination', *Bulletin of Indonesian Economic Studies*, Vol. 25(2), pp. 100–10.

Bank Indonesia (2000), *Annual Report 2000*, Jakarta: Bank Indonesia.

Booth, A. (1999a), 'The impact of the crisis on poverty and equity', in H.W. Arndt and Hal Hill (eds), *Southeast Asia's Economic Crisis: Origins, Lessons and the Way Forward*, Singapore: Institute of Southeast Asian Studies.

Booth, A. (1999b), 'Survey of recent developments', *Bulletin of Indonesian Economic Studies*, Vol. 35(3), pp. 3–38.

Cameron, L. (1999), 'Survey of recent developments', *Bulletin of Indonesian Economic Studies*, Vol. 35(1), pp. 3–40.

Cameron, L. (2001), 'The impact of the Indonesian financial crisis on children: an analysis using the 100-Villages data', *Bulletin of Indonesian Economic Studies*, Vol. 37(1), pp. 43–64.

Central Bureau of Statistics (CBS) (1995a), *Sensus Pertanian 1993 Seri D1, Pendapatan Rumahtangga Pertanian dan Indikator Sosial Ekonomi,* Jakarta: Central Bureau of Statistics, November.

Central Bureau of Statistics (CBS) (1995b), *Penduduk Indonesia: Hasil Survei Penduduk antar Sensus 1995 (Results of the 1995 Intercensal Population Survey)*, Jakarta: Central Bureau of Statistics, September.

Central Bureau of Statistics (CBS) (1998a), *Pendapatan Nasional Indonesia (1994–7) (National Income of Indonesia (1994–7)*, Jakarta: Central Bureau of Statistics.

Central Bureau of Statistics (CBS) (1998b), *Keadaan Angkatan Kerja di Indonesia (Labor Force Situation in Indonesia) August 1997*, Jakarta: Central Bureau of Statistics.

Central Board of Statistics (CBS) (1999a), *Produk Domestik Bruto Indonesia Menurut Penggunaan, 1993–1998* (Indonesian GDP 1993–98), Jakarta: Central Board of Statistics, March.

Central Board of Statistics (CBS) (1999b), *Sistem Neraca Sosial Ekonomi Indonesia 1998* (Social and Economic Accounting System for Indonesia 1998), Jakarta: Central Board of Statistics, March.

Central Board of Statistics (CBS) (1999c), *Keadaan Angkatan Kerja di Indonesia (Labor Force Situation in Indonesia) August 1998*, Jakarta: Central Board of Statistics.

Central Board of Statistics (CBS) (2000), *Keadaan Angkatan Kerja di Indonesia (Labor Force Situation in Indonesia) August 1999*, Jakarta: Central Board of Statistics.

Central Board of Statistics (CBS) (2001a), *Statistik Indonesia (Statistical Yearbook of Indonesia) 2000*, Jakarta: Central Board of Statistics, June.

Central Board of Statistics (CBS) (2001b), *Keadaan Angkatan Kerja di Indonesia (Labor Force Situation in Indonesia) August 2000*, Jakarta: Central Board of Statistics, February.

Department of Information (1998), *Lampiran Pidato Kenegaraan Presiden Republik Indonesia di depan Sidang Dewan Perwakilan Rakyat, 15 Augustus 1999*, Jakarta: Department of Information.

Department of Information (1999), *Lampiran Pidato Kenegaraan Presiden Republik Indonesia di depan Sidang Dewan Perwakilan Rakyat, 16 Augustus 1999*, Jakarta: Department of Information.

Filmer, D. *et al.* (1999), 'Impact of the economic crisis on basic education in Indonesia', *World Bank East Asia and the Pacific Watching Brief*, Issue 2, January.

Frankenberg, E., D. Thomas and K. Beegle (1999), 'The real costs of Indonesia's crisis: preliminary findings from the Family Life Surveys', Santa Monica: Rand Corporation, Mimeo.

Goldsmith, R. (1982), 'Comment on Hyman Minsky: *The financial-instability hypothesis: capitalist processes and the behaviour of the economy*', in C.P. Kindleberger and J.-P. Laffargue, *Financial Crises: Theory, History and Policy*, Cambridge: Cambridge University Press.

Hull, T.H. (2001), 'First results from the 2000 Population Census', *Bulletin of Indonesian Economic Studies*, Vol. 37(1), pp. 103–12.

ILO/UNDP (1998), *Employment Challenges of the Indonesian Economic Crisis*, Jakarta: International Labour Office and United Nations Development Programme.

Jones, G. and P. Hagul (2001), 'Schooling in Indonesia: crisis-related and longer-term issues', *Bulletin of Indonesian Economic Studies*, Vol. 37(2), pp. 207–32.

Kenward, L. (1999), 'Assessing vulnerability to financial crisis: evidence from Indonesia', *Bulletin of Indonesian Economic Studies*, Vol. 35(3), pp. 71–96.

Li Kheng Poh *et al.* (1999), *Manufacturing a Crisis: The Politics of Food Aid in Indonesia*, Manila: Southeast Asia Council for Food Security and Fair Trade.

Manning, C. (2000), 'Labour market adjustment to Indonesia's economic crisis: context, trends and implications', *Bulletin of Indonesian Economic Studies*, Vol. 36(1), pp. 105–36.

Oey-Gardiner, M. (1999), 'The value of education and the Indonesian economic crisis', Paper presented to the LPEM-FEUI/PEG-USAID Conference, 'The Economic Issues facing the New Government', Jakarta: 18–19 August.

Papanek, G. and B.S. Handoko (1999), 'The impact on the poor of growth and crisis: evidence from real wage data', Paper presented to the LPEM-FEUI/PEG-USAID Conference, 'The Economic Issues facing the New Government', Jakarta: 18–19 August.

Potter, L. (2000), 'Rural livelihoods and the environment at a time of uncertainty: the situation outside Java', in C. Manning and P. van Dierman (eds), *Indonesia in Transition: Social Aspects of Reformasi and Crisis*, Singapore: Institute of Southeast Asian Studies.

Pradhan, M., A. Suryahadi, S. Sumarto and L. Pritchett (2000), 'Measurements of poverty in Indonesia: 1996, 1999, and beyond', Jakarta: SMERU Working Paper, June.

Skoufias, E., A. Suryahadi and S. Sumarto (2000), 'Changes in household welfare, poverty and inequality during the crisis', *Bulletin of Indonesian Economic Studies*, Vol. 36(2), pp. 97–114.

Sumarto, S., A. Suryahadi and L. Pritchett (2000), 'Safety nets and safety ropes: comparing the dynamic benefit incidence of two Indonesian "JPS" programmes', Jakarta: SMERU Working Paper, February.

Sunderlin, W.D., A. Angelsen, D.P. Resosudarno, A. Dermawan and E. Rianto (2001), 'Economic crisis, small farmer well-being and forest cover change in Indonesia', *World Development*, Vol. 29(5), pp. 767–82.

Suryahadi, A., Y. Suharso and S. Sumarto (1999), 'Coverage and targeting in the Indonesian social safety net programmes: evidence from 100-Village Survey', Jakarta: SMERU Working Paper, August.

Suryahadi, A., S. Sumarto and L. Pritchett (2000), 'Update on the impact of the Indonesian crisis on consumption expenditures and poverty incidence: results from the December 1998 Round of 100-Village Surveys', Jakarta: SMERU Working Paper, 30 October.

Suryahadi, A., S. Sumarto, Y. Suharso and L. Pritchett (2000), 'The evolution of poverty during the crisis in Indonesia, 1996 to 1999 (Using the Full SUSENAS Sample)', Jakarta: SMERU Working Paper.

Sutanto, A. (1999), 'The December 1998 poverty in Indonesia: some findings and interpretation', Paper presented at the roundtable discussion on The Number of Indonesian Poor People (Method and Forecasting), Jakarta: National Development Planning Agency, July.

(UNSFIR) (1999), 'The social implications of the Indonesian economic crisis: perception and policy', *Discussion Paper No. 1*, United Nations Support Facility for Indonesian Recovery, Jakarta: UNDP, April.

Wetterberg, A., S. Sumarto and L. Pritchett (1999), 'A national snapshot of the social impact of Indonesia's crisis', *Bulletin of Indonesian Economic Studies*, Vol. 35(3), December, pp. 145–52.

World Bank (1993), *The East Asian Miracle*, New York: Oxford University Press for the World Bank.

World Bank (1996), *Managing Capital Flows in East Asia*, Washington, DC: World Bank.

World Bank (1998), *Indonesia in Crisis: A Macroeconomic Update*, Washington, DC: World Bank.

World Bank (2000), *East Asia: Recovery and Beyond*, Washington, DC: World Bank.

7
Estimating the Poverty Impact of the African Green Revolution

Paul Mosley and Andrew McKay

Introduction

In Asia at least the green revolution is now acknowledged as a major factor in reducing poverty and in contributing to the growth-with-equity of the East Asian miracle. But the Asian green revolution has slowed since the middle to late 1980s (IFAD 2001: 2); and there were very many whom it bypassed in the first place. As it now spreads, haltingly, to poorer and drier areas, in particular Africa, it becomes the more important to maximise its poverty impact and therefore to understand better the channels through which it diffuses.

Conceptual approach

A major contribution to understanding the distributional effects of the green revolution has been made by the IFPRI study of Kerr and Kolavalli (1999). This decomposes poverty impacts into four categories: increases in food production; increases in labour demand; increases in wages; and declines in food prices. In the schema of Table 7.1, transcribed from Kerr and Kolavalli's paper, each of these impacts is decomposed by beneficiary.

This is an extremely valuable start. Our own methodology, developed independently, is two-pronged. The first part, which we call the 'quick and dirty' approach, also uses a four-channel methodology; however, in relation to the four columns of Table 7.1, the 'wage' and 'employment' impacts are collapsed into one labour market channel, and an additional channel is added corresponding to linkage effects. In addition, we seek to attach actual numbers to magnitudes of impact – and we use as our basic frame of reference mainly least-developed, and in particular African, countries. The exercise is carried out on seven countries of which four are 'least-developed' – Uganda, Malawi, Lesotho, Ethiopia. The surveys were conducted between 1997 and 2000, and in general cover two samples of 150 producers,

Table 7.1 Possible categorisation of distributional impacts of the green revolution

Household's initial asset position	Direct and indirect effects of agricultural technology improvement					
	Food production rises, costs fall	Labour demand rises	Wage rises	Food price falls	Net effect	Comments
Net seller of food, net seller of labour	+	+	+	−	Ambiguous	Shift more land to cash crops and sell more; employment income rises
Net seller of food, net buyer of labour	+	+	+	+	+	Food expenditure falls, employment income rises
Net buyer of food, net buyer of labour	+	−	−	−	Ambiguous	Shift more land to cash crops and sell more; wage expenditure rises
Landless: buyer of food, seller of labour	Not applicable	+	+	+	+	Food expenditure falls, wage expenditure rises

Notes: + denotes net benefit for the household category in question, − denotes net loss.
Source: Kerr and Kolavalli (1999), Table 4.1.

one of them taken in a 'wet' area (rainfall more than 1000 mm) and the other in a 'dry' area (rainfall less than 800mm). The focus is on the green revolution in foodcrops – maize, cassava and sorghum and millets in dry areas.

In this approach, then, the four channels of potential poverty impact are:

(1)   *Effects of technical change on the productivity, and thus the incomes, of individual cultivators.* Modern (hybrid) varieties typically raise productivity per unit of land, increasingly often without aggravating risk; and the effect of this on household incomes may by itself raise individuals over the poverty line.

(2)   *Effects transmitted through the labour market.* Modern varieties produce larger crops and therefore require more labour for harvesting; labour-intensive practices such as deep ploughing, soil conservation, fertiliser application, and frequent weeding are often associated with the use of modern varieties and much less often associated with the use of traditional varieties[1]; irrigation, if used, enables multiple cropping in many dry areas, thus creating a large boost in labour use. Finally, modern varieties generally reduce yield variability and therefore the uncertainty associated with the hiring of labour.

(3)   *Effects transmitted through the prices of grains and other products consumed by poor people.* If technical change reduces the prices of key items in the consumption baskets of poor people, their real incomes increase. This effect has been found to be crucial in the Asian green revolution, and has been a key political motivation impelling the mass import of new seeds by Asian governments.

(4)   *Effects transmitted through linkages from agriculture to non-agricultural activities.* If the consumption linkages (incremental demands for consumption goods generated by income increases under (1)–(3)) and the production linkages (incremental demands for agricultural inputs) resulting from increases in agricultural productivity generate income increases, these will, to the extent that they take people out of poverty, add to the poverty reduction channels listed under (1)–(3) above. Again, these have proved extremely important channels of poverty reduction in India and China, where the growth of the rural non-farm sector has by a large margin exceeded the growth of farm production.

This approach, although serviceable, is indeed quick and dirty. It essentially examines effects in only three markets – product markets, labour markets and 'linkage activities'. In this way many effects – such as those operating through capital markets and the prices of other agricultural products – are omitted. Our second method of impact assesment is intended, in principle, to compensate for some of these deficiencies. It aims to examine all channels of impact through all markets, using a multi-market model. This is applied in one country only (Uganda); the results are derived from McKay and Mosley (2001).

The 'quick and dirty' method

Channel (a) Effects on innovator farm households

The most obvious link between yield improvement and poverty reduction is that farm households which experience higher yields derive higher incomes (or improved values of some other poverty indicator), and some of these thereby move from the poor into the non-poor category.

In Table 7.2 we offer, for our case-study countries, an estimate of the extent to which net poverty reduction was achieved through this channel.

There is a tendency, across our samples, for exit from poverty to be correlated with high levels of access to education (including in the non-formal sense, such as extension contact), infrastructure and financial services (see Dercon and Krishnan's Chapter 8 in this volume). It is also negatively correlated with risk aversion, suggesting the presence of a vicious circle in which people are poor because they do not innovate, and do not innovate because they are poor; in terms of Figure 3, they are trapped in low-input technology for fear of being forced out of the 'safe zone'. The impact of landholding on poverty is more complex. The general pattern from the literature is for the relationship between landholding and yields to be inverse, reflecting the Boserup hypothesis (Mosley 2001: Table 3). Several exceptions to this general rule have been reported, both in Asia (Singh 1990: Table 4) and in Africa: for example, in several countries, including Zimbabwe and Malawi, landholding has a U-shaped relationship with yields and thus with incomes (Mosley 2001: Figure 6). The general conclusion is that redistribution of land to the landless, in those LDCs where it is a realistic option (e.g. Mozambique), will certainly also increase equity and possibly the efficiency of land utilisation.

Channel (b) Labour market effects

As noted earlier, modern varieties of foodcrops tend to require the employment of more labour than traditional varieties, and to the extent that the labour thus absorbed is thereby moved from below to above the poverty line, this may be an important channel of poverty reduction: Singh (1990) argues that has been perhaps the most important channel by which the green revolution made possible 'the great ascent' of the South Asian peasantry, but whether such a thing has also happened in Africa and the LDCs, with their thinner labour markets, remains to be ascertained. Table 7.3, derived from survey data, examines this issue. The basic 'driver' of the table is the difference between labour intensity in modern and traditional varieties, as represented in column (1), which on our data amounts to a minimum of four person-months per cultivated hectare, higher in Western Kenya and North-Central Malawi,the regions of higher population density (one recalls Boserup's point

Table 7.2 Poverty reduction among farm households: nine country samples, 1994–2000 (LDCs in italics)

| | (1) Percentage of sample moved out of poverty | (2) Percentage of sample moved Into poverty | (3) = ((2)−(1)) Net movement out of poverty | (4) Net movement out of poverty owing to: | | | (5) Estimated net movement out of headcount poverty P_0 (in entire country, for period stated) owing to improved maize, sorghum and cassava yields within cultivators' families |
				(a) Technical change (intensification) in foodcrops	(b) Extension of the land area (extensification)	(c) Other cause	
Uganda, various locations, 1994–6 (sample size = 96)	21	7	14	1.3	3.2	9.5	
Uganda, Mbale, 1998–2000 (sample size = 90)	11	1	10	2.8	1.3	5.9	−23,000 (−0.1%)
Kenya, Bungoma, 1994–6							
Kenya, Rongo, 1998–2000 (sample size = 79)	4	1	3	0.9	0.3	1.8	−26,300 (−0.1%)
Malawi, Dowa and Mwanza, 1994–6 (sample size = 153)	13	8	5	0.7	1.6	2.7	−17,000 (−0.2%)
Zimbabwe, Zvishavane, 1998–2000	22	10	12	1.8	3.0	7.2	+2,000 (+0.1%)

	(14)	(8)	(6)	(0.7)	(0.9)	(6.4)	
Cameroon, Muyuka,1994–6							
South Africa, Phokoane, 1992–2000							−7,000 (<0.1%)
Average	11	6	5	1.2	1.5	4.7	−0.2% (1998–2000) −0.3% (1995–2000)

Note: The data in this table are based on provisional estimates of national crop yields in 2000 and should therefore be treated as provisional overall.

Sources: Percentage of sample moved out of and into poverty: National poverty lines used (in household income per month) are:

• Uganda: Sh 76,700 per household in 1996, increasing to Sh 100,500 in 2000
• Kenya: Sh 3,287 per household in 1996, increasing to Sh 4,325 in 2000
• South Africa, Lesotho: R 379 per household in 1996, increasing to R 499 in 2000
• Zimbabwe: Z$ 1,620 per household in 1996, increasing to $ 2,160 in 2000
• Malawi: MK 704 per household in 1994, increasing to MK 810 in 1996.
• Cameroon: FCFA 2,6211 per household in 1994, rising to FCFA 29,786 per household in 1996.

The percentage entered in this column is the proportion of the sample who crossed the poverty line over the period stated.

Apportionment of poverty reduction between causes: Pro rata according to the ratio of different components in the income of those who moved out of poverty during the period stated. If one-fifth of total increases in income over the period specified derives from increases in yield (multiplied by the value of the crop), one-fifth from increases in the sown area and three-fifths from external sources (agricultural income not derived from cereal crops, off-farm businesses and remittances), this is the ratio used to divide between columns (a) and (c). *Example:* in Uganda (Mbale) during 1998–2000, average incomes increased by about Sh 200,000/month. Within this, crop incomes increased by about Sh 82,000/month. The average sample increase in yields, multiplied by acreage, accounts for Sh 56,000, or 28 per cent of this income increase, with expansion of the sown area accounting for the remaining Sh 26,000 or 13 per cent. What is left over from crop income (Sh 118,000 or 59 per cent of thr total income increase) is assigned to the third part, 'other cause' of column (4).

Estimated movement out of poverty due to cause stated. The percentage of the sample estimated to have moved out of poverty over the period specified is grossed up to the total rural population by multiplying by (total number of producers) times (ratio of sample yield change to national yield change).

Example: in the Uganda (Mbale) sample 2.8 per cent are estimated to have moved out of poverty due to intensification, and the sample yield change (1998–2000) was 11 per cent. The national yield change for all cereals plus cassava (1998–2000) was 5.7 per cent, and the number of households producing these crops is estimated (*Background to the Budget 2000/01*) at 1.6 million. Thus the estimated poverty impact of the observed productivity change from this source is (5.7/11) times 2.8 per cent times 1.6 million = 23,000 people.

Table 7.3 Poverty impact of shift from traditional to modern varieties: labour market (LDCs in italics)

	(1)	(2)	(3)	(4) = $((1)\times(2)\times(3))$ Change in poverty indices (per cultivated hectare):			(5) Change in national head-count poverty 1998–2000 (col 4a × col 5 from table below)	
	(1) Change in labour demand (person-months) per hectare switched from local to modern varieties	(2) Average wage in locality (US $/month)	(3) Percentage of poor in household sample	(a) Total	(b) Male	(c) Female	(numbers)	%
Cameroon, Muyuka (cassava)	4.20	39.9	43	$P_0=0.2$ P_1:72 $P_2=5184$	$P_0=0.1$ P_1:55 $P_2=3025$	$P_0=0.1$ P_1:57 $P_2=289$	(low) 720 (high) 1320	
Uganda, Iganga (maize)	4.00	27.2	55	$P_0=0.18$ P_1:60 $P_2=3600$	$P_0=0.13$ P_1:35 $P_2=1225$	$P_0=0.05$ P_1:25 $P_2=625$	(low) 278 (high) 463	
Uganda, Soroti (cassava)	8.95	22.5	64	$P_0=0.20$ P_1:86 $P_2=129$	$P_0=0.14$ P_1:53 $P_2=2809$	$P_0=0.06$ P_1:33 $P_2=1089$	(low) 1340 (high) 2278	
Kenya, Bungoma (maize)	10.8	32.0	61	$P_0=0.26$ P_1:211	$P_0=0.16$ P_1:131	$P_0=0.10$ P_1:80	(low) 5304 (high) 9016	
Kenya, Tharaka (sorghum)				$P_2=44521$	$P_2=17161$	$P_2=6400$		
Malawi, Dowa (maize)	6.0	(19.5)	80	$P_0=0.09$ P_1:93 $P_2=8648$	$P_0=0.05$ P_1:52 $P_2=2704$	$P_0=0.04$ P_1:41 $P_2=1681$	(low) 3969 (high) 6336	
Overall average							(low) 2322 (high) 3882	0.1 (1998–2000) 0.2 (1995–2000)

Sources and guiding assumptions:

Column (1), change in labour demand: difference between mean labour demand for hybrid and traditional varieties for crop and country stated, as specified in component parts of Mosley (2000b: Table 4.12).

Column (2), wage rate: data for each survey location from Mosley (2000b: Table 4.3).

Column (3), percentage of poor: from Table 4.6. (UNICEF poverty line used for each country; national figures varied from $45–$70 per month).

Column (4): poverty indices reported are:

p_0 – the 'headcount index'. Number of persons crossing the poverty line during the period stated. Measured as columns $((1)/(2))$ times a 'transition coefficient' representing the proportion of employed poor who could be expected to cross the poverty line during the period stated per unit reduction in the poverty gap. This is derived from the measures of income distribution and yield impact given in Table 7.2.

p_1 – the 'poverty gap'. Changes in poverty multiplied by number of persons experiencing a change in poverty. Measured as columns $((1) \times (2) \times (3))$.

p_2 – an indicator of the depth of poverty: the sum of the squares of the poverty gaps measured under p_1. Measured as columns $((1) \times (2) \times (3))^2$. (Note that each of p_0, p_1 and p_2 can be represented as $\Sigma((Y_i - Z)/Z)^\alpha$ where $\alpha = 0, 1, 2$, respectively)

Column (5): The headcount estimate of 'poverty reduction per cultivated hectare' is grossed up to the number of hectares which could be expected to shift from traditional to modern varieties over a transition period of five years:

The *'low estimate'* is: (hectarage under crop stated) × (hectarage still under traditional varieties) × (change in adoption rate over last five years), extrapolated for the next five years. The *'high estimate'* assumes a combination of favourable policy initiatives, as listed in Mosley (2002: Table 4.12b): extension of micro-finance to half of the bottom 30 per cent; doubling of extension coverage; 20 per cent cut in real exchange rate and restoration of input subsidies (Malawi, Cameroon).

Working data for column (5):

	(1) Acreage (from FAO Production Yearbook 1998) (000 ha)	(2) % not yet under modern varieties (from Mosley 2002 Table 3.3)	(3) = (2) × (1) Acreage not yet under modern varieties	(4) Increase in adoption 1993–8 (percentage change)	(5) = (3) × (4) × 40% Low-end forecast of acreage to be transferred to modern varieties, 1998–2000 (000 ha)
Cameroon – cassava	90	40	36	0.11	2
Kenya – maize	1,510	34	513	0.10	30
Uganda – cassava	342	45	153	0.12	8
maize	598	16	95	0.07	3
Malawi – maize	1,245	86	1070	0.10	44

that 'lower population densities make it possible to stick to an agricultural system with less labour input per unit of agricultural output' and vice versa; Boserup 1970: 32). Depending on the validity of the other assumptions we have used, this suggests that poverty reduction generated by the labour market effects of the green revolution is at least half of that generated by increases in the incomes of farm households, possibly more. And yet what has been achieved falls far short of potential, because African labour markets (and labour markets in LDCs elsewhere, with the exception of Bangladesh) are so thin: as one measure of this, more than half of the households we surveyed were below the national poverty line, and very few of those took on any hired labour at all.

The demand for labour, from basic microeconomics, depends initially on the demand for the activity for which it is required (and thence on the growth of local demand, and the rate of productivity change in foodcrops). Further inspection of the labour demand function in our African samples, however, suggests the following:

(1) *The demand for labour is highly responsive to the demand for loan capital.* The availability of finance often unlocks a constraint on the ability of households to hire labour (pushes the budget line outwards; see Table 7.4). Thus development of the weak and undiversified capital markets of LDCs may be a precondition of labour market development.

(2) *The demand function for labour is kinked* – typically in the shape of a clock with its hands at a quarter to two, with the kink some way in excess of the poverty line, since low-income households do not hire labour for cash (see Mosley 2003, Chapter 5). Why this is so – across a huge range of

Table 7.4   Labour hiring and access to capital

	Cameroon (Muyuka)	Kenya (Bungoma)	Uganda (Iganga)	Lesotho (Butha-Buthe)	Malawi (Dowa)
All those with no access to capital market	3.0	2.0	2.5	1.2	1.1
N	36	138	116	64	130
All credit users	10.5	5.7	8.0	4.6	3.5
N	124	45	44	44	23
t-statistic for difference between sample means	4.37**	6.08**	1.95*		4.16**
Elasticity of demand for labour in relation to credit availability	*0.67*	*0.51*	*1.43*		*0.20*

** denotes significance of *t*-statistic at 1 per cent level.
* denotes significance at 5 per cent level.
Labour hiring measured in person-years per cultivated hectare.
Source: Mosley (2000b: Table 4.1).

microbusinesses, and not only in small-farm agriculture – requires further research, but we interpret it in terms of risk aversion – poor microentrepreneurs are risk-averse, and see labour as a 'quasi-fixed cost', imposing big risks on them, since even if casual it cannot easily be laid off without incurring serious relational costs. The implication is that any measures which are capable of smoothing out the demand side of the labour market, such as insurance, may be positive for labour demand and poverty reduction.

(3)   *The demand for male and female labour is asymmetric*, with women doing most of the unpaid work in agriculture and men most of the paid work[1]: this is already apparent from Table 7.3, which distinguishes between the demand for male and female labour. As in the labour markets of industrialised countries, this creates misallocation of resources and causes output to fall below its potential if men and women, having the same marginal productivities, are paid different amounts, as they are. The inefficiencies in different markets are interlocked, with female-headed households typically having less secure land rights and thus less access to collateralised loan capital,[2] less access to extension services and thus lower yields (Boserup 1970: 53–5, Saito 1994; see also Mosley 2000: 40) and less freedom to migrate in search of better income opportunities, all of which reduce their ability to bargain for higher wages or employment contracts which better suit their own preferences. Any policy measures which are able to augment the demand specifically for *female* paid labour are likely to have particularly strong leverage in poverty reduction. Our survey research (Mosley 2000b, Table 4.7), using a household bargaining model, suggests that among the factors which favour female participation in rural labour markets, given the wage level, are; education: a small number of children; membership of community organisations; and, as earlier discussed, access to loan capital. The policy discussion below, therefore, will use this short list – together with the variables mentioned under (1) and (2) above – as its point of departure.

As a medium-term objective, therefore, it is vital to do everything possible to increase rural labour utilisation; especially the absorption of women into the cash labour force.

However, these effects may diminish over time, depending on the pattern of technical development. The IFAD report (IFAD 2001: 135) claims that 'the response of employment to a given yield enhancement in Asia is now about one-third of 1970s levels, owing to the increasing use of tractors and herbicides'.

Channel (c) Consumer price effects

In Asia, a major influence by which the green revolution has reduced poverty has been by reducing the cost of foods consumed by the poor; indeed, an important trigger for pro-green revolution state policies in India and Indonesia was the desire to avoid politically risky surges in the price of rice imports.[3] In the LDCs of Africa and elsewhere, yield and production gains have of course been smaller and thus this element in the impact of technical change has been less significant; but in several countries it is possible to observe an impact of increased foodgrain productivity on the consumer price of food within and sometimes (as in the case of the maize surpluses of South Africa, Zimbabwe and Uganda and the cassava surpluses of Cameroon) outside the country. This has derived from a combination of influences operating alongside technical change itself, notably improvements in infrastructure and the liberalisation during the 1980s and 1990s, across most of Eastern and Southern Africa, of monopolistic food marketing arrangements previously controlled by the state. Food grains are typically the main element in the consumption of the poor, and thus any price reduction which can be achieved by this means has substantial poverty leverage, although, to the extent that it is realised, it mitigates the production-based gains to producer households described under channel (a) above. The approach we take here is quintessentially 'quick and dirty', and ignores this caveat, focusing only on the within-country reduction in the consumer price.

Table 7.5 seeks to measure the impact of food price changes on poverty by multiplying, for specific countries, the number of consumer households by a 'transition coefficient' which estimates the proportion of households which improvements in technology carried over the poverty line. In some LDCs within the sample (e.g. Lesotho) the 'trigger' is so small as to make the level of poverty reduction attributable to this source insignificant. But in Zimbabwe, Kenya, Uganda and Malawi – the last two of these being LDCs – substantial poverty reduction can be ascribed to this source. We believe, without having the data to hand, that the same is true for Ethiopia, one of the countries where a state-controlled marketing structure was reformed in the 1990s, and Bangladesh.

To what policy factors is this measure sensitive? We seek to answer this question by examining a panel data regression of price and other factors on production.

The estimated cross-section equation for the pooled data is the following:

Change in the real consumer price of maize (1980–97) = 0.14

$$(1.66)$$

-0.0003** (productivity change in maize 1980–97)
    (4.64)

-0.0034* (liberalisation index) -0.016** (food aid inflows)
    (2.19) (3.79)

$+0.07$ (growth in real personal disposable income)
    (1.14)

$+0.06$** (weather index), $r^2 = 0.59$, n = 98 observations.
    (3.65)

Table 7.5 Estimated price effect of technological changes in foodcrops on poverty

	(1) Estimated number of poor consumer households (thousands)	(2) 'Transition coefficient' = % of beneficiaries taken across poverty line by technology-induced price falls	(3) = ((1) × (2)) Estimated number of individuals carried across poverty line (1998–2000) by technology-induced food price cuts
Cameroon	2,100	0.0027	567
Uganda	4,400	0.0053	2,332
Kenya	8,600	0.0046	1,462
Malawi	3,900	0.0072	2,808
Zimbabwe	3,650	0.0044	1,606
Lesotho	850	0.0051	348
Pooled data	3,920	0.0049	1520
% of poverty head count P_0			−0.02 (1998–2000) −0.05 (1995–2000)

Sources: Column 1: estimated number of individuals buying crops mentioned for cash; data from household budget surveys as specified in Mosley 2002, Table 10.

Column 2: data from household budget surveys as specified in Mosley 2002, Table 10.

On this analysis, the 'shift parameters' most likely to affect the downward influence of food prices on poverty emerge as the liberalisation index – and, indeed, in many LDCs most gains from this source have now been secured – and infrastructure, which exercises an analogous influence on linkage effects (p. 159). In addition, food aid has an ambiguous influence – it reduces poverty via the *consumption* channel currently under analysis, but of course it increases it via the *production* channel (a).

Channel (d) Linkage effects

The linkage effects of the green revolution consist of economic activities which come into being as a result of technical change in the foodcrop sector. In Asia especially, these effects have been substantial: in the *World Development Report 2000/01*, the World Bank writes:

> Growth in agricultural incomes appears to have been particularly effective at reducing rural poverty because of demand spillovers to local markets in which the nonfarm rural poor have a large stake. Rural construction, personal services, simple manufacturing, and repair have been major channels through which poor people have shared in agricultural booms, even when they have not been direct beneficiaries of higher crop prices.
>
> (World Bank 2000/01: 67)

Indeed, the 'regional multiplier' from agricultural to total regional economic activity has been calculated, across a range of studies, at 1.8 (Haggblade *et al.* 1989): 1 dollar of agricultural output generates an additional 1 dollar and 80 cents of non-agricultural output. To the extent that employment or self-employment generated in these activities causes members of households to cross the poverty line, we have an additional channel of poverty reduction. Linkage effects arising from technical change may be:

- *Backward production linkages* – for example, the emergence of a group of farmers using modern inputs in a region causes local entrepreneurs to set up workshops for the production of hand tools, or a laboratory for the multiplication of hybrid seeds.
- *Backward consumption linkages* – for example, the additional incomes arising from the production of modern varieties that we have sought to measure (pp. 149–51) cause local entrepreneurs to produce locally goods and services that were previously obtained from outside the region.[4]
- *Forward linkages* – for example, local entrepreneurs begin to process locally produced foodcrops. The classical example is maize milling and the grinding of cassava into flour, but other possibilities exist, from beer brewing to the conversion of crop wastes into roofing thatch. In some cases, as with the conversion of cassava into 'chips' similar to potato crisps, these forward linkages have an export potential.

A first estimate of the size of these linkages and their poverty impact, in relation to data from a range of African countries including three LDCs, is provided in Table 7.6. As might be expected, the *size* of estimated linkage effects appears to vary with income in the locality and in the wider national economy: thus rural areas of eastern Uganda have much stronger linkage effects than southern Malawi and Lesotho, reflecting both a more prosperous rural economy and a faster-growing level of domestic demand. However, there are some aspects of linkage which cannot be explained by income factors alone.

Table 7.6   Effects of linkages to technical changes in foodcrops on poverty (provisional data, subject to amendment. *LDCs in italics*)

	(1) Estimated linkage effect (production of local goods and services as a consequence of linkages from incremental foodcrop production) ($000)	*(2) Incremental employment in linkage activities, 1998–2000*, whole country (thousands)*	*(3) 'Transition coefficient': % of beneficiaries crossed poverty line, 1998–2000*	*(4) = (2) × (3) Change in poverty headcount induced by estimated linkage effects (thousands)*
Cameroon	33,900	24	27	6
Uganda	39,450	41	43	17
Kenya	46,765	58	36	21
Malawi	8,795	13	62	8
Zimbabwe	36,500	39	34	13
Lesotho	7,900	8	31	2
South Africa	87,200	65	22	14
Pooled data		34	39	12
% of poverty head count P_0				0.05 (1998–2000) 0.1 (1995–2000)

Notes: Column (1): The linkage effect consists of (i) *the share* of *the increase in income of foodgrain producers* (1998–2000) which was spent on locally produced inputs ('backward production linkages' or locally produced consumption goods ('backward consumption linkages' (Source: Mosley 2003, Chapter 6: 2000 Survey, Question F1, checked against case study inspection of local industries), *plus* (ii) *forward linkages* – i.e. the value of agricultural products processed locally. This is assessed from local case study interviews only.
This estimate is computed for the locality covered by the questionnaire and then grossed up to the country as a whole via the method of the 'transition coefficient'.
Column (2): Employment in linkage activities: from questionnaire returns, calculating an average employment coefficient from the survey region and applying that coefficient to all linkage activities in the country.
Column (3): Transition coefficient of beneficiaries crossing poverty line: from interviews in case study regions.
Source: 2000 Survey, described as in Mosley (2003), Chapter 6, Table 3.

Our own research on rural locations in the countries listed above suggests that the size of linkage effects depends, in addition to income, on availability of infrastructure, both physical and financial, without which the costs of setting up local linkage activities become prohibitive. In certain policy contexts, such as Zimbabwe in the early 1980s and Indonesia in the 1970s (in common with most countries of South-East Asia) governments have made it their business to force the construction of linkage activities, and by doing so added substantially to the regional employment (and poverty-reduction) multiplier.

In addition, the comparative review by Delgado *et al.* (1998) suggests that the size of linkage effects depends on relative equality of income (without which, rural consumption linkages especially will be weak) and Hazell (1999) highlights the political element, noting that 'in many countries these potential multiplier effects are constrained by investment codes and related legislation that discriminate against small, rural nonfarm firms'. The economic damage caused by harassment of shanty-based informal sector production units, first pointed out in colonial times but subsequently with great intellectual weight by ILO (1972), continues into the twenty-first century and is by no means confined to urban areas (see for example Nairobi *Daily Nation*, 24 May 2001, which provides a photograph of a food stall being torn down by police in a remote rural marketplace). Less negatively, as with agricultural extension, the sectoral composition of any support given to the rural nonfarm sector may be important both directly and for its gender implications. As emphasized by Kerr and Kolavalli (1999: 108):

> data suggest that commerce and services are the most important growth sectors in the nonfarm rural economy, but assistance programmes typically focus on the manufacturing sector, which may be much less important. Women operate many of the commerce and service businesses and it is important that support services be targeted to them.

These factors suggest a range of policy options to be discussed below. To these are to be added the general factors determining poverty elasticity (see p. 155) – labour intensity and the adaptation of services to use by lower-income groups.

A multi-market model: Uganda

Introduction

This section presents an alternative and more comprehensive methodology for the assessment of poverty impacts. This is considered only for the case of Uganda where, as in many African countries, foodcrop producers are disproportionately represented among the poor. Increased yield in the production of such crops could then have a powerful poverty reducing effect if poor producers also share in this (the latter depends on many factors, including the extent to which the diffusion of new technology reaches them, as well as the factors influencing their decision to adopt). But in assessing this, other effects besides the impact on output need to be considered; in particular important general equilibrium effects may occur through changes in prices as well as through labour markets.

The analysis in this chapter relies primarily on household-level data from the Ugandan Integrated Household Survey (IHS) of 1992–3. These data enable a detailed characterisation of different household groups, in particular focusing on the extent to which they produce and consume major food commodities in Uganda. Different household groups will be affected to the extent that they consume and produce the different commodities affected, and the to extent to which they transact in labour markets. A multi-market model with significant disaggregation of foodcrops is used to try to estimate likely price effects. Based on the estimated price changes from the model, in conjunction with information about historical changes in productivity for key foodcrops, the survey data are then used to predict likely impacts on different household groups distinguished by region of residence and poverty status. To the extent that the survey data permit, the same issue is then addressed at the level of individual households, in order to simulate effects on standard poverty indices.

The characterisation of the household groups considered in this section is presented on p. 162. We then explain the multi-market model used to estimate the price effects associated with increased productivity, and present some estimates of their effects. We then consider the effects of these changes on the different household groups, while the final section summarises the analysis to date, and describes potential future developments of this analysis.

Patterns of food production and consumption in Uganda: descriptive analysis

The Ugandan Integrated Household Survey, the data from which form the basis for this chapter, was a multi-purpose survey conducted on a nation-wide basis, collecting information on different characteristics of households including consumption, incomes, use of education and health facilities and so on. As well as a household questionnaire collecting this and other information, separate questionnaires were also used to collect information on the different production activities (enterprises) of households, and on community-level information. The results of the household questionnaire have been used to construct a consumption-based standard of living measure (Appleton 1998). This defines the standard of living as total household consumption per adult equivalent household member, adjusted for geographic variations in the cost of living (see Appleton (1998) for further details of this, as well as for a thorough analysis of consumption poverty and inequality in Uganda based on this measure in this and subsequent surveys).

Foodcrop production is disproportionately important among poorer groups in Uganda – and at the same time households whose livelihoods are predominantly reliant on foodcrop production have benefited relatively less from the poverty reduction Uganda experienced over the 1990s. Improved varieties and other practices and measures that increase food productivity could potentially have a substantial impact on poverty, both incidence and depth, if they reach and are adopted by the poorest. This section seeks to quantify the likely impacts of increased productivity in key foodcrops (cassava, maize, millet and sorghum, initially focusing on the first two) if the benefits of increased productivity were to reach the poor in the same proportion as other groups.

It is important that such analysis reflects the diversity of households in Uganda. Given the focus on poverty, households are disaggregated into four quartile groups based on the consumption-based standard of living measure above. Those in the first two quartiles, and some of the least well-off in the third quartile are identified as poor relative to the absolute poverty line set by Appleton (1998). Households are also disaggregated into five groups by locality to take account of their significant variations in production and consumption patterns; these groups are urban households as a whole, and rural households in each of the Central, Western, Eastern and Northern regions.

It is clear from this analysis, that in 1992–3 poverty was disproportionately a rural phenomenon, and within rural areas poverty – especially extreme poverty – was greatest in the Northern region, followed by the Eastern region. However, there was a diversity of living standards within each locality, and urban areas still account for about 22 per cent of households in the lower two quartiles. This highlights the importance of combining income group and geographic criteria in analysing the data.

The consumption and production patterns of these groups are examined in McKay and Mosley (2001). The commodity groups are defined to identify explicitly the foodcrops for which the effects of productivity changes are to be considered (maize, cassava, sorghum and millet), other staple foodcrops and the remaining categories of consumption are aggregated. As expected food accounts for a lower proportion of the budget of those in the highest quartile, though the share varies little in the other quartiles. Several of the food commodities explicitly identified are disproportionately important for the poor; specifically the budget shares for maize, cassava, sorghum, millet, beans and potatoes monotonically decline with the standard of living quartile. Hence these commodities are *relatively* more important in the consumption basket of poorer households, although in absolute terms the higher-quartile groups still probably purchase more. The opposite pattern is true of the (very heterogeneous) 'other food' category and is almost true for matooke.

The national average patterns, though, aggregate over significant geographic differences in consumption baskets (and, indeed, some of the changes in consumption patterns by quartile at the national level reflect regional differences in consumption patterns). Within the rural regions the differences between quartile groups are often not so strong. Of the commodities of specific interest here, cassava is disproportionately important among poorer groups in the rural areas of the Eastern and Western regions, but not so strongly in the others. Maize is disproportionately important among poorer groups in the rural areas of the Western region, and less strongly in the Central and Northern regions, but not in the Eastern region. The contribution of sorghum to the consumption basket falls monotonically with the standard of living quartile in rural areas of the Eastern and Northern regions, but not elsewhere. For millet the decline in the budget share with the standard of living quintile is observed in the rural Central and Eastern region, but not elsewhere. It is clear from this that the distributional effects of changes in prices of these commodities resulting from improved productivity will be different in different regions. The same general point applies to other commodities whose prices may be affected indirectly.

The pattern for urban areas (itself a geographically diverse group) is similar to the pattern at the national level, which is not surprising. If this group were disaggregated by region (which is of less relevance here given the focus on foodcrop production), similar regional differences to those seen in rural areas might be observed.

Of still greater relevance here are variations in production patterns. Overall the crops under specific consideration here (cassava, maize, millet and sorghum) collectively account for 19.4 per cent of crop revenue, with cassava comprising around one-half of this. But in fact these crops account for a much higher proportion of the revenue of the households in the poorest quartile (38.0 per cent of revenue from crops); these then are crops of disproportionate importance to the poorest groups (as indeed is coffee, the main cash crop). Of the remaining crops the most important are matooke, potatoes and the heterogeneous 'other' category (which aggregates together many different crop types which are individually of lesser importance); again their relative importance varies sharply by quartile group. Overall revenue from crops is highest in the second quartile, diminishing in value in the third and fourth quintile; thus though the third and fourth quartiles are (by definition) richer overall they rely less on revenue from crops (partly reflecting the greater number of urban households in the top two quartiles). Households in the first quartile have much lower levels of revenue from crops – this of course comprises the poorest households in Uganda.

The relative importance of the different crops to the poorest households varies from locality to locality. In each locality, though, one or more of the commodities under specific consideration here are disproportionately more important for lower-quartile groups than higher ones (e.g. cassava, maize and millet for the first two quartiles in the rural Western region; cassava, millet and sorghum for the first quartile in the rural Northern region).[5] As with consumption, the varying pattern of production by income group indicates that the distributional impact of increased productivity in these crops may vary from region to region. Nonetheless, overall the crops being considered in this chapter are those where increased productivity may have the greatest impact on poverty.

Estimating the price effects of increased foodcrop productivity in Uganda

The effects of increased productivity in foodcrop production affects producers of these crops directly (via increased output), and affects producers and consumers indirectly through changes in the price of these and other commodities resulting from the productivity increases. The direct effects can be estimated directly from survey data given information about the level of production of each commodity (and its importance as a source of household income). But the indirect effects are general equilibrium in nature. Increased productivity of a non-tradeable commodity will tend to drive its price down, other things being equal, though in reality *ceteris* paribus does not apply because the increased productivity also affects incomes, as well as the prices of other commodities that are substitutes in production or consumption. A general equilibrium framework is needed to consider these effects. Changes in the productivity in tradeable foodcrop sectors will affect the level of external transactions. The price of these tradeable commodities will not be affected if domestic produced commodities can be regarded as a perfect substitute for an imported variety of the same commodity, and if producers are indifferent between domestic and export sales.

These general equilibrium effects on prices will be estimated by means of a multi-market model, focusing specifically on the key agricultural sectors. Such models are based on the production and consumption relationships of several commodities within the economy, combined with equilibrium conditions; a general summary of the approach is set out in Appendix Table 2 of Mosley (2002). It is less data-demanding and computationally intensive than a full Computable General Equilibrium (CGE) model and more transparent, but this simplicity comes because it is a much more limited representation of the economy. But it is used here in preference to a CGE model because of the very limited disaggregation of the agricultural sector in the input–output tables for Uganda (those for 1989 and 1992). Thus existing CGE models of Uganda (e.g. McDonald and Chant 2002) provide little detail on the agricultural sector and so are not suitable for current purposes.

Appendix 1 of McKay and Mosley (2001) sets out the general principles of multi-market models, based on the summary by Sadoulet and de Janvry (1995). As regards the specific model to be developed for Uganda, a first issue in its specification is the choice of commodities whose production and/or consumption is to be modelled and the characteristics of these

Table 7.7 Commodities included in Uganda multi-market model, and their characteristics

Commodity	Produced commodity	Consumed commodity	Tradeable or non-tradeable
1. Maize	√	√	Tradeable
2. Matooke	√	√	Non-tradeable
3. Millet and sorghum	√	√	Non-tradeable
4. Cassava	√	√	Non-tradeable
5. Coffee	√		Tradeable
6. Beans, potatoes, etc.	√	√	Non-tradeable
7. Other (food/non-food)		√	Tradeable

Note: The initial version of the model incorporates one specific simplification relative to the more general algebraic model set out in McKay and Mosley (2001), in that factors are modelled as being in perfectly elastic supply, which of course implies that factor prices are fixed. Given this, it becomes no longer vital to model factor markets as they will have no impact on the solution of the model. In other respects, though, the model is the same.

commodities. Given the focus of this study on the impact of increased productivity in the production of some specific food commodities (maize, cassava, millet and sorghum), and given other characteristics of Ugandan agriculture, the commodities to be specified and their assumed characteristics are set out in Table 7.7.

In log-linearised forms the equations of the Uganda model can be represented as follows:

$$\frac{dq^s}{q^s} = A\frac{dp}{p} + B\frac{dz}{z} \tag{7.1}$$

$$\frac{dq^d}{q^d} = C\frac{dp}{d} + D\frac{dy}{y} \tag{7.2}$$

$$\frac{dq_i^d}{q_i^d} = \frac{dq_i^s}{q_i^s}, i \in 2, 3, 4, 6 \tag{7.3}$$

$$\frac{dq_i^s}{q_i^d} = \left(\frac{q_i^s}{q_i^s + m_i}\right)\frac{dq_i^s}{q_i^s} + \left(\frac{m_i}{q_i^s + m_i}\right)\frac{dm_i}{m_i}, i \in 1, 7 \tag{7.4}$$

$$\frac{dq_i^d}{q_i^s} = -\frac{dm_i}{m_i}, i = 5 \tag{7.5}$$

$$\frac{dy}{y} = \sum_{i = 2, 3, 4, 6} \left(\frac{p_i q_i^s}{y}\right)\frac{dp_i}{p_i} + \sum_{j = 1, 5, 7} \left(\frac{p_j q_j^s}{y}\right)\frac{dp_j}{p_j} \qquad (7.6)$$

where q^s is the vector of supplies (with typical element q_i^s), q^d is the vector of supplies (with typical element q_i^d), p the vector of prices (typical element p_i), y household income, z a vector of technology shifts (typical element z_i), m_i net imports of commodity i, $i = 1, 5, 7$.

These equations then solve for the endogenous variables of the model: the changes in the demand and supply for consumed and produced commodities, respectively; in the prices of non-tradeable commodities; in the net imports of tradeable commodities; and in household income. To implement the model then requires knowledge of the coefficients. In equations (7.4) and (7.6) these are shares; the share of each non-tradeable commodity in overall household expenditure (7.6) and the share of net imports in total consumption. However, for (1) and (2) the data requirements are predominantly estimates of elasticities. In (7.2) C is the matrix of price elasticities of demand for the consumption commodities, where this covers both own- and cross- price elasticities, while D is the matrix of income elasticities of demand. In (7.1) A is the matrix of the price elasticities of supply – again in principle including cross-price as well as own-price elasticities. The contents of the matrix B depend on how the variable z is specified; but if dz/z is specified as the percentage increase in production owing to improved technology, other things being equal, then B can be specified as a matrix of ones.

Once the coefficients have been specified then the model can be solved by matrix inversion; clearly, though, the reliability with which elasticities can be estimated will have implications for the degree of confidence that can be placed in the results.

At the present time there are very few estimates of demand or supply elasticities available for food commodities in Uganda. Moreover, only relatively short time series are available on production and prices of the different food commodities considered in the model. In any case any longer time series for Uganda would most likely be affected by the crisis experienced by the Ugandan economy in the 1970s and early 1980s, meaning that any regression relationship that could be estimated would most likely be affected by structural breaks. Short time series make it particularly difficult to estimate cross-price elasticities, given the reduction in degrees of freedom this implies. The available time series have been used to derive approximate estimates of own-price demand elasticities, and in one or two cases, cross-price elasticities for commodities considered close substitutes or complements. In practice many cross-price elasticities have had to be set to zero for cases where *a priori* judgement suggested little or no substitutability in consumption; other cross-price elasticities and most of the elasticities of supply have been based on estimates for other African countries.

Simulation results

Two particular simulations are considered in this chapter:

(1) The effect of increased productivity in the production of maize (estimated to be around 15 per cent over 1995–2000)
(2) The effect of increased productivity in cassava production (estimated as around 40 per cent over 1995–2000).

Table 5 of McKay and Mosley (2001) presents the effects on agricultural revenue, assuming all other things remain equal – specifically that prices of these and other commodities do not change. In the case of maize the effects are strongest in the rural Eastern region; in the case of cassava in the rural Northern region and in urban areas. Overall, though, the effects on revenue are much smaller than the increase in productivity for the commodity concerned, indicating that agricultural activities are very diversified with these commodities accounting for only relatively small proportions of agricultural revenue on average.

In a general equilibrium framework, though, the *ceteris paribus* assumption may not be tenable. What is critically important now is whether commodities are modelled as tradeable or non-tradeable in the framework of the multi-market model. Maize was modelled as a tradeable commodity, so that the price is exogenously set on world markets (which Uganda is assumed to be too small to be able to influence). Under these assumptions our estimates of revenue changes may be reasonable. But cassava was modelled as a non-tradeable commodity; as such, its price will tend to be driven downwards as a result of the increased supply; further the change in the price of cassava will affect the price of other non-tradeable commodities and incentives to produce all commodities. In these circumstances the overall revenue effects can be positive or negative.

This can be examined in the context of the multi-market model by considering the effects of an exogenous increase in productivity, which are represented in the model as changes in the relevant element of the vector z. Table 7.8 reports the estimated effects on several variables of an exogenous 1 per cent change in productivity in maize and cassava production, under the above assumptions.

With maize being modelled as a tradeable commodity, changes in its productivity have little effect on the endogenous variables in the model. Its supply increases, so demand for imports fall one-to-one in absolute terms, but as the maize price does not change this does not encourage substitution in production from one crop to another. Maize consumption is unaffected,

Table 7.8 Percentage changes in key variables following a 1 per cent increase in maize and cassava productivity

	1% change in maize productivity	1% change in cassava productivity
Supply: maize	+1.0	0
Supply: matooke*	0	−0.27
Supply: millet and sorghum*	0	−0.91
Supply: cassava*	0	+1.27
Supply: coffee	0	+0.18
Supply: beans and potatoes*	0	+0.45
Demand: maize	0	+0.68
Demand: non-food	0	+0.09
Price of matooke	0	+1.36
Price of millet and sorghum	0	+4.55
Price of cassava	0	−0.91
Price of beans and potatoes	0	−2.27
Maize imports	−9.0	+6.8
Coffee exports	0	+0.18

Note: * Indicates that demand = supply for these commodities (non-tradeables).
Source: Estimates based on multi-market model.

though the balance of trade improves owing to the reduced level of imports. However, this is because the impact on household incomes of increased maize output has not been captured in the current version of the model; in reality increased household incomes among maize producers should lead to increased consumption demand for maize, among other commodities.

Cassava, by contrast, has been modelled as a non-tradeable commodity. As such, its price will adjust following an increase in the productivity of cassava production. In the first instance the increased output that results would tend to drive the price down, but at the same time many other factors will change including incomes, prices of other consumption commodities and supply of other agricultural commodities. Several general equilibrium effects are in operation here, some of which may act in opposite directions, so the overall impact is ambiguous *a priori*.

The results in Table 7.8 indicate that the price of cassava is driven down substantially by its increased aggregate supply. The price of beans and potatoes is also driven sharply downward, while that for matooke and millet and sorghum experience large increases. This pattern of changing prices reflects changes in supply of and demand for these non-tradeable commodities resulting from the increased cassava productivity, which depends partly on substitutability relationships between the commodities.

What the overall effect on poverty of these changes induced by the increased cassava productivity will be will vary from case to case, depending on a household's production and consumption patterns. In some cases the increased productivity of cassava may leave households worse off as a result of the other accompanying changes (including the falling cassava price).

Poverty effects of changes in foodcrop productivity

As noted above, the changes in poverty associated with increased productivity of foodcrops have direct effects (that depend on the extent to which a household cultivates the crop) and indirect or general equilibrium effects that can affects households both as producers and consumers. The latter effects are much more difficult to quantify, and the results of attempts to do so will be sensitive to the assumptions underlying the model. But these effects can be quite large in practice, and so cannot be discounted.

In this case the indirect effects operating through changes in prices apply only in the case of cassava. Consider first the more straightforward case of maize. Table 7.9 reports the effect of a 15 per cent increase in maize productivity on Foster–Greer–Thorbecke P_α poverty indices for $\alpha = 0, 1, 2$. The effects of the increased maize productivity were calculated based on household income, taking account of the share of household income derived from agriculture (estimated based on the IHS data), and taking account of the proportion of the value of agricultural *revenue* which was due to maize (crop specific income data not being available). However, as household incomes in the IHS survey appear to be significantly underestimated on average relative to expenditure (a common feature of household surveys), the effect of the increase in maize productivity was scaled by the ratio of household expenditure to household income, to obtain an estimate of the increment to the household's standard of living.

The results of Table 7.9 indicate that the effects of the large increase in maize productivity are modest. The biggest effects are experienced in the rural Eastern region, reflecting the fact that this is the most important maize growing region. But even there the effects on poverty of a large productivity increase are modest. This reflects largely two factors: agriculture accounts for only about 40 per cent of income, and then only 20 per cent of agricultural income is obtained from maize. This obviously reflects highly diversified livelihoods within the rural Eastern region. Many households are not engaged in agriculture at all, or only to a small extent; even those that are engaged in agriculture cultivate a wide variety of crops. The increases in maize productivity have yet more modest effects on poverty in other regions, again reflecting diversified livelihoods and the fact that maize is a less important source of agricultural revenue in these other regions.

These modest effects reflect the fact that in each region a majority of households are not growing maize at all; what about the poverty reducing effects among that sub-set of households that grow maize (whether in large or small quantities)? This information is reported in McKay and

Table 7.9 Effects on national poverty indices of a 15 per cent increase in maize productivity

		Average standard of living	P_0	P_1	P_2	Share of agricultural revenue from maize (initial)
Urban	Initial	12,287	0.291	0.088	0.038	12.4
	Simulation	12,296	0.290	0.088	0.038	
Rural Central	Initial	6,873	0.542	0.186	0.087	7.5
	Simulation	6,903	0.539	0.184	0.086	
Rural Western	Initial	5,860	0.607	0.230	0.114	20.4
	Simulation	5,952	0.598	0.225	0.111	
Rural Eastern	Initial	6,235	0.538	0.192	0.093	7.3
	Simulation	6,263	0.534	0.190	0.092	
Rural Northern	Initial	5,005	0.752	0.311	0.163	7.0
	Simulation	5,029	0.750	0.310	0.162	
National	Initial	6,793	0.565	0.209	0.103	11.0
	Simulation	6,834	0.561	0.207	0.102	

Note: The simulation reports the effect of a 15 per cent increase in maize productivity, with maize being modelled as a tradeable commodity.
Source: Authors' computations based on data from Uganda Integrated Household Survey, 1992–3.

Mosley (2001: Table 8), and here of course the poverty reducing effects are much greater. On average these households obtain around 70 per cent of their income from agriculture, and 46 per cent of their agricultural revenue from maize. This translates into bigger reductions in poverty among these groups. But, as noted above, these groups represent only a small minority of households, hence the aggregate poverty reduction effects are very modest.

Farmers that grow cassava derive a smaller proportion of their agricultural revenue from this crop than is the case for maize, but the productivity change being considered is much larger. Table 7.10 reports the impact on the same set of poverty of a 40 per cent increase in cassava productivity under two scenarios. Simulation 1 presents the equivalent case to maize above, measuring the impact of the increased productivity as if cassava were a tradeable commodity – in other words, not allowing for the general equilibrium effects including the change in the price of cassava. Simulation 2 takes account of the general equilibrium effects on production as estimated by the multimarket model and that were reported (for a 1 per cent change in cassava productivity) in Table 7.8 consumption consequences of these general equilibrium effects are not incorporated here.

Table 7.10 Effects on national poverty indices of a 40 per cent increase in cassava productivity

		Average standard of living	P_0	P_1	P_2	Share of income from agricultural (initial)	Share of agricultural revenue from cassava (initial)
Urban	Initial	12,287	0.290	0.088	0.038	13.6	12.7
	Sim 1	12,307	0.290	0.087	0.037		
	Sim 2	12,328	0.285	0.090	0.041		
Rural Central	Initial	6,873	0.542	0.186	0.087	59.0	3.6
	Sim 1	6,919	0.537	0.184	0.086		
	Sim 2	7,518	0.482	0.186	0.105		
Rural Western	Initial	5,860	0.607	0.230	0.114	63.6	3.8
	Sim 1	5,903	0.605	0.229	0.113		
	Sim 2	6,286	0.573	0.223	0.115		
Rural Eastern	Initial	6,235	0.538	0.192	0.093	68.5	4.5
	Sim 1	6,282	0.533	0.190	0.091		
	Sim 2	6,586	0.524	0.214	0.117		
Rural Northern	Initial	5,005	0.752	0.311	0.163	66.4	11.0
	Sim 1	5,105	0.741	0.304	0.159		
	Sim 2	5,123	0.719	0.306	0.165		
National	Initial	6,793	0.565	0.209	0.103	58.2	5.6
	Sim 1	6,846	0.560	0.207	0.101		
	Sim 2	7,142	0.534	0.212	0.114		

Note: Simulation 1 (Sim 1) reports the effect of a 40 per cent increase in cassava productivity, without taking general equilibrium effects into account (as if cassava was a tradeable commodity). Simulation 2 (Sim 2) additionally takes account of these general equilibrium effects, as estimated using the multi-market model.
Source: Authors' computations based on data from Uganda Integrated Household Survey, 1992–3, and multi-market model.

Considering first Simulation 1, the poverty reducing effects are greatest in the rural Northern region, but even there are fairly modest. At the aggregate level the incidence of poverty falls by only 0.5 per cent. The explanations for these small changes are similar to those that applied in the case of maize, combined with the fact that cassava is on average a less important source of agricultural revenue for those that grow it than was maize. Incorporating the general equilibrium effects (Simulation 2) leads to generally modest (on average around 4 per cent) increases in the average value of the standard of living measure, but its effects on poverty indices are more complex. The incidence of poverty falls further in each region, but indices of poverty that take account of its depth ($\alpha = 1, 2$) generally display small increases. That general equilibrium effects bring about a diversity of experience is not surprising; they will affect some households positively and others negatively depending on their patterns of production.

If we focus only on those households that cultivate cassava, the poverty-reduction effects associated with Simulation 1 are bigger, although in some cases (notably urban areas) the benefits accrue mostly to households that were already above the poverty line. The poverty reducing effects among cassava cultivating households in rural areas are quite large, but again these households account for only a small minority of those in the region. In rural areas, taking the general equilibrium effects into account (Simulation 2) offsets some of the poverty reducing effects of the increased productivity; this is probably due predominantly to the associated fall in the price of cassava.

Conclusions

We can put together Tables 7.9 and 7.10 to get an estimate of the combined poverty impact of the productivity changes which actually happened (Table 7.11).

The provisional finding is that over the period 1995–2000 improved productivity in maize and cassava knocked about half of a percentage point off the poverty headcount index; in other words, they accounted for about 5 per cent (one-twentieth) of the fall in poverty, of about 10 percentage points, which occurred during that period. This is broadly consistent with the figures emerging from the 'quick and dirty' approach (Table 7.2–7.6) given that the multi-market approach does not take into account labour market impacts (which will be estimated in future work). In addition, as will be strongly argued in the following section, we believe that these modest impacts could be substantially enlarged, even in Uganda, with the adoption of appropriate innovations in policy and institutions.

Table 7.11 Uganda: combined impact of productivity changes in maize and cassava, 1995–2000

	Change in headcount poverty index (P_0) (%)
Urban	−0.06
Rural Central	−0.63
Rural Western	−0.43
Rural Eastern	−0.18
Rural Northern	−0.35
National	−0.35

Source: difference between 'initial' and 'simulation' values in Tables 7.9 and 7.10.

Table 7.12 Poverty impact of the African green revolution: summary of results from alternative approaches

Channel of impact	Impact of modern varieties' adoption over 1995–2001 (generally 1998–2000) on: Headcount index (%)	Source
'Quick and dirty' method:		
1 Cereal producers' incomes	−0.2	Table 7.2
2 Labour market	−0.1	Table 7.3
3 Crop price effects	−0.05	Table 7.4
4 Linkage effects	−0.1	Table 7.5
Estimated total impact (average for six countries)	−0.45	Tables 7.2–7.6
(Uganda only)	−0.29	Tables 7.2–7.6
CGE method (Uganda only):	−0.35	Table 7.11

Synthesis

We now put together, in Table 7.12 which acts as the pivot for this chapter, the summary table which gives the estimated value of these effects for the average of all the countries in the sample. The provisional message appears to be that:

(1) The impact of the green revolution in LDCs, even though weak and hesitant, has nonetheless been poverty reducing; and could be more so if more were done to nurture the potential indirect or 'spread' effects.

(2) 'Indirect' effects, especially those operating through the labour market and through linkages, are crucial and between them outweigh 'direct' effects operating through the incomes of cereal producers.

(3) Linkage effects, in Africa by contrast with Asia, are seriously under-developed but nonetheless of significance (particularly in Eastern Uganda and Zimbabwe) for understanding the poverty reduction process.

(4) Consumer price effects in Africa, by contrast with Asia, are minor.

In Uganda, where we ran the 'quick and dirty' model side by side with a cleaner but more data-intensive CGE model, the results come out fairly similar, suggesting that if both direct and indirect effects are taken into account, possibly one-tenth of all the poverty reduction which took place, taking into account labour market impacts, is due to productivity change in the two foodcrops on which we have focused. Much of this poverty reduction

Table 7.13 Channels by which technical change influences poverty, and policy instruments to which they may be sensitive

Influences to which sensitive Channel of influence	(1) Factors influencing size of initial green revolution stimulus (p. 167)	(2) Factors influencing size of poverty reducing channels (see pp. 149, 154, 156)	Policy instruments capable of exercising pro-poor influence (see pp. 149, 154, 156, 160)
	Given the level of population pressure: 1 Access to financial services and protection against risk 2 Access to physical infrastructure 3 Access to extension and education overall		
1 Farm households move across poverty line owing to increase in farm income derived from crops		Distribution of land holding Distribution of financial access between households Access to extension and education among lower-income groups Risk aversion	Land reform Appropriate agricultural microfinance Gender-sensitive, risk-sensitive extension Microinsurance
2 Households cross poverty line as a consequence of increased labour demand from farm households using new technology		Removal of obstacles to hiring of women for cash	Appropriate agricultural microfinance
3 Households cross poverty line as a consequence of increased demand from 'linkage activities'		Infrastructure; income equality	Removal of planning restrictions
4 Households cross poverty line as a consequence of lower consumer prices made possible by higher foodcrop productivity		Aid composition Marketing policy	Stop non-emergency food aid Possibly some scope for liberalisation in some cases

took place in the dry Northern region which had been bypassed by the first phase of poverty reduction in the early to middle 1990s, and was based on cassava, not the maize on which most of the international research effort in Africa had been focused. This draws attention to the need to adopt a crop and region-specific perspective in our discussion of the policies, which might enable the rather modest poverty reduction so far extracted from the African green revolution to be enhanced.

It is important to emphasise:

(1) That the linkages depicted in Table 7.12 are neither automatic nor always strong and significant. The price linkage, in particular, is often weak and insignificant, because only for certain years and countries did smallholder crop production achieve sufficient volume to exercise a measurable influence on the consumer price.
(2) That these linkages are highly sensitive to policy – we have indicated on pp. 149–52 what the key policy influences are likely to be and discuss these further in the final section. Econometric tests are not attempted here but will be in subsequent work.

Sensitivity analysis and policy implications

The key purpose of this chapter is to identify how the channels through which technical change influences poverty can be 'broadened' and made more pro-poor in specific African contexts. We have identified four of these channels, and Table 7.13 lists the variables to which they appear to be sensitive and the policy instruments which may be capable of influencing them.They spread across a number of areas (infrastructure, financial institutions, agricultural support services, land policy, aid policy) – but one cross-cutting theme is the need to make factors of production available on equal terms to women and men; readers will recall Pyatt's conclusion (p. 117) that 'development is the amelioration of the lot of women'.

In conclusion, we believe that the enhancement of technical change in foodcrops represents a modest but still significant pro-poor strategy, which would have still greater leverage with the support of the policies mentioned above.

Notes

1. Ester Boserup, in her pioneering work (1970), estimates that women in Africa do 70 per cent of unpaid agricultural work; Katrine Saito, in her empirical survey (1994), estimates 65 per cent across four samples drawn from Kenya and Nigeria.
2. Most microfinance loans – especially those given to women's groups – are however uncollateralised, and therefore present women with an important opportunity to break out of the vicious circle.

3. In the 1970s, Indonesia was the world's largest rice importer; by the 1980s the country had achieved self-sufficiency, and now sells rice and other foodgrains on international markets.
4. Hazell and Haggblade (1993: 195) report that 'a consistent finding of all the multiplier studies is the relatively greater importance of household consumption linkages compared with the production (interindustry) linkages. The consumption linkages typically account for some 60–90 per cent of the total multiplier'.
5. This Northern region, we recall, is the region where poverty declined almost imperceptibly in the mid-1990s against the background of a generally sharp national decline in poverty (Appleton 1998).

Bibliography

Appleton, S. (1998), 'Changes in poverty in Uganda 1992–96', Occasional Paper WPS/ 98-15, Oxford: Centre for the Study of African Economies.

Boserup, E. (1965), *The Conditions of Agricultural Growth*, London: Allen & Unwin.

Boserup, F. (1970), *Woman's role in agricultural development*, London: Earthscan.

Bundy, C. (1979), *The Rise and Fall of the South African Peasantry*, London: Macmillan.

Chapman, G. and associates (1980), *The Green Revolution Game*, Operating manual for simulation game, Department of Geography, University of Lancaster.

Cockcroft, L. (1997), 'Mastering mosaic: the fight for cassava production in Uganda', Gatsby Charitable Foundation, December.

Collier, P. and F. Teal (1994), 'African labor markets', Unpublished paper, Oxford: Centre for the Study of African Economies.

Delgado, C. *et al*. (1998), *Agricultural growth linkages in sub-Saharan Africa*, Washington DC: IFPRI.

Dercon, S. (1999), 'Changes in poverty in rural Ethiopia 1989–95: some evidence', Unpublished paper, Oxford, CSAE, Chapter 8 in this volume.

Dorward, A. (1999), 'Farm size and Productivity in Malawi smallholder agriculture', *Journal of Development Studies*, 35 (June), pp. 141–61.

Eicher, C. (1995), 'Zimbabwe's maize-based green revolution', *World Development*, Vol. 23.

Ellis, F. (1998), 'Household strategies and rural livelihood diversification', *Journal of Development Studies*, Vol. 35, pp.1–38.

Elson, D. (1999), 'Labour markets as gendered institutions: equality, efficiency and empowerment issues', *World Development*, Vol. 27, 611–27.

Freebairn, D. (1995), 'Did the green revolution concentrate incomes? A qualitative study of research reports', *World Development*, Vol. 23 (February), pp. 265–79.

Haggblade, S. *et al*. (1989), 'Farm-nonfarm linkages in rural sub-Saharan Africa', *World Development*, Vol. 17, pp. 1173–99.

Hazell, P. (1999), *The African non-farm sector*, Washington DC: IFPRI, press release.

Hazell, P. and S. Haggblade (1993), 'Farm-nonfarm growth linkages and the welfare of the poor', chapter 8 in M. Lipton and J. Van der Gaag, *Including the Poor*, Washington, DC: World Bank.

IFAD (2001), *Rural Poverty Report 2001: The Challenge of Ending Rural Poverty*, Rome: International Fund for Agricultural Development.

IFPRI (International Food Policy Research Institute) (2001), 'Beacons of hope in African agriculture', *The East African*, 27 August–2 September.

ILO (1972), *Employment, incomes and equality: report of a mission to Kenya*, Geneva: ILO.

Iliffe, J. (1987), *The African Poor*, Cambridge: Cambridge University Press.

Jones, C. (1983), 'The mobilisation of women's labour for cash-crop production: a game-theoretic approach', *American Journal of Agricultural Economics*.

Kerr, J. and S. Kolavalli (1999), 'Impact of agricultural research on poverty alleviation: conceptual framework with illustrations from the literature', Washington, DC: IFPRI, Environment and Technology Division Discussion Paper 56.

Lipton, M. with R. Longhurst (1989), *New Seeds and Poor People*, London: Allen & Unwin.

McDonald, S. and L. Chant (2002), *A computable general equilibrium model for Uganda: technical documentation*. Unpublished paper, University of Sheffield.

McKay, A. and P. Mosley (2001), 'The economy-wide effect of increased food production in Uganda', Universities of Nottingham and Sheffield: Gatsby Charitable Foundation Occasional Paper 10.

Morduch, J. (1999), 'The microfinance promise', *Journal of Economic Literature*, December.

Mosley, P. (1982), 'Government policy and agricultural development in settler economies: the cases of Kenya and Southern Rhodesia', *Economic History Review*, Vol. 35.

Mosley, P. (2000a), 'Overseas aid, technical change in agriculture, and national economic strategy in Africa and the least developed countries', University of Sheffield: Gatsby Charitable Foundation Occasional Paper 7.

Mosley, P. (2000b), *New Seeds. The Operation of Rural Labour Markets, and their Significance for Understanding the Effect of Adjustment: four African Case Studies*, Sheffield: Gatsby Foundation paper 4.

Mosley, P. and Kirsten J. (2001), *The poverty-reducing potential of farm-nonfarm linkages*: evidence from *seven African countries*, Sheffield: Gatsby Foundation, Occasional Paper 12.

Mosley, P. (2002), 'Poverty impact of the green revolution and possibilities for pro-poor growth in Africa and the least developed countries', DFID Research Programme on Pro-Poor Growth, Occasional Paper 1.

Mosley, P. (2003), *A Painful Ascent: The Green Revolution in Africa*, London: Routledge, forthcoming.

Osmani, L. (1998), 'Credit and women's well-being; a case study of the Grameen Bank, Bangladesh', PhD thesis, Queen's University Belfast.

Sadoulet, E. and A. de Janvry (1995), *Quantitative Development Policy Analysis*, Berkeley: University of California Press.

Saito, K.A. (1994), Raising the productivity of women farmers in sub-Saharan Africa, Africa Technical Department Discussion Paper 230, Washington, DC: World Bank.

Sen, A.K. (1983), *Poverty and Famines*, London: Allen & Unwin.

Singh, I. (1990), *The Great Ascent. . .*, Baltimore: Johns Hopkins University Press.

Thirtle, C. and associates (1992), 'Determinants of productivity change in Zimbabwe agriculture', *Economic Journal*, Vol. 102.

Udry, C. (1996), 'Gender, agricultural production, and the theory of the household', *Journal of Political Economy*, Vol. 104, pp. 1010–46.

Uganda Government (2001), 'Background to the budget 2001', Kampala: Government Printer.

United Kingdom (1975), 'More help for the poorest', White Paper on International Development, London: HMSO.

United Kingdom (2000), 'Making globalisation work for the poor', White Paper on International Development, London: The Stationery Office.

Weeks, J. (1971), 'Risk, uncertainty and wealth and income distribution in peasant agriculture', *Journal of Development Studies*, Vol. 8, pp. 28–36.

Whitehead, A. (2001), 'Trade, trade liberalisation and rural poverty in low-income Africa: a gendered account', Background Paper for UNCTAD Least Developed Countries Report, Unpublished paper, University of Sussex.

World Bank (1990), *World Development Report 1990: Poverty*, Oxford: University Press.

World Bank (2000), *World Development Report 2000/01: Attacking Poverty*, Oxford: Oxford University Press.

Van Zyl, J.H. Binswanger and C. Thirtle (1995), 'The relationship between farm size and efficiency in South African agriculture', World Bank Policy Research Working Paper 1548.

Van Zyl, J. and J. Kirsten (1995), Chapter 6 in R. Singini and J. van Rooyen (eds), *Serving Small-Scale Agriculture*, Midrand, South Africa: Development Bank of Southern Africa.

8

Poverty in Rural Ethiopia 1989–95: Evidence from Household Panel Data in Selected Villages

Stefan Dercon and Pramila Krishnan

Introduction

Identifying the pattern of change in welfare and poverty over time is of increasing importance in the policy debate about reform in Africa. It is recognised that the reform programmes are sustainable only in the long run if they also result in poverty alleviation. However, the data available on changes in poverty in Africa is surprisingly limited compared to Asia. Despite the various household surveys recently implemented (Deaton 1997), problems ranging from access to data to incompatible surveys, have meant that few studies on the changes in welfare since the 1980s have been attempted.[1] Cross-section data could be used to perform this task, provided coverage and sampling are done with great care (Deaton 1997). Panel data, although not without their own methodological problems, are more reliable in establishing changes at least within the sample collected. In the context of Africa, with the exception of the rolling panels in some LSMS surveys, such as in Côte d'Ivoire (Grootaert and Kanbur 1995), the number of panel data sets that could be used for assessing the changes in welfare are limited.

In this chapter we use data from a survey conducted in 1989 in six villages in the Southern and Central part of the country. In 1994, these households were re-visited as part of a larger household survey covering 15 villages throughout Ethiopia. Subsequently, the larger sample was interviewed again in the second half of 1994 and in 1995. The result is a twofold panel, the smaller one allowing the analysis of welfare changes between 1989 and 1994, and a larger panel, covering 1994 and 1995.[2]

The period analysed in this chapter is ideal for such an exercise in the context of reform in Ethiopia. The first survey, conducted in 1989, provides a picture of the situation in Ethiopia towards the end of a long period of strict economic controls, bad weather and civil war. The year 1994 marks the beginning of a structural adjustment programme, agreed by a new government that came to power after the end of the civil war in 1991. In 1990, a tentative set of economic reforms had already implied food market liberalisation and a reduction of rural taxation, which were expanded by the new government. Consequently, the smaller panel on about 350 households can address change in the period after the end of the war and after the first wave of the reforms. The second panel (on about 1,450 households between 1994 and 1995) can be used to examine the initial consequences of the structural adjustment programme.

Measuring welfare changes is not without its problems. In line with most studies, we use consumption as our basis for measuring the standard of living.[3] Furthermore, we use a cost-of-basic-needs poverty line to calculate poverty measures (Ravallion and Bidani 1994). The measures used are from the Foster–Greer–Thorbecke family of additively decomposable measures (Foster, Greer and Thorbecke 1984). We discuss explicitly some of the problems we face when conducting the analysis. In particular, we address issues of questionnaire design, robustness to the actual poverty line chosen (stochastic dominance) and whether the results are sensitive to the sources of the price data used.

The chapter does not present exhaustive analysis of these data. It is largely concerned to understand the patterns of change and its correlates. Much attention is paid to the careful analysis of the underlying data, illustrating the numerous problems related to poverty analysis. More detailed analysis and interpretation of the observed patterns, including the actual determinants of the observed changes and the role of policy in this respect, is left to other work. In particular, the short-term movements between 1994 and 1995, including an analysis of the role of risk and seasonality in explaining the findings, are discussed in Dercon and Krishnan (2000a, 2000b), while the extent to which the economic reforms have contributed to the observed changes between 1989 and 1995 is discussed in Dercon (2001).

This chapter is organised as follows. We first describe the data used. We then discuss the construction of consumption, the poverty line used and issues related to the price data. We then present the poverty findings and discuss their robustness. We finally interpret the results via a dynamic poverty profile. The final section concludes.

The data used

The data for 1989 come from a survey conducted in seven villages now located in the regions called the Amhara, Oromiya and the Southern Ethiopian People's Association (for details see Webb, Braun and Yohannes 1992). Six of the seven villages were re-visited in 1994, covering about 400 households (the remaining village in a semi-pastoralist area in Southern Ethiopia could not be re-visited because of violent conflict in the area). Nine additional villages were selected, allowing for a total of 15 village studies, covering 1,477 households (the Ethiopian Rural Household Survey, ERHS) and reflecting the full diversity in farming systems in the country. They were interviewed three times: in the first part of 1994 (1994a), again later in the same year (1994b) and in the first part of 1995.

In the 1989 survey, the households were randomly selected within each community, while the communities selected were mainly areas which had suffered from famine in this period (for details see Webb, Braun and Yohannes 1992; Dercon and Krishnan 1996). Food consumption information from the six villages surveyed in 1994 is available for 363 households (non-food on a much smaller sample). For 1994 and beyond we have complete food and non-food data for most households (1,411) for all three rounds. Within each village, random sampling was used, stratified by female-headed and non-female-headed households.

Obviously, with only 15 communities, but relatively large samples within each village, the interpretation of the results in terms of rural Ethiopia as a whole has to be done with care. No other sources allowing a comparison over time exist, however, so that the current data set is probably the only one currently available to make any statements about change in Ethiopia.[4] Attrition between 1989 and 1994 was only 7 per cent. In 8 per cent of cases, the head of the household had changed (owing to death, illness or transfer of headship to a son or daughter because of age). These households were retained. Attrition between 1994 and 1995 was about 2 per cent.

Constructing comparable consumption data and a poverty line

Several potential problems with comparing poverty over time exist and have been discussed in the literature. First, changes in the questionnaire over different rounds may affect the comparison.[5] For the 1994a, 1994b and 1995 round we do not have this problem since the questionnaires were not changed. For 1989 data there is no fundamental problem, since the 1994 questionnaire is modelled on the 1989 questionnaire. However, the list of specific items prompted for is longer in 1994. To deal with this problem, we include in our consumption measures for 1994 and beyond only items specifically prompted for in the 1989 questionnaire, at least when conducting the poverty comparison between these period. Since this is likely to underestimate total consumption from 1994 onwards, this may well bias our results against a reduction in the measured number of poor.

Another issue is the actual definition of consumption used. The actual consumption definition used is the sum of values of all food items, including purchased meals and non-investment non-food items. The latter was interpreted in a limited way, so that contributions for durables and house expenses were excluded, as well as health and education expenditures (see Hentschel and Lanjouw 1996). This will avoid our results being biased by temporary increases in consumption owing to durable purchases, although other procedures could be used as well.

Consumption data are available only at the household level so further corrections are needed. We use consumption expressed per adult equivalent. Household composition and size were transformed into adult equivalent units using World Health Organisation (WHO) conversion codes (details are in Dercon and Krishnan 1998). Since data on household size and composition was collected in each period, we adjusted the household size and the adult equivalent units in each period.

The study of poverty in a country is ultimately an attempt to compare living standards across households or individuals. It therefore suffers from all the usual problems associated with tastes, circumstances, price differences and behavioural responses. While economists may have little problem with using consumption measures, one still needs to make careful corrections to allow monetary measures to reflect poverty differences. As usual, poverty will be defined relative to a poverty line. Although alternative methods to define the poverty line are possible (Greer and Thorbecke 1986; Anand and Harris 1994), we use the cost-of-basic-needs approach to estimate a poverty line (Ravallion and Bidani 1994). A food poverty line is constructed by valuing a bundle of food items providing 2300 Kcal. A specific value for this basket is obtained per survey site. To this value, an estimated non-food share is added to obtain the total consumption poverty line per day per adult.

We identify two specific problems with this approach in the Ethiopian case. First, pricing a basic basket assumes the availability of all these commodities in the local market, which is difficult to believe especially for 1989. Indeed, we encountered problems with finding price data for some commodities in the local markets[6] even in 1994. A second problem is that in rural areas we are dealing with very different farming systems. Their diets are very different, implying very different product availability in markets affecting our pricing. The main consequence of the latter problem appears to be very different cost-of-living measures depending on which diet is used (specific per site or common for all sites). In this chapter we settled for a common diet for everyone, to increase comparability across sites.

As will be seen below, the issue of prices becomes even more crucial when attempting to do comparisons over time and space. We know from other work that price dispersion is high in Ethiopia, with markets taking considerable time to perform arbitrage (Dercon 1995). Also, rural areas are not well served by rural markets, probably due to very poor infrastructure, while even in small urban markets the availability is often poor. Even if markets always clear, price variability over time is high, and is not explained by seasonal factors. Such variability is very difficult to deal with in analysing poverty. Temporary price increases will make the minimum food basket very expensive, and the expected behavioural response is to reduce consumption as long as prices are very high. When prices return to lower levels consumption may then be boosted. Depending on whether consumption was measured when prices were high or low has important consequences for finding whether households were poor or non-poor. In fact, since allowing consumption to fluctuate may be part of the same consumption plan, the interpretation of the poverty figures is difficult: when prices are (temporarily) high, poverty is likely to be overestimated, while when prices are low, poverty is likely to be underestimated.[7] Seasonality presents a similar problem, but here, information about the likely patterns of prices is available since the seasons are always with us.

We decided to use the same basket of commodities for each period and site to increase transparency and comparability in the analysis, using 1994 as a base year to determine the basket of commodities included.[8] As in Ravallion and Bidani (1994), we constructed a typical diet for the poorest half of the sample in nominal consumption using the 1994 data and calculated its calorie contribution. We then scaled this measure to reach 2300 Kcal per day.

We used the approach described in Ravallion and Bidani (1994) to estimate the required non-food share by estimating an Engel curve and then determined the food share of the representative household whose total consumption is exactly equal to the food poverty line. The value of the non-food share at the poverty line can then be interpreted as representing the absolute minimum basic needs in terms of non-food items, for which households should be compensated, on top of the minimum food requirement. The resulting food share at the poverty line is 83 per cent on average. Note that this share is very high, so that the non-food share to be added to the food poverty line is actually quite low. The consequence is that this implies that the total consumption poverty lines calculated in this way are relatively low (less than 10 dollars per month per adult).

A few remarks on this 'low' poverty line are in order. Although the approach aims to establish an 'absolute' poverty line by measuring the actual cost of basic needs, its application does not necessarily result in a poverty line that could be directly used for comparisons across countries. We use data from the survey itself to decide the relevant minimum food bundle to establish the poverty line. In doing so, we limit it to calorie intake. Of course, calorie intake is only a limited part of a healthy diet; if a large part of the country is then to perforce forgo other more expensive nutrients to obtain a calorie-intensive diet, then the resulting diet to reach 2300 Kcal is biased against the inclusion of other nutrients. If other nutrients were included in the construction of the diet, then we would probably have reached a much more expensive food diet. For example, the only protein intake included is from pulses and milk; no meat or fish is included, since the poorer half of the sample simply do not consume it. Since food shares decline with total expenditure, non-food shares near these new food poverty lines with more nutrients would also be higher, resulting in an even higher total poverty line. An important consequence is that the poverty measures calculated in this way can hardly be used for cross-country comparisons; for such comparisons, 1-dollar-a-day or similar approaches may be more appropriate.

The poverty line used for each period uses the same basket throughout, but valued at the prices for the survey period. The poverty line can therefore also be thought of as a price deflator allowing comparisons across villages and over time. A potential problem is that in 1989 and 1994 we are forced to use different prices through lack of a specific price survey in the survey area during 1989, while during the three rounds since 1994, a site-specific price survey was collected. In order to handle this problem, we use regional price data from the CSA (Central Statistical Authority) when analysing the comparison between 1989 and 1995 in the smaller sample. For the comparison in the full sample between 1994 and 1995, we use the price data locally collected during the survey period. In Table 8.1 and 8.2, we give the average of the poverty lines used both for the longer and the shorter panel. We also express them as an index to compare it with other data sources on price changes.

In Table 8.1, columns (1) and (2) provide comparisons of the poverty line using the ERHS price survey, compared to the regional data from the CSA. The 1994a poverty line is 11 per cent higher when using the ERHS data. Since, for the 1989 poverty line, we use the CSA data, we may overestimate

Table 8.1   Poverty lines and implied inflation rates, 1989–95, panel sites only

Year	Poverty line ERHS (1)	Poverty line CSA (2)	Price index ERHS (3)	Price index CSA (4)	Price index CPI (5)	Price index Food CPI (6)
1989		22.3	(100)*	100	100	100
1994a	49.2	44.2	221	198	175	185
1994b	48.3		216		184	197
1995	50.8	48.0	228	215	180	193

Notes: * Using CSA 1989 = 100 as base.
Poverty lines for ERHS and CSA data are population weighted averages within the sample.
Sources: ERHS = Price survey of the Ethiopian Rural Household Survey; CSA = Regional price data based on Central Statistical Authority price data collection; CPI = Official Consumer Price Index based on urban price data; Food CPI = Food Consumer Price Index.

Table 8.2   Poverty lines and implied inflation rates, 1994–5, all sites

Year	Poverty line ERHS (1)	Poverty line CSA (2)	Price index ERHS (3)	Price index CSA (4)	Price index CPI (5)	Price index Food CPI (6)
1994a	44.5	44.4	100	100	100	100
1994b	47.0		106		105	106
1995	50.0	47.6	113	107	103	104

Sources: See Table 8.1.

the increase in the cost of living between 1989 and 1994 if we were to use the ERHS data for the latter period. Note that this difference is perfectly plausible, given the different markets in which prices were collected. The CSA data include many rural market towns, while our sample specifically uses the local market, closest to the village, which in some cases is quite remote.

The differences between these two data sources become relatively small, however, when comparing the results with the situation using the CPI (official Consumer Price Index) data. Irrespective of whether we use the overall or the food CPI, both the ERHS and to a lesser extent the CSA price data suggest much larger price increases between 1989 and 1994 than the official CPI. This points to the dangers if no careful choices are made with respect to price data: if we were to make poverty comparisons simply using the CPI as the appropriate adjustment of the cost of living over time, then we are likely to underestimate the cost of basic needs –, i.e. underestimate the level of poverty in our sample in 1994, in comparison to 1989. Part of the reason is likely to be the fact that the CPI is based on urban data only. Other methods to construct a poverty line over time, based on Greer and Thorbecke (1986), illustrate the problems associated with the CPI as well; details can be found in Dercon and Krishnan (1998).

Table 8.2 highlights another potential problem. Using the ERHS price survey, we observe much larger price increases between 1994 and 1995 than those implied by the CPI during exactly the same period: the ERHS data suggests a 13 per cent increase, while the CPI suggest only a 3 per cent rise. The CSA regional prices increased less than the ERHS, but still more than the CPI. Again, this illustrates the problems with using the CPI within the rural sample as a means of adjusting the poverty line over time.

Poverty levels and changes

Having constructed poverty lines and consumption measures, we can now analyse levels and changes in poverty. First, we focus on the panel households for the trends between 1989 and 1994. Recall that for four villages, we have data on total consumption for both 1989 and 1994. For the six villages (and 361 households) surveyed, we have data only on food consumption in 1989 for comparison with 1994. We construct food poverty levels using the full sample.

The poverty measures reported are from the FGT-family of poverty indexes (Foster, Greer and Thorbecke 1984). Let y_i denote consumption per adult equivalent which is ordered for all households from low to high, and z the poverty line and if there are q households with consumption per adult below the poverty line z, then the P_α family of poverty indexes can be defined as:

$$P_\alpha = \frac{1}{n} \sum_{i=1}^{q} \left(\frac{z - y_i}{z} \right)^\alpha \qquad (8.1)$$

for different values of α: if $\alpha=0$, this is the head count index, $\alpha=1$ is the poverty gap and $\alpha=2$ is the severity of poverty index. Since poverty measures are calculated using sample data, it is important to treat them as statistics.[9]

We report poverty levels for households, not at the level of the individual. Often poverty is reported by individuals by using the household sizes to convert the household level observations in apparent individual-level data. We do not follow this practice, because it artificially makes it appear that the sample size is much larger than actually is the case. This is important when calculating standard errors of the poverty measures: the larger the sample size, the lower the error and the levels and differences will more often be significantly different from zero. In principle, we could correct for this problem by calculating the corrections for clustering (Deaton 1997), but this is beyond the scope of this chapter.

Table 8.3 shows the results regarding food poverty declines between 1989 and 1995. These are based on consumption definitions that limit the items included to exactly those asked in both rounds and the prices used for valuing consumption and the poverty line are from the CSA. Furthermore, since we observe very high seasonality in the data (see below), it is worthwhile constructing a more careful comparison in poverty between 1989 and 1995. Given that the exact dates of data collection differ between 1989 and the first round of 1994 or 1995 data in some areas, we constructed a comparison, taking the closest month of data collection in the 1994–5 rounds to make the relevant comparison with the 1989 poverty levels. Consequently, only one of the rounds from the three rounds collected in 1994–5 is being used.

The observed decline between 1989 and 1995 is substantial: about a quarter lower for the headcount, more than a third lower in terms of the poverty gap measure and 45 per cent lower in terms of the severity of poverty index. In short, overall we find important decline in poverty in this period. Stochastic dominance tests were conducted to check the robustness of this result (Atkinson 1987). We find that, irrespective of the poverty line, a large decline in poverty can indeed be observed in this period. This decline however, hides, a diverging experience in the different communities surveyed in both years.

Table 8.3   Changes in food poverty, 1989–95, controlling for seasonality ($n=351$)

	1989	1994–5	
P_0	61.3	45.9	(-4.14)
P_1	29.2	18.4	(-5.17)
P_2	17.4	9.9	(-4.88)

Notes: 1. Debre Berhan and Dinki = 1994a; Garagodo and Domaa = 1995; Korodegaga and Adele Keke = 1994b.
2. *t*-test for difference in poverty measure in brackets.

Table 8.4 gives the resulting food poverty levels for each of the villages. In two villages we observe increases in food poverty, while in the others we observe substantive decreases in poverty. The increases in Dinki are not significant, but those in Garagodo are, for the poverty gap and the intensity of poverty. In the other villages, the decreases are generally significant. To conclude, overall we find an important poverty decline, but the experience is different for different villages, with some communities facing increased poverty.

Thus far, we have concentrated only on the households in the sample for which data exist in 1989. The ERHS household survey for 1994–5 has more extensive coverage and data were collected three times over the year. The data in 1995 were collected in more or less the same month as in the first round of 1994 (1994a). Therefore, they provide a test whether a year later, any change has occurred in the sample. The second round of 1994 (1994b) provides an interesting test on whether the exact timing of data collection matters for these welfare comparisons over time. In other words, seasonal effects can be captured. Table 8.5 presents the results for the P_α measures. In brackets, we give the t-values of the test in the difference in the estimated poverty measure with the equivalent measure in 1994a.

In terms of the full sample, there is a large and significant decrease in poverty between the first and second round of the 1994 survey: poverty decreased by a fifth in terms of the headcount and with even larger declines in the higher-order measures. The results for 1995 illustrate, however, that this is most likely to be a strong seasonal effect. Although there are differences between many areas in the exact timing of harvests, in the majority of the areas, the second round is the beginning of the harvest in most cereal areas, when food is relatively plentiful. The first (1994a) and the third round (1995) were conducted several months past the main harvest in most of these sites. Overall, we cannot detect a significant change between 1994a and 1995: aggregate poverty appears not to have been affected by the reforms initiated 1994, at least in the short run. Using stochastic dominance tests, we could confirm this result for a wide range of poverty lines. Poverty levels in 1994a and 1995 cannot be distinguished, but there is a large decline between 1994a and 1995.

As is to be expected, this obscures some differences between areas. In all areas, the decline in poverty between 1994a and 1994b is observed, and virtually in all cases it is significant. Only in the Southern cereal villages do we observe a significant decline in poverty between 1994a and 1995, while in the Southern non-cereal villages we observe a significant increase. A tentative explanation for the latter effect is that this is largely due to an increase in enset pests destroying some crops in one village and a large decline in the possibility of seasonal migration owing to ethnic conflict in another village, which affected slack-season earnings substantially in the area.

Table 8.4 Food poverty levels, 1989–94, panel villages

Survey	Dinki		Debre Berhan		Adele Keke		Korodegaga		Garagodo		Domaa	
P_0 89	41.5		33.9		41.9		74.7		80.0		84.9	
P_0 94	45.3	(0.39)	16.1	(2.33)	4.7	(3.04)	68.4	(0.97)	90.9	(1.64)	62.3	(2.74)
P_1 89	14.4		11.8		10.4		39.7		45.9		44.2	
P_1 94	15.3	(0.21)	2.4	(3.52)	4.3	(1.75)	25.8	(3.44)	58.3	(2.36)	30.5	(2.46)
P_2 89	6.6		5.4		4.7		24.8		30.2		26.5	
P_2 94	6.6	(0.03)	0.5	(3.33)	1.9	(1.30)	13.1	(3.90)	40.0	(2.12)	19.1	(1.63)
Obs.	53		43		62		95		55		53	

Notes: 94 = poverty measure using poverty line valued at CSA regional price survey and consumption per adult using definition of consumption, limited to items explicitly included in 1989 survey.

In brackets, *t*-test of difference of estimate with the estimates in 1989.

Table 8.5 Poverty levels, 1994–5, ERHS panel households

Survey	Northern cereal		Central cereal		Southern cereal		Southern non-cereal		All areas	
P_0 1994a	32.5		23.1		32.2		46.9		34.1	
P_0 1994b	23.1	(−2.53)	14.3	(−3.26)	26.7	(−1.46)	41.8	(−1.52)	26.9	(−4.14)
P_0 1995	28.7	(−1.00)	23.3	(0.08)	28.8	(−0.90)	55.9	(2.62)	35.4	(0.71)
P_1 1994a	11.6		6.8		13.6		19.6		13.0	
P_1 1994b	6.1	(−3.63)	4.0	(−2.79)	7.6	(−3.60)	13.9	(−3.39)	8.2	(−6.40)
P_1 1995	11.2	(−0.20)	6.7	(−0.13)	8.9	(−2.73)	24.0	(2.36)	13.3	(0.28)
P_2 1994a	5.9		2.9		7.3		11.1		6.9	
P_2 1994b	2.4	(−3.76)	1.9	(−1.69)	3.2	(−3.95)	6.7	(−3.84)	3.7	(−6.48)
P_2 1995	6.0	(0.06)	2.8	(−0.09)	4.0	(−3.24)	13.1	(1.56)	6.8	(−0.15)
n	286		407		292		426		1411	

Notes: Northern cereal are villages located in the Northern Highlands grain – plough complex; Central cereal are villages located in the Central Highlands grain – plough complex; Southern cereal are the villages in the grain – plough areas of Arsi/Bale or with sorghum plough/hoe; the Southern non-cereal are the enset villages with or without coffee/cereals.

In brackets, the *t*-values testing the difference in the estimate of the poverty measure in the particular period with the estimate in 1994a.

Finally, the pattern of results remains unchanged when considering different sources for the price data. Recall that our analysis was confronted by problems in finding consistent price data for all the different periods. However, it can be shown that the observed seasonal change in 1994 and the overall decline between 1989 and 1995 is sufficiently large to discount this explanation for the observed changes (for details, see Dercon and Krishnan 1998).

Decomposing poverty changes

The Foster–Greer–Thorbecke poverty measures used in the analysis are additively decomposable – i.e. they can be written as a weighted average of poverty measures for sub-groups, the weights being proportional to the population shares (Foster, Greer and Thorbecke 1984). Formally, for m different sub-groups, the poverty measures can be written as:

$$P_\alpha = \sum_{i=1}^{m} w_i P_\alpha^i \tag{8.2}$$

in which w_i is the population share of sub-group i and P_α^i is the poverty measure for the sub-group. This property carries over to changes in poverty as well. Let s and t be two periods in poverty measures are calculated and let (for simplicity) w_i be constant over time. Consequently, it follows from (8.2) that:

$$P_\alpha^t - P_\alpha^s = \sum_{i=1}^{m} w_i(P_\alpha^{ti} + (-P_\alpha^{si})) \tag{8.3}$$

It is then also possible to define θ_α^i, the contribution of each group to the change in poverty between t and s, as:

$$\theta_\alpha^i = w_i \frac{P_\alpha^{ti} - P_\alpha^{si}}{P_\alpha^t - P_\alpha^s} \tag{8.4}$$

If θ_α^i is larger (smaller) than w_i, then the sub-group i has experienced proportionately larger (smaller) changes in poverty than the total population. As a first step in the analysis of the dynamics of poverty, this is a useful statistic. Obviously, it is just a start and the interpretation suffers from all the problems static poverty profiles suffer from (Ravallion 1996). The results must be regarded as descriptive statistics.

Applying this decomposition to the data from Ethiopia, we focus on a few characteristics of the endowments of the households in the sample, which can be considered fixed in the short period under consideration. First, we look at some human capital variables in the broad sense: education (whether the head has completed primary school) and some labour supply characteristics of the head of the household (the sex and the age of the head). Next, we consider some physical assets: land owned in hectares and whether the household owns any oxen (or bulls). The former can be treated as exogenous to the household: land is not privately owned and is allocated by the peasant association to the household. Oxen are crucial in the main farming system for ploughing and cattle in general are an important source of wealth for accumulation. Of course, since markets exist, oxen ownership may well change over time, although the accumulation is generally slow. For the poverty profile below, we use the ownership of oxen in 1994a.[10] Finally, we look at some infrastructure and location variables. As discussed already, there are some critical differences in the experience of certain villages and village-level variables may well account for this. We grouped villages according to the distance to nearest all-weather road and to the distance to the nearest town.

We look at the contribution of different groups to changes over three periods: first, the change between 1989 and 1994–5 for the core panel villages, secondly, the change within 1994 allowing for some assessment of the sensitivity to seasonal variation. We do not look into the change between 1994 and 1995, since it is insignificant. For the first, we use the food poverty measures and use food poverty in 1994–5 in the equivalent period of the data collection in 1989. We group the households in two (using the median value for continuous variables[11]). We provide a *t*-test of the changes in poverty for each sub-group and the contribution of each sub-group to the total poverty change.

Tables 8.6(a)–8.6(g) give the results of the decompositions for the changes between 1989 and 1994–5 for the panel villages. Recall that poverty declined by about 15.4 percentage points in this period (Table 8.3). Human capital variables matter in accounting for the changes in this period. Although very few heads of household are educated, they contributed proportionately more to the poverty decline. Similarly, households with younger heads experienced a larger decline in poverty than those with an older head of the household; the decline for the latter is not significant even for the head-count index. The sex of the household also matters: female-headed households experienced no significant decline in this period. Oxen and land ownership is also important: those owning oxen and those with relatively large land holdings contributed proportionately more to the decline in poverty. Land holdings particularly affect the poverty gap and the severity of poverty measure. The decline in poverty for those not owning oxen is not significantly different from zero at the 5 per cent level for all measures. Finally, distance to roads and to towns also matters a lot. At least with respect to the headcount index, those close to all-weather roads contributed

Table 8.6 Decomposing changes in food poverty, by sub-groups, 1989 to 1994–5 (n = 351)

(a) Education

	Household head did not complete primary school (97%)					Household head completed primary school (3%)				
	Poverty 89	Poverty 94	Change	t-test	Contrib. to change (%)	Poverty 89	Poverty 94	Change	t-test	Contrib. to change (%)
P_0	0,60	0,47	−0,14	−3,65**	87	0,83	0,25	−0,58	−3,54**	13
P_1	0,29	0,19	−0,10	−4,74**	90	0,42	0,11	−0,30	−3,38**	10
P_2	0,17	0,10	−0,07	−4,59**	93	0,22	0,06	−0,15	−2,61**	7

(b) Age of the household head

	Head of the household is at least 45 years (45%)					Head of the household is below 45 years (55%)				
	Poverty 89	Poverty 94	Change	t-test	Contrib. to change (%)	Poverty 89	Poverty 94	Change	t-test	Contrib. to change (%)
P_0	0,59	0,50	−0,09	−1,84	33	0,64	0,41	−0,23	−4,18**	67
P_1	0,27	0,20	−0,08	−2,67**	39	0,31	0,16	−0,15	−4,81**	61
P_2	0,16	0,11	−0,06	−2,70**	42	0,19	0,09	−0,10	−4,34**	58

(c) Sex of the head of the household

	Female-headed household (17%)					Male-headed household (83%)				
	Poverty 89	Poverty 94	Change	t-test	Contrib. to change (%)	Poverty 89	Poverty 94	Change	t-test	Contrib. to change (%)
P_0	0,57	0,48	−0,09	−0,93	9	0,62	0,45	−0,17	−4,12**	91
P_1	0,29	0,20	−0,10	−1,85	15	0,29	0,18	−0,11	−4,84**	85
P_2	0,18	0,11	−0,07	−1,79	15	0,17	0,10	−0,08	−4,55**	85

(d) Oxen ownership

	Household does not own oxen (33%)					Household owns at least one ox (67%)				
	Poverty 89	Poverty 94	Change	t-test	Contrib. to change (%)	Poverty 89	Poverty 94	Change	t-test	Contrib. to change (%)
P_0	0,65	0,55	−0,10	−1,62	22	0,59	0,42	−0,18	−3,93**	78
P_1	0,32	0,25	−0,08	−1,92	23	0,28	0,15	−0,12	−5,13**	77
P_2	0,20	0,14	−0,05	−1,82	24	0,16	0,08	−0,08	−4,89**	76

(e) Land ownership

	Large land holdings (50%) (above 0.45 ha)					Small land holdings (50%) (below 0.45-ha)				
	Poverty 89	Poverty 94	Change	t-test	Contrib. to change (%)	Poverty 89	Poverty 94	Change	t-test	Contrib. to change (%)
P_0	0,54	0,38	−0,17	−3,15**	54	0,68	0,54	−0,14	−2,76**	46
P_1	0,27	0,13	−0,14	−5,26**	66	0,32	0,24	−0,07	−2,38**	34
P_2	0,16	0,06	−0,10	−5,36**	68	0,19	0,14	−0,05	−2,04*	32

Table 8.6 (Continued)

(f) Distance to all-weather road

	At least 5 km from all-weather road (56%)					Less than 5 km from all-weather road (44%)				
	Poverty 89	Poverty 94	Change	t-test	Contrib. to change (%)	Poverty 89	Poverty 94	Change	t-test	Contrib. to change (%)
P_0	0,67	0,59	−0,08	−1,67	30	0,54	0,29	−0,25	−4,54**	70
P_1	0,34	0,25	−0,10	−3,35**	50	0,23	0,11	−0,12	−4,39**	50
P_2	0,21	0,13	−0,08	−3,61**	59	0,13	0,06	−0,07	−3,53**	41

(g) Distance to nearest town

	At least 10 km from town (47%)					Less than 10 km from town (53%)				
	Poverty 89	Poverty 94	Change	t-test	Contrib. to change (%)	Poverty 89	Poverty 94	Change	t-test	Contrib. to change (%)
P_0	0,52	0,58	0,06	1,11	−19	0,70	0,35	−0,34	−7,08**	119
P_1	0,23	0,25	0,02	0,50	−7	0,34	0,13	−0,22	−7,99**	107
P_2	0,14	0,14	0,00	0,13	−2	0,21	0,06	−0,14	−7,04**	102

Notes: ** Significant at the level 1 per cent; * Significant at the level 5 per cent.

proportionately more to the decline in poverty. Those households living more than 10 km outside towns experienced no significant change in poverty; consequently, the entire decline between 1989 and 1994–5 can be accounted for by those in villages in the vicinity of urban areas.

Turning to the larger sample, Table 8.6 showed that poverty declined substantially between the two rounds in 1994 (1994a and 1994b), but between 1994a and 1995, two rounds collected at roughly the same point in the seasonal cycle, poverty remained unchanged. The change within 1994 clearly reflects seasonal fluctuations. Table 8.7 shows which groups are more affected by these fluctuations. First, note that households with older, female or uneducated heads have higher poverty levels in both periods. However, the gap in poverty levels becomes smaller in 1994b. For example, those households whose heads have completed primary education constitute only one-tenth of the sample, but they did not experience any significant fluctu-ation – i.e. the entire decline in poverty is experienced by those households without educated heads. Female-headed households, while constituting about 22 per cent of the sample, contributed to about 40 per cent of the change in the poverty measures between 1994a and 1994b.

Higher asset ownership in terms of land and oxen, and distances to roads or towns, implies consistently lower poverty levels – but also accompanies larger fluctuations in consumption.[12] Living closer to all-weather roads or towns is also correlated with lower poverty in both periods, but linked to lower fluctuations. In particular, those living further away from towns contribute the lion's share of the total poverty decline in this period. This may suggest that access to infrastructure and markets allows households to better smooth consumption. These are clearly issues that need to be researched further.

Conclusions

This chapter investigates the problems of comparing poverty over time in a panel household survey collected between 1989 and 1995 in rural Ethiopia. We used Foster–Greer–Thorbecke measures of poverty and implemented significance tests for changes in poverty. We found that poverty declined substantially between 1989 and 1995, but remained largely unchanged between 1994 and 1995. We found substantial differences in poverty levels between the two rounds of data collection in 1994, suggesting substantial seasonal fluctuations.

These results were found to be robust to several possible problems, including small changes in questionnaire design, problems with price data, the choice of the poverty line and seasonality. The latter was shown to be potentially a serious problem in this type of analysis. As the results for 1994 showed, the exact timing of the data collection matters for the magnitudes of the poverty measures. This point is rarely considered when comparing poverty

Table 8.7 Decomposing changes in poverty, by sub-groups, 1994a–1994b ($n = 1411$)

(a) Education of the head of the household

	Household head did not complete primary school (91%)					Household head completed primary school (9%)				
	Poverty 94a	Poverty 94b	Change	t-test	Contrib. to change (%)	Poverty 94a	Poverty 94b	Change	t-test	Contrib. to change (%)
P_0	0,35	0,28	−0,08	−4,26**	99	0,20	0,20	−0,01	−0,16	1
P_1	0,14	0,08	−0,05	−6,62**	101	0,05	0,06	0,00	0,26	−1
P_2	0,07	0,04	−0,04	−6,68**	101	0,02	0,03	0,00	0,39	−1

(b) Age of the household head

	Head of the household is at least 45 years (52%)					Head of the household is below 45 years (48%)				
	Poverty 94a	Poverty 94b	Change	t-test	Contrib. to change (%)	Poverty 94a	Poverty 94b	Change	t-test	Contrib. to change (%)
P_0	0,39	0,31	−0,07	−2,91**	52	0,29	0,22	−0,07	−3,00**	48
P_1	0,15	0,09	−0,06	−5,11**	60	0,11	0,07	−0,04	−3,90**	40
P_2	0,08	0,04	−0,04	−5,20**	61	0,06	0,03	−0,03	−3,90**	39

(c) Sex of the head of the household

	Female-headed household (22%)					Male-headed household (78%)				
	Poverty 94a	*Poverty 94b*	*Change*	*t-test*	*Contrib. to change (%)*	*Poverty 94a*	*Poverty 94b*	*Change*	*t-test*	*Contrib. to change (%)*
P_0	0,40	0,28	−0,12	−3,17**	37	0,33	0,27	−0,06	−2,99**	63
P_1	0,17	0,08	−0,09	−4,93**	40	0,12	0,08	−0,04	−4,52**	60
P_2	0,10	0,04	−0,06	−4,84**	40	0,06	0,04	−0,02	−4,63**	60

(d) Oxen ownership

	Household does not own oxen (48%)					Household owns at least one ox (52%)				
	Poverty 94a	*Poverty 94b*	*Change*	*t-test*	*Contrib. to change (%)*	*Poverty 94a*	*Poverty 94b*	*Change*	*t-test*	*Contrib. to change (%)*
P_0	0,38	0,34	−0,04	−1,59	28	0,30	0,20	−0,10	−4,37**	72
P_1	0,15	0,11	−0,03	−2,87**	34	0,12	0,05	−0,06	−6,60**	66
P_2	0,08	0,05	−0,02	−3,08**	38	0,06	0,02	−0,04	−6,71**	62

(e) Land ownership

	Large land holdings (50%) (above 0.23 ha)					Small land holdings (50%) (below 0.23 ha)				
	Poverty 94a	*Poverty 94b*	*Change*	*t-test*	*Contrib. to change (%)*	*Poverty 94a*	*Poverty 94b*	*Change*	*t-test*	*Contrib. to change (%)*
P_0	0,28	0,16	−0,11	−5,22**	80	0,40	0,38	−0,03	−1,10	20
P_1	0,10	0,04	−0,06	−6,46**	58	0,16	0,12	−0,04	−3,34**	42
P_2	0,05	0,02	−0,03	−6,02**	50	0,09	0,06	−0,03	−3,90**	50

Table 8.7 (Continued)

(f) Distance to the nearest all-weather road

	At least 5 km from all-weather road (44%)					Less than 5 km from all-weather road (56%)				
	Poverty 94a	Poverty 94b	Change	t-test	Contrib. to change (%)	Poverty 94a	Poverty 94b	Change	t-test	Contrib. to change (%)
P_0	0,47	0,36	−0,11	−4,09**	69	0,24	0,20	−0,04	−1,87	31
P_1	0,20	0,11	−0,09	−6,61**	77	0,08	0,06	−0,02	−2,33**	23
P_2	0,11	0,05	−0,06	−6,78**	80	0,04	0,03	−0,01	−2,11*	20

(g) Distance to the nearest town

	At least 10 km from town (45%)					Less than 10 km from town (55%)				
	Poverty 94a	Poverty 94b	Change	t-test	Contrib. to change (%)	Poverty 94a	Poverty 94b	Change	t-test	Contrib. to change (%)
P_0	0,38	0,24	−0,14	−5,44**	88	0,31	0,29	−0,02	−0,67	12
P_1	0,15	0,08	−0,07	−6,17**	68	0,11	0,08	−0,03	−2,88**	32
P_2	0,08	0,04	−0,05	−5,76**	65	0,06	0,04	−0,02	−3,34**	35

Notes: ** Significant at the level of 1 per cent; * Significant at the level of 5 per cent.

over time in developing countries, especially since data collection usually takes many months to be completed, which implies that consumption changes are not readily comparable.

The overall decline between 1989 and 1995 hides important differences between villages and households. In some villages, poverty had in fact increased or remained largely unchanged. In the final section, we provide a simple decomposition of the findings across different groups. We found that those households with relatively better human capital or labour supply characteristics (better education, male-headed households and relatively young heads of households) experienced levels of poverty in each period. They also had larger poverty declines between 1989 and 1995 and lower seasonal fluctuations in poverty. Households with better physical capital endowments, in terms of land and oxen had lower poverty levels and saw larger poverty declines. They seem to face larger poverty fluctuations across seasons. Finally, those with good access to road infrastructure and those close to towns also had lower poverty levels throughout. They experienced a larger poverty decline between 1989 and 1995 and experienced lower within-year fluctuations.

These decomposition results are only the first step in the analysis of the dynamics of poverty. Nevertheless, the results appear to suggest that not only did physical, human and infrastructural capital matter in explaining levels of poverty, but that poverty declines during a period of reforms and the return to peace appear to be influenced by the initial levels of these sources of capital, so that better-endowed households were better placed to benefit much more from the changed circumstances. Similarly, access to infrastructure and proximity to towns, as well as better human capital circumstances, implied lower fluctuations in seasonal poverty levels, presumably linked to more opportunities for alternative income generation and lower food price fluctuations. Clearly, these issues need to be investigated further.

Dercon (2001) presents such analysis for the changes in poverty between 1989 and 1995. A detailed econometric analysis of the factors determining the changes of income and poverty and further decompositions reveal the factors that appear to have caused the changes. It is found that the observed changes are genuine and not caused, for example, by better weather only. Much of the decline in poverty can be explained by improved agricultural terms of trade for many of the villages, as well as increased return from off-farm activities in the post-reform period. But the role of initial endowments and infrastructure is shown to be crucial as well: the entire decline in poverty can be linked to households with relatively good-sized and quality land, and sufficient adult labour, as well as living in relative proximity to town and good roads. In fact, without these characteristics, households could not take advantage of the better opportunities offered, and remained trapped in deep poverty. Further analysis of more recent data from the panel villages appears to confirm the earlier patterns (Dercon 2000).

Notes

1. Demery and Squire (1996) review six countries in which some attempt has been made to compare welfare over time.
2. The data for 1989 were collected by the International Food Policy Research Institute (IFPRI). The data for 1994 and subsequent rounds were collected by the Economics Department, Addis Ababa University and the Centre for the Study of African Economies, Oxford. Data collection was financed by Sida (Sweden), the Economic and Social Research Council (ESRC) (UK) and the Fund for Scientific Research (Belgium).
3. Obviously, this is not without its critics, although there are good reasons to use it in practice (Anand and Harris 1994; Ravallion 1994; Hentschel and Lanjouw 1996).
4. The survey collected also extensive information on health and anthropometric outcomes of all persons in the sample. In the same year, the Central Statistical Office (CSO) collected a data set as part of the Welfare Monitoring System. Many of the average outcome variables, in terms of health and nutriton were very similar to the results in the ERHS, suggesting that the resulting sample may well be broadly representative of the general situation in rural Ethiopia. See Collier, Dercon and Mackinnon (1997).
5. Grosh and Jeancard (1994) and Lanjouw and Lanjouw (1997) discuss some of the consequences if this were to happen. Appleton (1996) discusses the consequences for poverty comparisons in Uganda.
6. These problems are common in this type of survey. See Deaton (1997) and Capéau and Dercon (1998) for a discussion and some alternative solutions.
7. If the problem is mainly intertemporal variability, a possible solution is to make the minimum basket of commodities dependent on the time period – effectively adjusting over time the quantities needed to obtain the minimum level of consumption. If the variability is mainly spatial then one may argue in favour in taking location-specific diets. However, this raises again the problem of comparability.
8. The poverty line then effectively becomes a cost-of-living index with budget weights taken from the poorer half of the sampled households.
9. Kakwani (1993) provided standard errors and showed the conditions under which differences between poverty measures are asymptotically normally distributed.
10. The analysis of the dynamics of oxen ownership in relation to poverty is beyond the scope of this chapter.
11. For land, we considered both a grouping according to median land per village and according to median land per adult in the entire sample. If there are large differences in fertility, climate and farming systems across villages in the sample, then the results may have been sensitive to the alternative groupings. However, the results were very similar, so we report only the results relative to the median of land per adult in the entire sample.
12. This appears partly linked to the fact that households with smaller land holdings are often specialising more in permanent foodcrops such as enset, which provide a more stable return over the season, which may help them to keep relatively smooth consumption.

Bibliography

Anand, S. and C.J. Harris (1994), 'Choosing a welfare indicator', *American Economic Review Papers and Proceedings*, Vol. 84(2), pp. 226–31.

Appleton, S. (1996), 'Problems of measuring changes in poverty over time: the case of Uganda 1989–1992', *Institute of Development Studies Bulletin*, Vol. 27(1), pp. 43–55.

Atkinson, A.B. (1987), 'On the measurement of poverty', *Econometrica*, Vol. 55(4), pp. 749–64.

Capéau, B. and S. Dercon (1998), 'Prices, local measurement units and subsistence consumption in rural surveys: an econometric approach and an application to Ethiopia', Oxford: Centre for the Study of African Economies, mimeo.

Collier, P., S. Dercon and J. Mackinnon (1997), *Social Sector Review – PER II, Ministry of Finance*, Addis Ababa: Government of Ethiopia.

Deaton, A. (1997), *The Analysis of Household Surveys: A Microeconometric Approach to Development Policy*, Washington, DC and Baltimore: The World Bank and Johns Hopkins University Press.

Demery, L. and L. Squire (1996), 'Macroeconomic adjustment and the poverty in Africa: an emerging picture', *The World Bank Research Observer*, Vol. 11(1), pp. 39–59.

Dercon, S. (1995), 'On market integration and liberalisation: method and application to Ethiopia', *Journal of Development Studies*, Vol. 32(1), pp. 112–43.

Dercon, S. (2000), 'Changes in poverty and social indicators in the 1990s', mimeo, http://www.economics.ox.ac.uk/members/stefan.dercon/research.htm.

Dercon, S. (2001), 'The impact of economic reform on households in rural Ethiopia 1989–1995', unpublished paper.

Dercon, S. and P. Krishnan (1996), 'A consumption-based measure of poverty in Ethiopia 1989–1994', in M. Taddesse and B. Kebede, *Poverty and Economic Reform in Ethiopia*, Proceedings of the Annual Conference of the Ethiopian Economic Association, Addis Ababa.

Dercon, S. and P. Krishnan (1998), 'Changes in poverty in rural Ethiopia 1989–1995: measurement, robustness tests and decomposition', Centre for the Study of African Economies, Working Paper Series, April.

Dercon, S. and P. Krishnan (2000a), 'In sickness and in health: risk-sharing within households in rural Ethiopia', *Journal of Political Economy*, Vol. 108(4), pp. 688–727.

Dercon, S. and P. Krishnan (2000b), 'Vulnerability, seasonality and poverty in Ethiopia', *Journal of Development Studies*, Vol. 36(6).

Foster, J., J. Greer and E. Thorbecke (1984), 'A class of decomposable poverty measures', *Econometrica*, Vol. 52, pp. 761–6.

Greer, J. and E. Thorbecke (1986), 'A methodology for measuring food poverty applied to Kenya', *Journal of Development Economics*, Vol. 4, pp. 59–74.

Grootaert, C. and R. Kanbur (1995), 'The lucky few amidst economic decline: distributional change in Côte D'Ivoire as seen through panel data sets, 1985–88', *Journal of Development Studies*, Vol. 31(4).

Grosh, M. and H.-P. Jeancard (1994), 'The sensitivity of consumption aggregates to questionnaire formulation: some preliminary evidence form the Jamaican and Ghanaian LSMS surveys', Poverty Research Department, World Bank, Mimeo.

Hentschel, J. and P. Lanjouw (1996), 'Constructing an indicator of consumption for the analysis of *poverty*: principles and illustrations with reference to Ecuador', *Living Standards Measurement Survey Working Paper*, 124, Washington, DC: World Bank.

Kakwani, N. (1986), 'Measuring poverty: definitions and significance tests with application to Côte d'Ivoire', in M. Lipton and J. van der Gaag, *Including the Poor*, Baltimore : Johns Hopkins University Press, pp. 43–66.

Kakwani, N., (1993), 'Statistical Inference in the Measurement of Poverty', *Reveiew of Economics and Statistics*, Vol. LXXV, pp. 632–9.

Lanjouw, J.O. and P. Lanjouw (1997), 'Poverty comparisons with non-compatible data: theory and illustrations', Washington, DC: World Bank, mimeo.

Lipton, M. and M. Ravallion (1995), 'Poverty and policy', Chapter 41 in J. Behrman and T.N. Srinivasan, *Handbook of Development Economics*, Vol. IIIA, New York: Elsevier Science, pp. 2551–657.

Ravallion, M. (1994), *Poverty Comparisons*, Chur. Harwood Academic Publishers.

Ravallion, M. (1996), 'How well can method substitute for data? Five experiments in poverty analysis', *The World Bank Research Observer*, Vol. 11(2), pp. 199–217.

Ravallion, M. and B. Bidani (1994), 'How robust is a poverty profile?', *The World Bank Economic Review*, Vol. 8(1), pp. 75–102.

Webb, P., J. von Braun and Y. Yohannes (1992), 'Famine in Ethiopia: policy implications of coping with failure at national and household levels', *Research Report*, 92, Washington, DC: International Food Policy Research Institute.

Part IV

Social Protection, Governance and Poverty Targets

9
Mobilising the Poor Effectively: Rights and Institutions

*Anuradha Joshi and Mick Moore**

Introduction

There is a substantial disjuncture between what international aid and development agencies say they want to do, and what they actually do. Most have for many years accepted the principle that effective poverty alleviation should have significant *collective* and *mobilising* dimensions: they talk in terms of 'empowerment', 'participation', and of framing programmes that are responsive to the demands of poor communities. In practice, they do little to advance these goals. Indeed, in some respects they have regressed: in recent years, large amounts of money have gone to *new* programmes that may undermine the scope for collective action on the part of the poor – while proclaiming that to be the goal. Aid and development agencies are probably forced into hypocrisy mainly because of the structural contradictions they face, notably the pressures to continue to disburse money and to find ways of legitimating their activities that appeal to very diverse constituencies. But genuine inability to see through the fog of fashionable jargon and to think clearly about the political and institutional issues may be part of the problem. The purpose of this chapter is to develop a set of concepts and a language that help us better to understand how 'external agencies' could contribute to the (collective) empowerment of poor people through the ways in which they design, organise and implement anti-poverty programmes in poor countries.

This definition of the problem raises several questions about meanings of the terms we use. For present purposes, some of them can be left fairly open. 'External agencies' refers essentially to government and to other organisations,

* We are grateful to participants in the DSA conference for helpful observations on an earlier draft; to Peter Houtzager and Judith Tendler for detailed comments; and to the Department for International Development for support to the IDS Poverty Research Programme, within which the ideas here were developed.

mainly NGOs, that are involved in development activities. 'Anti-poverty programmes' covers any programmes that are directed mainly or solely at poor people, whether or not 'poverty' is formally part of their brief. Primary education in rural areas of most poor countries would therefore be included. 'Mobilisation', that we use as a synonym for collective empowerment, connotes both action (i.e. people being involved in doing things) and organisation. Forms of mobilisation vary widely.

How might 'friends of the poor' in government or other external agencies help increase the effectiveness of anti-poverty programmes by designing organising, or implementing them so as to stimulate the mobilisation of the poor? They cannot provide, *qua* bureaucrats, the full range of resources that contribute to creating mobilising structures. In particular, they are poorly placed to provide ideological resources: the ideas and values around which collective action can be built. They are however potentially better placed to provide certain kinds of *organisational resources* and *political opportunities*.[1] In principle, one can distinguish four different mechanisms (or strategies) that external agencies can use to encourage the mobilisation of the poor. Two or more may be combined in practice, but they are best treated separately for purposes of exposition.

Provocation

This may in reality be the most widespread mechanism through which governments in particular succeed in mobilising the poor: angering them by treating them badly in some way – failing to truck in emergency drinking water supplies during drought; forcibly displacing people to build highways, dams or shopping malls; compulsorily acquiring foodgrains from producers at low prices, etc. Provocation is potentially a powerful instrument, but one that rarely can be wielded with finesse or precision – and which anyway involves first hurting the poor. It does not merit further discussion.

Conscientisation

This is the practice of despatching 'social mobilisers' to mobilise the poor by encouraging them to examine their situation (usually collectively) and, hopefully, to decide collectively to do something to change it. This technique is most commonly adopted by non-state organisations – political parties, religious organisations, and other NGOs of various kinds. Agencies that employ social mobilisers to work with the poor in relation to their own programmes – and there are plenty of such cases in the development field, including government agencies – are vulnerable to two kinds of moral hazard. First, they have every incentive to discourage mobilisation once it becomes uncomfortable for them, and thus to keep it closely under control. Second, as we illustrate in the next section, the agencies and their field staff easily slip into the role of salespersons, trying to 'market' to their clients (the poor) the products that the agency has available, even if they are inappropriate.

Casual evidence and logic suggest that, where both the conscientisation process and programme management are in the same hands, authentic mobilisation is unlikely. Conscientisation is far more likely to be effective if employed by one external agency to mobilise the poor in relation to the activities of other agencies or parties.

Organisational preference

Government agencies, in particular, are well placed to mobilise the poor by giving preferential treatment to particular grass-roots organisations that (claim to) represent the poor. This preference can have two main components, that tend to go together: recognition and licensing of certain categories of organisations (and not others); and channelling resources to the poor through those organisations, to encourage the poor to become involved. These kinds of arrangements are generally labelled 'corporatist'. But corporatism has a bad reputation. Whose interests might be served? Are we not just opening the door to cooptation: institutional arrangements through which the state mobilises and organises socio-economic groups in its own interests, and in ways that closely circumscribe the autonomy of the organisations and their capacity genuinely to represent societal interests? The ambiguities in the corporatist relationship are captured in Philip Selznik's description of participation as 'a technique for turning an unorganized citizenry into a reliable instrument for the achievement of administrative goals'. Cooptation is a potential threat whenever a grass-roots organisation enters into any relationship with a powerful external agency;[2] this is especially true within corporatist structures. But cooptation and demobilisation of the grass-roots organisation is not the only potential 'unbalanced' outcome of corporatism. There is an equally well established tradition of political analysis that focuses on the opposite process: the 'capture' of state agencies by the societal interests that they are attempting to organise. True the poor have limited resources through which to effect such capture. But they do have some room to manoeuvre. Grass-roots organisations may be exploited by external agencies, but at the same time exploit those relationships for their own purposes. In particular, they can enjoy leverage and bargaining power if the external agencies (a) are disunited, with elements seeking support and allies from elsewhere, (b) focus their attention and energies elsewhere, leaving grass-roots organisations with considerable local autonomy by default;[3] or (c) are dependent in some way on a level of performance from grass-roots organisations that can be achieved only through permitting them autonomy and initiative. Even explicitly corporatist systems can generate organisations that bring to the poor both resources and some degree of – often heavily contested – organisational autonomy. For grass-roots political entrepreneurs have incentives to move into these organisations and to try to expand their scope and autonomy. For example, the corporatist rural workers' unions that were established in rural Brazil by military regimes in the 1960s provided both (a) 'cover' behind which local politicians, trades unionists and social activists could operate, and (b) legitimacy for parallel organising activities conducted by the Catholic Church. They helped to lay the basis for the rich network of social movements for the rural poor that are found in present-day Brazil (Houtzager 1998). The very existence of privileged corporatist unions encouraged opposition trades unionists to enter them and compete for power. In some cases this has generated levels of union activism and responsiveness to members well in excess of the standard expectations of corporatist arrangements (Pinhanez 1997). Similarly, the corporatism practised by Mexico's once dominant ruling party (the PRI) has provided the means for the development of partly autonomous local movements of the poor by opening up competition for control of public resources at local level. For example, locally organised Food Councils were given control of food stores, supplies of subsidised basic foods and means of transport. Not all Food Councils were dominated by the local elites or by the local representatives of the PRI. There was continual struggle, that partly reflected divisions within the PRI itself. Jonathan Fox (1994) views the struggles around these programmes as an important part of the story of the gradual widening of the scope for autonomous associational activity in Mexico.

Depending very much on the political context, corporatist arrangements for giving organisational preference can encourage the poor to organise on their own behalf. We should not dismiss them as irrelevant to our concerns. They are however less than ideal. There are three significant characteristic problems:

- Any degree of local organisational autonomy that is achieved is constantly under threat, and has continually to be reasserted
- Insofar as the organisations receive and redistribute public money, they may become a major charge on the government budget, with much of the benefit going to the non-poor (e.g. the Mexican case above)
- Granting permanent organisational preference may result in local organisational monopoly, and then in lack of accountability and misuse of resources and power; this was often the case, for example, with the corporatist rural workers' unions in Brazil, with their guaranteed income from the state and monopoly control over pension funds (Houtzager 1998).

Corporatist sponsorship of poor people's organisations is potentially a useful means through which 'friends of the poor' within state agencies can help empower the poor. But there are further options.

Creating an enabling institutional environment

The *conscientisation* and *organisational preference* strategies are activist: they involve external agencies and agencies directly doing things on behalf of the poor – and that activism itself leads to moral hazard. The main argument of this chapter is that there are considerable opportunities to stimulate the effective, autonomous organisation of the poor by adopting a more *parametric* strategy: establishing and maintaining a framework that would encourage poor people themselves to take a more active role. This is now orthodoxy in the context of government policy toward the private sector: do less directly, and concentrate more on creating an enabling environment. We suggest that the same argument applies to public action and the political organisation of the poor. The environment in which poor people and external organisations interact is frequently inimical to collective action by the poor. It is characterised by so much uncertainty, arbitrariness and inequality that investment in collective action is not worthwhile. External agencies should focus more on creating incentives to collective action, above all by removing the obstacles that they themselves create. Four dimensions of the performance or behaviour of external agencies are of special interest to us:

- *Tolerance*: We take it as given that collective action on the part of the poor is more likely where the political environment is not hostile and punitive; the fact that no more is said on this reflects our belief that the point is obvious, not that it is unimportant.
- *Credibility*: This is essentially a behavioural concept: the extent to which, in their relations with the poor, public officials can be relied on to behave like good partners in an enterprise – i.e. to do their job correctly, and to be reliable.
- *Predictability*: This refers to the form of external programmes: the extent to which they are stable over time in content, form, and procedural requirements.
- *Rights*: The extent to which (a) the benefits received under external programmes are recognised as moral or, better, legal entitlements, and (b) there are recognised (preferably legal) mechanisms that the beneficiaries can access to ensure that these entitlements are actually realised.

This looks like a wish list. The key point, illustrated by the case studies in the next two sections, is that it is not a list of the *necessary* conditions for the creation of an enabling institutional environment. A relationship can be highly enabling in one or two of these dimensions even when the general environment appears quite bleak. External agencies do not have to perform well on every dimension in order to generate positive results. Context is all. The relationship between poor people and external agents may be enabling, in the sense in which we have defined it, both when it appears concordant (i.e. cooperative and harmonious), and when it is discordant.

Water in Nepal: credibility and concordant collective action

The first case is a programme for constructing rural drinking water infra-structure in Nepal that was funded by the Finnish aid agency, FINNIDA, and implemented by a Finnish consultancy company with expatriate and local staff.[4] The programme design was relatively orthodox. Water projects in the mountains of Nepal are expensive; most costs were met by FINNIDA. Communities that chose to participate were required to organise themselves to make inputs into planning, construction, fee collection and maintenance. Although they contributed only a fraction of construction costs, their total commitments, in terms of cash, labour and self-organisation, were significant to them: this was not an exercise that a community would embark on lightly. Nepali government agencies undertook the investigation and design work, and much of the construction, under the supervision of the aid project staff. The programme had been in operation for six years when we researched it – long enough for us to judge it a success in terms of both process and outcome. A large number of water-supply schemes had been built, without glaring design or construction failures. As far as we could judge, villagers had made a substantial input in most cases and exhibited a degree of ownership.

We asked villagers why and how they became involved in this pro-gramme. The lessons we learned are encapsulated in two responses:

> *Village A*: 'We had wanted water for a long time. We heard that the Fanta Company had done a good job in Villages V and W, so we talked to them about their experience and then approached the Company.' (In many places, the term FINNIDA had been transmuted into 'Fanta Company'; Fanta is a popular soft-drink in South Asia.)
>
> *Village B*, where we asked why it had taken the villagers three years from the time the water project was first mooted until they began to make serious progress to get themselves organised and raise resources: 'We have had at least four different survey teams here from the Local Government Department over the past 15 years, promising us water. They come when there is an election. We don't really trust people who come and talk about bringing us water. It took us a long time to learn to trust these Fanta people. We discovered that they had done good work elsewhere and seemed reliable.'

The reliability of which the villagers talked is what we have termed *credibility*. It refers to both technical competence and dependability when interacting with others. Water projects are expensive and vulnerable to poor location (especially via landslips), poor design and bad construction. If Nepali villagers invest their efforts and savings in a water project that fails – or is simply never completed – they lose a great deal. The perceived *credibility* of the external agent is central to the willingness of communities to mobilise their own contributions. These conversations heightened our awareness that much of the interaction between poor people and external agencies is shaped by rational lack of trust on the part of the poor. Increasingly, they are bombarded by visitors from outside who ask for something from them (even if only their time in meetings) and often promise or imply some reward for cooperation. 'Someone will be back.' 'You will hear more.' 'Ask the Council Chairman in a couple of months.' To us, these outsiders fall into distinct categories: politicians; researchers; government officials; students; census officials; aid agency staff on familiarisation tours; Christian missionaries; NGO staffers; consultants, etc. It is much more difficult for villagers to draw such distinctions, to get any accurate sense of what the agenda actually is – or, above all, to get any kind of binding commitment from outsiders in return for cooperating with them. By contrast, external agencies that have established a reputation for reliability on the basis of their performance are at least serious candidates for trust.

While formally in the public sector, the 'Fanta Company' in practice enjoyed the operational and budgetary autonomy of an NGO. People who know the rural water sector in Nepal might therefore be tempted to read this case as an illustration of the badness of the government sector and the virtues of NGOs. There is, however, a clear and important contrast between the strategies employed by the 'Fanta Company' on the one hand and most NGOs on the other to tackle the problem of villagers' rational suspicion of outsiders promising water. The staff of Nepali NGOs working in the sector presented an image of their relative strengths that could have been obtained in almost any developing country. Government agencies were inefficient and corrupt; they took a very long time to get anything done; did it at high cost; and then delivered only standard designs in standard ways, completely disregarding the specific needs, preferences and capacities of different groups of clients. By contrast, we were told that NGOs could find out what people wanted, work with local communities, ensure that appropriate low-cost designs were used, and generally get a good job done cheaply. There was in Nepal at that time friction between NGOs and government water agencies, fuelled by competition for aid funds. This was articulated in terms of relative professional competence. The government water agencies were equally critical of the NGOs, claiming that the NGOs were working with shoddy designs that of course could be constructed cheaply and quickly, but soon fell apart; and that they were experimenting so much, without consistency or good records, that the government agencies were left with an almighty mess when they were asked to maintain and rehabilitate the water facilities that the NGOs had constructed in ones and two all over the country.

It was no surprise to us that spokesmen of government agencies made little reference to what we have termed *credibility* issues. Such concerns rarely feature in the public discourse of government officials in South Asia. That the NGOs were aware of these issues is implicit in the procedure they typically adopted: sending social mobilisers into villages for weeks or months to gain the trust and cooperation of the population before initiating construction work. This is a variant of the *conscientisation* strategy mentioned on p. 206. One might usefully term it an 'active marketing' strategy, for it involves taking the initiative to *persuade* villagers to cooperate. But was this the best solution to the distrust problem? The 'passive marketing' strategy employed by the 'Fanta Company' – i.e. set some good examples of reliability and then rely on reputation to interest other villagers and elicit requests for assistance – appears superior. It assumes a high and often justified faith in the capacity of communities to organise themselves once they are confident that they have reliable external partners. This obviates the need for external social mobilisers, and provides a more valid test of community engagement and sense of ownership than do commitments made in response to 'active marketing' strategies employed by influential outsiders. The employment of social mobilisers raises the possibility of moral hazard problems. One has to assume that social mobilisers generally are biased in favour of obtaining formal commitments from communities to engage on projects. This will enhance their sense of job satisfaction (mission accomplishment) and is likely to advance their careers. The organisations that employ them are vulnerable to similar temptations. What is to stop an effective social mobiliser from persuading villagers to cooperate on schemes that are badly designed or constructed but look good on the papers that go to the aid donors? The social mobiliser is anyway leaving the village once the project is complete, and the relative inaccessibility of most of rural Nepal means that few aid projects are ever independently and properly assessed. Could it be true, as alleged to us, that NGOs sometimes 'saved' vast sums of money and cut short construction times by, for example, hanging polythene water pipes between trees rather than burying them deep in the ground out of harm's way? Perhaps the impressive performances that some of them were reporting really were based on misuse, unintended or conscious, of a position of power that they had established through their marketing techniques? Note that there was a clear affinity between this 'active marketing' strategy and the fact that many NGOs were working on a very small scale, often spreading their resources widely over more than one locality – a village here and a village there. This wide scattering of activities provides little scope for building up local reputations for reliability and performance. The more sceptical view is that it protected NGOs against performance scrutiny and helped maintain their dominance in their relationships with the communities where they were working.

The water projects we have discussed here work better if local people engage in collective action and invest substantial resources in collaboration with external agencies, all the time ensuring that the collaboration takes place on equal terms. If they are to make substantial investments in planning and construction, communities need a concordant relationship with external agencies – both generalised trust and extensive cooperation in implementation. The *credibility* of the external agency, and the reputation it thereby acquired, were central to project success. Programme *predictability* was a secondary factor, of some significance. Communities needed some assurance that their external partner would be around long enough to ensure completion of individual projects. Although the programme that we studied was aid-funded and very likely to come to an end within a few years, it had been operating for six years and worked through the permanent Nepali government agencies. *Rights* played no significant role. There was no legal recourse for villagers if projects went wrong, and very little political recourse: the programme was relatively insulated from Nepali politics, and, in the mountains of Nepal, implementation mistakes and failures are easily concealed from external evaluators.

Public works in India: programme predictability, rights and discordant collective action

Our second example deals with a different type of anti-poverty intervention; and a relationship between the poor and external agencies that has frequently been discordant. The core of the story is the way in which programme *predictability* and, more especially, an ingenious set of *rights* mechanisms, have provided significant opportunities and incentives for local politicians and social activists to intermediate between organised groups of poor people and the public bureaucracy.

In the mid-1970s, the state of Maharashtra, India, introduced an Employment Guarantee Scheme for its rural population – assured unskilled manual employment on local public works on request. The Employment Guarantee Scheme (EGS) appeared innovative and in its early years received considerable attention from the outside world. Over the 23 years from 1975–6 to 1998–9, it provided an annual average of 132 million work days, on 341,661 separate work sites – soil and water conservation, small-scale irrigation, reforestation, and local roads. Despite many problems, EGS continues to provide relatively cost-effective and reliable income support for significant sections of the rural poor of Maharashtra. We have conducted field and documentary research on EGS, focusing on the 'guarantee' and the role of client mobilisation in making the scheme work.[5] The conclusions are encouraging.

EGS is an innovative scheme for providing paid work for the rural poor on a self-selection basis, with (a) a substantial in-built guarantee of work and (b) a set of procedures for using this labour to construct public infrastructure. The precise procedures and conditions offered under EGS to achieve these goals have changed over the years. It is convenient here to summarise the rules when the scheme was formalised in the mid-1970s. All rural adults over the age of 18 who were willing to do manual unskilled work on a piece-rate basis were offered a guarantee of employment within 15 days of the demand being made, provided that (a) jobseekers registered with the local administration; and (b) there were at least 50 jobseekers in one locality. In principle – although almost never in practice – the government was obliged to pay an unemployment benefit (originally Rs 1 per day) if it was unable to provide suitable work for registered jobseekers. More significant, if the job offered were more than 8 km from the residence of the jobseeker, the government was required to provide a specified set of amenities, including temporary housing. Although there is no single comprehensive set of figures, most sources indicate that around half of all EGS employment went to women. On the government side, EGS committees identified and designed groups of projects, so that the scheme could be operationalised at short notice during the dry, lean season and during unusual droughts. Projects were required to create productive assets. At least 60 per cent of expenditures were to be on unskilled labour. Soil and water conservation and drought-prevention works were given priority. EGS operates through two parallel lines of administration: the Revenue Department (i.e. territorial administration) that controls the financing, opening and closing of projects and directs workers to appropriae sites; and various technical departments (Irrigation, Agriculture, Forestry, Highways, etc.) that identify and design particular projects and manage the construction process.

What makes EGS distinctive is the fact that it is enshrined in law. The implementation details – wage rates, eligibility conditions, criteria for projects, etc. – can be, and are, changed by the executive authority of the state government. But the Maharashtra Employment Guarantee Act of 1977 obliges the Government of Maharashtra to operate an Employment Guarantee Scheme for the rural poor. Equally important, the Maharashtra State Tax on Professions, Trades, Callings and Employments Act of 1975 provides a dedicated financing mechanism, i.e. a revenue stream devoted only to EGS. There are five specific taxes, of which the most important is the 'professional tax', that is borne mainly by registered professionals and formal sector employees in the urban sector. The state government is obliged to make a contribution to the Employment Guarantee Fund that matches the yield from these dedicated taxes. Once the Secretary to the Government of Maharashtra (EGS) has certified in an appropriate fashion that funds are required to honour the employment guarantee, the state government is legally obliged to release the money.

How did such progressive ideas ever get onto the statute books? One part of the story is the pioneering role played by a group of progressive politicians and social activists, notably the Congress politician V.S. Page, who had been experimenting with similar pilot projects since 1965. A more structural factor was the major drought that affected large areas of Western Maharashtra in 1970–4. The massive public works programme mounted to deal with the consequences of drought provided the basis on which EGS became a state-wide programme. The state government responded effectively to the drought in part because the Communist and left political parties and trades unions rooted in Mumbai (Bombay), the state capital, had established bases in the drought areas. They organised many 'agitations' and sparked a fear of more general unrest.[6]

The more important question for us is why EGS has continued to be implemented relatively effectively, in a country where there often appear to be several public programmes for every conceivable development problem, many of them quickly mired in clientelist politics and/or corruption. The major reason is that *EGS jobseekers, via political representatives of various kinds, have continuously been mobilised to demand their rights.* That mobilisation is far from predictable. For this is in no sense a variant of a standard story about public sector trades unions. Few EGS workers belong to a union; the scheme is far from the labour organisers' dream. The work force is casual and fluctuating, and work sites dispersed and temporary. There is no basis for solidarity around a common, long-term employment relation or permanent work place. There is no scope to use the strike weapon: if eligible jobseekers strike, the government simply saves money. Because implementation is shared locally between several government agencies, it is difficult to find one clear target against which to mobilise. Yet there is a great deal of mobilisation. There have been *morchas* (marches) *dharnas* (sit-ins) and *gheraos* (sieges of government offices) at many levels. Activist coordinating committees develop around EGS issues. The Government of Maharashtra has several times been taken to court by trades unions and social activists over EGS issues. This level of mobilisation, and the consequent relative success of EGS as a social insurance scheme for the rural poor, results from the interaction of several factors, listed here in ascending order of importance:

(1) Incentives to collective action are built into the scheme: a minimum number of people need to be in search of employment before work sites can be opened.
(2) The funding mechanism for EGS is near-automatic and funds have not generally been scarce at the aggregate level. Consequently, there have been limited incentives for politicians to undermine the scheme by concentrating allocations on their own supporters, thereby punishing particular localities, caste groups or other population categories.
(3) While there are recurrent problems with the execution of the scheme, the public agencies involved enjoy a degree of *credibility*. EGS is implemented more honestly and effectively than many public anti-poverty programmes. One reason is that there is a balance of power and mutual accountability between two distinct sections of the state apparatus: the 'line departments' that directly manage EGS projects (Irrigation, Agriculture,

Forestry, Highways); and the Revenue Department (general territorial administration) that controls the finances and constitutes the channel through which demands for work are expressed and, more generally, political concerns and pressures are treated. Neither part of the state apparatus can abuse EGS too far without risking complaints and exposure from the other. It is also important that, in response to past revelations of corruption, the mechanisms for checking and approving EGS expenditures have become relatively demanding and transparent.

(4) EGS is characterised by a high degree of programme *predictability*, in three important respects:

- *Longevity*: the scheme has been in place in much the same form for 20 years, is well institutionalised and operates virtually throughout the state. Knowledge of how to 'work' it has accumulated over time.
- *Security*: it is worthwhile for politicians and social activists to invest in developing their knowledge of the scheme because they have a high degree of confidence that EGS will be in place next year and the year after. EGS is legislated. Unlike other government programmes, it cannot easily be abolished and replaced with another anti-poverty programme.
- *Continuity*: EGS work is always in process. Projects are always being prepared and implemented. Even during the monsoon period, when labour is needed for agriculture, the Forestry Department is rearing seedlings and planting trees with EGS funds. And a substantial amount of employment is given every year during the driest months of March–May. Contrast the permanency of EGS with the more typical situation, where large-scale public employment is offered on an ad hoc basis whenever drought strikes. The administrative machinery to provide this employment is disbanded at the end of each drought, and re-created some years later. Without programme continuity, public servants have to re-learn how to do the job each time. Politicians and social activists representing the poor also have to re-learn the rules, and put a great deal of effort into stimulating government action on each occasion – e.g. securing a declaration of emergency and a commitment of public funds – and in trying to re-write operational rules.

In Maharashtra, with EGS in place, political and organisational energy need not be dissipated on these 'first-stage' responses to crisis. It can be focused instead on much more concrete, locally-specific, questions of what will be done, where, and by whom. Government agencies are required to be ready to deal with these questions. They have incentives to be cooperative because the funding is generally available (the line agencies that manage projects obtain a significant fraction of their regular funding from EGS); the procedures are known; and EGS administration is not burdensome: there is a separate office within the Revenue Department that does nothing but coordinate EGS work. Because implementing EGS does not pose major problems for government agencies, they are responsive to pressures to provide work. That itself is an incentive for politicians and social activists to demand it. From the perspective of providing incentives to activists to invest in pro-poor mobilisation, the permanency and continuity of EGS provide a functional substitute for the absence of strong workforce solidarity around the workplace (see above). It is the character of the public programme, rather than workforce and workplace conditions, that makes feasible the mobilisation of EGS jobseekers.

(5)   Above all, the legal *rights* enshrined in EGS create incentives for jobseekers and their (potential) political representative to engage in political mobilisation of various kinds at both local (*taluka* and district) and state levels. Action at these two levels is mutually reinforcing. EGS legislation in principle guarantees a range of *rights* in addition to the core entitlement to employment under the conditions set out above. These include: payment if workers use their own tools; plastic spectacles for people employed in stone-breaking; provision of on-site drinking water, first-aid and child-care; compensation payments ('unemployment pay') in the case of failure of government to provide work; and, for work sites more than 8 km from employees' homes, camping facilities and access to fair-price shops. Except for drinking water provision, few of these additional formal entitlements have been realised regularly. They have however provided the focus for mobilisation, along with the grievances typically found on all public works sites: delays in initiating work; disputes over piece-work norms (e.g. payment per m^3 for digging and shifting different types of soil and rock); delays or cheating in paying wages; and corruption of various kinds. These rights and grievances have led to a wide range of local-level political activities, including filing cases against the state government in district courts. Some of these issues have also been taken up by organisations campaigning at state level. However, at state level it is general policy issues that have dominated, above all the recurrent question of revising EGS wage rates in line with inflation, and the related issue, now settled, of whether EGS wages should be the same as the minimum agricultural wage rates. Petitions relating to EGS have twice been heard in the High Court in Mumbai.

The significance of the *right* to EGS employment can be illustrated by comparing it with the Employment Assurance Scheme (EAS), that was introduced in all Indian states in 1994. EAS is a central government scheme. Impressed by the reputation of EGS, and no doubt wishing not to appear less effective or concerned than a state government in dealing with rural unemployment, the Government of India created and directly funded EAS. In one respect EAS appears better targeted than EGS because preference is given to members of households below the poverty line. EAS was often described to us as 'identical to EGS – except for the lack of a guarantee of work'. That is the administrators' perspective. For phrase 'except for the guarantee' is crucial. There is no client mobilisation around EAS, because the lever of *rights* is lacking. It is the entitlement to employment that limits bureaucratic discretion and ensures that, to a substantial degree, EGS opportunities really are self-targeted on the poor. The implementation of the scheme does involve a great deal of routine friction between activists and the local state apparatus. Local administrators have used the discretion they enjoy to try to suppress local activism. They have had some success, but are still constrained by the strong *rights* element built into EGS, the relative autonomy and power of the Indian courts and the institutionalisation of mobilisation around the right to work.

The EGS is far from perfect. It is unlikely to be directly replicable elsewhere. But it provides a great deal of inspiration, and illustrates clearly how clever political and institutional design can encourage the mobilisation of the poor around public programmes in a non-corporatist fashion while helping to make those programmes more effective.

Enabling institutional environments and contemporary development policy

How relevant are our concerns about *enabling institutional environments* to the shape of contemporary anti-poverty interventions in poor countries? Although contemporary anti-poverty policies tend formally to be justified in terms of concepts like 'participation' and responsiveness to client needs, there appears in practice to be little concern for the issues and relationships we have discussed here. Indeed, there is a problem of *disabling institutional environments*. Two development policy trends give grounds for concern.

First, there has been a big expansion in the use of NGOs as agents for the delivery of public services to the poor. We can look again at Maharashtra to illustrate the consequences. Maharashtra is a relatively developed and politically aware state in the Indian context. It enjoys a history of extensive popular and leftist political activity and, since the 1980s, has shared in the big expansion of the activities of development NGOs. Some rural activists blamed the slackening of political activity around the EGS and related issues in the late 1980s and early 1990s on the growth of (foreign-funded) NGOs. These NGOs are said to be attractive employers, and to have 'seduced' the rural activists who had previously helped mobilise the poor around issues of a broadly 'class' nature (Joshi 1998). Whatever the truth of that charge, it is clear that the development activities of NGOs do not elicit the same kind of countervailing popular organisation that the EGS has generated. This is especially true of NGOs that (a) are not strongly rooted in the populations they serve; (b) are oriented mainly to obtaining external financial resources; and (c) are engaged more in service delivery than advocacy. These types of NGOs in particular provide pure 'benefits', not *rights* in either the moral or legal sense of the term. There is no moral or legal basis on which to organise to ensure that NGOs deliver what they promise. Equally important, NGO activities are invariably small-scale and dispersed, and frequently experimental and in practice flexible, temporary and unstable. To the NGO staffers and their funders, flexibility and experimentation are positive values that constitute 'learning experiences'. To potential social activists these same values are disabling, for the central role of NGOs undermines the scope for mobilisation of the poor around programme implementation. We will not dwell too much on the impact of the induction of grass-roots activists into an NGO and programme implementation 'establishment.' This is certainly a widespread phenomenon (e.g. Clarke 1998: 208). More important are the points made above that (a) NGO programmes typically are diverse, fragmented and unstable (they lack programme *predictability*); and (b) they are not even potentially formally enforceable in the way that programmes run directly by government agencies may be. The wider use of NGOs for service delivery is sometimes defended or justified on the grounds that NGOs are better able to mobilise the poor: some element of mobilisation is often built into the programmes they implement. To that degree, there is a potential counter-argument to the one we have advanced. We are however sceptical of the capacity or willingness of any but the most exceptional organisations to encourage or even tolerate the autonomous and potentially antagonistic mobilisation of their own client groups.

Second, and despite the rhetorical and substantive shift to the NGO sector, there has been a massive expansion of one particular type of public anti-poverty programme on the 1990s: the so-called 'Social Funds'.[7] The amounts of money involved are enormous. Social Funds are thick on the ground in Latin America, and fairly common in Africa. They were originally justified mainly in terms of coping with the social costs of economic adjustment. They have become the dominant anti-poverty instrument of the International Financial Institutions (IFIs) and banks, and are spreading to Asia. The main aid donors committed substantial money to deal with the social costs of the implosion of the Indonesian economy only when a Social Fund was put in place in late 1998. It is estimated that, since the late 1980s, the World Bank, the Inter-American Development Bank (IDB) and the main European aid donors spent about US\$ 4 billion on Social Funds in Latin America and Africa (Tendler 1999: 1).

Although Social Funds come in many shapes and sizes, a core component, both substantively and ideologically, is the idea of response to 'community demand'. Much Social Fund expenditure is committed by asking poor, territorially defined 'communities' to decide how they would like to spend an external cash injection for community purposes. Do they want a water supply system or a toolshed? A road or a new school building? A tractor or latrines? Social Funds are often managed by a special bureaucratic agency, and private firms and NGOs are frequently contracted to undertake preparation, design and construction work. The rhetoric is of decentralisation: moving away from the monolithic state and its 'old-fashioned', unresponsive specialist departments (Water, Irrigation, Health, Agriculture, etc.); tapping the strengths of the private sector and NGOs; and shifting from 'supply-driven' to 'demand-driven' service delivery. From our particular perspective on anti-poverty programmes then, Social Funds are expected to encourage the mobilisation of beneficiaries.

The reality is not only more complex but substantially different. To a large degree, the real choices are made somewhere up the line: by politicians, by bureaucrats, or by the private companies and NGOs who are formally supposed to elicit community desires. There are a number of interacting reasons for this situation. But the dominant factor is that Social Funds programmes are neither designed nor implemented to produce what we have labelled an *enabling institutional environment* for the mobilisation of the poor. While characterised by tolerance, they are deficient in respect of *credibility*, programme *predictability* and *rights*. Communities are presented with their Social Funds opportunity out of the blue. They face what appears to be a once-in-a-lifetime opportunity, since the programmes are not so well funded or established that they become a regular part of the annual round in any community. Information on the resources actually available is limited. Publicity campaigns are poor – not because governments do not know how to run such campaigns, but because every agency in a position of authority has a strong interest in limiting information, so that they can influence community choice. Politicians do not want accurate and transparent information, since that would (a) reduce their discretion to grant access for political reasons and (b) lead to excess demands for access to Social Funds that would generate political disappointment. Government agencies do not want to generate more demand than they can handle; and generally find some types of community projects easier to handle than others. They want both to limit demands and standardise the types of facilities they supply. And the private companies that design and construct projects also want to standardise, because that reduces costs and increases profits. Since these are all 'one-shot games' as far as any individual community is concerned, there is little opportunity to build up knowledge of what is really on offer, and how best to bargain with these better-informed external agencies.

The Social Funds case is very similar to that of the NGOs: a new set of institutional arrangements for delivering public services to the poor are justified through the rhetoric of 'community', 'client demand', 'localism' and 'decentralisation', while little real attention is paid to creating an organisational context that will enable the poor actually to organise to help ensure that programmes work in their favour. Both cases illustrate the main point of our argument: mobilising the poor effectively might better be done by paying less attention to sending emissaries, organisers and propagandists down to the grass-roots, and putting more effort into providing the poor with an *enabling* external bureaucratic and programme environment – one characterised by more tolerance, credibility, predictability and rights. A little more of some of these things might go a long way.

Notes

1. For a useful discussion of the types of resources needed and used by social movements, see McAdam, Tarrow and Tilly (1997).
2. It was an acute awareness of this possibility that led Piven and Cloward (1971), for example, to argue that 'poor people's movements' could be effective only if they totally rejected cooperation of any kind with state agencies, and pursued the strategy of making a nuisance of themselves.
3. The general argument that the inferior party in an unequal relationship may be able to benefit from the limited attention paid to the relationship by the superior party is presented in Hirschman (1981).
4. We undertook some research on this programme in 1996 (see Moore *et al.* 1996).
5. There is a large literature on EGS, most of it published in India. The more internationally accessible sources are Herring and Edwards (1983); Acharya (1990); Echeverri-Gent (1993); Dev (1996); Gaiha (1996, 1997). For more details on the arguments put forward in this chapter, see Joshi (1998).
6. Another part of the story is found in changes in state boundaries and in the fact that in the late 1960s power within the ruling Maharashtra Congress Party shifted decisively from Mumbai-based industrial and commercial capitalists, most of them non-Marathi speakers and thus 'outsiders' to the new linguistic-based state of Maharashtra. The people who inherited power were mainly big farmers and rural commercial interests of the Maratha caste, many based in the drought-affected areas of Western Maharashtra. EGS was essentially funded by a tax on Mumbai, it was in part an expression of the political dominance of this new Marathi-speaking, rural-based class.
7. This section is based heavily on Judith Tendler's thorough review of the Social Funds (Tendler 1999). (See: http://www.worldbank.org/html/oed/eprconf/assets/images/01New.pdf.) For more corroborating analyses from the agencies financing Social Funds, see for example, Inter-American Development Bank (1998) and Cornia (1999).

Bibliography

Acharya, S. (1990), 'The Maharashtra Employment Guarantee Scheme: a study of labour market intervention', ARTEP Working Paper, International Labour Organisation/Asian Regional Team for Employment Promotion.

Clarke, G. (1998), *The Politics of NGOs in South-East Asia. Participation and Protest in the Philippines,* London: Routledge.

Cornia, G.A. (1999), 'Social Funds in stabilization and adjustment programmes', Research in Action Paper 48, Helsinki: World Institute for Development Economics Research.

Dev, M. (1996), 'Experience of India's (Maharashtra) Employment Guarantee Scheme: lessons for development policy', *Development Policy Review*, Vol. 14(3), pp. 227–53.

Echeverri-Gent, J. (1993), *The State and the Poor. Public Policy and Political Development in India and the United States*, Berkeley: University of California Press.

Fox, J. (1994), 'The difficult transition from clientilism to citizenship: lessons from Mexico', *World Politics*, Vol. 46, pp. 151–84.

Gaiha, R. (1996), 'How dependent are the rural poor on the Employment Guarantee Scheme in India?', *Journal of Development Studies*, Vol. 32(5), pp. 669–94.

Gaiha, R. (1997), 'Do rural public works influence agricultural wages? The case of the Employment Guarantee Scheme in India', *Oxford Development Studies*, Vol. 25(3), pp. 301–14.

Herring, R. and R.M. Edwards (1983), 'Guaranteeing employment to the rural poor: social functions and class interests in the Employment Guarantee Scheme in Western India', *World Development*, Vol. 11(7), pp. 575–92.

Hirschman, A.O. (1981), 'Beyond asymmetry: critical notes on myself as a young man and on some other old friends', in A.O. Hirschman, *Essays in Trespassing. Economics to Politics and Beyond*, Cambridge, London, and New York: Cambridge University Press.

Houtzager, P.P. (1998), 'State and unions in the transformation of the Brazilian countryside, 1964–1979', *Latin American Research Review*, Vol. 33(2), pp. 103–42.

Inter-American Development Bank (1998), 'The use of Social Funds as an instrument for combating poverty', *IDB Sector Strategy*, POV-104, Washington, DC: Inter-American Development Bank.

Joshi, A. (1998), 'Mobilizing the poor? Activism and the Employment Guarantee Scheme, Maharashtra', IDS, mimeo: University of Sussex.

McAdam, D., S. Tarrow and C. Tilly (1997), 'Toward an integrated perspective on social movements and revolution', in: *Comparative Politics. Rationality, Culture and Structure*, Cambridge: Cambridge University Press.

Moore, M. *et al.* (1996), 'Ownership in the Finnish aid programme', *Evaluation Study*, 1996: 3, Helsinki: Ministry of Foreign Affairs of Finland, Department for International Development Cooperation.

Pinhanez, M.F. (1997), 'Shattered power, reconstructed coalitions: an analysis of rural labor unions in Maranhao, Brazil', Master's thesis in City Planning, Cambridge, MA: Massachusetts Institute of Technology.

Piven, F.F. and R.A. Cloward (1971), *Regulating the Poor. The Functions of Public Welfare*, New York: Vintage Books.

Rodrik, D. (1999), *The New Global Economy and Developing Countries: Making Openness Work*, Washington, DC: Overseas Development Council.

Stiglitz, J.E. (1998), 'More instruments and broader goals: moving beyond the post-Washington Consensus', *Wider Annual Lectures*, 2, Helsinki: WIDER.

Tendler, J. (1997), *Good Government in the Tropics*, Baltimore: Johns Hopkins University Press.

Tendler, J. (1999), 'The rise of Social Funds: what are they a model of?', *Draft Report for MIT/UNDP Decentralisation Project*, Cambridge, MA: Massachusetts Institute of Technology.

10
Gendering Poverty: A Review of Six World Bank African Poverty Assessments[1]

Ann Whitehead and Matthew Lockwood[*]

Introduction

Concern with poverty within the World Bank has ebbed and flowed over time. Its most recent appearance dates from the late 1980s, which saw the emergence of a 'New Poverty Agenda' and the *1990 World Development Report* on poverty (Lipton and Maxwell 1992). However, a key difference between the 1990s and, for instance, the MacNamara period is that awareness of issues to do with 'women in development' and 'gender and development' is far more pervasive. The literature on gender and poverty is now a mature, and very large one (see Baden and Milward 1995; Kabeer 1994, 1997 for reviews).

At one level, the relationship between gender disadvantage and poverty appears straightforward, and this approach has been readily taken up by development agencies such as the World Bank within a general set of arguments about the 'feminisation' of poverty (Buvinic 1983, 1997). However, on closer inspection, and at a deeper analytical level, the relationships between gender and poverty are far from straightforward, and there are

* This chapter is a shorter version of Whitehead and Lockwood (1999), which presents the evidence and arguments in greater detail. The not inconsiderable task of editing a lengthy paper down to manageable proportions was undertaken by Bridget Byrne, to whom we are very grateful. We would like to thank Caroline Moser, Andy Norton, Alison Evans, Shahrashoub Razavi, Rosemary McGee, Jo Beall, Naila Kabeer and participants in workshops in Trivandrum and Oslo for helpful comments on earlier drafts of this chapter. We have also benefited from the comments of anonymous reviewers who read the chapter for *Development and Change*. The responsibility for the chapter's findings, including errors of fact or judgement, of course remains with us, as the authors.

concerns that objectives about unequal gender relations will become subordinated to an agenda about increasing welfare (Jackson 1996).

This is the context within which this chapter examines gender in the World Bank's Poverty Assessments. Poverty Assessments (PAs) have emerged as the most important statements by the World Bank about poverty in particular countries. By 1996, almost 50 Assessments had been carried out, and for some countries there is more than one Assessment. The approach we have taken is to look at a relatively small number of Assessments (six from four countries) in some detail. Our chosen four countries are Ghana, Zambia, Tanzania and Uganda in sub-Saharan Africa.[1] Partly because both African populations and poverty are mainly in rural areas, and partly because our own experience has been in rural, as opposed to urban Africa, we have focused particularly on what the Assessments have to say about poverty and gender in rural areas. In our review, we have been helped by the fact that a number of high-quality evaluations of the PAs already exist which focus on complementary themes: a review of Assessments and public expenditure reviews in Africa by the Institute of Development Studies at Sussex (IDS 1994); a comprehensive examination of 38 Assessments by a team at the Institute of Social Studies (ISS) in the Hague (Hanmer, Pyatt and White 1996); an internal evaluation by the World Bank which focuses on the links between Assessments and other Bank processes (World Bank OED 1996); and a review of the Participatory Poverty Assessments for the UK's Department for International Development by the Centre for Development Studies at Swansea (Booth *et al.* 1998).

The first section of the chapter outlines the ways in which gender concerns actually appear, or do not appear, in each of the six PAs we examined, and the institutional and organisational context in which they were produced. The rest of the chapter then seeks to explain exactly why gender appears in the forms it does, and at the points it does, in these documents. In this process, a number of points emerge not simply about the approach to gender within the World Bank, but also about the approach to poverty, to methodological issues, and to policy.

Gender in the Poverty Assessments: an overview

How does gender appear?

There is enormous variation in the extent to which women and/or gender issues are present in the six PAs under scrutiny. Moreover, as the clumsy phrase 'women and/or gender' signals, the language adopted for the analysis and description of gender issues also varies widely. In some PAs, the issues are addressed through talking about 'women'; other PAs use the language of 'gender' and some of these have an elaborated set of concepts, including those of the gender division of labour, gender relations, gender discrimination and so on. By far the most common way in which women appear in the Assessments is in the guise of female-headed households. This is a frequently used way of disaggregating the quantitative nationally representative household surveys. Here, as elsewhere, gender is largely used to describe a relatively fixed status or category with little reference to its relational implications. Where there is an attempt to specify the link between gender and poverty, it mainly consists of identifying women's specific poverty characteristics. Most markedly, even where the main body of the PA has addressed the particular characteristics of poor women or gender issues in other ways, there is a substantial gap between these discussions and the extent to which gender is addressed in the final policy section of the main volume of each Report. In these policy sections, gender sensitivity appears in highly fragmented references, largely to women and education and sometimes to the role of women in agriculture.

Readers will hardly be surprised at this lack of consistency. It mirrors the complexity – and confusions – of gender conceptualisations, analysis and language use in the development field as a whole. Academic attention to gender and development began with debates about language and appropriate concepts and recently public institutions and the donor community have come under increasing pressure to elaborate their languages of gender. There has been a commonly occurring shift away from women in development (WID) to gender and development (GAD) formulations within public policy, usually as a result of highly politicised debates about what the shift from women to gender means.[2] As Razavi and Miller (1995a) document, several important institutions have changed their gender language and we can see a trend towards a more uniform language in their public documents.

However, this has not happened at the World Bank. A recent review by Moser, Tornqvist and van Bronkhorst (1998) contends that there is no agreement on what the term 'gender' means in Bank policy documents. Arguably, this complexity and lack of coherence in gender language and gender approaches arises out of the relatively weak commitment to WID/gender issues within the Bank. Razavi and Miller (1995b) document the history of the relatively limited resources allocated to gender specialists in the Bank and their weak mandates and institutional position. There is a tendency to locate WID/gender concerns in the 'soft' areas – such as human resources – in an organisation giving strong analytical and policy priority to economics. In the period leading up to the Poverty Assessments, gender thinking in the Bank was relocated in a WID Division of the Population and Human Resources Department. Ravazi and Miller (1995b: 38) cite the Gender Team in the Africa region of the Bank arguing that the 1993 reorganisation of the institution had led to a 'temporary slowdown of momentum in building up and sustaining staff gender capacity'. It is significant that poverty measurement was being expanded rapidly at a time when efforts to mainstream gender in the Bank had stalled.

By the late 1990s, this weak capacity had contributed to producing a diversity – in approaches to gender and development; in definitions of what gender analysis is; and in the potential components of a gender analysis – that Moser, Tornqvist and van Bronkhorst document (1998). Their paper argues the need for a common framework of gender analysis within the Bank. However, no attempt is made to associate the use of particular approaches or definitions of gender with other differences (for example, crudely between different schools of economic analysis, or between social development sections and others). As a result, it is unclear whether this diversity is accidental, whether it is associated with particular perspectives within different sections of the Bank and, crucially, whether it is the outcome of contestation.

Given this background, it is not unexpected that the six PAs of our case study have such wide variations in their approach to gender. *Uganda II* and *Ghana I*[3] are two studies in which women and/or gender hardly figure at all in the documents. In *Ghana I*, for example, the only mention of gender issues is an occasional reference to female-headed households and a sudden appearance in an assertion that the agricultural labour force is becoming feminised. No evidence is offered for this generalisation and it is not linked with any previous data discussion. It returns in the final section on policy, where the main mention of women is a recommendation for improvements in agricultural extension work with women farmers.

It is a very similar story in *Uganda II*. Household survey data is analysed in terms of differences in *per capita* expenditure between male-headed and female-headed households. Women are hardly mentioned anywhere else in the Report. The policy section does not refer at any point to the gender of the beneficiaries and agents of economic growth, nor to the rural infrastructure and human capital programmes that it recommends.

Since both Uganda and Ghana have two successive PAs, this allows us to examine whether there is evidence of a learning process. We might expect the gender sensitivity of PAs to have grown through the early 1990s. This seems to be borne out in the Ghana case. *Ghana I*, which is one of the earliest PAs (1992), was followed by a 1995 assessment which is much more gender-sensitive (*Ghana II*). A general trend is belied, however, in the contrast between the two Uganda studies. *Uganda I*, undertaken in 1992, contains much more about gender than *Uganda II*, undertaken in 1995. What the *Uganda II* and *Ghana I* Poverty Assessments (with their scant attention to gender) seem to have in common is that they are the documents most dominated by a poverty strategy centred on macroeconomic growth. These PAs are also largely content to use poverty lines – that is, income or consumption money-metric household definitions of poverty.

Tanzania and *Uganda I* are more eclectic in their approach. Each has an initial gender sensitivity in that a separate Report on gender/women's issues was commissioned, with a summary appearing as a separate chapter in the final Report. The content of these chapters is dominated by the kind of gender analysis that is prevalent in the country concerned, influenced by national literature and local feminist policy priorities. They have a much better developed language to describe gender issues. In *Uganda I*, there is a wholesale use of the language of gender. It appears, for example, in the idea of the gender division of labour, and in arguments about the need for gender-responsive actions and growth. The framework of gender analysis makes use of the idea of rights and obligations between men and women and the use of the law to establish women's rights to land, labour and other resources. The problem of women's time burdens, because of domestic responsibilities and their disadvantages in access to education, are also prominent, as are the effects on women of the high incidence of HIV and AIDS. The treatment of gender in a separate chapter does mean, however, that there is much less focus on women throughout the rest of the Report, with the exception of female-headed households which are identified as one of the poverty categories. When it comes to the policy chapter, there is no mention of gendered agents, until a separate section makes a series of recommendations about women which arise directly out of the analyses in the gender chapter.

In the *Tanzania* PA, the dominant gender language in the chapter on women concerns the 'status of women', with a stress on women's legal status and educational disadvantages, on advocacy and political mobilisation. The *Tanzania* PA is also one of three out of the six PAs that adopts new methodologies for the identification of poverty, with the commissioning of a Participatory Poverty Assessment (PPA). The women's chapter has a good discussion of the link, or lack of it, between poverty and female-headed households which draws on both household survey data and data from the PPAs. It also discusses intra-household gender equity, using as its sources already published qualitative case studies.

Despite all this, the main chapter on incomes, inequality and poverty barely mentions women, except in a suggestion that women choose under-employment. In the policy chapters, gender issues are reduced to two: female education and targeted social spending. There are other missed opportunities and inconsistencies, as for example when women (as an otherwise unqualified social category) are described as a 'vulnerable group'. The account of agriculture and rural livelihoods is completely silent on the sex of farmers and the gender division of labour in agriculture. There is a rather good account of the causes of poverty in households with agricultural livelihoods that owes much to the findings of PPAs. Yet, while several of these findings have clear gender dimensions – such as the supply of inputs, savings, credit, access to livestock and labour – rural poverty is discussed in wholly gender-blind ways.

The final pair of studies – *Zambia* and *Ghana II* – are documents in which gender is a palpable part of the PAs, although neither has a separate chapter on women/gender. Rather, gender is integrated into the analysis with different degrees of success. In the *Zambia* case, the language of the gender analysis shifts around quite a lot. Gender is referred to as a 'social status'. 'Female-headed households' appear, as do 'women without support', but the 'gender division of labour' is a significant element of the arguments in the rural volume. Here the analysis centres on a model of the agricultural household which examines the effect of the gender division of labour on income from agriculture under a number of conditions. Female headship is listed as a cause of poverty in urban areas and female-headed households in general are included as a poverty category.

In *Ghana II*, the language of gender is largely descriptive, with frequent references to women, or women and girls. The report gives prominence to the role of women in agriculture and to some of the conditions which affect poor rural women, such as the time burden of water collection in the dry North. There is no data on gender and poverty in the account of the household quantitative data, except in a disaggregation by sex of household head, where there is also a discussion of some of the problems of defining female household heads and of the importance of intra-household differences. There is an innovative discussion of gender biases in social spending.

Along with *Tanzania, Zambia* and *Ghana II* are the other two PAs that have combined national-level poverty line methodologies with specially undertaken PPAs. The influence of the findings from the participatory exercises is evident throughout the accounts and appears to be one vehicle for greater gender sensitivity. Additionally, in each of these Assessments, gender has been examined in one or more of the other studies commissioned to inform the findings. In the *Ghana II* case, this is apparent in the analysis of who benefits from social spending and in the *Zambia* case, in the agricultural modelling, which is the centrepiece of the rural analysis. Even in these two PAs, the policy sections fail to match the visibility of gender in the rest of the reports. In the *Zambia* case, the implications have been reduced to the need for labour-saving technology for 'female' tasks on smallholdings and a prioritising of girls' education in human resource development (HRD) policy. In *Ghana II*, the policy section contains very little reference to women. There is a final paragraph to the Report listing the need for more research on gender and poverty as one of a series of priorities for future research.

The picture that emerges from this overview is one of inconsistencies, fragmentation and gaps, both between and within the six PAs being reviewed here. Where it is not ignored, gender is made visible in many different ways, with no attempt to systematise the gender analysis implied by these discussions. The inconsistencies between the PAs suggest that the project teams had a good deal of autonomy about how they interpreted and prioritised gender issues. Indeed, the PAs are very different from one another in a large number of respects. They do not appear to have a common work plan, yet, at the same time, the concluding policy sections, in which much less attention is given to gender or women, are much more uniform. All this raises questions about the organisation of, and background to, the PAs. What briefs were the project teams working to? How were the Assessments planned and carried out? What were the procedures for producing the final Reports? What is the link between the PAs and the Bank's move to prioritise poverty as its development goal since 1990?

How were the assessments done?

The publication of the *1990 World Development Report* (*WDR*) signalled a significant break from the past for the World Bank. It was the product of an evolving approach to poverty and policy within the Bank, influenced by thinking on growth and liberalisation in Africa in the early 1980s, debates on the social costs of adjustment and the UNICEF critique. Since then, the approach to poverty and policy has continued to evolve under the influence of the *East Asian Miracle* Report (World Bank 1993b). In general, there has been a move away from the preoccupation with the perceived conflict between the market and the state. Poverty, and policy to reduce poverty, have moved to centre stage.

As a result of these shifts, by the late 1980s, the World Bank had begun to step up its country-specific analysis and measurement of poverty in order to fill the information gap. As noted in the *1990 WDR*: 'The absence of reliable inter-temporal statistics on income distribution in most Sub-Saharan African countries makes any comprehensive account of trends in poverty there impossible' (World Bank 1990: 42). In 1991, various directives and strategy papers were combined and released as a new *Operational Directive 4.15: Poverty Reduction* (World Bank 1991). This was accompanied by a *Poverty Reduction Handbook* (World Bank 1992a) containing 'examples of good-practice analytical and operational work' (World Bank 1991: 1). The Directive was intended to guide operational work for poverty reduction, including the collection of information on poverty.

The approach to policy in OD 4.15 is explicitly based on the *1990 WDR*. The policy recipe consisted of: broad-based growth brought about by the removal of price distortions and the provision of credit and infrastructure (World Bank 1990: 73), basic social services (World Bank 1990: 88–9); and safety nets (World Bank 1990: 101–2). There is a guide for content for the Assessments, based on this approach, clearly aimed at standardisation across countries. However, the Directive does recognise that the scope of issues will vary across countries, as will data availability. The level of government commitment to poverty reduction is seen as a key variable for shaping individual Assessments. Further guidance on measurement, analysis and policy is spelled out in detail in the *Poverty Reduction Handbook* accompanying OD 4.15 (World Bank 1992a).

In practice, almost all of the PAs we looked at did follow a common overall structure, roughly similar to the model laid out in OD 4.15 and in the

Poverty Reduction Handbook.[4] Each starts with an attempt to lay out a poverty line, and provide an overall headcount indicator of poverty. Most then go on to provide associations of poverty with household characteristics, such as location, education and sex of head. The format does vary, with some including separate chapters on particular issues (for example, urban poverty in *Zambia*, and women in *Tanzania*). However, what is common across all of the examples is a concluding policy section. Not only is the policy section an inevitable feature of all the PAs; there are also core elements in that section which are common. Not surprisingly given the *1990 WDR* background, these centre on achieving growth through macroeconomic policies, public sector reform for the delivery of social services, especially education, and targeting of safety nets.

Bearing in mind the enormous variation in approaches to gender within our sample of six PAs, it is noteworthy that OD 4.15 gives no guidance on whether and how gender considerations should be included in the content of PAs. The only mention of gender is the general statement which appears at the beginning of the document that: 'The burden of poverty falls disproportionately on women: so it is essential to increase their income-earning opportunities, their food security and their access to social services' (World Bank 1991: 2). Gendered statements in the *Poverty Reduction Handbook* are confined to a breakdown of data by gender, a discussion of female education under public expenditure, women's land rights, and the targeting of agricultural extension services to women.

According to OD 4.15, overall responsibility for operational work on poverty, which includes the PAs, was vested in Regional Vice Presidents. Country department directors were to ensure the quality of analytical work and consistency with Bank policies, while regional chief economists were responsible for determining the satisfactory completion of a PA and the position of the poverty line (World Bank 1991: 3).

In practice, many PAs ended up with only a loose articulation with the Bank itself. Many were funded directly by external donors, especially European ones. A team of national and expatriate consultants headed by a task manager from Bank staff typically carried them out. This relative autonomy meant that although PAs did contain certain overall elements dictated by OD 4.15 and the *1990 WDR*, other aspects varied between countries, and even between two Assessments in one country (for details, see World Bank OED 1996). The PAs are also products of country governments, with national consultants and government staff involved in their production. OD 4.15 makes it clear that PAs provide 'the basis for a collaborative approach to poverty reduction by country officials and the Bank... [helping] to establish the agenda of issues for the policy dialogue' (World Bank 1991: 4). As a result, there are different approaches to poverty lines, to poverty analysis, to background studies, and to themed chapters. Crucially, there are also important differences in methodologies for poverty measurement and analysis, especially in how far the team embraced information beyond quantitative surveys.

As noted, variation in the PAs disappears in the final sections dealing with policy. The key factor seems to be the peer review process, by which drafts of the Assessments circulated within the relevant parts of the Bank, and especially through the hands of the country director and regional chief economist. While relatively little attention was paid to the empirical details of poverty measurement and analysis, policy sections attracted heavy comments and, we suspect, rewriting.

The process by which PAs are produced gives some insight into where we should look to understand how gender issues are made visible, or rendered invisible, within the Assessments. The team approach goes some way to explaining variation in how gender appears in the document described above. Since there is no common analysis of gender in the Bank (let alone among PA consultants), different teams tended to bring their own approaches, and task managers weighted the significance of gender differently. The 'terms of reference' for the Assessments encapsulated in OD 4.15 and the *Poverty Reduction Handbook* give minimal guidance. They contain virtually no gender analysis, and a limited range of fragmented pointers to where teams might single out women.

Understanding gender in the Poverty Assessments

At one level, then, we can see the variable treatment of gender in the PAs simply as the outcome of an absence of a clear analytical gender framework linked to the loose and overdirected manner in which the Assessments were carried out. However, these problems are themselves symptoms of a more subtle and pervasive malaise. Methodological choices have a powerful influence in shaping the ways in which gender appears or is made invisible in the evidence on poverty in the PAs. Moreover, rather different factors shape the ways in which gender is treated in the analysis of poverty, and discussion of policies to reduce poverty. In the absence of a clear analytical framework for understanding gender, the treatment of gender in the Assessments is effectively driven by, on the one hand, a set of epistemological and methodological choices about measuring poverty, and on the other, a set of prescriptions for reducing poverty which originate in the *1990 WDR*.

In the remainder of this study, two central questions are taken up. The first focuses on the empirical evidence collated in the poverty profiles, and asks why gender appears as it does – or, indeed, why it is rendered invisible in certain ways. Central to the question of how far and in what ways gender issues could be discussed in the PAs is the issue of how evidence is generated and presented. While all of the Assessments exploited data collected in surveys using households as units, some also used various other sources, including evidence collected through participatory techniques. These various approaches to data collection imply different possibilities for raising gender issues.

The second question asks why gender appears as it does (or again, does not) in the policy analysis of the Assessments. In most of the Assessments, there are significant gaps, as we move from the evidence on gender and poverty to the policy analysis. Unlike the country-specific poverty profiles, the policy sections of the PAs are heavily influenced by peer review, and hence by both the *1990 WDR* model and by subsequent evolving ideas about poverty within the Bank. To understand how gender appears in the analytical and especially the policy sections of the PAs, it is therefore crucial to examine these ideas.

The PAs display an instance of one of the most fundamental, yet at the same time difficult to grasp, aspects of gender and poverty. Gender considerations are not an add-on to poverty, or a way of finessing a basically sound analysis or policy. Rather, the ways in which we (or the World Bank) define, measure and analyse poverty will have profound consequences for the way in which we characterise gender relations and inequalities. Equally, a proper gender analysis makes possible a useful approach to poverty.

Measuring poverty and gender: I – household surveys

The PAs follow in a long line of attempts to define and measure poverty. The definition of poverty determines the approach to measurement and the types of evidence to be considered. Of the Assessments we examined, most start by asserting the multiple dimensions of poverty. This multi-dimensional approach has led some (four out of six) of the PAs to adopt specialist methodologies to get at the poor's own perceptions of poverty, or at least local understandings of what poverty is. None of the PAs translate the multi-dimensional nature of poverty into an interest in wellbeing, or quality of life indicators, and so ignore the whole debate about social indicators and their relation to poverty.

Table 10.1, which looks at the various ways in which poverty is measured in the PAs under review, makes it clear that there is no standard, agreed way of defining and measuring poverty across the Assessments. Money-metric poverty lines dominate the introductory sections on evidence on poverty but, at various points, additional or complementary evidence is also drawn upon, including health and nutritional outcome indicators. Ultimately, however, all give priority to an income and/or consumption definition, a money-metric poverty line and a quantitative estimate of the percentage in poverty. There is also a great deal of variation in how that poverty line is established. Of our six Assessments, half define poverty lines in absolute terms and half in relative terms. Absolute poverty lines are in two cases determined in relation to a 'minimum' food basket and in *Tanzania* simply as a level of expenditure. Relative poverty lines range from 0.33 to 0.5 of mean expenditure for lower poverty lines, and between 0.66 and 0.8 of

Table 10.1 Measures of poverty in six Poverty Assessments

	Money-metric	Participatory poverty line assessment	Nutritional and health data	Education data
Uganda I	x	x	x	x
Uganda II	x	x	x	
Ghana I	x			
Ghana II*	x	x	x	x
Tanzania	x	x	x	x
Zambia	x	x	x	x

Note: * Also contains a discussion of social spending by gender.

mean expenditure for upper poverty lines. Finally, while most Assessments deflate household expenditure by average household size, *Uganda II* and *Zambia* use expenditure per adult equivalent. This variation makes cross-national comparisons impossible, although one of the rationales for using quantitative data is precisely that they are (in theory at least) comparable.[5]

Basing the definition and measurement of poverty on a single, money-metric dimension makes poverty into a simple characteristic. In a sense, this is a fundamental methodological choice, since it locks the PAs into reliance on expenditure data from surveys. As a result, poverty lines are a relatively weak guide to the *processes* of impoverishment. This point is strongly made in the ISS review which recommends dropping money-metric poverty lines in favour of a socio-economic analysis approach because of the way in which the former fails to produce an account of poverty processes and dynamics (Hanmer, Pyatt and White 1996). There are gender implications here, since a gendered account of poverty must be based in an analysis of poverty processes and dynamics.

Money-metric poverty lines also lead to a heavy dependence on survey data collected on a household basis. None of the PAs attempt a quantitative exploration of poverty *within* households. However, both *Zambia* (p. 3) and *Uganda I* (p. 33) show an awareness of the problems arising from the limitations of aggregated data, particularly in terms of masking inequities within households. These insights are not, however, followed through in the analysis of the household survey data. In considering gender, all the PAs are confined to analysing their household survey data according to the differences in the sex of the household head. Lying behind the aggregated household approach is an implicit assumption of pooled income and consumption within the household, despite considerable evidence to the contrary, especially for West Africa. Such a household has a head and the characteristics of this head – age, sex and marital status – are invariably collected and form a ready basis for sorting the data. Thus, women can be made visible only as female heads of household. Consequently, some of the approach to gender in the PAs is driven by data whose mode of collection embodies prior decisions about the level at which human agency and personhood can, or should be, appropriately conceptualised in policy analysis of this kind.

The contemporary analysis of gender began with the understanding that the family-based household is never a terrain of equality. Wellbeing, power and often access to economic resources are all differentially distributed. Intra-household relations themselves have been shown to be a powerful determinant of individual access to utilities and capabilities. Twenty years of feminist argument and evidence about the need to analyse the household as a system of a social relations (Whitehead 1981; Evans 1991; Kabeer 1994; Folbre 1996), plus the evidence of gender differentiated poverty outcomes, has led to several developments in the formal economic modelling of households (see Haddad, Hoddinott and Alderman 1997). These important developments are not reflected in the methodologies adopted in the PAs we are considering. All lack any intra-household dimension to income.

Female-headed households

Despite the limitations, it is important to compare female- and male-headed households, if only because of some claims that growing poverty in sub-Saharan Africa is associated with the growth of female-headed households, or that female-headed households are disproportionately poor.[6] When female-headed households are compared with male-headed within each PA, using the poverty measurement from the household surveys, there is no clear finding as to which is likely to be poorer. So, in *Tanzania* and *Ghana II*, female-headed households are reported as richer, while in *Uganda I*, and *Zambia*, they are poorer. There was no comment on the level at which the sometimes very small differences have been shown to be significant, or indeed *if* they are. We were surprised that there had been no effort to compare female and male heads of households divided into urban and rural dwellers, or to make regional comparisons given differences in labour markets, climatically linked types of agriculture and social organisation. Such a comparison is positively crying out to be made in the *Ghana II* PA, in the light of the interesting finding in the PPA that female headship in the South is not perceived to be associated with poverty, whereas in the North it is.

The evidence of the six PAs, as well as the extensive literature deconstructing the idea of female-headed households,[7] suggest that disaggregation by gender of 'household head' does not provide a very meaningful approach to gender and poverty. The category of female headship lumps together categories of household, generated by different processes at different life cycle stages and for different reasons, which are likely to have a variety of socio-economic circumstances and opportunities.[8] This makes any simple comparison between male-headed and female-headed households impossible to interpret.

A further point is that even where certain types of female-headed households are found to be poorer, this begs a further set of questions for which we need a processual, rather than snapshot approach to household formation. In discussions of the household characteristics of poor and poorest households, the household variables are always treated as if they were independent, but it is perfectly possible that the chain of causation runs the other way round. For example, lone widows may well be a significantly poor category of households in sub-Saharan Africa, but why do some widows end up living alone and others don't? Widowhood may be a calamitous event for the poor only because it is those widows who are poor whose children leave the household – perhaps on labour migration. When more economically secure women are widowed, they do not end up living alone. This suggests the need for policies that support the social management of household membership, which is such a priority concern for African people in very many areas (Bledsoe 1995; Lockwood 1997).

The decision then to prioritise money-metric poverty lines, based on households, as the unit of analysis as the measurement of poverty has profound consequences for any gender profiling of poverty. It is one of a number of methodological decisions which underlie the way in which gender is present, or absent, in the PAs. It undermines any perspective on the ways in which intra-household inequalities might contribute to gendered poverty outcomes. Poverty lines may be politically useful for establishing entitlement in welfare states or as baselines for assessing changes in incomes. However, it is difficult to make a link between the measurement of poverty in this form and its causes, and therefore to any explanation and rationale for alleviation strategies. A major reason for this is the difficulty of establishing poverty processes using static measurements of this kind.

Measuring gender and poverty: II – gender and the Participatory Poverty Assessments

These kinds of limitations of conventional household-level surveys of quantitative poverty indicators have been widely discussed. They undoubtedly influenced the Bank's decision to experiment in the PAs with methodologies that incorporate a qualitative, or subjective, element through using participation as a key tool. The Participatory Development Group that was established within the Bank, promoted the idea of commissioning PPAs to operational managers (Holland and Blackburn 1998).

The growing popularity in participatory methodologies reflects an interest in both the values embodied in the use of participatory methodologies and in the use of specific methods, as both a planning aide and a form of research method. There are many different kinds of participatory methodology. Guijt and Shah (1997) list 33 separate approaches and sets of techniques, each with its attendant acronym and a substantial and multi-faceted literature on their advantages and disadvantages over more traditional methods (for Participatory Rural Appraisal, PRA, see Chambers 1994).

The core idea in participatory methods is that of using a variety of techniques to elicit knowledge, characterisations and understandings which do not use the language, concepts and categories of the interviewer and researcher, who by definition does not share the economic and social reality of poor people. The open-endedness of participatory techniques, and especially their stress on local perceptions of poverty, allows for a fuller range of poverty concepts. In addition, participatory methodologies also incorporate a philosophy that valorises the direct involvement of people in problem identification. They draw on a critique of literacy practices which argues that these are more than a set of technical skills, but are also a key element in a nexus of power–knowledge relations. Participatory methodologies aim to deliver a bottom-up approach and to report the voices of the poor.

One contentious area in participatory methodologies is their use of more traditional qualitative techniques as part of participatory methods. We were initially surprised to find interviews with key informants and unstructured interviews with farmers or urban traders being described as 'participatory', since we are accustomed to think of these as standard qualitative research methods. However, techniques such as conversational interviewing and semi-structured interviews are now normal practice in some kinds of participatory methodologies. Proponents argue that it is the participatory context in which these semi-structured interviews were carried out which is the important feature of the methodology (Norton: personal communication). Furthermore, the participatory element in using informal interviewing of individuals, as part of a PPA, does become difficult to pin down.

Contestation about what constitutes a participatory method and its relation to qualitative methods is not simply a turf war. It is an important link to the long-standing epistemological competition in the social sciences between quantitative and qualitative approaches to research. Within economics, the quantitative paradigm has a foundational status. The use of the new participatory methods within the Bank, whose research culture has been dominated by economics, represents a foothold for non-quantitative methods. However, this does beg the question of whether there should not be a greater role for the findings from more conventional research using qualitative methods in the Bank's discussions of poverty. Our six PAs make relatively little use of the existing published local-level case studies that have used a variety of qualitative research techniques to produce data appropriate for the analysis of socio-economic processes.[9]

Four Participatory Poverty Assessments

Given the emphasis on flexibility and local ownership in participatory methods, we were particularly interested in how each of the PPAs had been done and how the findings were integrated into the PAs. Moreover, as men and women experience poverty rather differently, we would expect gender to be made more visible through PPA methodologies.

In our four examples, the *Uganda* study stands out. The PPA was conceived as providing an adjunct to existing data and was used in the war zones where the household-level survey work, on which the rest of the poverty assessment depends, could not be carried out. This was a very early example of a PPA and the decision to use it as an 'adjunct' clearly had a lot to do with local circumstances. There is very little evidence that the results of the *Uganda* PPA in any way influenced the analysis in the PA, especially its policy discussion. Nevertheless, according to Robb (1998), the *Uganda* PA generated a widespread discussion in the Bank of the value of using qualitative methods.

The other three examples of PAs with PPAs, dated 1994, 1995 and 1996, all had the participatory element funded as a separate piece of research. The most comprehensive published PPA in our set is that from *Zambia* (1994). The account of the methods of the PPA in Volume 5 of the PA is detailed and it is immediately clear that the participatory data collection exercise includes many forms of semi-structured interviewing of individuals and groups as a significant part of the research.

In contrast to the *Uganda* PA, it is much easier to see the influence of the PPA in the case of the *Zambia* assessment. However, moving backwards from the PPA Volume 5, through Volume 3 (on rural poverty), to the main report, Volume 1, we witness a loss of many themes from the PPA. The specificities of rural poverty, which are well described in the PPA report itself, become dominated by analytical and policy agendas which are extraneous to the local situation.[10] It is in this process that the gender insights from the PPA become lost. First, because they are not used in the rural volume, which is dominated by other specially commissioned work, notably that on agricultural modelling. Second, when these Volume 3 findings make their way into Volume 1, evidence there that the gender division of labour is not nearly as rigid as the model specified, is ignored in favour of the findings of the model.

The design of the *Ghana* PPA and its findings are much less transparent. Very little of the design of the research and the findings appear in the PA itself. They are instead described in a separate discussion paper (Norton *et al.* 1995) in the *Poverty and Social Policy Series*. The *Ghana II* case (1995), shows clear slippage or gaps between the PPA and the PA. In the PA itself, the findings from the qualitative interviews and the various participatory exercises appear as a separate chapter. This follows on immediately from the quantitative data description. Care is taken to discuss the linkages between the two kinds of findings; however, some of the key messages from the local conceptions of vulnerability and poverty of the PPA are not carried through elsewhere in the PA. Further slippage occurs when we come to the final chapter on the policy agenda. The prescription is a three-pronged set, namely broad-based growth (especially in agriculture); deepening of human capital through education and health; and the use of a targeted social fund. The appraisal of the health and education sectors made in the PPA are taken on board. However, the discussion of agriculture seems to derive little from the PPA findings. In the *Ghana II* case, there is no doubt that certain findings of the PPA are relatively well integrated into the PA and it does appear to influence the overall policy recommendations. Nevertheless, the internal evidence suggests that it is a very selective reading of the PPA findings. The gender findings of the PPA are among those that are subject to this selective reading.

Our final case is that of *Tanzania* (1996) which is both very individual and very interesting. Policy makers were consulted on what they wanted to know and this was incorporated in the terms of reference for the PPA. The research team's stress on credibility led them to design one part of their PPA as a semi-structured interview format, with a sample of households which was drawn in a statistically rigorous way as a sub-sample for the main survey. This methodology enables some of the PPA findings to claim statistical significance; others have a more strictly illustrative or qualitative role. There are several chapters of the PA where the findings of the PPA are apparently widely integrated into the analysis and discussion. The PPA results are not *only* used when they can be backed up by household economic survey evidence. A telling example of this occurs in the discussion of female-headed households. There is a stark difference in the findings from the main quantitative and PPA surveys about the poverty of female-headed households. According to the PPA data, 29 per cent of female-headed households are very poor, but the main survey data gives only 18 per cent. In the interesting discussion of this difference, it is suggested that people themselves perceive poverty as being about more than current income and resources, but also about long-term security. The discrepancy arises because more female heads lack long-term security, since they are less likely to own capital assets than male heads and are also more isolated from supportive family networks. This discussion is judicious in its attempt to reconcile differences in the findings. This kind of serious comparison is rare and rarer still is a preference for the PPA evidence over that from a household survey.

Do the Participatory Poverty Assessments improve gender analysis?

Our most important question, of course, is whether the PPAs improve the gender analysis in the PAs. Participatory methodologies might potentially deliver a gendered profile of poverty because of their capacity to come closer to people's experience of poverty. However, despite the fact that those PAs with PPAs in our sample do show greater gender sensitivity, this does not seem to come from a direct delivery of gendered poverty analysis from the PPA findings. Given the various claims made for participatory methodologies, this is both striking and disappointing. In the following analysis of several claims frequently made for participatory methodologies, we show that the potential for PPAs to improve gender analysis fails precisely because it is only a potential, not an intrinsic feature. In the absence of existing gender awareness, the PPA will add little that is new.

Booth *et al.* (1998) argue that one major benefit of the PPAs lies in the potential for *triangulation*. We are in complete agreement about the huge benefits of triangulation in an analysis of poverty, its incidence, characteristics and causes in sub-Saharan Africa, but there are few examples in our case studies that PPAs are being used in this way. The PAs appear to have a limited understanding of non-quantitative non-survey-based methodologies, poor conceptualisation of what PPAs can do, and very little idea about triangulation and how multi-stranded methods can be successfully combined. Indeed, as we have indicated, the PPAs sit very uneasily within the PAs. The PAs almost inevitably privilege the authority and use of quantitative data from household surveys over qualitative information, which effectively comes from the participatory PAs. The lack of methodological sophistication in resolving the tension between the different types of data represents yet another barrier between the potential for the PPAs to contribute a gendered perspective on poverty and their actual failure to do so.

The claim that PPAs give a more dynamic picture of poverty is an important one (see Booth *et al.* 1998). It is made explicit in the *Ghana II* Assessment and is followed by a discussion of seasonal aspects of poverty and malnutrition, which introduces the idea of poverty as vulnerability. The qualitative PPA accounts certainly include the reporting of long-term changes in the environment which are having a critical effect on vulnerability. This is an important discussion. But it is 'dynamic' only in the simple sense that long-term trends are addressed; what is absent is an account of the economic and social dynamics related to environmental trends. In our three examples where there is a full PPA component, this has not produced a substantial account of poverty causes and poverty processes. Both methodologies – participatory and conventionally statistical – can be deployed to produce static pictures of poverty (cf. Baulch 1996).

The politics of poverty

Booth *et al.* (1998) point out that participatory methodologies have come to be seen as 'a powerful tool' to establish how poor people perceive and understand poverty. Indeed one of the most frequently cited advantages of using participatory methodologies in the Bank's documents lies in their capacity to access the *'voices of the poor'*. There is, however, unease as to what this means, and how it should be done. In one or two cases, the results of the country's PPA are introduced with a composite picture of a poor person that is very close to being banal. This is not very different from the simple addition of human interest – to show poverty is a human tragedy, experienced by flesh and blood people, not by statistical units.

Nonetheless, there are some cases where the poor's perceptions have been used properly as evidence. Perhaps the most promising aspect of the PPAs is the detailed information they have provided on the reality of public service provision. Norton (1998b) identifies these policy areas as ones in which there has been a successful translation of findings into public policy. It is worth pointing out that the data collection in some PPAs was specifically geared to these aspects of public service provision. For example, in the *Ghana* PPA, the third round of data collection was specifically about this and this is reflected in the findings. It represents a priority of the data collectors and it is not clear how far it matches poor people's priorities.

There is scarcely any reporting on how the PPAs ensured that the voices of women were heard. One of the major literatures criticising participatory methodologies has concerned their capacity to represent multiple and different voices (Mosse 1994; Guijt and Shah 1997). There has been a lot of concern that the voices of the farmers and the voices of the poor picked up through participatory methodologies may turn out to be the voices of men (and slightly wealthier men at that).[11] Without much more detail on the processes by which (and by whom) the PPAs were conducted, it is impossible to assess how widespread and systematic a gender-blind application of participatory method has prevented the PAs from including the voices of poor women.

Participatory methodologies were originally developed within the context of the design and implementation of projects, and were intended to change the ways in which decisions were made. Such issues of power are of course very different where they are directed towards national-level issues of measurement and policy. But within this new context, an important claim made for the PPAs was that, since they are locally owned in a way that conventional poverty measurement is not, they open up a national debate on poverty, making it visible and a legitimate issue for political discourse. Certainly, there is evidence that the Assessments are opening up lively and productive debates at national and international levels (Norton, personal communication). It is too early to judge whether, or how soon, this will lead to shifts in political priorities and policies.

The PPAs have involved larger numbers of people in the process of direct engagement with fellow citizens as a source of research evidence. Here, the key issue is the relatively neglected one of the politics of poverty research, which takes us back to the problem of voice. National debates my be generated, but existing political structures have important effects on the outcomes of these debates. These political issues have urgent relevance for the local politics of gender, as well as the local politics of poverty. The greater awareness of poverty created by the PPAs does not necessarily lead to a more gender-aware national poverty debate or to capacity building for gendered poverty analysis. The national political discourses about poverty that are being promoted may remain aloof from the national debates about gender, depending on the existing character of the local and national politics of gender. Changing the politics of poverty in Africa – whether in national arenas or in research culture – will not in itself change the politics of gender.

An overall assessment

The analysis in this section suggests that there are severe constraints militating against the potential capacity of the PPAs to produce gender-sensitive accounts of poverty. Participatory methodologies are neither intrinsically gender-sensitive nor gender-neutral (cf. Kabeer 1997). It depends how they are conducted. There is a range of reasons why the PPAs do not deliver a set of gender messages that are then picked up and used in the PAs. Some gender differences did emerge in many of the PPAs, but so much of the PPA findings are left out of the final Reports that this potential for gender analysis is completely lost.

At a more fundamental level, one factor explaining the gender weaknesses in the PPAs is the absence of gender analysis, of any depth, in the participatory methodologies that underlie them. Some feminist methodologies had very similar starting premises of participatory methodologies, especially in their analysis of the relationship between knowledge and power. The two schools also share sophisticated discussions of the link between research, empowerment and social differences.[12] Yet these feminist influences are often unexplored and unacknowledged by those advocating participatory methodologies.[13] In the last analysis then, it is not simply the marginalisation of PPA findings within the PAs that reduces their gender impacts. Serious shortcomings in the theory and practice of participatory methodologies also play an important part.

We have addressed the participatory methodologies at some length because they are an important innovation in the PAs. Their use reflects widespread misgivings about the potential of money-metric poverty line measurements and definitions for dynamic and poverty analysis. The use of the PPAs has been a learning experience, so that what they are meant to do in each PA is a bit of a moving target. Many of our criticisms of these PPA examples, which represent early attempts to incorporate the new methods, are being addressed in the plans for future PPAs. For us, two issues stand out. First, successful use of participatory methodologies has breached the monopoly over poverty measurement hitherto held by money-metric poverty methodologies. It opens up a space for more careful consideration of the use of alternatives to national household surveys. Our own view is that there is an important role here for integrating the findings of qualitative case studies with national-level findings, as well as instituting new studies using participatory methodologies. Secondly, there is an urgent need for future PPAs to be much more gender-aware in how they are carried out and to be much more fully grounded in a gendered analysis of poverty.

Gender and policy in the Poverty Assessments

There is a deeply embedded paradox in the Assessments. On the one hand, there is considerable variation in the approaches to measurement, to the identification of poverty causes and to the analysis of gender relations in the PAs. On the other hand, there is a remarkable consistency of views expressed on how to reduce poverty, with usually implicit, but occasionally explicit, implications for the treatment of gender. These consistent views can be traced to an orthodoxy in the World Bank regarding the nature of poverty and policy on poverty reduction, which has its fullest expression in the *1990 WDR*. The policy sections of the Assessments may therefore be read as exercises in applying the framework of the *1990 WDR* to particular countries, rather than being generated out of the study of poverty in those countries itself. We suggested earlier that the resulting gaps between evidence and analysis on the one hand, and policy, on the other, reflect a process by which policy sections of the Assessments came under much heavier peer review. While differing empirical specifics of poverty are consistent with the Bank's position on poverty reduction, different models for poverty reduction are not.

The implications for gender, and particularly for the ways in which a gender analysis informs, or fails to inform, policy in the Assessments, are considerable. A major problem is the 'filtering out' of gender issues and gendered perspectives. For example in the *Tanzania* PA, a lack of rural infrastructure, education and safety nets are picked up on in the policy section, while other issues, such as the detailed discussion of gender, are not mentioned there. We noted above that this process starts as we move from the PPAs to the main PAs, but it continues as we move from evidence to analysis and, finally, to policy.

The resulting 'gaps' in the treatment of poverty are analogous to those in the treatment of gender. One of the most striking aspects of the six PAs is that the relationship between evidence about poverty and its causes on the one hand, and policy recommendations on the other, is highly selective and highly partial. In the *Zambia* PA, the sophisticated programming model of household farming is used in the policy section, producing recommendations which are belied by the relatively rich evidence and analysis produced elsewhere in the report. Issues present in the evidence appear with changed emphasis, or sometimes do not appear at all. For example, issues highlighted in the PPA in the *Ghana II* report receive a much lower emphasis in the policy section. Problems and solutions raised in the analysis are overlooked in the policy section. Again, in the example of the *Tanzania* PA, the issue of remoteness is addressed by proposing more roads, rather than rethinking the liberalisation of marketing that is suggested by the earlier analysis. In reports where country-level evidence is less extensive, there is a tendency to rely on international comparisons to make arguments and policy recommendations (for example, *Ghana I* or

Uganda II). In the case of *Uganda I*, the policy section is explicitly based on the *1990 WDR*.

The 1990 WDR model of poverty

Other reviews of the PAs also refer to the deep influence of the *1990 WDR*. As we described above, the analysis and policy prescriptions in the PAs reflect not only this orthodoxy, but also an evolving approach to poverty and policy within the Bank over a longer period. We see the implications for gender emerging in three areas in the Assessments, matching the three-pronged *1990 WDR* approach. These are the idea of market-led growth (particularly export-led agricultural growth), the role of education and vulnerability.

In the early 1980s, the World Bank was embarking on structural adjustment as its core policy. The key World Bank document on Africa over the 1980s was known as the 'Berg Report' (World Bank 1981). This put forward a view of African agriculture and an account of agricultural stagnation that is still clearly visible in the PAs in the mid-1990s. The PAs also reflect the shift marked by the Bank's (1989) Report, *Sub-Saharan Africa: From Crisis to Sustainable Growth*. A more nuanced agenda was introduced, emphasising institutional reform, increased efficiency of service delivery and re-direction of expenditure towards primary rather than tertiary services. All the Assessments advocate liberalisation of trade and domestic marketing. They state variously that farmers should not be overtaxed, need liberalised export markets and inputs such as roads, fertilisers and credit, as well as price incentives.

Until recently, the conceptual, largely microeconomic framework underlying the market-led growth approach was gender-blind. With the sole exception of the *Zambia* PA, there is no sustained thinking about gender in relation to the broad-based export-led growth model in our six PAs, except for brief assertions that agricultural extension services must target women. Even this last point usually enters under the policy sections on agriculture, not on broad-based growth.

The *Zambia* Assessment frames gender as a question of efficiency: rigidities in the gender division of labour are identified as potential barriers to the expansion of agricultural production. This approach very much reflects the main way in which microeconomists both inside and outside the World Bank (as opposed to social scientists), have taken up gender over the 1990s (see for example, Collier 1994). Gender equity arguments have been recast as arguments about efficiency (Razavi and Miller 1995b: 40–2, 47). This process has currently reached the stage that gender relations are now seen by some within the Bank as the main constraint to growth in sub-Saharan Africa (Blackden 1998). The issues raised by feminist economists – of gender equity within households and the balancing of the productive and reproductive economies – are not reflected in the growth agenda.

Vulnerability

Social safety nets as they appear in the Assessments have picked up the UNICEF idea of vulnerability. UNICEF, in the publication *Adjustment with a Human Face* (Cornia, Jolly and Stewart 1987) emphasised that adjustment involved costs to which some sections of the population were particularly vulnerable. This combined with the recognition that 'getting prices right' would not alone bring investment, stability and growth. In practice, the social dimensions of adjustment programmes introduced in Africa rarely addressed the problems of the poor, especially the rural poor. They largely went to compensate public sector workers who lost incomes through cuts in public employment. The successors to SDA programmes – Social Funds – have also failed to act as proper safety nets (Tjonneland *et al.* 1998: 73).

There are sometimes considerable continuities between the UNICEF approach and the poverty groups that emerge in the PAs: compare, for example, the *Ghana I* PA with Cornia, Jolly and Stewart (1987). However, when the social safety nets concept appears in the policy sections of the PAs, it does so in a different context from its original use. The concept of vulnerability in the PAs is not used to mean vulnerability to economic change (including reform), but a more static sense of vulnerability to drought, other natural disasters, and a 'common-sense' notion of social vulnerability. This approach is consistent with the Bank's continuing position that adjustment causes only 'transitional' poverty and that the majority of the poor have generally gained from adjustment (see Demery and Squire 1996).

'Common-sense' vulnerable groups often include orphans, the disabled, widows, female-headed households and rural producers in certain marginalised regions. These are of course not categories that have been identified by the statistical analysis. They do, however, represent a kind of analysis of what poverty is (vulnerability), as well as referring to particular policy needs. Women are over-represented in these 'common-sense' vulnerable groups. This is explicitly or implicitly linked to a static gender-as-characteristic understanding of gender inequalities.

The role of education

Recognition of the limits of 'getting prices right', and the criticism levelled by UNICEF and others at school fees and health care charges, has resulted in a new orthodoxy within the Bank on the pivotal role of human capital. This orthodoxy has been strengthened by the Bank views on the role of education in enhancing growth rates in East Asia. Female education in particular, began to be seen as a synergistic 'magic bullet' which would not only increase child welfare, but also reduce population growth and increase economic growth.[14]

It is widely stated in the Assessments that education is intimately related to agricultural productivity, and thus the escape from poverty. However, the evidence given is often weak, with apparent associations only loosely established and poorly analysed. One concern here is that a relationship between education and income might beis being read spuriously as causal, when both education and household income may be affected by underlying patterns of wealth organised through families. An alternative hypothesis – seeing educational outcomes as the result of patterns of wealth and poverty rather than the other way round – would be more consistent with the striking fact that, while there are strong statements about the desire for more and better schools in the PPAs, education is not mentioned as an important *cause* of poverty in any of those the PPAs reported.

The Bank orthodoxy concerning gender and education (see for example, Summers 1994), if not about gender issues more broadly, is reflected within the Assessments, where female education appears in strikingly uniform ways. The analysis of female education in the Assessments is based exclusively on efficiency arguments: how female education is more efficient than male education in increasing child and household welfare, and development indicators more widely. It is not an analysis that says anything about the reproduction of structural gender inequalities, or anything substantive about how gender inequalities underlie educational outcomes. A gender gap in primary or junior secondary education is found in all cases (*Uganda II*: 64; *Uganda I*: 38–9; *Zambia*: 53; *Ghana I*: 19; *Tanzania*: Chapter 5; *Ghana II*: 33). The explanations of why these gender gaps exist are particularly problematic. They are either purely economistic, about expected future returns, or they are anodyne ('parental reluctance' and 'gender bias' are both cited by *Uganda I*, which seem so self-evident as to be virtually meaningless).

In conclusion, it is clear that there are gaps between the evidence on both gender and poverty issues in the Assessments, and their treatment in the policy sections, because the policy and analysis are much more heavily influenced by peer review and by the evolution of Bank thinking since the late 1980s. As a result, the discussions of growth and poverty in the Assessments we examined is almost entirely gender-blind, even in the case where the analysis of rural growth was more gendered (*Zambia*). This is a fairly striking invisibilisation of the role of gender relations in rural African economies, considering that 30 years have already passed since Ester Boserup's pioneering work in this area. The sole exception is the mention of targeting agricultural extension services to women, an approach that merely reinforces the sense that policy-makers find it very difficult to engage with the gendered analysis of the economy.

Gendered policy appears to be more visible in the area of vulnerability and safety nets. However, it typically takes the form of 'common-sense' statements about groups taken to be vulnerable as a whole, such as widows. Finally, the gender jewel in the policy crown is female education. This is the only high-profile gendered policy prescription in most of the Assessments, and reflects the fact that this is the only gender issue on which Bank staff – from country level right up to the President – can express clear consensus. It is also a prescription based on ideas about the developmental efficiency of female education, rather than gender equity.

Gender and poverty: paying attention to process

At the beginning of this chapter, we suggested that the PAs of the 1990s were conducted in a climate of development and aid which was much more alert to issues of gender equity as compared with the 1970s. Perhaps the most disappointing aspect of our review of these six case studies is how little influence the accumulating evidence – that men and women experience poverty differently – has had. The Assessments betray a lack of any substantial appreciation of the issues raised by the study of gender and poverty in Africa since the 1980s.

In our view, the quantitative evidence in the Assessments (on which so much importance is placed) is both underinterpreted and overinterpreted. In the 'poverty profiles', an opportunity to explore poverty dynamics through a series of comparative analyses is ignored in favour of a set of statistical associations which produce a static view of who the poor are. At the same time, the quantitative data are taken up selectively to illustrate *a priori* arguments about causes of poverty. The relationship between poverty and education discussed above is a good example.

The PPAs, which were done in four out of the six cases, have a greater potential to unpick this methodological lock, in that they can have the capacity to say something about perceptions of gender and poverty and of gender relations. Our review confirms the point made by a number of critical, but sympathetic, observers that PPAs are not intrinsically gender-sensitive, and that considerable effort needs to be made to ensure that they are so.

There is, in our view, a further problem with the participatory methodologies as they are currently discussed, and their capacity to deliver a gendered analysis. The methodological tradition that has emerged within the participatory approach, as opposed to that underlying more conventional locality-specific case studies of poverty by sociologists or anthropologists, emphasises the importance of how data is collected, but underplays the importance of interpreting or 'reading' data. This stage of participatory methodologies is relatively underdiscussed but it is an important point where the voices of women, which may well be muted by local gender relations, become heard. 'Reading' PPA data also means becoming aware of, and open to, implictly gendered statements about poverty coming from poor people.

Above, we suggested that there was a gendered gap between the main findings of the Assessments and their policy sections. While some of the gender findings of the PPAs did find their way into the reports, and the separately commissioned background papers on gender were also represented in some PAs, this evidence and thematic discussion was usually lost when the policy section was reached. These gaps arise because the PAs are, above all, policy documents. The status of the documents as World Bank papers means that they are situated within a particular policy context or climate, which effectively imposes assumptions about what can or cannot be done, and what should or should not be done, in the realm of policy.

A major influence on the policy recommendations in the PAs is the underlying model of poverty causes developed within the Bank, and the associated approach to policy for poverty reduction policy. This strong Bank orthodoxy on poverty reduction strategy interferes with any detailed interpretations of the evidence and findings of the poverty assessments. It is the policy sections of the PAs that are the most influenced by the Bank's evolving but relatively universal model of poverty and poverty reduction. This model has built into it certain assumptions about gender.

The PAs apply a standard, pre-existing analysis, with its attached policy agenda, to each country. The model applied is largely based on the *1990 World Development Report*, with some additional features that evolve out of the Bank's interpretation of East Asian experience. One of the important characteristics of the *1990 WDR* analysis of poverty is that it is fundamentally about the actions of individuals or individual households in markets. With the exception of the relationship between the market and the state, social and economic relations are absent from this analysis. We would therefore agree with the ISS evaluation that one of the main shortcomings of the PAs is the limited poverty analysis which they contain, and we would point to this lack of analysis of *relational processes of impoverishment or accumulation* as the critical limitation. This is similar to the point made by feminist economists, that gender-blind economics has failed to analyse how men and women are positioned differently in relation to the economy, and to each other.

A particularly clear example of this is in the discussions of agriculture. Many of the policy chapters of the PAs have long discussions of agriculture, which reflects the fact that huge numbers of poor people in sub-Saharan Africa gain their livelihoods in that sector. Increasing the productivity, output and returns to smallholder agriculture must be core objectives in any strategy of labour intensive and pro-poor growth. Yet, we found it hard to feel very confident about either the diagnosis of the processes which produce poverty among African agriculturalists, or the proposed remedies.

Absent from the analysis in the PAs are examinations of rural livelihoods, agrarian socio-economic processes, rural social relations and, despite the centrality of the gender division of labour to African agriculture, of course, gender relations. Only by including such examinations would the PAs produce the socio-economic categories of poor people that Hanmer, Pyatt and White (1996) call for as a prerequisite for an analysis of poverty. The accounts of rural processes found in sociological, anthropological, and in some cases historical, case studies hardly seem to have penetrated discussions of agricultural policy in the PAs. It is true that women sometimes make momentary appearances in the agricultural policy sections of the PAs. However, they usually do so in ways that are unrelated to the previous findings and analyses, but at the same time are highly similar to the few appearances of 'women' and 'gender' in the *Poverty Reduction Handbook.*

The only sustained discussions of women and agriculture centre on land rights, and occur in those PAs that have stressed the legal basis for gender bias. Gender equity demands attention to the land rights issue, and for some women discriminatory inheritance laws and poor land access are significant constraints. But in our view, it is only in a minority of cases that inadequate access to land, because of an inability to secure usufruct rights, is by itself a cause of poverty for the two-thirds of rural African women who are poor. The fact that land rights rarely emerged as a voiced concern of rural women in the PPAs lends some support for this view.

Access to land, as with other significant resources, is secured or lost through the dynamics of gender relations as they intersect with socio-economic processes, which are often, but not always, ones of impoverishment. Once again, the issue here is a contrast between the static analysis of categories and characteristics, and the dynamic analysis of social and economic relations. The link between gender and poverty lies at the level of process and relations. For this link to be established, poverty must be analysed as relation and process, as must gender.

Notes

1. These were chosen so as to give a geographic spread, but also to take advantage of the countries in which we have experience of first-hand field research. The PA documents are World Bank 1992b, 1993a, 1994, 1995a, 1995b, 1996.
2. See, for example, the change from 'women in development' to 'gender and development' by the Development Assistance Committee (DAC) of the OECD. Whitehead (1998) dicusses this shift. Goetz and Baden (1997) includes an interesting discussion of contentions around the use of the language of gender and/or women at Beijing.
3. In our sample countries, both Uganda and Ghana have two successive PAs, conducted in 1992 and 1995. In each case, the 1992 PAs are denoted I and the 1995 PAs are denoted II. The 1992 *Uganda* PA was published in 1993 (World Bank 1993a).
4. The exception to this was *Uganda II*, which was in effect not a full poverty assessment, but a *Country Economic Memorandum* with an Quantitative Appendix on poverty.
5. For example, for Uganda, a relative poverty line approach in 1992 is followed by an absolute food-basket-based approach in 1995, making comparison across time very difficult (Appleton 1996).
6. For discussions see, for example, Baden and Milward (1995); Buvinic (1983, 1997); (Chant 1997a); Jackson (1996).
7. See Appleton (1996), Chant (1997a, 1997b); Lloyd and Gage-Brandon (1993).

8. Persistent definitional problems with SSA households (see Guyer 1981; Guyer and Peters 1987; Yanagisako 1979) underlie some of these difficulties. Many household surveys (for example, the *Uganda Household Budget Survey*, the *Ghana Living Standards Survey*) contain relatively little discussion of how these difficulties have been resolved, but most of the country studies throw up examples of culturally-specific household forms that do not tally with standardised definitions of household. A particular issue here is that we get very little sense of how polygamy is treated in relation to household definition and hence of what contribution polygamy makes to the category of female headship.

9. Some recent PAs have examined this literature with many positive effects (see World Bank 1995c),

10. A fuller and more informed discussion on the influence of the Zambian PPA findings on the PA and other aspects of the policy process is to be found in Norton (1998a); Norton is one of the authors of the PPA.

11. See Cornwall (1997) for a full exploration of gender sensitivity in participatory methodologies.

12. See Maguire (1984) and Mies (1983) for a positive assessment of the potential of participatory methodologies from a feminist perspective, and Mosse (1994) and Guijt and Shah (1997) who point out its limitations in practice. See also Cornwall (1997).

13. Robert Chambers' (1997) account of the theoretical influences on PRA is a case in point.

14. Summers (1994). For a critique see Green (1994) and Jackson (1992).

Bibliography

Appleton, S. (1996), 'Problems of measuring changes in poverty over time: the case of Uganda 1989–92', *IDS Bulletin*, Vol. 27(1), pp. 43–55.

Baden, S. and K. Milward (1995), 'Gender and poverty', Bridge Report for Sida, Brighton: Institute of Development Studies.

Baulch, B. (1996), 'The new poverty agenda: a disputed consensus', *IDS Bulletin*, Vol. 27(1), pp. 1–10.

Blackden, M. (1998), 'Gender, growth and poverty reduction in sub-Saharan Africa', Washington, DC: World Bank, mimeo.

Bledsoe, C. (1995), 'The social construction of reproductive outcomes: social marginalisation in sub-Saharan Africa', in T. Locoh and V. Hertrich (eds), *The Onset of Fertility Transition in Sub Saharan Africa*, Liège: Ordina Editions, pp. 221–34.

Booth, D., P. Lanjouw, J. Hentschel and J. Holland (1998), *Participation and Combined Methods in African Poverty Assessment: Renewing the Agenda*, London: Department for International Development.

Buvinic, M. (1983), 'Women's issues in Third World development: a policy analysis', in M. Buvinic (ed.), *Women and Poverty in the Third World*, Baltimore: Johns Hopkins University Press, pp. 14–33.

Buvinic, M. (1997), 'Women in poverty: a new global underclass', *Foreign Policy* (Fall), pp. 38–53.

Chambers, R. (1994), *Participatory Rural Appraisal: Challenges, Potentials and Paradigms*, Brighton: Institute of Development, University of Sussex.

Chambers, R. (1997), *Whose Reality Counts? Putting the Last First*, London: Intermediate Technology Publicaions.

Chant, S. (1997a), *Women Headed Households: Diversity and Dynamics in the Developing World*, London: Macmillan.

Chant, S. (1997b), 'Women headed households: poorest of the poor?', *IDS Bulletin*, Vol. 28(3), pp. 26–48.

Collier, P. (1994), 'Gender aspects of labor allocation during structural adjustment: a theoretical framework and the Africa experience', in S. Horton, R. Kanbur and D. Mazumdar, *Labour Markets in an Era of Adjustment*, Washington, DC: World Bank.

Cornia, G.A., R. Jolly and F. Stewart (eds) (1987), *Adjustment with a Human Face. Protecting the Vulnerable and Promoting Growth*, New York: Oxford University Press.

Cornwall, A. (1997), 'Gender politics and the politics of difference', in I. Guijt and M. Shah (eds), *The Myth of Community: Gender and Participatory Development*, London: Intermediate Technology Publications, pp. 46–57.

Demery, L. and L. Squire (1996), 'Macroeconomic adjustment and poverty in Africa: an emerging picture', *World Bank Research Observer*, Vol. 11(1), pp. 39–59.

Evans, A. (1991), 'Gender issues in household rural economics', *IDS Bulletin*, Vol. 22(1), pp. 51–9.

Folbre, N. (1996), 'Hearts and spades: paradigms of household economics', *World Development*, Vol. 14(2), pp. 245–55.

Goetz, A. and S. Baden (1997), 'Who needs (sex) when you can have (gender)? Conflicting discourses on gender at Beijing', *Feminst Review*, Vol. 56, pp. 3–25.

Green, C. (1994), 'Poverty, population and environment: does "synergism" work for women?', *IDS Discussion Paper*, 343, Brighton: Institute of Development Studies.

Guijt, I. and M. Shah (1997), 'General introduction: waking up to power, process and conflict', in I. Guijt and M. Shah (eds), *The Myth of Community: Gender and Participatory Development*, London: Intermediate Technology Publications, pp. 1–23.

Guyer, J. (1981), 'Household and community in African studies', *African Studies Review*, 24(2–3), pp. 87–137.

Guyer, J. and P. Peters (eds) (1987), 'Conceptualizing the household: issues of theory and policy in Africa', *Development and Change*, 18(2), Special Issue.

Haddad, L., J. Hoddinott and H. Alderman (eds) (1997), *Intrahousehold Resource Allocation in Developing Countries: Models, Methods and Policy*, Baltimore and London: Johns Hopkins University Press for the International Food Policy Research Institute.

Hanmer, L., G. Pyatt and H. White (1996), *Poverty in sub-Saharan Africa: What Can we Learn from the World Bank's Poverty Assessments?*, The Hague: Institute of Social Studies Advisory Services.

Holland, J. and J. Blackburn (eds) (1998), *Whose Voice? Participatory Research and Policy Change*, London: Intermediate Technology Publications.

IDS (1994), *Poverty Assessment and Public Expenditure: A Study for the SPA Working Group on Poverty and Social Policy*, Brighton: Institute of Development Studies.

Jackson, C. (1992), 'Questioning synergism: win–win with women in population and environmental policies', Norwich: University of East Anglia, mimeo.

Jackson, C. (1996), 'Rescuing gender from the poverty trap', *World Development*, Vol. 24(3), pp. 489–504.

Kabeer, N. (1994), *Reversed Realities: Gender Heirarchies in Development Thought*, London: Verso.

Kabeer, N. (1997), 'Tactics and trade-offs: revisiting the links between gender and poverty', *IDS Bulletin*, Vol. 28(3), pp. 1–13.

Lipton, M. and S. Maxwell (1992), 'The new poverty agenda: an overview', IDS Discussion Paper, No. 306, Brighton: Instititute of Development Studies.

Lloyd, C. and A. Gage-Brandon (1993), 'Women's role in maintaining households: family welfare and sexual inequality in Ghana', *Population Studies*, Vol. 47, pp. 115–31.

Lockwood, M. (1997), 'Reproduction and poverty in Sub-Saharan Africa', *IDS Bulletin*, Vol. 28(3), pp. 91–100.

Maguire, P. (1984), *Women in Development: An Alternative Analysis*, Boston, MA: University of Massachusetts, Center for International Education.

Mies, M. (1983), 'Towards a methodology of feminist research', in G. Bowles and R. Duelli-Klien (eds), *Theories of Women's Studies*, London: Routledge, pp. 173–91.

Moser, C., A. Tornqvist and B. van Bronkhorst (1998), 'Mainstreaming gender and development in the World Bank: a review of progress to date and recommendations for next stages', Washington, DC: World Bank, mimeo.

Mosse, D. (1994), 'Authority, gender and knowledge: theoretical reflections on the practice of participatory rural appraisal', *Development and Change*, Vol. 25(3), pp. 497–526.

Norton, A. (1998a), 'Some reflections on the PPA process and the lessons learned', in J. Holland and J. Blackburn (eds), *Whose Voice? Participatory Research and Policy Change*, London: Intermediate Technology Publications, pp. 143–8.

Norton, A. (1998b), 'Analysing participatory research for policy change', in J. Holland and J. Blackburn (eds), *Whose Voice? Participatory Research and Policy Change*, London: Intermediate Technology Publications, pp. 179–91.

Norton, A., E. Bortei-Doku Aryeetey, D. Korboe and D.K. Tony Dogbe (1995), 'Poverty assessment in Ghana using qualitative and participatory research methods', PSP Discussion Paper Series No 83, Washington, DC: World Bank.

Razavi, S. and C. Miller (1995a), 'From WID to GAD: conceptual shifts in the women and development discourse', Geneva: UNRISD.

Razavi, S. and C. Miller (1995b), 'Gender mainstreaming: a study of efforts by the UNDP', the World Bank and the ILO to Institutionalize Gender Issues', Geneva: UNRISD.

Robb, C. (1998), 'PPAs: a review of the World Bank's experience', in J. Holland and J. Blackburn (eds), *Whose Voice? Participatory Research and Policy Change*, London: Intermediate Technology Publications, pp. 131–42.

Summers, L. (1994), *Investing in All the People: Educating Women in Developing Countries*, Washington, DC: World Bank.

Tjonneland, E., H. Harboe, A.J. Jerve and N. Kanji (1998), 'The World Bank and poverty in Africa: a critical assessment of the Bank's operational strategies for poverty reduction', Oslo: Norwegian Ministry of Foreign Affairs.

Whitehead, A. (1981), 'I'm hungry mum: the politics of domestic budgeting', in K. Young *et al.* (eds), *Of Marriage and the Market*, London: CSE Books, pp. 88–111.

Whitehead, A. (1998), 'Women in development (WID), gender and development (GAD): the new politics of an old distinction', University of Sussex Development Lectures, Brighton: University of Sussex.

Whitehead, A. and Lockwood, M. (1999), 'Gender in the World Bank's poverty assessments: six case studies from Sub-Saharan Africa', Geneva: UNRISD.

World Bank (1981), *Accelerated Development in Sub-Saharan Africa: An Agenda for Action (Berg Report)*. Washington, DC: World Bank.

World Bank (1989), *Sub-Saharan Africa: From Crisis to Sustainable Growth*. Washington, DC: World Bank.

World Bank (1990), *World Development Report for 1990*, Oxford: Oxford University Press.

World Bank (1991), 'Operational Directive 4.15: Poverty Reduction', Washington, DC: World Bank.

World Bank (1992a), *Poverty Reduction Handbook*, Washington, DC: World Bank.

World Bank (1992b), *Ghana I: 2000 and Beyond: Setting the Stage for Accelerated Growth and Poverty Reduction* (one-volume PA), West Africa Department, Washington, DC: World Bank.

World Bank (1993a), *Uganda: Growing out of Poverty* (PA), Washngton, DC: World Bank.

World Bank (1993b), *The East Asian Miracle: Economic Growth and Public Policy*, Oxford: Oxford University Press.

World Bank (1994), *Zambia: Poverty Assessment* (five-volume PA), Human Resources Division, Africa Regional Office, Washington, DC: World Bank.

World Bank (1995a), *Ghana II: Poverty Past, Present and Future* (one-volume. PA), Population and Human Resources Division, Africa Region, Washington, DC: World Bank.

World Bank (1995b), *Uganda: The Challenge of Growth and Poverty Reduction*, CEM, Country Operations Division, Washington, DC: World Bank.

World Bank (1995c), *Cameroon: Diversity, Growth and Poverty Reduction*, Population and Human Resources Division, Africa Region, Washington, DC: World Bank.

World Bank (1996), *Tanzania: The Challenge of Reforms: Growth, Incomes and Welfare* (three-volume PA), Country Operations Division, Washington, DC: World Bank.

World Bank Operations Evaluation Department (OED) (1996), *Poverty Assessment: A Progress Report*, Washington, DC: World Bank.

Yanagisako, S. (1979), 'Family and household: the analysis of domestic groups', *Annual Review of Anthropology*, Vol. 8, pp. 161–205.

11
Attaining the International Development Targets: Will Growth be Enough?

*Lucia Hanmer and Felix Naschold**

Introduction

During the course of the late 1980s and early 1990s, improvements in health and education and progress in poverty reduction ground to a halt, or began to be eroded, in many developing regions and in the transition economies. In 1996 the OECD Development Assistance Committee (DAC) agreed the International Development Targets (IDTs) shown in Box 11.1, reflecting the concern of development agencies and their developing country partners about these trends. This chapter considers whether these targets are attainable.

The following section reviews the economic literature on modelling poverty and human development and the next section examines what data from the 1980s and 1990s can tell us about the determinants of changes in poverty and human development over this time period. We then examine how the poverty projections have been made, and present estimates of poverty in 2015 under various future scenarios. We then describe how the projections for the human development targets have been made, and present results for estimates of infant and under-five mortality, maternal mortality and primary school enrolment rates for 2015 under various future scenarios. The final section draws together the key conclusions regarding the attainability of the DAC targets.

Modelling poverty and human development

Earlier attempts to assess the attainability of the DAC targets (Demery and Walton 1999 and Hanmer *et al.* 1999) are based on the premise that poverty reduction and human development improvement can be specified as

* This research was commissioned by DfID. The authors would like to thank Peter Grant, Peter Balacs and Rachel Turner (DfID) for comments on this chapter and discussion of the issues it addresses. The usual disclaimer applies.

> **Box 11.1   The International Development Targets**
>
> 1   The proportion of people living in extreme poverty in developing
>   countries should be reduced by at least one-half by 2015.
> 2   There should be universal primary education in all countries by 2015.
> 3   Progress towards gender equality and the empowerment of women
>   should be demonstrated by eliminating gender disparity in primary
>   and secondary education by 2005.
> 4   The death rates for infants and children under five should be reduced
>   in each developing country by two-thirds the 1990 level by 2015.
> 5   The rate of maternal mortality should be reduced by three-quarters by
>   2015.
> 6   Access should be available through the primary health-care system to
>   reproductive health services for all individuals of appropriate ages, no
>   later than the year 2015.
> 7   There should be a national strategy for sustainable development, in
>   the process of implementation, in every country by 2005, so as to
>   ensure that current trends in the loss of environmental resources are
>   effectively reversed at both global and national levels by 2015.
>
> *Source*: DAC (1996).

functions of income growth alone. However, this is a simplification that could produce misleading results. Research shows that other variables, besides income, are important determinants of poverty reduction and human development improvement. We review below research findings on the influence of income inequality and the qualitative characteristics of the growth path on poverty reduction and research on the non-income determinants of human development indicators and consider the implications for specifying models for predicting future poverty and human development.

Poverty elasticity estimates and income inequality

The relationship between income growth and poverty reduction (Human Development Indicators (HDI) improvement) is given by the poverty (HDI) elasticity. The elasticities show the percentage change in the poverty head-count incidence (HDI) that result from a 1 per cent change in *per capita* GDP.[1] It is impossible to predict in the abstract how overall income inequality will affect poverty elasticity as the outcome will depend on how the income distribution varies over time, and the specific properties of the poverty measure (Ravallion 1997). One finding that is emerging as robust from the literature is that the size of the poverty elasticity varies system-atically with income inequality (Ravallion 1997; Hanmer *et al.* 1999). Ravallion (1997) tests the hypothesis that the poverty elasticity falls as inequality rises. He uses a general model of the rate of poverty reduction that can be tested for the restrictions that leaves growth alone, as opposed to a distribution-corrected growth rate, determining the rate of poverty reduction. His results confirm that higher initial levels of inequality are associated with lower rates of poverty reduction for any given positive rate of growth.

Poverty reduction and the growth path

While growth is important for poverty reduction it has also been recognised for a long time that the type of growth, that is the particular processes and sectors that generate growth, also matters. Here we investigate the proposition that broad-based (labour-intensive) growth reduces poverty more effectively than other types of growth. It is frequently argued that the agricultural sector is particularly important as a source of broad-based growth as it often possesses the characteristics that can stimulate the sort of growth that reduces poverty rapidly (see Lipton 1977; Stewart 1978; Ranis 1979 for an early statement of these views and Mellor 1999 for a more recent one). Recent studies of poverty reduction in India support this view (Datt and Ravallion 1990, 1996a, 1996b). One finding is that poverty reduction is the result of growth within agriculture, rather than a shift of labour and capital out of agriculture into large-scale industry.[2] Hence growth of agricultural output and small-scale enterprises and services (which are related to the rural economy and linked to the development of a labour-intensive agricultural sector) have a large effect on the reduction of poverty, whereas large-scale industrial and manufacturing growth does not. Thorbecke and Jung (1996) come to similar conclusions for Indonesia.

The significance of agriculture for poverty reduction is also confirmed by results from cross-section data sets. Timmer (1997) finds that manufacturing reduces poverty directly owing to an increase in the income of employed workers, but it also worsens the distribution of income, reducing the overall benefits to the poor. By contrast, agricultural growth is not associated with worsening income distribution.[3] Bourguignon and Morrison (1998) using a sample of 38 small and medium-sized developing countries find that growth in agriculture and in basic services reduces poverty more than expanding industrial output.

The conclusion that agricultural growth is 'best' for poverty reduction is, however, conditional on equitable land distribution. Mellor (1999) argues that agricultural growth is especially effective in reducing poverty because, in addition to generating income for poor farmers, it generates demand for goods and services that can easily be produced by the poor (non-durable consumer goods sold by small shops, market trading services, hoes, ploughs and other capital goods, etc.). However, if land and income distribution is highly skewed, as is common in Latin America and some sub-Saharan

African countries, consumption patterns of landowners are skewed towards imported or capital-intensive consumer goods rather than the products of the small-scale labour-intensive domestic manufacturing and services. De Janvry and Sadoulet (2000) analyse poverty reduction in 11 countries in Latin America and the Caribbean which account for 87 per cent of the region's population. Their findings confirm Mellor's conclusion. They find that, owing to the highly unequal pattern of land ownership, agricultural growth increases overall income inequality. The inequality effect is so strong that agricultural growth produced greater poverty in Latin America and the Caribbean between 1970 and 1994.

De Janvry and Sadoulet's work has important implications for poverty elasticity estimation and for projections based on estimated future growth rates. They find that the qualitative and structural features of the growth path have strong effects on poverty and inequality reduction.[4] In fact, once these variables are included in the poverty reduction model they find that the role of income growth is very small and its total effect is often perverse. The perversity results from the fact that late growth (roughly, growth periods in the 1980s) was usually accompanied by rising urban poverty and rising inequality, though it reduced rural poverty in Latin America. Their findings suggest that simple bivariate models of poverty reduction (e.g. Demery and Walton 1998 and Hanmer *et al.* 1999) may be mis-specified as they fail to control for variations in the poverty reduction capacity of different types of growth paths. Model misspecification is the source of bias in estimators of coefficients which implies that predictions will not be accurate.

To sum up, recent analysis of the determinants of the poverty reduction suggest that using elasticities derived from a bivariate regression model of *per capita* GDP growth on poverty to generate projections is likely to be highly misleading. Economic growth and variables that capture:

(1) Labour productivity growth (real labour income growth)
(2) The volume of employment creation
(3) The sectoral origin of economic growth

should together be considered as determinants of poverty. Furthermore, it may be important to control for initial levels of income inequality when estimating the poverty reducing effects of growth.

Finally, research has also established the importance of the government's policy stance in creating the economic environment for sustained growth and poverty reduction (see, e.g., Wade 1990 and Burnside and Dollar 1998). Maintaining competitive exchange rates and an open trade regime, fostering domestic price stability and controlling deficits on the balance of payments and the government's budget are generally considered to be important preconditions for sustained economic growth.

Modelling Human Development Indicators

Hanmer *et al.* (1999) established that improvements in HDIs are highly correlated with the rate of growth of real *per capita* GDP and with technological progress, which is independent of national rates of *per capita* GDP growth.[5] However, HDIs are imperfectly correlated with *per capita* income and the explanatory power of models can usually be improved with the addition of further socio-economic variables (see for example, UNDP 1996; Ramirez, Ranis and Stewart 1997). However, it is important to establish that explanatory variables included in specified models are robust, that is their coefficients have a significant effect of approximately the same magnitude across a various model specifications.[6] We therefore base our choice of explanatory variables for the infant and under-five mortality rates (*IMR* and *U5MR*) on Hanmer and White's (1999) identification of robust determinants of *IMR* and *U5MR*.[7] The following variables are robust across model specifications:

(1) *Per capita* GDP
(2) The availability of health services (as measured by an output variable rather than an expenditure variable)[8]
(3) Immunisation rates
(4) Education
(5) Gender inequality.

In many countries in the developing world the HIV/AIDS epidemic has had significant effects on progress in reducing infant and child mortality. In some countries in sub-Saharan Africa infant and child mortality has begun to increase again after years of steady improvement (see for example Hanmer and White, 1999 and UNICEF 1999). Whether the HIV/AIDS virus could mean that the infant and child mortality target is unattainable is obviously an important question and new data published by UNAIDS (1998) means that it is possible to include its effects in our model.

In conclusion the literature suggests that socio-economic variables that are robust to model specification should be included in addition to income *per capita* in models of HDIs. There is a large literature on modelling infant and child mortality and the robust independent variables identified by Hanmer and White (1999) should be included in these models. In addition it seems critical to assess what the effect of HIV/AIDS will be on the acheivability of DAC mortality targets.

Accounting for changes in poverty and human development in the 1980s and 1990s

In order to produce projections of poverty and HDIs in the future we estimate base-run models using past observations of poverty incidence and human development indicators for a cross-section of developing countries. These base-run models thus show how, on average, changes in poverty and human development are related to economic growth and the other independent variables. The final models presented below shows the relationship between the dependent variable and a set of independent variables that have been selected on the basis of the results of model specification tests. This model is then used to make projections for the future value of poverty and HDIs.

Poverty

The World Bank (1999) and Chen, Datt and Ravallion (1994) have produced estimates of the percentage of people living below a poverty line of $1 (1985 PPP) a day for 58 developing countries. We used poverty observations between 1985 and 1995 (a total of 121 observations) as the dependent variable in the poverty model.

We considered the following independent variables:

(1)   GDP *per capita* (*GDP*)
(2)   Openness (Sachs–Warner dummy) (*OPEN*)
(3)   Ratio of value added per worker in modern sector to value added per worker in agriculture (*VA*)
(4)   Incremental labour: capital ratio (*dL/dK*)
(5)   Incremental capital: output ratio (*ICOR*)

The last four variables are qualitative variables that seek to capture the characteristics of the growth path. The Sachs–Warner dummy gives a broad indication of the government's policy stance. The dummy is equal to one if the black market exchange rate premium is larger than 20 per cent for at least 10 years, and/or there is a public sector export monopoly for crops, and/or the country is classified as socialist, and/or more than 40 per cent of customs import code lines are affected by some sort of quantitative restrictions. Otherwise the dummy equals zero. Hence government policy is 'good' if the dummy equals zero and 'bad' if the dummy equals one. The *VA* variable is introduced to capture the sectoral origins of growth. The incremental labour: capital ratio aims to capture the employment-creating capacity of the growth path, the argument being that new investment has to keep pace with the increase in the labour force coming onto the market each year if labour-intensive growth is to be poverty reducing. The *ICOR* is included as a broad proxy for labour productivity growth, on the basis that the more efficiently capital is used, the more likely it is that labour productivity will grow too.

Table 11.1 shows that in addition to economic growth several of the growth path variables and the policy variable are significant determinants of the poverty headcount, indicating that bivariate models are misspecified.

Table 11.1   Poverty regression model

Dependent variable: Poverty headcount[1]	Constant	Independent variables 1				Adj. R^2	n
Sample		OPEN	dL/dK	ICOR	GDP		
Low Gini	10.77	0.25	0.16	0.016	− 0.93	0.61	49
	(7.31)*	(0.85)	(0.97)	(2.00)*	(− 2.66)*		
High Gini	8.54	0.88	0.35		− 0.34	0.58	55
	(9.74)*	(3.12)*	(2.07)*		(− 1.73)**		

Notes: [1] Dependent variable and independent variables *dL/dK* and *GDP* in logs.
T-statistics in brackets: * *t*-statistic significant at 5 per cent confidence level or above; ** *t*-statistic significant at 10 per cent confidence level.
n is the number of observations.

Our results also show that the poverty elasticity was systematically related to income inequality. Table 11.1 presents the regression for results for two groups of countries, one with low-income inequality (average Gini = 0.34) and one with high-income inequality (average Gini = 0.55).[9]

What is immediately striking from Table 11.1 is the large difference between the poverty elasticity for low- and high-inequality countries. In low-inequality countries economic growth of 10 per cent reduces the poverty headcount by around 9 per cent. In high-inequality countries economic growth of 10 per cent reduces the poverty headcount only by about 3 per cent.[10] In other words, with a given predicted rate of growth, low-inequality countries will be more effective in reducing the poverty headcount than high-inequality countries. The absolute values of the poverty elasticities are lower than the ones derived from the bivariate specification used in Hanmer *et al.* (1999) which is consistent with De Janvry and Sadoulet's (2000) findings for Latin America.

Turning now to the effects of the qualitative variables we can identify the following effects:

(1) The openness variable is significant and its sign shows that, for a given level of GDP, poverty is higher if government policies fit the Sachs–Warner definition of 'bad' policies.
(2) The incremental labour: capital ratio is negatively correlated[11] with the poverty headcount implying that the higher investment is relative to the rate of growth of the labour force, the lower is the poverty headcount.
(3) The incremental capital: output ratio is positively correlated to the poverty headcount, meaning that poverty is lower the more efficiently capital is used.

The significance of *dL/dK* and *ICOR* for poverty reductions is consistent with the view that investment growth can have a key role to play in poverty reduction if it contributes to a growth strategy that is characterised by growing labour productivity and increasing real wages. The values of both the variables are lowest (most favourable) for the East Asia and Pacific region where long-run growth has been associated with growing labour productivity and increasing real wages.

The ratio of modern to agricultural productivity has a significant effect in the regression models for the sub-Saharan African and South Asia country sub-samples but not for the total sample. In sub-Saharan Africa and South Asia, higher rates of productivity per worker in agriculture relative to the modern sector productivity are associated with lower poverty headcounts. In other words the performance of the agricultural sector is critical for poverty reduction in these two regions.[12] The total effect of the qualitative variables on poverty reduction is quite large, as we show below. Hence if the growth path is broad-based and policies are 'good', then poverty reduction will be greater than is implied by the coefficient on the *GDP* term alone. This means that success in reducing poverty depends critically on the type of growth that occurs. High growth alone does not guarantee rapid poverty reduction.

Human development

Base-run models were estimated for the HDIs relating to the DAC targets for infant and child mortality; maternal mortality; primary school education and gender equality.

Infant and under-five mortality

Infant and under-five mortality are modelled as a function of GDP *per capita*, education, access to health services and HIV/AIDS. All the data (apart from HIV prevalence) are drawn from the 1998 *World Development Indicators* CD-ROM. The mortality rates used are from the 1990s as these are based on Demographic and Health Surveys and other cited surveys and censuses. The HIV prevalence data are drawn from the UNAIDS Report on the Global HIV/AIDS Epidemic (1998). We considered the following independent variables:[13]

(1) GDP *per capita* (GDP)
(2) HIV/AIDS prevalence of women attending ante-natal clinics
(3) physicians per thousand population
(4) births attended by trained personnel
(5) primary school enrolment ratio.

Physicians *per capita* is taken as a proxy for the availability of health services. Births attended by trained personnel can be expected to have a direct effect

Table 11.2 IMR and U5MR regression results

Dependent variable	Constant	Independent variables			Adj. R^2	n
		GDP	HIV	PHY		
IMR	197.92	− 20.42	3.49	− 11.28	0.81	32
	(3.99)*	(− 3.62)*	(1.64)**	(− 3.5)*		
U5MR	347.48	− 37.86	3.26	− 26.33	0.73	32
	(2.87)*	(− 2.87)*	(0.65)	(− 3.59)		

Notes: All independent variables are logged.
t-statistics in parentheses.
* *t*-statistics significant at 0.05 confidence level or above, ** *t*-statistics significant at 0.10 confidence level.
n = Number of observations.

on child survival prospects and also indicate access to and availability of primary health care services. Table 11.2, shows the regression results for the infant and under-five mortality models. We found that HIV/AIDS is positively correlated with levels of infant and under-five mortality. GDP *per capita* and the quantity and availability of health services (as proxied by the number of physicians per thousand population and the number of births attended by trained personnel) is negatively correlated with infant and child mortality. In other words high HIV/AIDS prevalence levels result in higher infant mortality rates, and higher average income levels and greater availability of health services increases the prospects for child survival. Model restriction tests showed that primary school enrolment could be dropped from the model with no loss of explanatory power. This challenges the commonly held belief that education in general, and female education in particular has an effect over and above the effects of a higher standard of living.[14] Table 11.2 thus shows the final models that are used to make projections.[15]

Maternal mortality

Data on maternal mortality rates are scarce. We use data from the 1990s and specify maternal mortality as a function of *per capita* GDP, access to health services, adult literacy and HIV/AIDS. The percentage of births attended by trained personnel is used as a measure of access to and the quality of health services for maternal mortality.[16] We use the reported HIV prevalence rate of women attending antenatal clinics for the HIV/AIDS variable. Table 11.3 shows the final specification that we used for our maternal mortality model. All signs are as expected. HIV/AIDS is strongly and positively correlated with levels of maternal mortality. Higher adult literacy and percentages of births attended by skilled health personnel (doctors, nurses and trained midwifes) are associated with lower maternal mortality. The level of GDP *per capita* has

Table 11.3   Maternal mortality regression results

Dependent variable	Constant	Independent variables			Adj. R²	n
		Birth att.	Ln HIV	Literacy		
MatMR	8.03	−0.03	0.15	−0.008	0.88	27
	(35.00)*	(−8.79)*	(3.98)*	(−2.43)*		

Notes: * *t*-statistics significant at 0.05 confidence level or above, ** *t*-statistics significant at 0.10 confidence level.
n = Number of observations.

little influence on maternal mortality once the effects of HIV/AIDS and access to health services and adult literacy are controlled for and model restriction tests show that the variable can be dropped from the model. In other words, maternal mortality rates can be explained by access to health services (and, presumably health service quality) and the HIV prevalence rates. This suggests that maternal mortality could be reduced in many countries in the absence of increases in *per capita* income if maternal health services were improved and HIV prevalence reduced.

Primary school enrolment rates

The education target is that by 2015 there should be universal primary education. The indicator chosen to proxy this is the primary school enrolment ratio. Two key factors are likely to determine whether a child is enrolled in primary school. First, the family needs to be able to afford to send its children to school. Even if there are no school fees to be paid, parents still need to spend money on books, other materials and uniforms. Secondly schools have to be accessible by the whole of the population. We use GDP *per capita* and school expenditure per student as explanatory variables in our model.

Table 11.4 shows that primary school enrolment is positively related to *per capita* income. However, overall the model's explanatory power is weak

Table 11.4   Primary school enrolment regression results

Dependent variable	Constant	Ln GDP	Adj. R²	n
Net primary school enrolment	−36.59	14.55	0.38	48
	(−1.73)**	(5.47)*		

Notes: * *t*-statistics significant at 0.05 confidence level or above, ** *t*-statistics significant at 0.10 confidence level.
n = Number of observations.

as only 38 per cent of the variation in the data is explained by the level of *per capita* GDP. School expenditure per student, on the other hand, is not a significant determinant of primary school enrolment rates. However it is probably a very imperfect measure of the accessibility of schools to the whole population. Projections are therefore based only on the forecasts of future GDP *per capita* and we have much less confidence in these results than the projections for the other IDTs.

Gender equality in primary and secondary school enrolment rates

We use the ratio of female to male primary and secondary enrolment (*PSER*) as the dependent variable and consider the relationship between gender inequality on the one hand and the level of GDP *per capita* and income inequality on the other. Table 11.5 shows the regression results for this model. It shows that that there is only a very weak correlation between gender equality in school enrolment on the one hand and *per capita* income. Income inequality is positively and significantly correlated with the ratio of female to male primary school enrolment rate. Thus the higher the Gini the lower the level of gender inequality in school enrolment rates.[17] However the overall explanatory power of the model is weak (R^2=0.20). No significance can be attributed to the effect that income inequality or *per capita* income have on gender equality and hence the model cannot be used to predict whether the gender target will be met, given projected future growth.

This result confirms both the country studies conclusions and the gender and development literature, which finds that the role of women, and hence gender equality, very much depends on local culture and customs. The country studies on the attainment of the IDTs argue that policies to promote women's economic and political empowerment, rather than economic growth, are the critical determinants of advances in gender equality. Such policies need to address the overall position of women in society if the incentive system is to be changed so that parents want to send their girl

Table 11.5 Gender equality regression model results

Dependent variable	Constant	Ln GDP	Gini	Adj. R^2	n
Ratio of female to male primary school enrolment rate	46.8 (2.24)*	3.18 (1.27)	0.52 (2.86)*	0.21	29
Ratio of female to male secondary school enrolment rate	− 20.35 (−0.41)	9.26 (1.7)**	1.00 (2.5)*	0.20	29

* *t*-statistics significant at 0.05 confidence level or above, ** *t*-statistics significant at 0.10 confidence level.
n = Number of observations.

Table 11.6 Poverty regression model: sample country characteristics, 1990

	No. of countries	Population (million)	% of population included in sample	Headcount % of population under $1/day	No. of people in poverty (million)	Average Gini coefficient	Average GDP per capita (US$ PPP)
Sub-Saharan Africa	19	336	66	44.1	148	43.7	1267
High-inequality countries	11	129		43.0	56	56.2	2198
Low-inequality countries	8	207		44.7	93	35.9	686
Middle East and North Africa	4	60	24	2.5	2	39.2	3228
High-inequality countries	0						
Low-inequality countries	4	60		2.5	2	39.2	3228
East Asia and Pacific	5	1449	88	31.2	453	35.9	1621
High-inequality countries	2	73		4.7	3	44.9	4084
Low-inequality countries	3	1376		32.7	449	35.5	1490
South Asia	5	1108	98	46.7	517	31.7	962
High-inequality countries	0						
Low-inequality countries	5	1108		46.7	517	31.7	962
Latin America and Caribbean	15	369	84	27.9	103	55.4	4768
High-inequality countries	12	350		28.2	99	56.1	4859
Low-inequality countries	3	19		22.5	4	42.5	3111
Eastern Europe and Central Asia	10	110	27	9.3	10	26.8	4023
High-inequality countries	0						
Low-inequality countries	10	110		9.3	10	26.8	4023
All Developing Countries	*58*	*3433*	*78*	*35.9*	*1233*	*37.2*	*1817*
High-inequality countries	25	552		28.6	158	54.6	4134
Low-inequality countries	33	2881		37.3	1075	33.9	1373

Notes: All data from *World Development Indicators 1999* except Gini coefficients which are from Deininger and Squire (1996) and *1998 WDR*. The percentage of the population covered in our sample cannot be calculated separately for the high- and low-inequality categories as denominators are unknown.
Eastern Europe and Central Asia data are unreliable (see Mosley and Kalyuzhnova 2000).

children to school and girls want to remain there and have the opportunity to succeed when they do.

Poverty projections

Whether the income poverty target is met or not will be judged by whether the 1990 poverty incidence has been halved or not by 2015. The following section describes how the base-run model outlined in the previous section is used to produce poverty projections for 2015.

Country sample

The poverty regression models specified in Table 11.1 are combined with economic growth rate forecasts to produce a projection of poverty incidence for 2015. The projections for high- and low-inequality countries are run separately and then combined in a population weighted regional average. The projections are based on the countries which were used to produce the base-run model which, as Table 11.6 shows, contain 78 per cent of the population of developing world, covering 66 per cent, 88 per cent and 98 per cent of the populations of sub-Saharan Africa, East Asia and the Pacific, and South Asia respectively. The World Bank's estimates of $1 a day poverty at 1985 PPPs are shown in Table 11.6; 1990 poverty incidence is highest in sub-Saharan Africa and South Asia at 44 and 47 per cent, respectively, and the number of people living in poverty is highest in East Asia and the Pacific and South Asia at 453 and 517 million, respectively.

Growth rates

The projections use two economic growth scenarios, one based on the latest forecasts available for the regions and the other on the rates of growth achieved between 1965 and 1997. They are shown in Table 11.7.

Table 11.7 Growth rate assumptions

Annual growth in GDP per capita	Global economic prospects projections 2001–8[a]	Historic growth rates 1965–97
Sub-Saharan Africa	1.4	0
Middle East and North Africa	1.4	0.1
East Asia and Pacific	5.6	5.4
South Asia	3.7	2.3
Latin America and Caribbean	3.0	1.3
Eastern Europe and Central Asia	4.8	3.2
All developing countries	4.0	3.0

[a] The Global Economic Prospects (World Bank 1998) projections are for 2001–8. We assume they remain the same between 2008 and 2015.

Future scenarios

Four scenarios are considered for the poverty projections:

(1) No change and high growth combines the growth forecasts from World Bank (1998) with the base-run model, assuming that there is no change in the qualitative features of the growth path until 2015.[18]
(2) No change and low growth combines economic growth at historic averages achieved between 1965 and 1997 (World Bank 1999) with the base-run model, assuming that there is no change in the qualitative feature of the growth path until 2015.
(3) Broader based and high growth combines the optimistic growth forecasts with the base-run model, assuming that policies improve the qualitative variables having an increased poverty reducing effect until 2015.
(4) Broader-based and low growth combines economic growth at historic averages achieved between 1965 and 1997, assuming that policies result in the qualitative variables having an increased poverty reducing effect until 2015.

The broader-based growth scenario makes the following assumptions:

(1) Sachs–Warner openness dummy (*OPEN*): all regions become open by 2015.
(2) Incremental capital output ratio (*ICOR*): sub-Saharan Africa, South Asia and Latin America and Caribbean reach the East Asian and Pacific 1990 *ICOR* by 2015. East Asia Pacific converges to the lowest 1990 ICOR in the region by 2015.
(3) Incremental labour capital ratio (dL/dK): improves by 25 per cent by 2015.

The broader-based growth scenario assumptions, that is a growth process in which the poor participate and benefit from, have the effect of increasing the absolute value of the poverty elasticity to 1.5 per cent for low-inequality countries and 1.45 per cent for high-inequality developing countries.

Meeting the income poverty target: halving the incidence of poverty by 2015

Table 11.8 presents our forecasts of the poverty headcount in 2015 for developing regions overall. A number in bold indicates that the poverty target is met. It shows that there is a good chance that poverty will be half its present level by 2015, as long as policies are in place to induce a broader-based growth path.

Table 11.9 shows how income inequality affects the attainability of the income-poverty target. High-inequality developing countries had *lower*

Table 11.8 Poverty incidence (per cent), developing countries 1990 and 2015 (for a range of $1 a day at 1985 PPP estimates)

Scenario	1990	2015	
		High-growth	Low-growth
Poverty incidence		–	
No change	36	**18**	20
Broader-based	36	**13**	**14–26**
Poverty incidence as % of 1990 poverty			
No change		**50**	56
Broader-based		**35**	**40**

Note: **Bold** numbers indicate that the target has been attained.

Table 11.9 Poverty, 1990 and 2015: the effect of income inequality under no change and broader-growth paths in the high-growth scenario

1990	1990	2015	
		No change	Broader-based
Poverty incidence			
High-inequality countries	29–39	19	14
Low-inequality countries	38–48	**18**	**13**
Poverty incidence as % of 1990 poverty			
High-inequality countries		68	**49**
Low-inequality countries		**47**	**33**

Note: **Bold** numbers indicate that the target has been attained.

levels of poverty in 1990 than low-inequality countries. However, they are less likely to attain the poverty target than low-inequality countries. Good policies and broader-based growth improve poverty reduction prospects in high and low-income inequality countries alike. However in high-income inequality countries it is not certain that even broader-based high growth will be enough to meet the target, as poverty incidence falls only to 49–62 per cent of its 1990 level by 2015.

Table 11.10 shows whether the poverty incidence target is attained at the regional level. We present the upper and lower bounds of the projection results:

(1) The worst-case scenario assumes low growth and no policy change
(2) The best-case scenario assumes high and broader-based growth.

Low-inequality East Asia and Pacific meets the target in all scenarios.[19] Eastern Europe and South Asia are likely to meet the target in the best case

Table 11.10   Poverty incidence, 2015, as a per cent of poverty incidence in 1990

	1990 headcount	2015 headcount as % of 1990	
		High broader-based growth Best case	No change, low-growth Worst case
Sub-Saharan Africa	44	56	95
High-inequality	43	57	87
Low-inequality	44	56	99
Middle East and North Africa	3	51	75
High-inequality			
Low-inequality	3	51	75
East Asia and Pacific	31	27	**38**
High-inequality	5		
Low-inequality	33	27	**38**
South Asia	47	**35**	64
High-inequality			
Low-inequality	47	**35**	64
Latin America and Caribbean	28	**44**	68
High-inequality	28	**44**	68
Low-inequality	23	**44**	81
Eastern Europe and Central Asia	9	**32**	55
High-inequality			
Low-inequality	9	**32**	55
Developing countries	36	**33**	56
High-inequality	29	**49**	73
Low-inequality	38	**33**	53

Note: **Bold** numbers indicate that the target has been attained.

scenario. Reaching the poverty target in Latin America and the Caribbean is possible but less certain even in the best-case scenario. Prospects for halving income poverty are worst for sub-Saharan Africa. In the worst case, poverty in Africa in 2015 is as almost as widespread as in 1990. Overall the attainment of the DAC income poverty target for 2015 is strongly driven by the performance of China and India. Both fall into the low-income inequality country sample and the population share of these two countries means that the overall developing country result is driven by their performance.

Growth rates required to halve poverty by 2015

Forecast growth is sufficent to halve poverty by 2015 for developing countries as a whole as long as the growth path is broad-based. Without change in the growth path, *per capita* growth of 7.1 per cent in high-inequality and 3.7 per cent in low-inequality countries is needed to halve poverty by 2015.

Table 11.11 Forecast growth and growth required to halve poverty by 2015 (average annual real growth in GDP *per capita*)

| | Forecast growth[a] | Growth required to halve poverty by 2015 | |
		Broader-based	No change
Sub-Saharan Africa	1.4	2.4	5.9
High-inequality		3.5	10.4
Low-inequality		2.1	4.6
Latin America and Caribbean	3.0	0.6	7.0
High-inequality		0.5	7.0
Low-inequality		2.1	4.5

[a] World Bank (1998), Projections 2001–8.

For Latin America and the Caribbean the difference in the poverty reducing capacity of the two scenarios is particularly marked, especially for high inequality countries as Table 11.11 shows. This table also shows that growth rates of 2.4 per cent under the broad-based growth scenario and 5.9 per cent under the no change scenario would be needed to halve poverty in sub-Saharan Africa. The latter rate is well above the forecast rate and far in excess of growth rates achieved in the region since the 1960s.

Thus, without policies in place that alter the growth path to favour the poor, the growth rates required to halve poverty are high enough to be considered not feasible in these regions. Between 1960 and 1990 the high performing Asian economies grew at about 5.5 per cent per annum – less than the minimum growth rates of 6 and 7 per cent required to halve poverty in sub-Saharan Africa and Latin America and the Caribbean respectively, under the no change scenario. The equality of income distribution also has a significant impact on the growth rate required to halve poverty. Under both scenarios, high-inequality developing countries need *per capita* income growth which is roughly twice as high as that of low inequality countries. Hence policies that reduce inequality in high-inequality developing countries and stabilise it in low-inequality ones are another route to ensuring that the DAC targets are achieved.

Attaining the human development targets

Whether the human development targets are met will be judged by whether by 2015:

(1) The infant and under-five mortality rate has been reduced by two-thirds of its 1990 level.

(2)   The maternal mortality rate has been reduced by three-quarters of its 1990 level.
(3)   There is universal primary school enrolment and whether by 2005.
(4)   Gender disparity in primary and secondary education has been eliminated.

We use the base-run models described on pp. 265–6 to estimate levels of the indicators for each of the human development targets under various future scenarios.

Future scenarios: meeting the infant and under-five mortality rate targets; reducing infant and under-five mortality rates by two-thirds

The World Bank (1998) growth rates were combined with assumptions about changes in the other independent variables and changes in the constant term – the technology effect – to produce three future scenarios:[20]

(1)   The Better Health Scenario keeps HIV/AIDS infection rates at their present level and assumes that the availability of health services *per capita* increases and that technological progress continues to have effects in the twenty-first century.
(2)   The No Health Gains scenario keeps HIV/AIDS infection rates at their present level and assumes that the availability of health services *per capita* does not increase, but that technological progress continues to have effects in the twenty-first century.
(3)   The AIDS Pandemic Scenario projects HIV/AIDS infection rates spreading throughout all developing regions at the rate predicted by epidemiological models currently used in developing countries. All regions have adult HIV/AIDS prevalence rates of 22.5 per cent by 2015.[21] The benefits of technological progress are assumed to be wiped out by the spread of AIDS in this scenario.

Table 11.12 shows that for developing countries as a whole attaining a reduction of two-thirds the 1990 level of infant mortality is possible in the Better Health Scenario. However, without improvements in health services, and greater access to them, the target is unlikely to be met. The course of the HIV/AIDS epidemic is a crucial factor in the attainability of this target, as the infant mortality rate (IMR) remains at 76 per cent of its 1990 level in the AIDS Pandemic Scenario. The corresponding IMR of 42 per 1,000 live births is more than twice as high as projection for the Better Health scenario.

The regional breakdown shows that, even with the AIDS pandemic, infant mortality is expected to fall in all regions apart from Middle East and North Africa. East Asia and Pacific is the only region that is likely to reduce infant mortality by two-thirds under any circumstances. Latin America and Eastern Europe need to control the spread of the AIDS epidemic to meet the target,

Table 11.12   Infant mortality rate (*IMR*) per 1,000, 1990 and 2015, as a percentage of 1990 levels

	1990 IMR (000)	*IMR in 2015 as % of 1990 level*		
		Better Health	*No Health Gains*	*AIDS Pandemic*
Sub-Saharan Africa	93	56	65	94
Middle East and North Africa	51	**18**	34	110
East Asia and Pacific	36	**14**	**14**	29
South Asia	83	34	44	79
Latin America and Caribbean	43	**12**	**12**	74
Eastern Europe and Central Asia	21	**24**	**24**	89
All developing countries	56	**33**	40	76

Note: **Bold** figures indicate that the target (down to 33 per cent of the 1990 level by 2005) is on course to be met. The constant figures for East Asia, Latin America and Eastern Europe in the Better Health and No Health Gain scenario reflect the lower bound of 5 per thousand imposed by the projection model.

Table 11.13   Under-five mortality rates (*U5MR*), 1990 and 2015, as a percentage of 1990 levels

	U5MR 1990	*U5MR as per cent of 1990 level*		
		Better Health	*No Health Gains*	*AIDS Pandemic*
Sub-Saharan Africa	149	64	77	96
Middle East and North Africa	62	**15**	41	107
East Asia and Pacific	42	**12**	**12**	30
South Asia	105	**33**	46	79
Latin America and Caribbean	49	**10**	**10**	70
Eastern Europe and Central Asia	26	**29**	19	**26**
All developing countries	72	36	47	77

Note: **Bold** figures indicate that the target (reducing by two-thirds, which is 33 per cent of the 1990 level) has been met. The constant figures for East Asia, Latin America and Eastern Europe in the Better Health and No Health Gain scenario reflect the lower bound of 5 per thousand imposed by the projection model.

while the Middle East and South Asia, in addition, have to improve health services.

Table 11.13 shows that for developing countries as a whole under-five mortality is likely to fall to 36 per cent of its 1990 level (72 per thousand) if better health policies increase access to health services and contain the spread of HIV/AIDS. In the worst-case scenario (AIDS Pandemic) under-five mortality decreases slowly compared to past trends, falling by less than 20 per thousand over the 15-year time period and remaining at about three-quarters of its 1990 level. Although developing countries overall do not reach the target all regions, apart from sub-Saharan Africa, do so under the Better Health Scenario.

Future scenarios: meeting the maternal mortality rate target

The estimated rates of growth of adult literacy[22] are combined with the assumptions about access to reproductive health care and the spread of HIV/ AIDS to create three scenarios:

(1) The Better Health Services scenario keeps HIV/AIDS infection rates at their present level and assumes that the 80 percent of births in 2015 are attended by skilled health personnel.[23]
(2) The Slower Health Gain scenario keeps HIV/AIDS infection rates at their present level and assumes that improvements in births attended by skilled health personnel take place at only half the rate necessary to meet the births target (and that around 70 percent of births are attended in 2015).
(3) The High AIDS scenario makes the same births attended assumption as the Slower Health Gain scenario, but also assumes that HIV/AIDS infection rates spreading throughout all developing regions at the rate predicted by epidemiological models. All regions have adult HIV/AIDS prevalence of 22.5 per cent by 2015.

Maternal mortality data are available for very few countries. Table 11.14 shows the country which has the largest weight in the result for each region in the case where the regional country sample is small.

None of the regions, or countries, under any of the scenarios reaches the target of reducing maternal mortality rates by three-quarters by 2015. This would imply a value of 25 percent of the 1990 level in 2015. Starting from a very high level, sub-Saharan Africa gets close to reaching the target, but that is contingent on achieving a target of 80 percent births attended by skilled personnel and on halting the spread of HIV/AIDS at current rates of infection. In terms of percentage change the best-case outlook for Africa is better than for other regions, as currently the ratio of births attended is very low and hence there are bigger potential improvements to be made. If the health gains take place at only half the rate necessary to hit the birth attended target, sub-Saharan African maternal mortality in 2015 falls only to 60 percent its 1990 level.

Comparing the Slower Health Gains and the High AIDS scenario, Table 11.15 shows that for Africa the effect of AIDS on maternal mortality is smaller than the effect due to births attended. This is because HIV/AIDS

Table 11.14 Maternal mortality rates (*MMR*) per 100,000, 1990 and 2015, as a percentage of 1990 levels

		2015 MMR as a per cent of 1990 level		
	1990 MMR (per 100,000)	*Better Health Services*	*Slower Health Gains*	*High AIDS*
Sub-Saharan Africa	768	30	60	68
Middle East and North Africa	221	50	72	153
Vietnam[1,2]	1356	45	65	101
Pakistan[1,3]	263	60	75	96
Latin America and Caribbean	98	45	68	86
Poland[1,4]	109	72	73	129
All developing countries	694	44	65	94

Notes:
[1] Data for Vietnam, Pakistan and Poland represent more than 75 percent of the population in their region for which data is available.
[2] Plus Mongolia, Cambodia and some Pacific Islands.
[3] Plus Afghanistan, Bhutan, Maldives and Nepal.
[4] Plus Moldova and Georgia.

Table 11.15 Net primary school enrolment rates, 2015, by region

	1990	*2015*	
		High-growth	*Low-growth*
Sub-Saharan Africa	54	68	65
Middle East and North Africa	84	98	96
East Asia and Pacific	99	100*	100*
South Asia	62	83	79
Latin America and Caribbean	90	100*	100*
Eastern Europe and Central Asia	96	100*	100*
Developing countries	82	**100***	**98**

Note: 100* = full net primary school enrolment.

infection rates in the region are already very high, nearing the epidemiological maximum. The situation is reversed for a region such as the Middle East and North Africa, which currently has low HIV/AIDS infection rates but a higher percentage of births attended. Though the relative importance of the births attended and the AIDS effect differs by region, it is clear that, to improve maternal mortality rates in developing countries, it is crucial to enhance health services and contain the spread of the AIDS epidemic.

Future scenarios: achieving universal primary school enrolment by 2015

Table 11.15 shows the 1990 levels and 2015 projections of the net primary school enrolment rate for the high- and low-growth scenarios by region. At a regional level only three regions, East Asia and the Pacific, Latin America and the Caribbean and Eastern Europe and Central Asia will have universal enrolment by 2015. The other regions are unlikely to reach the target. Middle East and North Africa gets very close, and South Asia is projected to at least reach around 80 percent enrolment. Forecasts for Sub-Saharan Africa suggest that even in 2015 more than three out of ten children will not attend primary school.

An important caveat must be kept in mind in considering efforts to improve education. Enrolment does not ensure education. A country case study of the Universal Primary Education (UPE) policy in Uganda shows that quality concerns can be critical. Teacher: pupil ratios have soared to 70:1 in government schools with UPE and the challenge facing the Ugandan government is to ensure that all pupils leave primary school literate and numerate and that the overall standard of education does not fall (McGee *et al.* 1999). Our case study from Tanzania shows that deteriorating standards of education can lead to education becoming highly price elastic. The recent imposition of a charge of 1,000 Tanzanian shillings per year (about £1) led to falling enrolments as parents would not pay 'something for nothing' (Eele *et al.* 1999).

Conclusions

This chapter set out to examine whether the DAC targets were achievable. It sought to improve on models which predicted whether or not these targets could be met on the basis of forecast future growth alone. Our analysis demonstrated that although economic growth was an important determinant of both poverty and human development, analysis of data from the 1980s and 1990s showed that other independent variables also played an important role in determining poverty reduction and human development improvements. The projected future levels of poverty and human development indicators are therefore based on models that take account of this finding.

We have established that halving income poverty by 2015 is possible. There is a good chance that this ambitious target can be met, provided that policies are in place to induce broader-based growth paths. And growth does not have to be as high as forecast if the growth path becomes more broadly-based. Developing countries overall will meet the target if they achieve the 3 per cent *per capita* per annum real average growth rates that they achieved between 1965 and 1997. Growth is important but attaining the poverty targets crucially depends on actions being taken by developing country governments and donor agencies to influence the qualitative nature of the growth path. These actions include policies to ensure that growth is rooted in sectors of the economy that the poor are able to participate in, to create conditions for rising labour productivity through increasing the rate and efficient use of investment and policies to increase openness. Our results also point to the critical role of income inequality in attaining the income poverty target. The prospects for reducing poverty are much better in low-income inequality countries than high-income inequality countries. High-inequality developing countries are unlikely to attain the target even if growth is rapid and broad-based. Our projections show that they need growth rates about twice as high as low-inequality countries to meet the income poverty target.

Despite the good prospects for reducing poverty in the world's developing regions overall, there are some sobering findings. Sub-Saharan Africa is unlikely to reach the target, given the forecast rates of growth. If the growth path were broader-based, then growth of about 2.5–5 per cent *per capita* per annum would be needed to halve poverty. Other developing regions have achieved growth rates of this magnitude, but it will take a major effort by the international community and African governments alike to launch sub-Saharan Africa on such a growth path. Contrary to widespread assumptions, sub-Saharan Africa contains a large number of high-inequality countries and there is certainly scope for increasing the rate of poverty reduction for any given growth rate, if policies that induce high growth and falling income inequality can be devised and implemented. Further research is needed to establish exactly what these policies should be but, if the experience of Latin America is anything to go by, making sure that land tenure reforms have the net effect of increasing equality – including gender equality – seems likely to be a critical ingredient of a successful anti-poverty policy in many African countries.

There are good prospects for meeting the human development targets, too, as long as policies are in place that support the gains that higher-income levels can bring. Reducing infant and under-five mortality rates by two-thirds will depend on policy interventions that can halt the spread of HIV/AIDS, increase the capacity of developing countries' health sectors to deliver more health services and ensure that technological progress spills over to benefit the developing world. Making strong progress towards the maternal mortality rate target requires investment in health services that increase women's access to maternal health services. It is also essential that the spread of HIV/AIDS is halted. In developing regions as a whole primary school enrolment can become universal. However, South Asia and particularly sub-Saharan Africa are unlikely to reach the universal primary enrolment target. Moreover, attaining universal primary education must be combined with policies to ensure improvement in the quality of teaching in primary schools. Finally, we find that there is no evidence that gender equality in enrolment in primary and secondary education increases automatically as development proceeds. This suggests that the achievement of this target depends critically on pro-active policy measures that promote the cultural, political and economic empowerment of women.

Notes

1. There are two approaches to poverty elasticity estimation – the analytic and the econometric methods (see Hanmer *et al.* 1999 for a discussion of the relative merits of the two approaches).
2. That is the effect of resource reallocation from low- to high-productivity sectors; this is the sectoral shift that is associated with Kuznets' inverted 'U' trajectory of inequality rising then falling in the course of development.
3. The Timmer sample of the Deininger and Squire (1996) data set covers 3.3 billion people in 1995 or two-thirds of the population in low- and middle-income countries, where agriculture comprises a quarter of GDP and employs half the labour force.
4. Qualitative features are: predicted growth of the Gini; length of growth or recession sequence; difference in growth of value added between agriculture and manufacturing: difference in growth of value added between agriculture and services; hyperinflation; real exchange rate growth; coefficient of variation of GDP *per capita* around its trend; migration rate; urban minimum wage. Structural features are: initial GDP *per capita*; share of agriculture in GDP; initial level of inequality; initial urban–rural poverty; natural growth rate of urban–rural poverty; initial share of urban–rural in total population (de Janvry and Sadoulet 2000).
5. This study found that between 1970 and 1990 the intercept of the regressions of real GDP *per capita* on life expectancy and adult literacy, respectively, shifted upwards. Hence at the same level of *per capita* GDP life expectancy (literacy) was higher in 1990 than in it was in 1970.
6. There are a large number of empirical studies of the determinants of infant and under-five mortality rates from the perspective of various disciplines, including medical science, demography and economics. The choice of independent variable is for the most part contingent on the disciplinary approach.
7. We know of no similar study that identifies robust variables for primary school enrolment rates.
8. Health sector expenditures are not necessarily representative of the quantity and availability of health services. Money can be inefficiently spent and some health care systems are more expensive than others are and so the cost of the same health services varies widely between countries. An output rather than an input indicator of health services can better capture the effect of increasing health expenditures.
9. Chow tests show that the sample should be divided into two groups containing countries with Gini coefficients of above and below 0.43, respectively. Model specification tests showed that *VA* could be dropped from the model.
10. The systematic difference in poverty elasticities holds at the regional level for sub-Saharan Africa, Latin America and the Caribbean. Numbers of observations limited testing for systematic differences in poverty elasticities in other regions.

11. The logarithm of a ratio < 1 is negative and all observations for $dL/dK < 1$.
12. For all developing countries, however, this variable was not significant and small sample size for each of the regions meant that it was better to use the parameters derived from the model using all developing countries for projections.
13. We could not include immunisation rates and gender inequality in the model as the number of countries which had a complete set of observations for all the independent variables once these two are included is fewer than 20.
14. The finding that education is insignificant in this model does not mean it is not a policy relevant variable. It means education is highly correlated with *per capita* GDP and the other independent variables and so no inferences about its effect can be drawn from the model.
15. The HIV/AIDS data is for the early 1990s (and not the mid-1990s). Therefore, they represent the mortality rates towards the beginning of the epidemic, which do not yet fully reflect the impact of HIV/AIDS on mortality. A 1990 observation of *U5MR* would include children born in 1985 – before the epidemic had become widespread. We therefore include HIV/AIDS as an explanatory variable in the *U5MR* model, despite the fact that it is insignificant in the model.
16. This would probably be a better measure of access to and the quality of health services for the IMR model as well, but it was not used as its inclusion restricted the sample size to fewer than 20 observations.
17. The dependent variable is a ratio less than 1 for almost all observations hence higher Ginis are correlated with higher values of the ratio – i.e. it increasing to 1 or above. This result may be driven by East Europe and Central Asian economies that frequently have high levels of inequality and higher female than male school enrolment rates.
18. The values of all the independent variables, apart from *per capita* GDP, are the same in 2015 as they were in 1990.
19. The high-inequality sample for East Asia and Pacific (only Thailand and Malaysia) is too small to use for projections.
20. Hanmer *et al.* (1999) found that some improvements in infant and child mortality over time could be attributed to autonomous effects of improved technology and knowledge. We incorporate this finding in our model.
21. Epidemiological models (e.g. Stover 1997) plot the course of the AIDS epidemic as a 'S'-shaped curve. Infection spreads very slowly in the initial years and then, after prevalence levels of about 5 per cent are reached, the epidemic spreads rapidly. After about 15 years it stabilises at a maximum value of 22.5 percent. This rapid spread of AIDS throughout the developing world's population may, of course, not actually happen. In Western Europe and North America the rapid spread of AIDS has to date only affected particular high risk sub-sets of the population.
22. A model of adult literacy as a function of GDP *per capita* is used to estimate future adult literacy rates given the growth rates predicted by the World Bank.
23. A subsidiary IDT is that 80 per cent of births are attended by trained personnel by 2015.

Bibliography

Bourguignon, F. and C. Morrisson (1998), 'Inequality and development: the role of dualism', *Journal of Development Economics*, Vol. 57: pp. 233–57.

Burnside, C. and D. Dollar (1998), 'Aid, the incentive regime and poverty reduction', The World Bank, Policy Research Department, Working Paper 1937.

Chen, S., G. Datt and M. Ravallion (1994), 'Is poverty increasing in the developing world?', *Review of Income and Wealth*, 40(4), pp. 359–76.

Collier, P. and D. Dollar (1998), 'Aid allocation and poverty reduction', Washington DC: World Bank, mimeo.

DAC (1996) *Development Assistance: Efforts and Policies of the Members of the Development Assistance Committee*, Paris: OELD.

Datt, G. and M. Ravallion (1990), *Regional Disparities, Targeting and Poverty in India*, Washington, DC: World Bank.

Datt, G. and M. Ravallion (1994), 'How important to India's poor is the urban–rural composition of growth?', Washington, DC: World Bank, Policy Research Department.

Datt, G. and M. Ravallion (1996a), 'How important to India's poor is the sectoral composition of economic growth?', *The World Bank Economic Review*, Vol. 10(1), pp. 1–25.

Datt, G. and M. Ravallion (1996b), *Why Have Some Indian States Done Better than Others at Reducing Rural Poverty?*, Washington, DC: World Bank.

Datt, G. and M. Ravallion (1998), 'Farm productivity and rural poverty in India', *Journal of Development Studies*, Vol. 34(4), pp. 62–85.

Deininger, K. and L. Squire (1996), 'A new data set measuring income inequality', *The World Bank Economic Review*, 10(3), pp. 565–91.

Deininger, K. and L. Squire (1997), Data set for *A new data set measuring income inequality*, available at http://www.worldbank.org/html/prdmg/grthweb/dde-isqu.htm.

De Janvry, A. and E. Sadoulet (2000), 'Growth, poverty and inequality in Latin America: a causal analysis, 1970–94', *Review of Income and Wealth*, 46(3), pp. 267–87.

Demery, L. and M. Walton (1998), 'Are poverty and social goals for the 21st century attainable?', Paper presented at conference 'What Can be Done about Poverty?', Institute for Development Studies, Sussex University.

Eele, G. *et al.* (1999), 'Meeting the international development targets in Uganda', Paper presented to the workshop, 'Meeting the International Development Targets', ODI, London, 26–27 April, mimeo.

Hanmer, L., N. de Jong, R. Kurian and J. Mooij (1999), 'Are the DAC targets achievable? Poverty and human development in the year 2015', *Journal of International Development*, 11, pp. 547–63.

Hanmer, L., R. Lensink and H. White (1998), 'Infant and child mortality in developing countries: analysing the data for robust determinants', unpublished Working Paper.

Hanmer, L. and H. White (1999), 'The impact of HIV/AIDS on under-five mortality in Zambia and Zimbabwe', in *Human Development in Sub-Saharan Africa: The Determinants of Under-Five Mortality*, The Hague: ISSAS, January.

IADB (1999), 'An exercise on the sensitivity of poverty headcount estimates to different adjustment methodologies', www.iadb.org/sds/doc/1404eng.pdf.

ILO (1996), LABORPROJ 1996 (diskette), Geneva: International Labour Organisation.

Kanbur, R. and N. Lustig (1999), 'Why is inequality back on the agenda?', Paper prepared for the Annual Bank Conference on Development Economics, Washington, DC: World Bank, 28–30 April.

Lipton, M. (1977), *Why Poor People Stay Poor: Urban Bias in World Development*, London: Temple Smith.

McGee, R. *et al.* (1999), 'Meeting the international development targets in Uganda', Paper presented to the workshop 'Meeting the International Development Targets', ODI, London, 26–27 April, mimeo.

Mellor, J. (1999), 'Poverty reduction – sequences and priorities', Abt Associates, Inc. Bethesda, MD, 29 August, mimeo.

Mosley, P. and J. Hudson (1997), *Aid Effectiveness: Tests of the Robustness of Macro-Relationships*, Report to Overseas Development Administration.

Mosley, P. and Y. Kalyuzhnova (2000), 'Are poverty and social goals attainable in the transition region?', *Development Policy Review*, Vol. 18(1), pp. 107–20.

OECD Development Assistance Committee (1996), *Shaping the 21st Century: The Contribution of Development Cooperation*, Paris: OECD/DAC, May.

OECD Development Assistance Committee (1999), data from their website http://www.oecd.org/dac/.

Ramirez, A., G. Ranis and F. Stewart (1997), 'Economic growth and human development', Center Discussion Paper 787, New Haven: Yale University Economic Growth Center.

Ranis, G. (1979), 'Appropriate technology in the dual economy: reflections on Philippine and Taiwanese experience', in A. Robinson (ed.), *Appropriate Technologies for Third World Development*, New York: Macmillan.

Ravallion, M. (1997), 'Can high-inequality developing countries escape absolute poverty?', *Economics Letters*, Vol. 56(1), pp. 51–7.

Ravallion, M. and Shaohua Chen (1997), 'What can new survey data tell us about recent changes in distribution and poverty?', *World Bank Economic Review* 11(2), pp. 357–82.

Sachs, J. and A.M. Warner (1995), 'Economic Convergence and Economic Policies', National Bureau of Economic Research Working Paper, 5039.

Stewart, F. (1978), *Technology and Underdevelopment*, London: Macmillan.

Stover, J. (1997), *AIDSproj spreadsheet model to project HIV, AIDS and TB*, Glastonbury: The POLICY Project, The Futures Group International.

Thorbecke, E, and H.S. Jung (1996), 'A multiplier decomposition method to analyse poverty alleviation', *Journal of Development Economics*, Vol. 48(2), pp. 279–300.

Timmer, C.P. (1997), 'How well do the poor connect to the growth process?', CAER Discussion Paper 178, Cambridge, MA: Harvard Institute for International Development.

UNAIDS (1998) *Reports on the Global AIDS Epidemic*, Geneva.

UNDP (1996), *Human Development Report, 1996*, New York: Oxford University Press.

UNICEF (1998), *State of the World's Children 1998*, New York: UNICEF.

UNICEF (1999), 'Progress in the social sectors in Eastern and Southern Africa in the 1990's: a UNICEF perspective', Nairobi: UNICEF Eastern and Southern Africa Regional Office.

Wade, R. (1990), *Governing the Market: Economic Theory and the Role of Government in East Asian Industrialization*, Princeton: Princeton University Press.

World Bank (1993), *East Asian Miracle*, New York: Oxford University Press.

World Bank (1996), *Poverty Reduction and the World Bank*, Washington, DC: World Bank.

World Bank (1998), *Global Economic Prospects for Developing Countries 1998/99: Beyond Financial Crisis*, Washington, DC: World Bank, December.

World Bank (1999), *World Development Indicators*, Washington, DC: World Bank.

Index